To John Bressler
Best Wishes

Legends & Legacies
Anchorage 1910–1935

John Bagoy   3/10/02

John P. Bagoy

ISBN Number: 1-888125-91-8

Library of Congress Catalog Card Number: 2001038581

Copyright 2001 by John P. Bagoy
— First Edition —

Manufactured in the United States of America

DEDICATION

This book is dedicated to those hardy men and women who braved the elements and bore the hardships of life on the frontier, seeking their fortunes or seeking a new life or just someplace to put down their roots, to those women who bore their children in a cold tent, without medical assistance, and who followed their men regardless of how rough the trail was, and especially to my mother and father, Marie and John Bagoy, whose life in Alaska since 1894 epitomizes the true Pioneer.

ACKNOWLEDGEMENTS

Putting this book together was a monumental task and required the talents of many people. With the help of Dianne Brenner and Mina Jacobs at the Museum Library, and Bruce Merrill and Dan Fleming at the Loussac Library, my research efforts were minimized, and these fine people have my deepest appreciation for their assistance.

My appreciation also goes to my "ruthless" copy editor, Letha Schwiesow Flint, whose command of the English language and grammar kept me on the right side of the dictionary. When my slang and unorthodox speaking style got out of line, she was there to get me straight again. My young granddaughter Lindsay Larson did a bang-up job scanning in the photographs and creating the page layout. She tried in vain to get me computer oriented and was there when I was on the verge of tossing it out of the window.

Last, but not least, to my patient and understanding wife Thelma, who put up with the paper, the clutter, books, boxes, and four letter words for the past three years, and who lost her sitting room to me and a computer, I can only say she has my undying gratitude and affection.

PHOTO CREDITS AND BIBLIOGRAPHY

The family photos and various general photos were all supplied by the participating family members. The Alaska Aviation Heritage Museum furnished photos of Don Glass, Hakon Christenson, Alonzo Cope, Cecil Higgins, Roy Holm, Al Jones, Art Woodley, Steve Mills, Frank Dorbrandt, and Harold Gillam.

The Anchorage Museum of History and Art furnished the following photos: all of the photos of Anchorage Mayors, Russian Jack, Bob Bragaw, Tom Bevers, President Harding, A. Settlemier, E. Kjosen, Ken Laughlin, W. E. Dunkle, Tony Dimond, Ora D. Clark, A. E. Lathrop, Mears, Christenson, Edes, Hunt and Riggs, Dick Tousely, Tom O'Dale, Elmer Simco, Oscar Vogel, Hurricane Gulch Bridge, Hotel Parsons, Moosemeat John Hedberg, Marie Silverman, Mother White and White House, Sydney and Jeanne Laurence, Charles Odermat, and Joe Spenard.

Sources of information concerning the participating families that came from outside of the family information were as follows: Evangeline Atwood's *They Shall Be Remembered, Anchorage, All American City* and *Who's Who in Alaska*, the *Seward Gateway*, the *Cook Inlet Pioneer*, the obituary columns of the *Anchorage Daily Times* and *Anchorage Daily News*. All of the photos of the high school graduates were furnished by individuals who held their original annuals, and, in particular, Dorothy Miller Markley, who had most of them. "The Outlet on the Inlet" by the Anchorage Chamber of Commerce, written in 1916, had much of the dated information, and Louise Potter's *Old Times on Upper Cook Inlet* held much information on navigation.

There were many individual contributors of information who had personal knowledge of many of the people in the book, and they were Jim Arness of Kenai, Chris Terry, Bob Winslow, Barbara Hendrichs, Phil Ames, Harry Bartels, Sven Ericksson, Peter J. Bagoy, Sr., Hazel Warwick, Lucy Whitehead, Wanda Griffin, and Christine Gill.

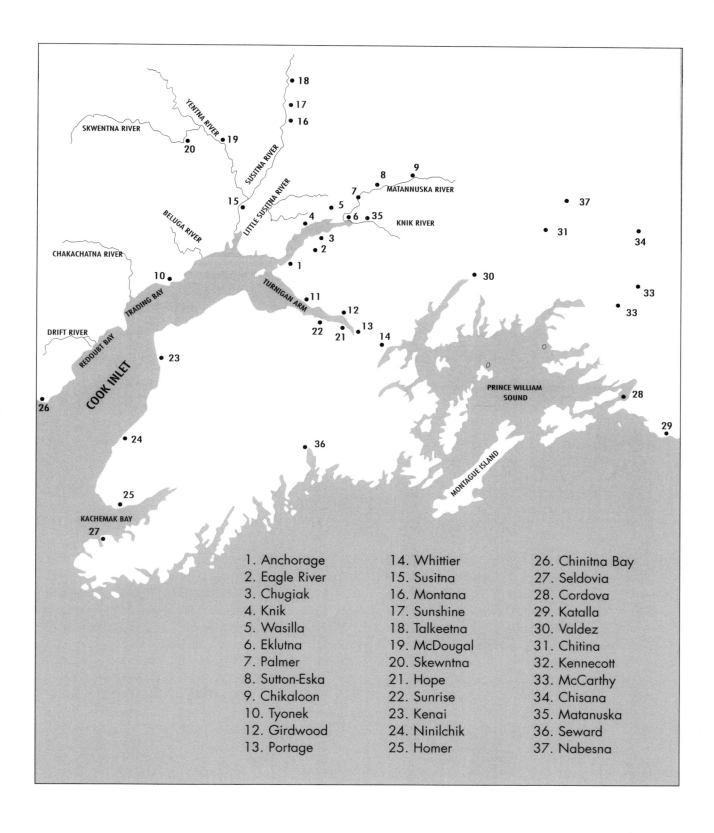

1. Anchorage
2. Eagle River
3. Chugiak
4. Knik
5. Wasilla
6. Eklutna
7. Palmer
8. Sutton-Eska
9. Chikaloon
10. Tyonek
12. Girdwood
13. Portage

14. Whittier
15. Susitna
16. Montana
17. Sunshine
18. Talkeetna
19. McDougal
20. Skewntna
21. Hope
22. Sunrise
23. Kenai
24. Ninilchik
25. Homer

26. Chinitna Bay
27. Seldovia
28. Cordova
29. Katalla
30. Valdez
31. Chitina
32. Kennecott
33. McCarthy
34. Chisana
35. Matanuska
36. Seward
37. Nabesna

Historic Monuments Collage, Anchorage Memorial Park circa 2001

Preface

This book is not a treatise on the history of Anchorage, it is not a collection of self-told stories and escapades of individuals, nor is it a collection of anecdotal or personal accomplishments by its residents, nor is it a Who's Who of Anchorage. This book is an accumulation of true histories of those Anchorage and Alaska Pioneers who came here for whatever reason and lived here for some period of time during its formative years. It depicts the history of those hardy pioneers who came, put down their roots, built their homes and planted the seeds that germinated into the city of today. It is a collection of the histories of many of these families and individuals who had a hand in the developing and molding the future of the community, or, to quote the vernacular, "the people that cut the brush" and gave Anchorage its start.

I have tried to contact all families and persons that were here or came here between 1910 and 1935, however, the first generation is gone, and the second and third generations are difficult to find, as names change and people move. If any one is left out that should be in this book, believe me, it was not intentional. Many did not respond to my request for information, and there is nothing that I could do about that, however to those that did respond, I wish to thank you profusely for your time and effort as without your input this book would not have been possible.

The 1994 Pioneer family exhibit in the Museum was the inspiration for this book. The idea was to preserve the histories of all of these hardy souls that came to Alaska and Anchorage and had a part in the development of this great city. The criteria was different, and the time frame setting from 1910 to 1935, the first twenty-five years, was used, as the year of 1935 was the turning point in the growth of Anchorage. After this year the population started to change, concrete buildings were being built, running water, street lights, sewage systems, automobiles, airplanes and whatever else were becoming commonplace. Modern conveniences were becoming the norm.

No one more clearly defines the true PIONEER, and the spirit, than Judge James Wickersham when he penned his "POEM OF THE YUKON AND ALASKA PIONEERS" and here it is.

Who first explored the Kwik-pak wide,
Who floated down the Pelly's tide,
Who built the fur posts for the indian trade,
And brought the book to the Yukon glade.

Who blazed the trail o'er the Dyea divide,
Who built the boats on Lindeman's side,
Who worked the Stewarts bars a while,
And found the paystreak on the forty-mile.

Who mined the Circle and Klondike Creek,
Who camped at Nome neath Anvil's peak,

Who founded Fairbanks, opened its mines,
And prospected where the Iditarod twines.

Who built its towns, its roads its trails,
Who planned its railroads, and laid the rails,
Who guided in council, in creating homes,
And in laying a State's foundation stones.

Table of Contents

FOREWORD

by
PROFESSOR STEPHEN HAYCOX
UNIVERSITY OF ALASKA ANCHORAGE

John Bagoy has been in love with Anchorage's Pioneers for a long time. It's a grand and glorious love that has produced an extraordinary amount of good. In this volume the reader will find some of its results, the carefully documented record of just about all of the City's early residents. In the first instance this commemorates those Pioneers' commitment to build a new community, to put down their stakes with the faith that this place was their proper place. At the same time, the record presented here provides the researcher with invaluable information, representing an inestimable investment of time and energy. When it becomes important for someone to know the facts about who lived in early Anchorage, when, what they did, where they came from, what happened to them, and who their children were, John Bagoy will provide the answer. It's right here in LEGENDS AND LEGACIES.

Whatever else history is, and it is many things, it is as accurate a reconstruction of the facts of the past as can be assembled. It takes hard work, tenacity, patience, and dedication. John Bagoy has all of these as he has demonstrated over more than a decade of carefully piecing together biographical data on thousands of Pioneers. It is impossible to place a value on what he has done; it simply can't be calculated. But the legacy of what he has done will be as eternal as human memory because it is so valuable. Anchorage will have many libraries over time. Information will be stored using a variety of technologies. But wherever it's located and in whatever form, one of the fundamental documents will be Bagoy's LEGENDS AND LEGACIES. Among the community of librarians and students of history, the name will be second nature; everyone will know what it means.

History matters. Not only does it keep alive the memory of those who came before, it inspires curiosity and wonder at what their lives were like and how and why they made the decisions they did. That's because what came after was built on the foundation of that which was built before, by the Pioneers. What qualifies the people in this volume as Pioneers is that they were here before anyone else. There was no Native community where the City of Anchorage now stands, though the Natives used the area, as artifacts collected along the bluff of Knik Arm northeast of the city testify. The Pioneers in LEGENDS AND LEGACIES decided to embark on a new enterprise, building a new community. The opportunity to do that was provided by the federal government. Anchorage was the construction, and later the administrative, headquarters for the federally owned and operated Alaska Railroad. Until 1940 the Railroad was the economic mainstay of the town. It provided its largest direct payroll, and thus was the principal indirect support for all the other businesses. But as the biographies here show, by the businesses they started and the dedication they manifested, the town's Pioneers attracted still more settlers. Town boosters cleared the land for an airstrip, helped launch a guiding business, and invested in an airplane company, among other things. Canneries found the location attractive and established operations in the dock area. The seat of the judicial district was transferred from Valdez "temporarily," and never made it back. Over time, the federal "brigade" grew substantially, and became a significant addition to the economy and the character of the town.

But the grist of the town was the Pioneers who decided to stay here, built their homes and supported the businesses, sent their children to the town's schools and fostered their development, nurtured the civic activities, and created a community. Thus, increasingly, John Bagoy will be associated with the Pioneers he so loves. That's a many-layered and entirely appropriate tribute to his work and life, and to his achievement in this book.

CHAPTER I

THE FIRST ARRIVALS - 1910-1914

It is nothing less than remarkable that during ninety years Ship Creek and the upper Cook Inlet area turned into the great city of Anchorage. A mere ninety years ago there were only three homesteaders living on Ship Creek flats, THOMAS J. JETER, J. D. "BUD" WHITNEY and JACK BROWN.

―――――

TOM JETER is believed to have built a cabin in 1910 and lived off the land intermittently for almost four years. He filed for patent on the land in 1915 but was turned down by Federal Judge J. Brown. The Court based its decision on the fact that, even though Jeter built a livable cabin and cleared an amount of land, he had settled thereon "without due authority and subsequent to the creation of the National Forest."

―――――

J. D. WHITNEY, hereinafter referred to as "Bud," was born in Illinois in 1875 and migrated to Washington in 1895. In 1898 he landed in Kikatar, Alaska, now known as Kotzebue. He and a partner traveled to Nome, where they staked and mined a few claims. In 1901 he moved to Candle where he continued his prospecting. There in 1903 he met and married Daisy Kincaid. Seven years later they went to Seward where they built a boat and floated the Kenai River to the town of Kenai where they spent the winter.

The following spring they moved to the mouth of Ship Creek where they built a cabin. Arriving on May 5, 1911, they had only a three-month supply of food and three dollars cash in their pockets. Knik was the closest source of supply and was accessible only by boat or winter trail.

The following year they moved up the creek several miles and located a new homestead. Their new site was located approximately where the Boniface gate to Ft. Richardson is now. Raising hogs seemed to be a good idea, and before long they were selling meat to the Alaska Engineering workers who were starting to build the railroad. By 1914 Bud also had the opportunity to acquire a little extra cash by guiding the engineers who were surveying the route. After the completion of the railroad, Bud and Daisy lived a quiet and peaceful life on the ranch until 1935 when they decided to move into town. Bud took a job with the Alaska Road Commission and later was the custodian of the new City Hall in Anchorage.

When the Railroad was completed the first section north of Anchorage was named Whitney Station and remained as such until Bud and Daisy sold the property to the Army. However, Whitney Road remains to this day.

Daisy and Bud on Their Homestead

In 1945 Bud and Daisy left Alaska for warmer climes, moving to Oregon, where they resided in Ashland for the rest of their years. Bud passed away in 1955 and Daisy in 1979. Thus ended a story of two Anchorage and Alaska Pioneers who actually cut the brush and left their mark on Anchorage history.

———

The life and times of JACK and NELLIE BROWN would certainly fill a book, and I am sure someone someday will write one. Jack Brown was born in Glasgow, Scotland in l872 and at an adult age migrated to Canada. He eventually worked his way across Canada to the west coast and finally landed in Alaska in l906. He found employment with the United States Forest Service and reported to Valdez where he was assigned as forester of the Cook Inlet and Kenai Peninsula area. He was living in a tent at the mouth of Ship Creek on upper Cook Inlet in 1910. Using this as his headquarters, he did his survey work and monitored the activities of the miners in the Turnagain Arm area.

Pencil Sketch of Nellie, by Jack

On frequent trips to Cordova, he met a young lady named Nellie Shepard whose mother was the daughter of an Eyak Indian Chief and whose father was a local merchant and fisherman who later became postmaster of Cordova. Jack was smitten with this young lady and she with him, and in 1912 they were married in Cordova. That same year they proceeded by boat to their Ship Creek honeymoon tent, arriving in June. After a short sojourn in the tent, they moved into the cabin that Bud and Daisy Whitney had vacated and remained there until they moved into the new townsite where they built a log cabin.

Jack built a boat to use as a lighter carrying freight and passengers ashore from the ships at anchor in bay. He also was establishing a homestead near Green Lake and used the boat to haul supplies. The homestead was just off the bluff at Cairn Point and had water access.

Jack in Forestry Tent

Jack and His Boat

Returning to town after seven years on the homestead, Jack went to work for the Alaska Railroad in the power plant until his retirement in 1940. When the Railroad started selling off the cottages on Government Hill, Jack and Nellie purchased Cottage #7 and remained there for the rest of their years.

In 1940 Nellie, with Margaret Abercrombie, opened a diner downtown on E Street between 4th and 5th

Avenues and appropriately named it Nellie's Diner. Nellie sold her interest in the Diner in 1943 and retired from business.

Nellie had a close relationship with Alaska's great artist Sydney Laurence. The story told on how this relationship developed has many versions, all of which are questionable. It seems that Sydney Laurence, when prospecting in the wilderness, became a victim of Alaska weather by breaking through shell ice while crossing a glacier stream and got completely soaked. The temperature was below zero when he was found by a good Samaritan who took him into a cabin and saved his freezing legs and feet. The Samaritan was supposedly Nellie's father. This is supposed to explain the numerous Laurence paintings hanging on Nellie's walls in her Government Hill home.

The legendary Browns were two of the earliest Anchorage residents. Even though Nellie has been characterized as the first lady of Anchorage, it seems that Daisy Whitney would also hold that title as she was on the scene one year prior to Nellie. Let them take equal billing! Jack Brown died in 1972 at the age of ninety-four and Nellie in 1978 at the age of eighty-six.

The Homestead

Nellie at Age 30

Jack at Age 85

At this point I think it appropriate to explain the Loop Road, Whitney Road and other landmarks. The Loop Road was the beginning of the Anchorage highway system and the Glenn Highway. It was completed around 1920-21 at the behest of homesteaders such as Jack Brown and Bud Whitney, who actually cleared the brush on their original wagon roads. The later homesteaders extended these wagon roads, and finally the Alaska Road Commission started grading them and made them passable to the public. The Loop Road started at the Ship Creek bridge, proceeded north across the railyards to the foot of Government Hill, angled up the hill to where the Elmendorf Gate is now, proceeded north again to Green Lake, then turned east to Otter Lake, went around Otter Lake south of Eagle River, proceeded south to approximately the edge of Fort Richardson, thence west again to the railroad tracks which intersected Whitney's ranch, then followed Ship Creek west on what is now Post Road to the intersection of Whitney and Post, then on Whitney Road to the point of origin, Ship Creek Bridge.

On March 12, 1914, President Woodrow Wilson signed a bill authorizing the Secretary of Interior to select a route for the construction of a railroad from Seward to Fairbanks, Alaska. The secretary set up the Alaska Engineering Commission (AEC), composed of Mr. W. C. Edes, Lt. Frederick Mears, both experienced railroad builders, and Mr. Thomas Riggs, Jr., a geologist. Under the direction of the Commission, eleven parties were sent out to select a route for the railroad. The western, or Susitna, route was chosen because of the deep-water port in Seward and the already begun Alaska Central Railway. Seward was the first choice for the railroad headquarters; however, the cost of the land rose too high due to the greed of one man, who owned most of the land involved. As a result, Ship Creek landing was selected, and Anchorage was born.

The following poem was written by a man who suffered financial losses due to the change of location of the railroad headquarters. He put the blame on Edes, Mears and Christenson, thus the poem. It was distributed widely in Seward and Anchorage, however it was not signed by Mr. Cotter. Our copy was.

THE UNHOLY TRINITY
By Pat P. Cotter

A little group of willful men,
Eades and Mears and Christensen,
Are running a scheme of common cause,
And barely keeping within the laws,
Wrecking a country they were sent to save
And this will follow them to the grave,
This self same group of little men,
Eades and Mears and Christensen.

The first is a relic of bygone days,
Too old to curse, to poor to praise,
The dean of the willful Trinity
Is a relic of scrap from the old S. P.,
Doddering, old, decrepit and all,
He could only hear "his country's call"
When they told him the wages paid this mob,
He tottered North on his farewell job.

And Mears, the ward of the Grape Juice King,
A political pet from the Panama Ring,
Sulky and silent and fearing a fall,
Though raised to a Captain, he hears no call,
Clings like grim death and obsessed by fear
Lest someone might steal his ten thousand a year,
Wanting to go and fearing to flee,
The first and the last of the Trinity.

And Andy, the Czar of official greed,
Cunning and crafty, a red tape Swede,
Staking his all on a side track spur,
Sneaking his scraps like an alien cur;

Selling townsites and missing the pen
By rating as one of "Our Government men."
Shall we stand for this Swede in this north country,
The brains and the boss of the Trinity.

Tell us ye group of little men,
Eades and Mears and Christensen;
Tell us the money you've spent and lost
Give us the Anchorage townsite cost,
The money you spent on graded roads,
Thrice built bungalows for your abodes;
Ships that your incompetence lost.
Oh! Tell us, Trinity, what was the cost?

Christ cleared the temple in olden days
And drove the grafters and thieves away.
Won't Congress do what Christ has done,
And give this Trinity gang the run,
And send us one man to build the road,
Forgetting townsites and his own abode;
And there is only one thing we want him to do
It's open the country and put the road through,
And tie the can to three little men,
Eades and Mears and Christensen.*

*Note, Thomas Riggs is not mentioned here, but Christensen
is, probably because it rhymes.

Andrew Christensen was appointed superintendent of lot sales in the new townsite. "The sale of lots in the new townsite will begin at 9 a.m. July 9th 1915, and will continue until all reasonable demand for lots has been met." Mr. Christensen was honored in that Christensen Road was named after him.

Phineas P. Hunt, official photographer of the AEC, dropped dead of heart failure in front of the post office at Seward, October 14, 1917. He had been in Seward on official business and was preparing to return to Anchorage. He was a Pioneer Alaskan, having come to Valdez in 1898, and had been an employee of the AEC since 1916. He did a magnificent job of preserving the history of the railroad construction in photography.

Phineas P. Hunt

Andrew Christensen

COLONEL FREDERICK MEARS was born in Ft. Omaha, Nebraska on May 25, 1878. His father was in the military, and he attended the Shattuck Military Academy in Faribault, Minnesota, graduating in 1897. In 1907 he met and married Jennie Wainwright in Ft. Clark, Texas. They had three children, two daughters and one son. He was employed by the Great Northern Railroad in Idaho from 1897 to 1899 and enlisted in the army in 1899. He served in the Philippines and was promoted to Second Lieutenant in 1901. He returned to the United States in 1903 and was sent to the Panama Canal Zone as chief engineer and general superintendent of the Panama Railroad and S.S. Line. In 1914 he was sent to Anchorage as the chairman of the Alaska Engineering Commission, responsible for the construction of the Alaska Railroad.

Colonel Frederick Mears

In 1917 he was sent to France for two years and returned a Lieutenant Colonel. He returned to Anchorage in 1919 and was appointed general manager of the Alaska Railroad, which he served until 1923. He retired from the ARR in 1923 and moved to Seattle, Washington. He moved then to Minnesota and became assistant chief engineer for the Great Northern Railway in charge of construction of tunnels through the Cascade Mountains from 1925 to 1939. He died in Seattle in 1939.

William Cushing Edes

Born in Bolton, Massachusetts in 1856, WILLIAM CUSHING EDES graduated from M.I.T. in 1875 with a degree in civil engineering. In 1876 and '77 he was a surveyor for the Southern Pacific Railroad; in 1882-86 he was assistant engineer on the Southern Pacific Railroad and the Atchison, Topeka and the Santa Fe; in 1907 he was the chief engineer of the Northwestern Pacific Railroad. When he came to Anchorage in 1914 he was construction and consulting engineer for the AEC. He retired in 1922 due to ill health and died in California in 1922.

THOMAS CHRISTMAS RIGGS, JR. was born in Ilchester, Maryland on October 17, 1873. He graduated from Princeton with a degree in civil engineering. In 1913 he married Rene C. Coudert and they had two children. The family moved to Washington in 1893 where Thomas was employed as a newspaper reporter. He left for Dawson and the gold fields of the Klondike in 1897 and then went to Nome in 1900. Returning to Seattle in 1901 he was engaged as a surveyor with the Alaska Canada Boundary Commission, and in l913 he was sent to Anchorage as engineer in charge of the northern terminus of the Alaska Railroad.

In 1918 he was appointed Governor of Alaska and served in this capacity until 1921. He left Alaska in 1921 for New York where he engaged in construction, mining and oil exploration. In 1935 he was appointed as a member of the American Canadian Boundary Commission and the International Highways Commission. He passed away in Washington, D.C. in January 1945.

The information on Riggs, Mears, Edes, Christenson and Hunt was taken from E. Atwood, *Who's Who in Alaska Politics.*

Thomas Riggs, Jr.

———

ROYDEN D. CHASE was another member of the AEC who was sent to Anchorage to participate in the construction of the Alaska Railroad. He was born in Washington, D.C. in 1875. He served under civil service as storekeeper, disbursing officer, paymaster and special assistant disbursing officer until 1925 when he returned to Washington, D.C. where he was appointed traveling auditor for the Public Works Administration. He died in Washington in 1935.

———

Another appointee to the AEC, BURNTON H. BARNDOLLAR came to Anchorage to join the original survey crews and to serve as legal adviser and examiner of accounts. He was born in Bedford, Pennsylvania in 1878 and lived there until 1893. He was a graduate of the Washington University Law School and spent several years in Chicago before moving to Washington, D.C. with the Department of Interior. He was sent from Washington to Alaska and became legal advisor to the governor of Alaska after completion of the Railroad. He died December 2, 1944.

———

GEORGE COLWELL, who was the chief engineer of the Railroad until his retirement, describes the first engineering party to arrive at Ship Creek on June 15, 1914. *Anchorage Times*, June 1944:

"It was on June 15, 1914, and a fine day when we came ashore at a spot just below where the Ship Creek Bridge is now," Colwell said. "There was one log cabin there as far as we could see. [Note: Jeter or Whitney cabin] No people around at all. We pitched our camp and four days later the survey parties had started out. We had to cut a trail through the heavy timber where the City of Anchorage now stands, so the pack trains could get through. There were 84 men in this first party," Colwell said, "including eight Assistant Engineers, [of which he was one,] Instrument men, Packers, Cooks, Camp tenders, Axe men and sufficient supplies and equipment, including twenty horses to maintain six survey parties on the trail and the base camp at Ship Creek." Of the original engineering party arriving in 1914, and up until the time of the narrative given by Colwell, he was the only one of the party still living in Alaska.

George Colwell was born in 1884 in Yankee Jims, Placer County, California, a small mining community that is no longer on the

George Colwell, 1920

Ethel Colwell, 1920

George, Ethel, George, Sr.
and Jaqueline Colwell

George, Ethel and Jaqueline
Colwell

California maps. He spent his youth in the area around Auburn and Newcastle. Educated as a civil engineer, he was employed as a junior engineer on the Panama Canal project prior to coming to Alaska.

ETHEL LESLIE was born in San Francisco, California in 1886. Her family moved to Whitehorse, Yukon Territory in 1899, where her father was employed by the White Pass and Yukon Railway. In 1917 the family moved to Seward, Alaska where she met George Colwell. They were married in Seward in 1918.

George was in charge of the construction camp at Kern Creek near the famous tunnel and loop. Their first child, George Leslie, was born at Kern Creek in 1919. They moved to Anchorage in 1922 where their second child, Iris, was born the same year. In 1924 their third child, Jacqueline, was born, and George became roadmaster of the Railroad.

After thirty-five years of service, George retired as chief engineer, and he and Ethel moved to Seattle, Washington where they resided for the rest of their years. In 1958 George passed away at the age of seventy-five. Ethel survived him, passing away in 1985 at age eighty-seven.

George L. Colwell resides in Oceanside, California, with his wife Bonnie. Iris passed away at the age of sixteen, and the youngest daughter, Jacqueline Hartfield, passed away in 1995. There are three grandchildren: Anne Leslie Hartfield Ordway and John Peter Hartfield, both living in Woodinville, Washington; Jeffrey Colwell lives in Anchorage.

The lure of gold brought many to the new community. Brothers EUGENE and BYRON BARTHOLF, members of a New York and Colorado mining family, arrived in Knik in 1906 bent on prospecting for gold in the Willow Creek mining district. Their search for gold paid off in 1907 when, high on the side of Bullion Mountain overlooking Craigie Creek, they struck the lode. This was not the first discovery, as Robert Hatcher had made his discovery in 1906. However, the Bartholf discovery was the first one to develop.

The brothers returned to Seattle, telling of their discovery to relatives and friends. The rich vein of ore supposedly encircled the entire mountain. The following spring the brothers returned with horses and equipment and started developing Gold Bullion #1 Claim. They hauled ore down the mountain in one hundred-pound sacks, stockpiling it at the base of the mountain. The sacks were then loaded on packhorses and taken to tidewater at Knik. From Knik the ore was loaded aboard small boats and taken across the inlet to Ship Creek to be loaded on sea going vessels and taken "outside."

At the same time as the Bartholfs were working their claim, another group of claims known as the Carle Prospects were developing. They became the property of the Alaska Gold Quartz Mining Company, which eventually became the Independence Gold Mining Company. The three groups, Hatcher, Bartholf and the Independence, became the principal producers of gold in the district, with gold production second only to that of the A. J. Mine in Juneau.

Byron and Eugene Bartolf

In 1910 Byron Bartholf's family arrived in Knik. The children were promptly enrolled in the first school in Knik, and son John joined his father in the mining business.

When sons Chester and Ralph were about sixteen years old, they were out ptarmigan hunting and doing a little prospecting as well. After they had shot a few ptarmigan, they noticed a hole where a "whistler" or marmot had a den. In front of the hole Chet found a large chunk of quartz. Picking it up, he shouted to Ralph, "I found gold and it is rich." He was right. It was rich, and it was the beginning of the Lucky Shot Mine, and is how it got its name.

The family erected a mill, installed a tram, and went into full production. William, another son of Byron's, while working a shift with his brother John, got his pant leg caught in the drive shaft and was almost dismembered. By the time they were able to get him off the mountain and down to Wasilla to catch a special train sent out from Anchorage, he had passed away. After this accident, Byron sold the mine, even though some of the children wanted to keep it.

First School, Knik, 1913

In 1921 Charles and John Tyler, two of Byron's sons by his second wife, arrived and discovered the Mabel Mine, which was named after John's daughter. They also discovered another prospect which they named the Pearl after another daughter. The Pearl, however, did not pan out, although the Mabel became a producer.

The second generation Bartholfs, Charles and John Tyler, remained in Alaska. However, Byron and Chester moved to the west coast in 1918. Chester returned in 1919, in 1923, and again in 1975 for the last time. The family left their mark in the annals of the Alaska mining industry and, in particular, the Willow Creek district. The family tree is a book in itself as there are dozens of great grandchildren, grandchildren, cousins, nieces and nephews living all over the United States.

Ralph and Chester Bartolf

Lucky Shot Mine

Four Generations of Bartolfs

Bakery

Byron, Chester, John and Great-grandson Duane Bartolf

In 1915 a Bartholf bakery was operating in Anchorage townsite, and in 1916 and 1917 a Bartholf operated a lumberyard in Anchorage, and another one operated a leather and bridle shop. All of these are members of the same family. Jean Strong of Sacramento, California, the daughter of Chester Bartholf, contributed this family information. William, who was killed in the mine, is buried in Anchorage Memorial Park. Byron died in April 1939 and is buried in Klamath Falls, Oregon. Chester died in 1999 and is buried in Chico, California, as is Mabel, who died in 1994.

VIC BLODGETT was a pioneer mining engineer in Alaska and the Yukon. Born in Jefferson, Wisconsin in 1860, he became interested in mining in his youth. He spent five years in South America in the mining game and returned to California where he obtained more experience in the mines. He went over the Chilkoot pass in 1898 to Dawson and in 1914 moved to Knik and Ship Creek. After working as an engineer for the Gold Bullion Mine at Willow for several years, he decided to try his hand at mink farming. In 1934 he retired and moved to Anchorage. He passed away in 1941 in Anchorage.

Born in Kansas in 1880, JAMES ST. CLAIR originally planned to come to Alaska and start a marten farm; however, this ambition turned to mining and "horse skinning." He came to Alaska as a youth in 1900 and engaged in mining and working as a mine foreman at the Gold Bullion. In 1910 he married his wife Nellie and took up prospecting and finally homesteading in Matanuska Valley. He later worked on the ARR construction out of Ship Creek. It is said that he once struck it rich when he won a gold mine in a poker game from the well-known Alaskan artist Sydney Laurence. St. Clair passed away in Anchorage in 1965.

Old-timer FREDERICK ZORN was a well-known character who styled himself as the "Nome Dynamiter." He arrived in tent town in 1914, coming from Nome and points north. Holding several mining claims along the right of way of the Alaska Railroad, he spent considerable time corresponding with the AEC and members of Congress to interest them in the development of mining in the area. He lived in a small cabin at the corner of 4th Avenue and A Street. He was a quiet bachelor of unknown origin. He was a gentle man and was always friendly with children most of whom called him Santa Claus because of the full white beard he wore. He passed away in 1932 and now lies in an unmarked grave in Anchorage Memorial Park.

The railroad authorization bill and the sale of Anchorage townsite lots brought many people from Knik, Wasilla and all parts of Alaska, the rest of the United States and many foreign countries to Anchorage in 1914 and 1915.

The AEC became concerned about the hundreds of people squatting on the flats and decided the most important thing on the agenda was to move them out as rapidly as possible. With this in mind, they started letting clearing contracts and dividing the land into city blocks and lots. Blocks and lots were surveyed, with areas set aside for municipal buildings, schools and a cemetery.

One of the earliest occupants of the cemetery was FRANK AMESTOY, who with his brother had contracted to clear the trees in Block 108 of the original townsite, located on what is now Cordova Street between 7th and 8th Avenues. He was killed instantly by a falling tree and was buried in the "Government Cemetery" which is now Anchorage Memorial Park Cemetery. He was killed on July 11, 1915 and buried on July 13 just one-half block from where he was killed.

There were many small contractors who worked at clearing the timber off the townsite, as well as working on the railroad construction. The AEC let hundreds of small contracts, usually to a contractor who employed as few as four or five men. It has been said that some of the wages actually came down to as low as thirty-seven cents per hour.

One of the early contractors on the railroad as well as on the townsite, TONY MARTINOVICH was a Croatian immigrant who arrived at Ship Creek in 1914. He was a station contractor during the construction years, a prospector and miner in the Willow Creek area, and finally a foreman at the Independence Mine for many years until he retired in Anchorage in 1939. Tony was well known in the mining community and among Anchorage businessmen. He passed away in 1942 and is buried in Anchorage Memorial Park.

Another of the early contractors and miners in the area, TONY BUTORAC first came to Knik in 1910 and prospected and mined in the Willow creek area. He worked construction, building the terminal yards in Anchorage, as well as working during the winter months as a powder man at the Independence Mine. He passed away in Palmer in 1949.

"CYCLONE" BILL THOMPSON ended his life in his cabin near Six Mile Roadhouse. Bill Thompson was a native of Norway and came to Alaska during the gold rush of '98. It was said he came to Anchorage from Nome in 1915 and settled on the Herb Beebe homestead at six-mile, Loop Road. Very little is known about him, however the article in the *Times* gave a full ten column inches describing how his body was positioned and where the bullet entered and exited. It was said he had been in ill health for some time, and this was the second attempt to end his life. He was buried in Anchorage's Memorial Park Cemetery July 19, 1932 in an unmarked grave.

On the other arm of Cook Inlet, the gold rush towns of Sunrise, Hope and Girdwood were prospering, with the gold seekers concentrating on Resurrection and Palmer Creeks. Transportation to these areas was a problem due to the inability of ocean going vessels to enter the shallow waters of Turnagain Arm.

The demand was great for small lighters, barges, gas boats, schooners and all types of shallow draft vessels. With this in mind we will take up the more prominent vessels and sailors who operated from Seward and Seldovia to all points on the Inlet, namely Tyonek, Ladds, Sunrise, Hope, Knik, Girdwood, Susitna station, McDougal, Matanuska and Crow Creek.

The most prominent small boats operating in upper Cook Inlet in 1908 were the *Swan*, owned by "Cap" Ward and Tom O'Dale, the *P.V.* owned by Lee Ellikson, the *Lina K* owned by "Red" Jack Bartels and the *Valdez*. These gas boats served as the lighters to the communities that the ocean going vessels could not reach. The Alaska Commercial Company's *S. S. Bertha* and the *S. S. Dora* were the two most prominent ocean going vessels operating in the upper inlet.

TOM O'DALE was born in Arkansas and grew up in Oregon, one of a family of seven boys and one girl. One of his brothers had come to Alaska during the 1896 Cook Inlet gold rush, and Tom followed in 1900. He worked and prospected along the Kenai peninsula, Crow Creek and other locations, but kept hearing the stories of the prospects on the north side of the Alaska Range.

In 1906 he teamed up with a man named Jack Clouse, and the two of them put together a grubstake and headed out to cross the Alaska Range. They estimated a two year supply of grub including twelve hundred pounds of flour, five hundred of sugar, three hundred of beans, two hundred fifty of rice, two hundred fifty of bacon, seventy-five of dried fruit and twenty of lard, in addition to salt, tea and soda.

They left in October of that year on a rented boat, and headed up the Big Susitna River to Susitna Station. There they bought an old boat and towed and poled up the Yentna and the south fork of the Skwentna. On their way up they met two more old-timers, Jim Ward and Mike Stagner, heading in the same direction, so they partnered up with them. With freeze-up coming they had to prepare their outfit for snow travel, so they dismantled their boat and made two sleds to carry their gear. They chose to "neck" their sleds rather than using dogs, as caring for the dogs and carrying more food for them would make their outfit much larger and harder to handle. Their trip was a story in itself, and it lasted two years. They blazed the route over what is now Rainy Pass to the Kuskokwim. This same route is now part of the Iditarod Trail.

Upon their return to the Inlet area, they built a boat, named it the *Bydarky*, and acquired mail contracts traveling up and down the Inlet. They carried not only mail but also passengers and freight. Tom finally settled down and married Ada Holser in 1910. They took out a homestead on Tustemena Lake and built the first hunting lodge permitted on the Lake. Tom became a registered Alaska guide and guided hunters from all over the world. Tom and Ada separated in 1924. Ada returned to California with her daughter, and Tom stayed in Alaska operating his guide business and spending his winters in Anchorage. All of the information given here was taken from the *Alaska Journal*, Volume 4, and from information given by Louise Simonson, Tom's daughter.

Tom O'Dale and *The Swan*

JIM "CAP" WARD was born in Trempealeau, Wisconsin, moved with his family to the west coast, and a short time later went to sea at the age of fifteen. He worked aboard vessels up and down the coast and then to Alaska to the 1898 Gold Rush. He was in Nome in 1898 and witnessed the beach fight told about in Rex Beach's novel *The Spoilers*. After partnering with Tom O'Dale, he moved to Kodiak where he married Elizabeth Bowen, daughter of Captain Harry Bowen who at one time was in charge of all Alaska Commercial Company stores on the west coast. The Wards moved to Anchorage in 1916-17 where Cap joined the work force of the Alaska Railroad in the machine shops. In 1923 Elizabeth passed away leaving Cap with five children, Jess, James, Edward, Lorinda and Stanley.

Jim Ward at the Wheel of the *Bydarky*

Edward, who was employed by Heinie Berger as a deck hand on the *M. V. Kasilof*, was in port in Anchorage on June 25, 1935. He went swimming alone at Green Lake and accidentally drowned. Cap retired from the Alaska Railroad and moved south to Seattle where he passed away in 1943. Jess retired in 1965 and moved to Garden Grove, California where he passed away in 1984. Lorinda Ward Watson and her spouse were accidentally killed in California in the 1980's. The whereabouts of Edward and Stanley is unknown. The Ward family occupied Cottage #9 on Government Hill until 1940.

Tom O'Dale on the *Bydarky*

"RED" JACK BARTELS was born in Hamburg, Germany in 1860 and left home at the age of sixteen, signing on a British whaling ship. He sailed for a year, and in San Francisco he was employed by the Spreckels Sugar Company. When the Spanish American War erupted, Jack served as a cook while in the service.

After the war he sailed aboard a sealing ship bound for Alaska, but, after arriving at Unga, he left the ship to sign on a herring boat. He eventually wound up at Tyonek and was operating a boat named the *Lina K* on the Susitna River. It was at Susitna station that Tom O'Dale and Jack Bartels met. According to Tom, Jack was interested in purchasing the *Swan*, which was owned by Bill Murphy, and at the time both Murphy and Bartels were kept busy taking passengers down the Susitna river to Tyonek.

Jack's boat, the *Lina K*, was the only boat on the Inlet operating on kerosene rather than gasoline. There is a story that the boat had a regular gasoline engine, but once that engine got hot it would operate on kerosene. There are two versions to this story, however, whichever the true one is, gasoline was in short supply and kerosene wasn't, so these indomitable Pioneers made do with what they had.

"Red" Jack Bartels in Pilot House of *Sea Lion*

Jack and Tom met again in Tyonek, and Tom struck a deal to buy the *Swan* from Bill Murphy. It was the first of November, and ice was forming when they headed to Seldovia for the winter. They had no charts, but fortunately saw a steamer, which happened to be the *Bertha*, and followed her into Seldovia. Jack returned to Tyonek where he either built a boat named the *Sea Lion* or renamed the *Lina K*. He operated on the Inlet under a mail contract serving Hope, Sunrise, Knik and Susitna station. He eventually sold his boat to Nick Gaikema who was operating out of Knik. Jack then moved to Knik where he homesteaded two hundred fifty acres.

In 1916 he married Tuxenna "Minnie" Trenton, who was born in Tyonek in 1885. They had three sons: John born 1917 and died 1967, Harry born 1922, and Lee born 1923 and died in 1968. They also had two daughters that did not survive infancy.

In 1928 Jack and Minnie moved to Anchorage where they bought a house located at 8th Avenue and I Street. Jack operated cannery tenders for the

The *Sea Lion* at the City Dock

Far West Cannery, H. J. Emard and Al Jones Kustatan Packing Company for a number of years and decided retirement was something to look into. He was a member of the Pioneers of Alaska and was lodge secretary in 1933.

The community hall, which was also the local gymnasium, was owned by the Pioneers. It was located across the street from where the Elks lodge presently stands. Jack volunteered as caretaker for fifty dollars per month. He became a father figure with youth of the community, as all indoor athletics took place in the Community Hall. Every student who played basketball knew Jack as the custodian, and he was available every day of the week to open the gym to any of them.

Jack passed away in 1946 at the age of eighty-six, and his spouse, Tuxenna, died at Eklutna in 1958. All information was contributed by Harry Bartels or was taken from Tom O'Dale's *Alaskan Adventures*.

N. J. "NICK" GAIKEMA sailed around Anchorage before it was born on his many trips to Knik, Sunrise and Crow Creek. He was operating the gas-boat *Swan*, which he had acquired from Tom O'Dale about 1910. Just about a year later he acquired the *Sea Lion* from Jack Bartels and kept it on the mail run between the upper and lower inlet.

Nick was born in Muskegon, Michigan in 1879 and came to Anchorage the year the townsite was settled, moving up from Seldovia. He carried passengers, freight and mail for many years, however he was most well known for his charter trips to the duck flats in the twenties and thirties. The *Sea Lion* could accommodate six persons and was used as a "duck" shack when arriving at the flats of Theodore, Susitna, Lewis River or Trading Bay. His guests were primarily businessmen of the community, all ardent duck hunters and poker players. The days were spent hunting ducks, and the nights were spent playing poker. His regular clients were Z. J. Loussac, Bob Bragaw, George Kennedy, Dan Kennedy, Chris Eckman, E. R. Tarwater, George Mumford, Oscar Gill, Bill Mellish and many others.

In 1922 Nick was trying to develop interest in the Katmai area, in particular the Valley of Ten Thousand Smokes. The idea was to find a route to the area by water, which meant going up the Katmai River and into Katmai Lake.

This route would bring the parties within thirty miles of the crater, which was a much shorter route than what the National Geographic Society had used. Two women in the party were nurse Alice Bartholf, and Miss Thelma Hunt. They spent three weeks in the area and were in awe of what they found on their trip up to the mountain, as well as of the fantastic view they had of the crater, which was three miles long. The ground was so warm they mostly walked in stocking feet on the pumice. Nick felt that the region had great promise as a tourist attraction, however not for those faint of heart.

Nick served one term on the Anchorage City Council and was a long time member of the Elks Lodge. He and the *Sea Lion* were last employed by the Iniskin Oil Drilling Company at Chinitna Bay as boatman, carrying equipment and materials from Anchorage to the drilling site. After Iniskin shut down, Nick was kept on as watchman and custodian at the site.

On June 22, 1943 Nick had a fatal heart attack at the camp. He was accompanied by his son Jim and Jack Huston, but nothing could be done for him. He and

Standing, Chris Eckman, George Kennedy; Standing on Pilot House is Bob Bragaw, Dr. L. J. Seeley, Dr. A. S. Walkowski and E. R. Tarwater; Nick Gaikema Standing on the Stern

Lowering *Sea Lion* into Water after Winter Dry Docking

his wife had been separated for a number of years, and she passed away sometime in the seventies in Seattle. Son Jim passed away in the eighties also in Seattle. Nick is buried in the Elks Tract in Anchorage Memorial Park.

AUSTIN E. "CAP" LATHROP
ALASKA'S GREATEST INDUSTRIALIST

On June 26, 1950 "Cap" Lathrop met with a fatal accident at his Healy River coal mine at Suntrana, Alaska. The accident occurred as Cap was inspecting a string of loaded coal gondola cars. The engineer did not see him and released a car from the string on a short grade. Evidently Cap either tripped or fell under the wheels and was killed instantly.

Born in Lapeer, Michigan in 1865, he came west to Seattle to seek his fortune on the west coast, arriving shortly after a disastrous fire had razed a good part of Seattle. He was twenty-four years old when he started his first venture. Pitching a tent, he offered his services as a contractor to raze and clean up the burned structures and also to excavate for new structures. Before long he became known as the "boy contractor."

His next venture was to contract to construct an electric railway from Anacortes, Washington to Fidalgo Island. Soon after the dedication of the rail line, he leased six hundred acres of good land and developed a first class chicken ranch. Disaster struck in the form of the panic of 1893. This not only left him broke but in debt. Never looking back, he ran into an old acquaintance, onc Captain Kelly, who told him of the discovery of gold in the Turnagain Arm area of Cook Inlet in Alaska. Cap was extremely interested and, even though he was broke, he had three valuable assets in his favor: he had good credit, he was an honest man, and he had a reputation of being a hard worker.

An executive of the Fry Meat Packing Company staked him money to buy a one-half interest in the steam schooner *J. L. Perry*, and he and his partners sailed out of Seattle in 1896 bound for Alaska, arriving in Juneau with their first cargo destined for the Alaska Commercial Company.

Within one year, Cap bought out his partner O'Neill and acquired his master's ticket as well. Thus was born Cap Lathrop, the sea going captain, and the name Cap stuck from then on. He was plying the waters of Cook Inlet, carrying freight and passengers, when he changed to a new venture: coal. He began hauling and selling coal taken off the beach near Homer until 1900 when the business died.

Lulu Fairbanks, Cap and Eva McGowen

A new challenge arose that year: oil. Cap found backing from an eastern investor and started to develop the Cold Bay oil prospect. He experienced another failure when the federal government set aside millions of acres of public land for reserves, and Cap had to seal up his wells and withdraw from Cold Bay. However, he still had his boat and kept running the Inlet.

His next challenge occurred when he met an attractive widow, Lillian McDowell, mother of a fourteen year old daughter. On February 18, 1901 they were married in Valdez. It was the first recorded marriage in the town. Life aboard the *J. L. Perry* was not the most fascinating for the mother and daughter, so she returned to Seattle. Cap visited them on frequent trips, until Lillian passed away in 1910.

Cap went back to Valdez and scouted the copper country in the Kotsina district. He organized the California-Alaska Mining and Development Company in Cordova to prospect for copper. However, transportation was a problem, so he founded the Alaska Transfer Company. A year later he purchased the theater in Cordova, then an apartment house, and finally a cannery that he operated for several years.

His business interests brought him to the new town of Anchorage in 1915. The Alaska Railroad needed transfer men to handle the moves from Tent City to the townsite, so Cap obliged by organizing the Alaska Transfer Company. Around 1919 he sold the transfer business and started building the Empress Theater, and then an apartment house on the corner of 4th Avenue and H Street. Before long he had theaters in Valdez, Cordova, and Fairbanks, and also supplied film to the communities of Nenana and Seward.

In 1927, pushing North to Fairbanks, he built a new theater, from reinforced concrete, which was a first in Fairbanks. He acquired an interest in the Healy River Coal Corporation, operating in Suntrana, just one hundred seventeen miles south of Fairbanks. He finally purchased full control of the Healy Coal Company and was guaranteed stable management by doing so.

The next ten years saw him building another concrete building in Fairbanks, a four-story apartment building, with the *News Miner* newspaper on the first floor and a radio station, KFAR, which went on the air in 1939. His greatest dream however was the 4th Avenue Theater in Anchorage. Starting construction prior to WWII, he completed it in 1947, and it opened as one of the finest theaters on the west coast. He housed his radio station KENI over the theater and added a penthouse for his key employees.

Though Cap never remarried, there were two women in his life who influenced him over the years. For seventeen years Ruby DeGraff was his right hand until her death in 1927. Four years later he found someone he could trust in Miss Miriam Dickey, a young journalism graduate from the University of Washington, who remained with him for fourteen years.

Cap took a fling in politics and served a term in the legislature in 1921, then as the Republican national committeeman from Alaska for four years, 1928 to 1932. He served on the Board of Regents of the University of Alaska, the Fisheries Advisory Board, as a director of the Olympia Brewing Company, and as president and CEO of various corporations.

The distribution of his estate was evidence of his great faith and interest in his employees. He was buried in Forest Lawn Cemetery, Seattle, Washington, and thus ended the life of an Alaskan entrepreneur.

———

JOHN BALIOS arrived at the mouth of Ship Creek on June 24, 1915. This young Greek immigrant landed here before the tent town started. He was immediately employed as a cook by the AEC and watched the tent town mushroom practically overnight into a tent city.

At the advent of WWI, John enlisted in the United States Army and served for two years. He returned to Anchorage in 1920, and for the next few years he was employed as a chef for Bob Kuvara in the Frisco Café and also at the Union Café. In 1927 he decided to take a fling at being a store owner on LaTouche Island. He obtained a concession from the Kennecott Copper Company to open a store and operated it until 1934, when he decided that Anchorage held more promise for him.

He again plied his trade as a chef at various Anchorage restaurants, and in 1939 he took over the operation of the D and D Café from Fred Wright. He operated the D and D until the big fire of 1942 in which the café was destroyed.

Prior to the fire, Emil Pfeil and Tom Bevers remodeled the Hewitt building and established the Bevers and Pfeil Apartments, located at the corner of 4th Avenue and E Street. Walt Grohnert opened the Cheechako Tavern next door to Gus George Shoe Shop and John Balios took over the café in the rear of the Tavern. You had to walk through the bar to get to the café, which had no tables, just stools. He ran a successful café and was extremely popular with the breakfast and lunch crowd. He will long be remembered by oldtimers as having the greatest French doughnuts you ever tasted, made fresh daily.

John married in 1930, however very little is known of his family other than that there were three children. At the time of his death, his wife, Zona, and three sons were living in Lubbock, Texas, according to his brother-in-law Damon Polk.

John was born in Levathia, Greece in 1891 and died in Anchorage in 1957. He is buried in the Elks Tract in Anchorage Memorial Park.

CHAPTER II

1915 – 1919

TRIVIA

•ON APRIL 10, 1915 PRESIDENT WILSON CHOSE THE SUSITNA RIVER ROUTE FOR THE PROPOSED RAILROAD.

•IN MAY 1915 THE FIRST GOVERNMENT BUILDING WAS ERECTED IN ANCHORAGE, THE UNITED STATES POST OFFICE.

•ON JUNE 5, 1915 THE FIRST NEWSPAPER WAS ISSUED, VOL. I, NO. 1, *COOK INLET PIONEER* AND *KNIK NEWS*.

•ON JULY 10, 1915 THE FIRST AUCTION SALE OF LOTS WAS HELD AND WAS THE FORMAL OPENING OF THE ANCHORAGE TOWNSITE.

•AUGUST 2, 1915 WAS THE FIRST ELECTION OF THE SCHOOL BOARD.

•ON OCTOBER 21, 1915 THE FIRST DAILY NEWSPAPER WAS PRINTED, THE *COOK INLET PIONEER*.

•IN APRIL 1918 THE FIRST SCHOOL DISTRICT WAS ORGANIZED.

•ON OCTOBER 1, 1918 THE FIRST TRAIN RAN BETWEEN ANCHORAGE AND SEWARD.

•ON OCTOBER 5, 1918 THE FIRST PASSENGER TRAIN FROM ANCHORAGE TO SEWARD RAN.

•ON SEPTEMBER 13, 1919 THE FIRST OCEAN GOING VESSEL TIED UP AT THE ANCHORAGE DOCK.

Q: WHY DOES ANCHORAGE NOT HAVE A "J" STREET?

A: THE ALASKA ENGINEERING COMMISSION, THAT DID THE PLATTING OF THE TOWNSITE, WAS BASICALLY A MILITARY ORGANIZATION, AND, BECAUSE OF THE MILITARY CONNECTION, THE MILITARY HISTORIANS STATE THAT THE LETTER "J" WAS ELIMINATED IN 1816 WHEN THE ARMY STARTED IDEN-TIFYING ITS COMPANIES WITH LETTERS OF THE ALPHABET. AT THE TIME ALL ORDERS WERE HAND-WRITTEN AND THE SCRIPT LETTER FOR "J" WAS SO SIMILAR TO THE SCRIPT LETTER FOR "I" THAT THE "J" WAS DROPPED.

THE FACT THAT THERE WERE MANY SCANDINAVIANS HERE AT THE TIME MAY ALSO HAVE HAD SOMETHING TO DO WITH IT, AS THE LETTER "J" WAS PRONOUNCED "YAY" BY MOST SCANDINAVIAN IMMIGRANTS.

A COMBINATION OF BOTH OF THESE EXPLANATIONS WOULD PROBABLY BE IN ORDER.

Jane Mears

With the movement of people out of the tent town, and more people coming into the community, the demand for a school was paramount. The Anchorage Womans Club took the lead, and, with Jane Mears as chairperson, the school was on its way.

JANE WAINWRIGHT MEARS was the wife of the lead official of the Alaska Engineering Commission, which was the agency responsible for construction of the Alaska Railroad. She was prominent in Anchorage history because of her involvement on behalf of the development of the Anchorage school system between 1915 to 1923. She was the foremost organizer of the Anchorage Womans Club and was its first president. She was also the head of the steering committee for the construction of the first Anchorage schoolhouse and headed up the committee that canvassed local businesses for donations to pay the salaries of the teachers and other operating costs.

As the wife of Lieutenant Frederick Mears, she played a most important role in convincing the federal government, through her husband, that the school should be built with federal funds. This first school was the Pioneer Hall, now located at 3rd Avenue and Denali Street. The second school, built on 5th Avenue between F and G Streets, was also built with federal funds. As a result, public bonding was not necessary for financing schools until the year 1928.

The Mears family lived in Anchorage from 1915 to 1923. Upon leaving Anchorage, they settled in Seattle, where Lieutenant Mears became associated with the Great Northern Railroad. Little information is available on the Mears either before they came to Anchorage or after they left. What is known, however, is that Jane was the sister of General Jonathon "Skinny" Wainwright of Corregidor fame under General Douglas Macarthur, and that Skinny survived the Bataan death march after the 1942 surrender to Japan.

Miss ORA DEE CLARK was forty years old when she first arrived in Anchorage in August 1915. Tents were still in Ship Creek flats, and the frame buildings of the townsite were just being erected.

Ora Dee Clark

She was on her way to Susitna Station where she had accepted a teaching job. While she was waiting for transportation to Susitna, she was offered a similar teaching job in Anchorage. Since she had already committed herself to the Susitna community, she had to refuse. When she arrived in Susitna, she found that there was already a qualified teacher there, so she requested to be relieved of her obligation, and she returned to Anchorage to accept the position here.

First School House, Pioneer Hall

Miss Clark then became the first teacher of Anchorage schools, as well as principal and superintendent, and for all of this received the gross amount of one hundred twenty-five dollars per month. There were many difficulties to running an efficient school system: homemade furniture, wood stoves, over-crowded classrooms, poor lighting with coal oil lamps, no library, no gymnasium, and no multi-purpose rooms. The classroom was used for all functions.

Miss Clark first taught in the Pioneer Hall, which was the first school building in Anchorage, but was used for only one year. The building was subsequently sold to the Pioneers of Alaska to be used as a meeting hall, and is presently owned by the city of Anchorage. It is located at 3rd Avenue and Denali and is now being used by the Anchorage Womans Club for meetings and social functions.

Second School House, 5th Avenue Between F and G Streets

Miss Clark was born in Firth, Nebraska in 1867. She received her BA degree in zoology at the University of Washington, and her first teaching position was in Vancouver, Washington in 1893. She arrived in Alaska in 1906, first serving at Kodiak, then Tanana and Anvik prior to coming to Anchorage. Once the Anchorage school system was firmly established, she moved "up the tracks," developing other schools at Wasilla, Eska, Fairview and Matanuska. She later taught at Unga, Kennecott, Ouzinkie, Takotna, Kiana and other villages until ending her career at Moose Pass in 1944, after fifty-one years of teaching. Clark Junior High School was named in her honor in 1959. She was unable to attend the dedication when the school was completed in 1960 due to an illness that hospitalized her until her death in 1965 at the age of ninety.

While Jane Mears and the Womans Club were diligently pursuing the development of an Anchorage school, another person, deeply involved behind the scenes, was in his own inimitable way influencing Colonel Mears to acquire federal money to build a new and larger school for Anchorage. That man was ANTON J. "TONY" WENDLER.

Tony Wendler

Florence Wendler

Clarice Wendler

Myrtle Wendler

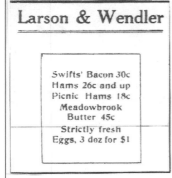

Store Advertising

Larson & Wendler Store

He was born in Gemen, Westphalia, Germany in 1868. He immigrated to the United States as a young man, stopping in Oregon long enough to meet and marry Florence Lucas who was born in Canyon City, Oregon in 1884. They lived in Canyon City where two daughters, Clarice and Myrtle, were born in 1906 and 1907. In 1909 the family took a trip to Valdez, expecting to stay only a few days; however, their stay turned out to be seven years. During this period Tony developed and opened a brewery, operating it until 1915 when the family packed up and moved to the tent city of Anchorage.

On July 5, 1915 the Wendler family debarked from the steamer *Mariposa* on the muddy shores of Ship Creek on upper Cook Inlet. They immediately set up two tents, one for sleeping and one for eating, and then set about to establish themselves in the new townsite. On July 17 one of the first sales of lots began, and Florence purchased Lot 1, Block 38 for $555. This lot was at the southwest corner of 4th Avenue and I Street, where the Captain Cook Hotel now stands.

Teaming up with Ray C. Larson, the Wendlers immediately began construction of a two-story building, the downstairs being a grocery store and the upstairs living quarters for the Wendlers.

Tony was deeply involved in the development of the townsite. His primary interest was the Pioneer Hall, which was built on the corner of 6th Avenue and F Street. He was then a prime mover with Colonel Mears to convince the federal government to provide thirty-six thousand dollars to build a new building on 5th Avenue between F and G Streets. This new building served as a school for all twelve grades, with the third floor being the high school and the lower floors the grade school.

Tony was elected to the first School Board, and was appointed clerk, serving for many years. He was also elected President of the first Chamber of Commerce, as well as Exalted Ruler of the Elks. Serving on various committees and commissions, he was acclaimed at the time as being the most public-spirited and active citizen of Anchorage. Because of his background of public service and dedication to the development of education in Anchorage, Wendler Junior High School was named in his honor.

In 1920 Tony closed his store and entered service with the Alaska Railroad, as supervisor of the cold storage department, until his death in 1935. Florence then converted the store building to an apartment house, and it remained as such until 1948 when she, with her daughters, opened the Club 25. It was initially opened for the exclusive use of women as a private club with a refined atmosphere. This use, however, did not last too long, and it was eventually changed to a supper club open to the public. The building now stands at the corner of 4th Avenue and I Street and is one of the oldest buildings in Anchorage.

Florence Wendler passed away in 1965 leaving a legacy of community service in support of her husband. She was a charter member of the Womans Club and participated in many committees and organizations in the city. In 1964 she was selected as Queen Regent of the Fur Rendezvous by the Women's Auxiliary of the Pioneers of Alaska.

Florence and Tony's daughter CLARICE WENDLER WEISS married John Weiss in 1942, after a career with the Anchorage telephone department from 1925 to 1942. She was the chief operator for many years, and her duties included keeping track of where the doctors were and calling people to tell them the northern lights were out. Husband John Weiss passed away in 1967, and Clarice in 1972. Surviving third generation family members are Tony Weiss of Anchorage, Myrtle Ellerbee Palmer of Kent, Washington, and Marita Ann Monroe of Chugiak, Alaska. Daughter Florence Marie Higgins passed away in 1996.

A second daughter of Tony and Florence, MYRTLE WENDLER STALNAKER, passed away in 1990. Her spouse, Homer Stalnaker, preceded her in death. Myrtle was first employed as a court reporter in the territorial court system, and she worked for the Alaska Railroad from 1929 until 1947. She opened the Marita Ann Shop, a store for children's clothing, in 1945 and then, with her mother and sister, opened the Club 25 in 1948.

Florence and Tony Wendler and Homer Stalnaker are all buried in the Elks Tract in Anchorage Memorial Park. Myrtle Stalnaker and Clarice and John Weiss are buried in the Pioneer Tract.

———

While the residents of Tent City were moving "uptown" into the new homes and businesses, the steamers were still bringing more people at Ship Creek landing. One of the lighter operators bringing in the passengers and freight from the steamers anchored off shore was FRANK JOHANSON, operator of the *Wilhelmina*.

Frank was born on the west coast of Sweden in 1880. He had served in the Swedish Navy prior to immigrating to the United States. Seeking their fortunes, he and two of his brothers

The Wilhelmina

Theresia and Frank Johanson

first traveled to San Francisco, but, hearing of the stampede to Nome, they decided that was going to be their destination. They did not intend to seek gold, but went to establish a boating business, lightering freight and passengers from the ships offshore.

THERESIA WESTERBERG traveled to Nome to join Frank in 1910. Their daughter Lillie was born there in 1912, and shortly thereafter she and her mother returned to Sweden for a visit. In the meanwhile, Frank and his brothers headed for Cook Inlet, arriving there in 1915 and finding the same boating opportunities they had found in Nome. Thea and Lillie joined Frank in Anchorage in 1916. Frank then went to work for the ARR and remained with them until his retirement in 1941.

The Johansons built their first home at the corner of 6th Avenue and I Street in 1916. In 1923 they purchased the Central Hotel at 5th Avenue and I Street, which became the home of many railroaders over the years.

The Johansons moved to Seattle in 1941 after Frank's retirement. Theresia died there in 1946, and Frank passed away in 1961. Both are buried in Acacia Cemetery, Seattle, Washington.

Johanson Home

Lillie graduated from Anchorage High School in 1930 and attended secretarial school in Seattle. She returned to Anchorage and worked for the Alaska Railroad. In 1935 she married Jack Waterworth, who, with Steve Mills and Charley Ruttan, established Star Air Service, the predecessor to Alaska Airlines. (More will be written about Jack in another chapter.)

Lillie and family moved to Seattle in 1943, where, with George Kennedy, they established a hardware store. They operated the store for eight years, after which Jack joined Boeing Aircraft Company. He remained in their employ until his death in 1969.

Central Hotel

Lillie Johanson Waterworth

The Johansons' grandchildren, Frank A. Waterworth, John Edwin Waterworth and Jane Marie Waterworth Levine, all live in Seattle, Washington.

Jack and Lillie Waterworth

Jack Waterworth

GEORGE GATES, who arrived in Ship Creek early in 1914, was another early Anchorage Pioneer. He came to Alaska before the 1898 gold rush and found his way to Knik in 1910 after sojourning in Nome and Ruby.

George was born in Muscatine, Iowa in 1860 and was raised in the badlands of the Dakotas. Migrating west to seek his fortune in mining, he covered much of Alaska and finally decided farming in Knik was his calling. He spent some years working in the Willow Creek mining district and developing a homestead on Loop Road, living there until the military acquired the property in 1941. He was a charter member of the Pioneers of Alaska Igloo #15, and was affectionately known as the "Colonel." George passed away May 24, 1944 and is buried in Anchorage Memorial Park.

A contemporary of George Gates, S. N. CAPPERS was an old-timer of the north who went over the Chilkoot in '98 and drifted to the forty-mile country, prospecting the Chicken and Forty-mile Creeks. He finally decided that it was more profitable to rent out his talents and took a job as mine foreman at Chicken, stating, "at least it's steady pay." Nome was his next stop, and then railroad building attracted him to Anchorage in 1914. He was in charge of the camp mess at Kern Creek in 1915 and worked in various camps including Girdwood, Anchorage and Curry.

Pioneer Cappers was born in the state of Minnesota March 15, 1856 and, as a young man, started moving west. He stopped long enough in Belvidere, Illinois to get married and was accompanied by his spouse in his travels in Alaska. He reached the end of the trail in Anchorage on April 25, 1928 and is buried in the Pioneer Tract, Anchorage Memorial Park.

An old friend of Cappers, JAKE MEYERHOFER landed in Dawson about the same time as George Gates and Cappers. Jake was born in Germany and came directly to Dawson, spending the years from 1901 to 1915 in and around Yukon Territory panning for gold with no great success.

Jake worked for the Railroad off and on and in later years for the city of Anchorage. He served as the garbage collector for several years, driving a horse and wagon. He passed away on October 21, 1948 at the age of eighty-four and is buried in the Catholic Tract, Anchorage Memorial Park.

———

Pioneer barber JOSEPH FLOWERS arrived in Anchorage in July 1915 and immediately opened a barbershop in a tent on 4th Avenue. Joe grew with the town and eventually became a prosperous property owner, acquiring buildings and land on 4th Avenue. In his later years he opened the Owl Bar and Card Room. Turning the operations of the business over to a lessee, Joe sat back and smoked his big cigars and cared for his best friend, Sam, a Chesapeake retriever. He was a well-known sight on 4th Avenue with his dog and his cigar. Joe lived in a small cabin between 4th and 5th Avenues and A and B Streets. As far as is known, Joe never married, however, he had a very good old friend in Ollie Gray, who operated Joe's establishment until he sold it in 1948. He never mentioned where he was from or where he was born, and he always called Anchorage his home. Joe died December 7, 1965 at the age of ninety-six. He is buried in the Pioneer Tract, Anchorage Memorial Park.

———

Like Joe Flowers, "BICYCLE" PETE DYKES, who arrived in Anchorage from the Seattle area in 1915, was a 4th Avenue shopkeeper. Pete was born in Greece and immigrated to the United States around 1900. He also never spoke of his past. He established himself as a plumber and ran a shop along with a second hand store on 4th Avenue between D and E Streets. He acquired the name of Bicycle Pete after he converted a bicycle to a motorized bike. Every evening during the summer months Pete could be seen, with a big cigar stuck in his mouth, riding his motorbike down 4th Avenue.

Behind Pete's store was a barn-like building with a huge attic. This housed hundreds of pigeons and was the home of almost all of the pigeons in Anchorage. Pete allowed the kids in town to catch them and keep them as pets and also to train them as carrier pigeons. He passed away June 14, 1954, and his body was claimed by a nephew from Mercer Island, Washington. It was later found that he was survived by a wife, Helen P., and a daughter, Georgia, living in Greece.

———

AL BENSON, one of the first Anchorage businessmen, was another Klondiker, like S. N. Cappers, who went over the Chilkoot and prospected the Bonanza in Dawson. After leaving Dawson, he made his way to Valdez and engaged in heavy freighting over the Valdez trail to Fairbanks. He hauled a good share of the machinery and equipment that established the Fairbanks mining district.

The excitement that pervaded the Territory when Anchorage was chosen as the Railroad headquarters brought Al to the new townsite, which promised great things to a freighter and transfer operator. The man who was the most prominent in the freighting business in Anchorage at the time was Cap Lathrop, and Al bought him out in 1916. Al was the second owner of the Alaska Transfer and operated it until ill health overcame him. Bob Romig and H. "Red" Hansen bought him out in 1938 and continued the business for many years. Al passed away in September 1938 in San Francisco and is buried in a cemetery there.

ERIK HILDING ANDERSON arrived in Anchorage in late 1914, after having spent some time working on the construction of the Copper River Railroad in Cordova. After completion of the C.R. and N.W. in Cordova, he joined the Alaska Railroad out of Anchorage as a powder man. When the ARR was completed he followed his trade with the Alaska Road Commission and other organizations throughout the Territory, building highways and airfields. His final employer was the city of Anchorage for which he worked until he retired.

Erik was born in Sundall, Sweden October 6, 1881 and came to America at the age of nineteen. Eight years later he joined the railroad construction crew at Cordova. He and his wife Lillian were married in Cordova in 1921. Lillian was a nurse and came north first to Latouche and then to Anchorage where she practiced her profession at the Alaska Railroad Hospital and also as a special nurse, giving aid to people in their homes.

Erik died in March 1943 in Anchorage and is buried in the Pioneer Tract of Anchorage Memorial Park. It is unknown where Lillian is buried.

CHAUNCEY PETERSON arrived at Cook Inlet in the fall of 1914 just in time to acquire Lot 4, Block 44 on 4th Avenue from Martin Scott for the huge amount of $450. He immediately set out to construct a hotel and aptly named it the Peterson Hotel.

As the years went by and Anchorage continued to develop, Chauncey saw the opportunity for a taxi service and auto repair garage. He vacated all of the rooms on the ground floor and converted them to a garage, maintaining only the upstairs for hotel rooms. The lobby was enlarged to accommodate an office for the taxi stand as well as for the hotel. His son Donald was the chief mechanic and serviced all of the taxicabs as his first priority before working on other vehicles.

Chauncey's fleet finally consisted of three Graham Paige four-door sedans. He employed one driver beside himself. Dressed in his leather leggings, choke-bore trousers and chauffeur cap, Chauncey met every train going north or south and also Heinie Berger's *Discoverer* and *Kasilof* boats as they brought passengers up from the lower Inlet. He was the agent for the Berger Navigation Company in later years and also established the Greyhound Bus Agency in Anchorage.

Due to ill health, Chauncey sold his property to Emil Pearl in 1944 and departed for the southern climes. He resided in Portland, Oregon for a short period of time, and there he married long time friend Vera Mae Broe. He then purchased some ranch property in Alsea, Oregon, and remained there until his death in 1952.

ELMER SIMCO, registered Alaska guide, trapper, prospector and mountain man, was born in Ohio in 1888. He arrived in Seldovia around 1912 and immediately established himself as

Dick Tousley, Tom O'Dale, Elmer Simco and Sydney Laurence

a trapper in the Susitna area and later in the Talkeetna River area. He ran a seventy-five mile trapline in the Kasina district, about sixty-five miles from Talkeetna.

Elmer was a trapper extraordinaire, his specialty being wolves. He took time out from trapping to enlist in the army during WWI and returned to Anchorage and his traplines in 1921. He became one of the first Alaska registered guides and conducted big-game hunts throughout Alaska along with his contemporaries, Oscar Vogel, Dick Tousley and Tom O'Dale.

Very little is known of his travels prior to coming to Alaska, other than that he had military service prior to WWI. In 1942 Elmer ended his lonely vigil on the trapline when he took his bride Julia Paulik for a five-month sojourn, spending the winter on their seventy-five-mile, eight-cabin trapline. The spring of 1943 brought them back to Anchorage to spend the summer months. Elmer bought the Morrisson Hotel, which was located on the corner of 3rd Avenue and H Street. Elmer and Julia operated the hotel until his death in 1964. Julia passed away in 1997, leaving a substantial estate in property.

The original Lot 6, Block 28 was bought by Mary Morrisson in 1915 for $280 and was sold in 1999 for $320,000. Both Julia and Elmer are buried in the Elks Tract, Anchorage Memorial Park.

CARL C. "DICK" TOUSLEY, a contemporary of Elmer Simco, arrived in Alaska and upon the Anchorage scene with the federal government survey parties in the early twenties. He left government service and, with Elmer Simco and Oscar Vogel, became one of the Territory's most prominent guides. He was born in Montana in 1876 and spent his life in the out-of-doors, for forty years of that in Alaska.

Dick and another old-time friend, seventy-nine year old DOC RISING, set out for the Tazlina Lake district, where they intended to set up a camp for the coming hunting season. It was a tough pack into the Tazlina, and Dick became exhausted after reaching the lake. He died of a heart attack within an hour after starting to set up camp. Doc Rising hiked all of that night to Copper Center to report the death of his partner and friend. Simco and Rising both expressed the same sentiments of their friend and partner: "he went the way he wanted to go." He died on the trail in 1946 and is buried in the Elks Tract, Anchorage Memorial Park, in an unmarked grave.

OSCAR VOGEL arrived on the Anchorage scne in 1924. He was born in Blommer, Wisconsin in 1905 and came to Alaska via Cnada. His first employment was as a commercial fisherman and later as a miner at the Latouche copper mines. He found his niche as one of the Alaska Guides and spent most of his life as a trapper and guide. Oscar wrote many articles for the *Alaska* magazine about his adventures hunting and guiding in Alaska. He passed away in 1979 and is buried in the Pioneer Tract, Anchorage Memorial Park.

Another Klondiker, and one of the first to arrive at Ship Creek in early 1915, ISADORE "IKE" BAYLES immediately pitched his tent and started business as a haberdasher while waiting for his store building to be built. He purchased Lot 12, Block 25, which was the northwest corner of 4th Avenue and D Street, from C. R. Dodge for $1000, and immediately started construction of his store.

He was born in the small Jewish village of Lilbau, Courland, Lithuania in 1876. He immigrated to the United States at the age of twenty-three and after one year joined the gold rush to the Klondike in 1899. He opened up his first store in Dawson, operated until things slowed down in 1903, and then moved to Fairbanks. While living in Fairbanks, Ike made a trip to New York. There he married Miss BEATRICE SWARTZ and returned with her to Fairbanks. On their return they came through Valdez and made the trip overland during the winter from Valdez to Fairbanks in a horse-drawn double-ender run by Bill Taylor. Taylor later owned the Reliance Grocery across the street from Bayles' store in Anchorage. Their first daughter, Dorothy, was born in Fairbanks. When the Iditarod rush began in 1910, he again joined that stampede and maintained a store there until he moved to Cook Inlet in 1915 with his wife and child. Second daughter, Edith, was born in Anchorage.

Beatrice Bayles

Ike readily established himself as an honest and fair businessman, and when the first municipal election was held in 1922, he was elected to the City Council and appointed to the City Finance Committee, holding the position of chairman for over ten years. During his term the City was kept out of most indebtedness and was on a solid fiscal foundation. There was no question that the reason the town was solvent was because of Bayles' financial policies. As busy as he was in running his business, he made the time for public service in addition to his council chores. He was also a member of the School Board, and for many years was the president of the Anchorage Times Publishing Company.

In 1925 Mrs. Bayles moved to Seattle while their two daughters attended the University of Washington. After the girls finished school she moved to Los Angeles with one of the daughters and resided there until her death in 1946.

Ike Bayles

Esther and Charles Balhiser

1915 Home

Ike sold his store to his faithful employee of fifteen years, Gene Smith, in 1950 and retired to live with his daughter Dorothy in San Francisco. He had been in ill health for some time and passed away in 1956. He is buried in the Mt. Zion Cemetery in San Francisco. There was no one more committed to the welfare of his community than was Ike Bayles, and the community benefited from his talents.

CHARLES BALHISER arrived in Anchorage in 1915 and immediately set about building a home to for his wife and daughter who were due to arrive as soon as the young daughter was old enough to travel. Charles had been given six months to live after nine mastoid operations and was advised to do whatever he wished to do, so he headed for Alaska.

Charles was born in Morrow, Ohio in 1884 and at the age of nineteen began his career as a railroad man. He began as a telegrapher in 1901 and worked as an agent and dispatcher on the Pennsylvania line. In 1905 he was a dispatcher on the Northern Pacific in Idaho, in 1908 a fireman, an engineer on the same line in 1912, and manager of Western Union in Lewiston, Idaho from 1913 to 1915.

In 1905 he met ESTHER JANETTE SLATTER. They were married in Spokane, Washington, on November 6, 1907 and their first child, Margery, was born there in 1915. The couple decided that Charles would proceed to Anchorage, and as soon as the child was old enough to travel Esther and daughter would follow. Mother and daughter embarked on the steamer *Mariposa* when Margery was three months old. When they approached Bella Bella in British Columbia, the ship hit a rock, and all passengers had to abandon ship. They were transferred to another ship and finally arrived at Ship Creek.

Bruce and Margery Cannon and Marie and Kenneth Balhiser

Charles spent his first year in Anchorage working to supply water for the community and was finally hired on as a locomotive engineer for the ARR. A second child, Charles Kenneth, was born in 1921 at the Railroad Hospital in Anchorage. Their last home was Cottage #20 on 3rd Avenue. The cottage was built by the AEC for their employees.

On January 4, 1934 Charles passed away suddenly. He had spent over twenty years as a locomotive engineer for the ARR and was second on the seniority list at the time of his passing.

Esther's life centered around her home and family, yet she found time to devote to public service. She served faithfully on the School Board for eight years. After Charles' death she was employed as housekeeper at the Curry Hotel from 1936 to 1951, retiring in 1951. She passed away in July 1972. Both she and Charles are buried in the Masonic Tract, Anchorage Memorial Park.

Daughter Margery and Bruce Cannon were married in Anchorage in 1935 and have three children. Bruce Everett, Jr. lives in Arizona, Anne Cannon Hawthorne lives in Kent, Ohio, and Mike lives in Wasilla. Son Charles "Kenneth" and Gussie Marie Good were married in 1946 and have two children. Patsy Balhiser Ellis lives in Olympia, Washington, and Susie Balhiser Marrs lives in Snohomish, Washington.

RAY C. LARSON entered the Territory of Alaska first at the turn of the century in time for the Shushana stampede northwest of Cordova. He was unsuccessful in his mining adventure and soon returned to Seattle where he and ANN THOMPSON were married in 1910. In 1912 they were blessed by the birth of a daughter, Helen, and were settling in to married life. Ray, however, had the Alaska adventure in his blood and in 1915 headed north again, this time to the new townsite of Anchorage. He immediately found a residence for his new family and awaited their arrival in 1916.

Ann Larson

Ray Larson

His first venture was a partnership with Anton Wendler, which involved a grocery store located in Wendlers' building at the corner of 4th Avenue and I Street. Ray soon left this venture and, with another partner, Harold Bliss, founded the Anchorage Lumber and Construction Company. He later left the lumber business and specialized in glasswork, operating this business for many years.

Ray took an interest in the growth of the new town, and his first volunteer effort was chief of the Volunteer Fire Department. He also expressed his athletic ability by helping to organize the first baseball team in Anchorage and was one of its valuable players. Ann kept her hand in volunteer work with organizations and was one of the first members of the Anchorage Womans Club.

Helen Larson Seeley

Ray was born in Seattle, Washington in 1877 and passed away in Seattle in 1942. Ann Thompson Larson was born in Eau Claire, Wisconsin in 1877 and passed away in 1968.

Helen's Wedding

Larson Home

Joe Seeley

Lawlor Seeley

Seeley Family

The JOSEPH SEELEY family became intertwined with the LAR-SON family in 1933, when Helen Larson became the bride of Lawlor Seeley.

JOE SEELEY was born in Detroit, Michigan in 1870 and as a young man, moved to Barrie, Ontario, Canada, where he met and married Miss Mary McCabe. The marriage produced two sons: Lawler, born in 1906, and Selby, born in 1908. Mary passed away in 1913, and Joe was left to raise the two boys. The opportunity arose for Joe to increase his income and seek a new life in Alaska. He accepted the position of chief accountant for the AEC in 1915 and had to leave the boys in care of his family in Detroit until he became established in Anchorage. In 1916 the two boys were taken to Seattle by family and began their trip north to be with their father.

In 1917 Joe married Katherine Oldfin, who was a nurse at the Railroad Hospital. Their first home was Cottage #8 on Government Hill. The family lived there until the boys graduated from high school. Soon thereafter, Joe and Katherine moved to Vancouver, British Columbia. Son Selby graduated from the University of Washington with an engineering degree and settled in Canada. He passed away in 1974.

Son Lawlor graduated from Marquette University Dental School in 1932 and returned to Anchorage to establish his dental practice here. He was the second dentist in Anchorage and held Territorial Dental License #36. In 1933 he and Helen Larson were married. They had eight children, all born in Anchorage. Lawlor passed away in 1974 in Seattle, Washington.

Grandchildren of the SEELEY-LARSON MAR-RIAGE are as follows: Joanne Marie Seeley Hodel lives in Anchorage; Lawlor Joseph passed away in 1961; James Raymond lives in Anchorage; John Selby lives in Olympia, Washington; David Arthur passed away in 1996; Marilyn Ann Seeley Hasenoehrl lives in Bellevue, Washington; Helen Yvonne lives in San Mateo, California; and Theresa Marie Seeley Waldock lives in Olympia, Washington.

Joe Bell with Grandson

It was late in 1915 when JOE BELL and his wife IDA MAE landed on Ship Creek to start life anew in the booming townsite of Anchorage. Joe was born in Wisconsin in 1877, and very little is known of his early life until he hit the Chilkoot in 1898. He had just turned twenty-one when the gold fever struck him, and he joined the rush to the Klondike. He gained a world of experience, but found no riches in his quest. He left the Klondike country in 1906 and spent a good share of his time in freighting over the Valdez trail between Valdez and Fairbanks.

In Valdez he met and married Ida Mae Corrigan. She was born in 1889 in Chippewa Falls, Wisconsin to a family of loggers who worked the woods and the timber country in various parts of Wisconsin and finally settled on a homestead in the Mineral Lake area.

After the Corrigan family lived several years on their homestead, the lumber mills began to slow down, and the family started to look west. When Dee (she was called Dee because of another relative named Ida Mae) was seven years old the family moved to Buckley, Washington. This did not prove to be a good move, and the family moved from one logging camp to another five times in six years.

Ida Mae Bell with Children Bonnie and Jean

When Ida Mae was sixteen years old she left school to go to Valdez, Alaska to live with her aunt and take on the duties of a nanny for her aunt's children. There she met Joe Bell, and they were married when Ida Mae turned nineteen. In 1915 they sailed for Anchorage, arriving in July of the same year. Immediately upon their arrival, they set out to buy town lots, which were being auctioned. Ida Mae bought Lot 1, Block 22, located on the southwest corner of 3rd Avenue and A Street, for $115. Joe obtained work right away with the ARR on the bridge crew and later with the security division. He worked on construction of his home each time he got into town and finally completed it in 1916.

Joe eventually became the United States deputy marshal in Anchorage, serving under both Marshal Harry Staser and Marshal Frank Hoffman. He was sent to Kenai and Homer during the summer months when the canneries were operating and the fishing was in full swing and was always accompanied by the family.

Joe Bell, Jr. with Bonnie and Jean

Bonnie Bell

The Bells had a son Joseph and two daughters, Bonnie and Jean. Joe, Jr., the oldest, was attending the University of Santa Clara in California when he passed away from a ruptured appendix in 1923. Tragedy seemed to follow the family after the death of Joe. Bonnie contracted TB and passed away at the age of twenty-six, just over two years after she and Stanley Parsons were married. Jean died just a few months later almost on her twentieth birthday. Tuberculosis was prevalent in Alaska during those years, and many local children were victims of this ravaging disease.

When the daughters became ill, Joe and Ida Mae decided to move south for the sake of the girls. They settled in San Fernando, California where Joe died in 1953. After Joe's death, Ida Mae moved to Oakdale, California where she was cared for by a dedicated cousin, Mrs. Pat Graham, until her death in 1971.

Ernest Amundsen

Victoria Amundsen

A business partner of Joe Bell, ERNEST INGRAM AMUNDSEN was born in Lake Preston, South Dakota in 1886. At the age of nineteen Ernest arrived in Valdez, Alaska seeking his fortune along with so many other boomers. After considerable moving around the Territory, he came to the tent city of Ship Creek in 1915, bought a lot at 810 8th Avenue, and immediately built a log cabin. In late 1915 and early 1916 in need of funds, he and partner Joe Bell contracted with the AEC to grade a portion of the railroad right-of-way.

In 1917 he moved to Halibut Cove to fish for herring and salmon, and when the herring run ended he moved to Kodiak where he operated a herring saltery. There he met a young Norwegian immigrant named Victoria Lampe, and they tied the knot in marriage in 1922.

Victoria Lampe was born in Lofoten, Norway in 1894 and arrived in Alaska in 1919. After Ernie's and Victoria's marriage, they moved to Anchorage in 1923 and occupied the log cabin that Ernie had built in 1915. Ernie was employed by the J.B. Gottstein Company, a wholesale grocer. They started a family, and suddenly the log cabin was no longer large enough. Ernie purchased a partially-built frame building and, after some additions, they had a home large enough for the family. In 1932 Ernie became postmaster of Anchorage, and, after serving four years, joined the Anchorage Police Department as chief in 1936.

Ernie passed away in 1938 after a long bout with cancer. He left a widow and four children who suddenly found themselves without a source of income. Victoria immediately turned the home into a boarding house for school children and mothered four to six children other than her own for several years in addition to working various jobs outside the home. After her own children were raised, she discontinued the boarding portion and rented out rooms until she was well into her eighties. Victoria was a true Alaska Pioneer woman, self-reliant, and never turning back in the face of adversity. She passed away in 1986. Both she and her spouse are buried in the Elks Tract, Anchorage Memorial Park Cemetery.

Ernie and Victoria's children were Iver, Ernie, Charles, and Betty Lou. The children of Iver and Lois Amundsen are: Sheryl Dainow, New Westminster, British Columbia; Jacqui Curtiss, Bremerton, Washington; and Matt Amundsen of Anchorage. Ernie and Mary Ellen Amundsen's children are Eric of Missoula, Montana, and Victoria of Los Angeles, California. Charles and Marion Amundsen have two children: Christopher of Alexandria, Virginia, and Nancy Peterson of Becker, Minnesota. Betty Lou and Howard Webster have a son, Mitch Webster, of Duluth, Minnesota.

The ROBERT COURTNAY, EVAN JONES, and JOHN TEELAND families are tied together as the result of second-generation marriages. We will present them all together here to make the relationships more understandable.

ROBERT COURTNAY went to the Klondike in 1898 with a load of hogs. When the barge carrying the hogs sunk on Lake LeBarge, Robert survived, but the hogs drowned. In 1900 he returned to Seattle where he married MARTHA GLASCOCK, and the following year they moved to Fairbanks. Their first

Original Cabin

Last Home

Iver Amundsen

Betty Lou Webster

Charles Amundsen

Ernie Amundsen

Martha and Ralph
Courtnay

Ralph and Vanny
Courtnay

Bronwen
Courtnay

Ralph
Courtnay, Jr.

child, Ralph, was born there in 1915. Shortly thereafter the family moved to Anchorage where Robert was employed as an accountant. In 1920 Martha moved to Seattle with the children. Robert was born in Oregon in 1877 and passed away in 1938. Martha Glascock Courtnay was born in Susanville, California in 1880 and passed away in 1943.

In 1924 son Ralph returned to Anchorage where he was employed alternately by the J. B. Gottstein Company, the Lucky Shot Mine, and the Alaska Road Commission. In 1934 he met and married MYFAWNY "VANNY" JONES, a fifth grade school teacher and daughter of the Pioneer Evan Jones family. Together they ran the Northern Commercial Company stores in Takotna and Bethel, and eventually moved back to Anchorage where Ralph was employed as an agent for Star Airways and later Pacific Northern Airlines.

Ralph suffered from Addisons disease for many years, and the family moved many times in search of a climate more suitable for him. Ralph died in 1948. After his death Vanny took a job teaching in a one-room school in Healy, where she met and married Lawrence Davenport. They moved back to Anchorage a few years later where Vanny worked for the National Bank of Alaska and as a librarian at the Bank's Heritage Library. Lawrence died in 1974. Vanny spent the last ten years of her life in the Anchorage Pioneers Home and died in 1996.

Ralph and Vanny had two children, Ralph W., Jr. and Bronwen Courtnay Jones, and four grandchildren. Craig Thomas and Julie Anne, the children of Ralph W., Jr., both reside in Menlo Park, California. Bronwen's two children are Megan Alyce, who lives in Phoenix, Arizona, and Christopher Evan, living in Rio Verde, Arizona. Vanny, Ralph Courtnay, Sr. and Lawrence Davenport are all buried at Anchorage Memorial Park Cemetery.

EVAN JONES and BRONWEN MORGAN were married in 1906 in Ravensdale, Washington. They had six children. Two sons died at birth and four daughters survived, one of whom was Vanny, who married Ralph Courtnay. Bronwen was born in Kirksville, Iowa in 1887, and Evan was born in Aberdare, Wales in 1880.

In 1917 after living in many coal-mining towns, they came to Anchorage where Evan became the superintendent of the Doherty Mine on Moose Creek. He later became superintendent of the ARR-owned Eska and Chickaloon Mines.

Evan and Bronwen Jones

In 1920 Evan organized the Evan Jones Coal Company with five other local Anchorage investors, including Oscar Anderson. The family then moved from Eska to Jonesville where he soon sold his interests in Jonesville and moved to Healy where he managed the Healy River Coal Company for Cap Lathrop. He returned to the Eska, Jonesville and the Wishbone Hill mines after leaving Healy. His last mining enterprise was in 1946 when he started developing the Homer Coal Company in Homer. He passed away in Homer in 1950.

Mine Camp in Jonesville

Bronwen supported Evan in all of his mining efforts and put up with the primitive life style that she faced in the mining camps, raising the children and making a good home wherever she was. After Evan's death, Bronwen lived in Wasilla with daughter Vivian Teeland, and eventually moved into the Pioneer Home in Palmer, where she passed away in 1980.

Miners

The grandchildren of Bronwen and Evan Jones include three Pioneer families, the Courtnays, the Teelands and the Evan Jones. We have already reviewed the Courtnay arm and will now address the Jones and Teelands. One of the four daughters, Vivian Jones, married Walter Teeland, and they produced three children. Colleen Teeland

The Jones Daughters

Cottle lives in Wasilla, Alaska; Walter lives in Brisbane, Australia; and Larry lives in Gavle, Sweden. Another daughter, Martha Bernice Jones Visger, bore four children: Frank John of Gillette, Wyoming; Margaret Visger Christie of Skwentna, Alaska; Jeff of Springfield, Oregon; and Sally now deceased. Daughter Margaret B. Jones Bennett bore three children: Richard of Jefferson City, Missouri; Evan of Redding, California; and Joanne Bennett Baker of Boise, Idaho. The fourth daughter was Vanny Jones Davenport.

The melding of three Pioneer Alaska families produced thirty-six children and grandchildren. Bronwen and Evan Jones are buried in Anchorage Memorial Park.

Although the JOHN and KATE TEELAND family did not arrive in Anchorage until 1923, we include them in this 1915 group simply for the family connection with the Courtnay and Jones families.

JOHN TEELAND arrived in Dyea, Alaska in 1898 enroute to the Klondike gold fields via Chilkoot Pass. He spent two years prospecting the famous Bonanza and Eldorado Creeks, and, like so many others,

John Teeland

Anchorage Legends & Legacies

Kate Teeland

he found the good claims were already staked and all that was left were the dregs. John soon departed for greener pastures in Fairbanks. When he heard of the strike at Pedro Dome he staked a claim or two on Cleary Creek and on Fox Gulch.

In about 1903 he decided to take a trip to Seattle, and there he met KATE NORRIS, who had just come from Ireland a few years earlier. John sold her on the idea of prospecting for gold, and they set out for Fairbanks. They got a grubstake and set themselves up in a cabin on Cleary Creek trying to strike it rich.

Following the big news of gold lying on the beach ready to be picked up at will, in the spring of 1908 they headed for Nome. As usual, all of the good stuff was staked, so they returned to Cleary Creek on the last boat up river from St. Michael.

Teeland Family: Walter, Hazel, May and Mabel

The next strike that attracted John's attention was at Ruby, on the Yukon River. The family included three children when they headed down the Yukon to Ruby on a raft. With the good gold claims already staked and not much of a chance to get a good one, John acquired some horses and did freighting and blacksmithing for the next ten years.

There was one more venture, and that was the strike at Wiseman on the Koyokuk River. Here the family spent a tough winter of minus sixty-degree weather, living in a small cabin. A near tragedy occurred when daughter May was attacked by three loose dogs. She was severely bitten about the face and required medical help, of which there was none in Hughes where the family had stopped to provision for the trip up to Coldfoot and Wiseman. John had to take her back down river to Nulato where there was a doctor. He had to leave the family at Hughes for three weeks while he made the one hundred mile trip. Before John left, however, he went dog hunting an found the three dogs tied up at the rear of the dog owner's store. He promptly dispensed them with a twelve guage shotgun.

Finally in 1921, with the gold fever almost subsiding, John moved the family to Nenana, where he obtained employment with the Alaska Railroad. In 1923 they moved down to Anchorage, making it their permanent home. John Teeland was born in Norway in 1865 and died in Anchorage in 1951. He is buried in the Pioneer section of Anchorage Memorial Park. Kate moved to Salem, Oregon to live with one of her daughters. She passed away in 1964 in Salem and is buried there.

Teeland Children with Kate

Walter and Vivian Jones Teeland had three children who are listed earlier with the Evan and Bronwen grandchildren. A second child of John and Kate Teeland, Hazel Teeland Ostrander, had two children: Loreen Ostrander Wells, living in Salem, Oregon, and Steve Jr. living in Medford, Oregon. May Teeland Bowman had two children. Eric lives in Rochester, Vermont, and Carol Bowman Goepford lives in Danville, California. Mabel Teeland Holbrook had no children.

A stampeder to the Iditarod in 1911, JOE BOWER was born in Austria in 1874 and immigrated to the United States at the age of twenty-one. He served a hitch in the United States Navy, where he received his citizenship and, soon after his discharge, headed for the new gold strike in the Iditarod. He had not done well in prospecting on his own, and, when he heard of the big railroad construction beginning in Anchorage, he headed this way. Upon arriving in Anchorage, he landed a job with the AEC, and, when the construction phase was complete, he stayed on with the ARR, retiring in Anchorage in 1937. Joe passed away in 1940 and is buried in the Pioneer Tract of Anchorage Memorial Park.

TOM D. MCRAE was born in Dunveyon, Canada in 1872 and, when he reached the age of twenty-six, he headed over the Chilkoot for Dawson to seek his fortune. He prospected and sluiced most of the streams on the Klondike tributaries without success and finally took on work as a mucker for the more successful miners. In 1906 he gave up on Dawson and headed for the new strike at Fairbanks, where he had the same lack of success. When the news broke about the Iditarod in 1909-1910, he headed down the Yukon to Holy Cross and the entrance to the Iditarod strike. In 1915 he moved back to Fairbanks and took on steady work as a bridge carpenter with the Alaska Road Commission, working not only in Fairbanks, but in Chitina and the Kuskokwim area and finally in Anchorage. He retired in ill health in 1938 and moved to a nursing home in Seattle, Washington. Tom passed away in Seattle in 1940 and is buried there.

A contemporary of Tom McRae, TOM D. CLARK came to Alaska via the Klondike gold rush in 1898. He prospected most of the streams around Dawson with about the same success as his old friend Tom McRae had. Tom Clark was born in 1862 in Missouri and was raised there, leaving his home in 1883 to head west. He found himself, along with thousands of others, heading north to the gold fields of the Yukon. Not having any success in mining, he headed for Anchorage in 1915-16 and took a job as a bridge carpenter foreman for the AEC in the northern section of the Railroad. He settled permanently in Anchorage in 1923 as carpenter foreman for the ARR. He was in semi-retirement from 1935 to 1939, working as a janitor at the McKinley Park Hotel, and in 1940 ill health forced him into full retirement. Tom died in Anchorage in 1940 and is buried in Anchorage Memorial Park.

BOB, CHARLIE, and JOHN MATHISON arrived at Cook Inlet, Turnagain Arm, in 1901 with their parents. They were all born in Texas and came to Hope in search of gold. They formed the Mathison Mining Company, which operated family-style for many years in Hope, and they were constant visitors to Anchorage after the 1915 stampede to Ship Creek.

Their family life, however, turned to the lucrative business of trapping the area around the Chickaloon River and the Chugach Mountains. Bob and brother Charlie developed the first "snowmobile" to be used in the area. They rigged a Model A Ford with three tracked wheels on each side and made the engine protrude over the front, with a counter-balance on the rear. Charlie said, "better than dogs for the trapline." With their snowmobile, the Mathisons opened up the country that was their home.

In 1941 these three indomitable brother pioneers built the first power scow to be used on the upper inlet. They named her the *Fairy Queen* and operated on the Inlet as far as Susitna Station and the Yentna. They built a second power scow called the *Yentna* and hauled freight, lumber and other goods for the settlers now occupying the upper Susitna River. "Passengers, mail, freight, you name it" was the Mathison motto.

All of the Mathisons are buried in the Hope area. A true Alaskan Pioneer family is now history.

LEOPOLD DAVID was born in Nordhausen, Germany in 1881. His family immigrated to Brooklyn, New York in 1884, where his parents established a soap factory. Some writings place Leopold's birthplace in Brooklyn, New York. We will use Germany as his birthplace, as information given by his daughter in 1978 indicates he was born there.

Leopold grew up in Brooklyn and, at the age of sixteen, after his parents passed away, he and his brother enlisted in the United States Army. He was under age; however, he managed to alter his birth certificate by three years and was finally accepted. The Philippine Insurrection was underway when he completed his advanced training in the Medical Corps. He and his brother were immediately shipped overseas and served on the Island of Luzon where his brother was killed in action.

Leopold David, Anchorage's First Mayor

Leopold reached the grade of First Sergeant in the Medical Corps and after hostilities ceased, was returned to the United States in 190l. In 1904 he was assigned to Fort Egbert, in Eagle, Alaska as assistant to the medical officer. He was sent on a mercy mission to Circle City, where a diphtheria epidemic had broken out in the native village. He and a private soldier, his assistant, were credited with saving many lives. They heard of another epidemic in Ft. Yukon and proceeded there immediately without authorization from their commanding officer. Upon their return to Ft. Egbert they received commendations for meritorious service for their efforts. They were not only commended for the service they performed, but for the arduous trip they made by dog team in fifty below zero temperatures, traveling over bad trails for nine days.

After his discharge from the Army, Leopold moved to Seward in 1908, where he met and married ANNA KARASEK in 1909. She had arrived in Seward the previous year as a schoolteacher. She was originally from Tacoma, Washington and had taught in Ketchikan prior to coming to Seward.

Leopold evidently started reading the law in Seward, as there is no information regarding his training as an attorney. Most of the available information indicates he was a physician practicing in Seward, when he actually was prospecting around Cooper Creek. Another story has him as United States Commissioner and deputy clerk of the Court.

1910 found the David family in Knik where Leopold was appointed United States Commissioner and evidently continued his education in reading the law. The family moved to Anchorage in August 1915. Here he apparently continued to read the law and was again appointed United States Commissioner until 1916 when he joined Mr. L.V. Ray of Seward in a law partnership. Mr. Ray had been practicing part time in Anchorage and part time in Seward. Now Leopold would run the Anchorage office.

Leopold was elected the first Mayor of Anchorage in 1921 and was elected again in 1922. Although he was active in local civic affairs, he never entered active politics, even though he was urged to do so by many of his friends. He died on November 21, 1924 at the age of forty-three in the middle of his second term as Mayor of Anchorage.

Soon after his death, Anna moved to Seattle with their two children, Caroline and Leopold, Jr. Anna passed away in Augus 1971 in Seattle, Washington. Her remains were shipped to Anchorage, and she is buried next to her spouse in the Masonic Tract, Anchorage Memorial Park Cemetery.

There is conflicting information concerning the life of Leopold David. His grave marker has an M.D. after his name, however, he was not a doctor. One story indicated he held the Congressional Medal of Honor, which is untrue. One story tells he practiced medicine in Seward and also in Knik, which also is untrue. We will probably never know the real story. Needless to say, whatever it is, this man was a true Alaska Pioneer who was devoted to his profession and his community and whose influence and direction served the City as well as his profession. Leopold was the first person to be awarded an honorary life membership in the Pioneers of Alaska Igloo #15.

———

"MARY MORRISSON, a woman who mushed the Chilkoot and went down the Yukon with her husband in a small boat in 1897 celebrated her 80th birthday today, September 4, 1936, by riding her horse through Anchorage visiting her friends." (Taken from the *Anchorage Times*, September 4, 1936.)

Mary Morrisson, who lived the history of Alaska since the gold rush, bought the present site of the Morrisson Hotel on the opening day of the Townsite lot auction. She bid on Lot 6, Block 28, and was awarded the bid for $280 cash. (See the Elmer Simco story.)

She landed in Skagway with her husband in August 1897 aboard the *Islander*, which was supposedly the largest boatload ever to land in Alaska at the time. It carried twenty-two hundred passengers, not to mention horses, mules and other equipment.

Mary staked out a lot in Skagway when the town was first laid out, and, in company with another woman, started a doughnut and biscuit business, selling them for fifty cents a dozen. After trekking the Chilkoot, she and her husband built a small boat and proceeded down the Yukon in the late fall. The ice floes already had started, and they had a perilous trip, arriving in Dawson on November 2.

Mr. Morrisson went to mining immediately, and Mary opened a restaurant, selling meals for not less than three dollars fifty cents each. She remained in business until 1905 and then sold out. She and her husband made a comfortable amount of money to carry them through retirement. They departed for warmer climes and settled in Arizona that same year. Mr. Morrisson died there, and the call of Alaska brought Mary north again, this time to Cordova.

She remained in Cordova until 1912 and then moved to the Matanuska Valley where, planning to start a horse ranch, she homesteaded one hundred sixty acres. Then she moved into nearby Knik and built another restaurant. The lure of the new townsite prompted her to move to Anchorage, where she built the Morrisson Hotel. She tore down the bakery in Knik and moved the material to Anchorage to build her hotel. Mary died in Tucson, Arizona, in 1946 at the age of eighty-eight, a true Pioneer woman who endured the hardships of Alaska with courage and never looked back.

JOSEPH and KATHERINE DIAMOND arrived in Tent City in 1915 and took up housekeeping in an eight foot by ten foot tent until they found permanent quarters. Joe was born in Gateshead, Durham County, England in 1877 and immigrated to the United States in 1897. He first settled in Philadelphia, Pennsylvania and opened up a small grocery store. In 1898 he met and married Katherine Farrell who had just arrived from Manchester, England. After a short period of time in Philadelphia, they moved westward and settled in Seattle, Washington, where Joe was engaged in the hotel business.

A son and daughter were born in Seattle and, when they were old enough to travel, Joe signed on for a job with the Alaska Railroad in Seward. They arrived in Seward in 1914 and spent a year there before moving into Anchorage in 1915.

The urge to be his own boss put Joe back into the grocery business in 1920. He opened a store on 4th Avenue next door to the Bank of Alaska and operated it with Katherine for many years, until competition from larger stores forced him to sell out. He took a job with the marshal's office and later was appointed as the Territorial school tax collector.

Katherine passed away in 1941 and is buried in the Catholic Tract, Anchorage Memorial Park. Joe died in 1945 in Seattle and is buried there. Their daughter Ann J. Swift, her husband L. J. Swift and daughter Carol Ann moved to California. Their son Charles, after retirement from the ARR, moved to Seattle, Washington.

Another of the many who came to Alaska seeking gold, ULYSSES GRANT "U. G." CROCKER was born in Placer County, California in 1864 and landed in Dawson in 1898. Like so many others, he found that all of the good claims were taken and immediately returned to Seattle where he purchased a load of assorted merchandise and returned to Dawson. He sold out his inventory in a short time and then headed for Nome. He went down the Yukon on a barge and sold baked goods enroute to Nome. He opened a bakery in Nome in 1905, and from 1905 to 1913 he established stores in Seward and Valdez. He still, however, had the gold fever and embarked on a prospect in the Koyokuk region. He hit a short pay-streak and then moved to Anchorage, where he opened a tent and awning store and a mattress factory.

MARY IDA ANDERSON was born in Helsinki, Finland in 1876 and came to Anchorage in 1916 to marry a local homesteader but met and married U. G. instead. Mary was a gourmet cook and took great pride in entertaining friends.

Mary Crocker

U. G. Crocker

The Crockers built a two-story frame building on the corner of 4th Avenue and G Street and developed a full-scale department store in 1916. The building still stands today on the northwest corner of 4th Avenue and G Street.

Original Store

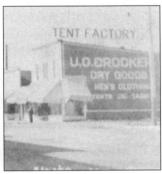

Store in 1929

In 1937 U. G., along with his son Gene and guide Elmer Simco, embarked on a boat trip up the Koyokuk River in search of a gold claim that he had worked some thirty years earlier. Before they had gone very far, he collapsed from a heart attack and died. Mary Ida and son Gene continued to run the department store until Ida retired. She moved to Seattle, Washington and passed away in 1968. Son Gene married Irma Wahl and had three children, Linda Gene White, Arlene Mary Bennett, and Eugene Charles, all reside in Anchorage. Gene passed away in 1990.

One time postmaster and grocer EVERETT MCPHEE was a veteran of the Chilkoot Pass and spent several years in Dawson where he met Bill Taylor. He stampeded to Fairbanks, Nome and Iditarod and finally arrived in

Son, Eugene

Store in 1942

Anchorage in 1915 where he and his old friend Bill Taylor opened a grocery store, aptly named McPhee and Taylor, on the corner of 4th Avenue and B Street. In 1934 he sold his interests to Taylor and, due to health reasons, departed for Seattle, Washington where he became associated in the wholesale grocery business.

———

BILL TAYLOR, Everett McPhee's business partner and old gold rush days friend, stampeded over the Chilkoot in '98 and staked a claim on Hunker Creek, adjacent to a claim worked by another old friend, John Bagoy. After leaving the Klondike, he stampeded to Fairbanks where he ran a freighting service over the Valdez trail and what is now the Richardson Highway.

Bill moved on to Iditarod where he met and married Lenore, and together they moved to Anchorage in 1916. Here Bill joined his old friend McPhee and opened a grocery store named McPhee and Taylor. After the departure of McPhee, Bill renamed the store the Reliance Grocery. While Bill busied himself in the store, Lenore opened and operated a bottling works, making soda pop in their garage on A Street between 4th and 5th Avenues. Bill and Lenore disposed of their business interests and moved to Seattle, Washington, where both of them lived out their lives in retirement. Bill passed away in Seattle in 1951.

———

An old friend of entrepreneur Ev McPhee, CHARLEY BOYLE navigated the Chilkoot pass at the same time in 1898. However, he spent a little more time in other parts of Alaska than McPhee did. While McPhee went to Fairbanks, Charley headed for Woodchopper, then Circle, Fairbanks and Iditarod. They met again in Anchorage in 1915 where Charley was engaged with the AEC in the Right of Way Department and later in the foundry of the ARR.

He was born in 1862, where, no one knew, and died in Anchorage in 1934, after spending many years with the Alaska Railroad. He is buried in the Catholic Tract of Anchorage Memorial Park.

———

One of the great bridge builders of the Alaska Railroad, PATRICK "INDESTRUCTIBLE" COHEN was born in Marquette, Michigan in 1889, came to Anchorage in 1915 to join the ARR, and became as much a part of the Railroad as the many bridges he helped build.

Hurricane Gulch Bridge (Museum Photo)

"Paddy" Cohen riveted on the Gold Creek Bridge when it was forty degrees below zero. He clung to the two hundred ninety-six foot high Hurricane Bridge structure, when, because of improper counterbalancing, it lurched over twenty feet to one side. And when, at the Nancy Bridge, a two thousand pound pile driver hammer fell through the platform he was working on and took his hand with it, he still held on.

Despite his handicap Paddy stayed with bridgework and earned the reputation of being the greatest bridgeman in the north. He had an unparalleled career as a bridgeman and construction boss which included his traveling by packhorse on the survey trails to bridge locations. He assisted a doctor performing an emergency operation in one of the camps, and he acted as a temporary officer of the court when a murder occurred in camp. It was no wonder that his reputation tagged him as "indestructible."

In 1934 Paddy married JOSEPHINE GEIS in Seattle, Washington. Jo was the daughter of a Pioneer Fairbanks family and was attending the University of Washington Nursing School and Swedish Hospital in Seattle when she met Paddy in 1933.

Paddy died in 1954 after twenty-one years of marriage. Jo went on with her nursing career, working as an intensive care nurse at Providence Hospital. She later worked as office nurse for Doctor Sedwick at the Anchorage Medical and Surgical Clinic. In 1957 Jo remarried to K. C. "Brick" Porter, a railroad conductor, who was also born and raised in Fairbanks. Upon Brick's retirement, the couple moved to Hemet, California and lived there until he passed away in 1990. Jo then moved to Palmer to be with her son and remained there until her death in April 1999.

One of "Paddy's" contemporaries in the bridge building business was JAMES M. "JIM" NICHOLSON. He was born in Scotland in 1865 and arrived in the United States in 1892. After traveling about the states for a number of years, he got the gold fever in 1897 and headed for Valdez. Crossing the Valdez glacier, he prospected the Copper River country for a number of years and finally headed for Nome.

Jim arrived in Nome in 1908 and sluiced the beach sands for a couple of years, then decided there was more money in the lighterage business, bringing people and freight ashore from the ships in the harbor. In 1912, hearing of the gold strikes along the Turnagain Arm, he headed for Girdwood and mined and prospected the Twenty-mile River, Crow Creek and finally into Hope.

Jim gave up the mining game and joined the Alaska Railroad in 1915 as a bridge carpenter. He was considered a master at this trade by his peers and stayed with the ARR until it was completed. Then he joined the Alaska Road Commission as bridge crew foreman. He stayed with the Alaska Road Commission until his retirement in 1930. Jim passed away in Anchorage in 1934 and is buried in the Elks Tract, Anchorage Memorial Park. Very little was known of his early life, as is the case of many of the single men who came to Alaska in the search for gold and never left.

ABEL C. CRAIG was another bridge builder and stampeder who found his way to Anchorage. Born in Denmark in 1859, he went to sea at the tender age of sixteen and landed in America in 1885, settling in Chicago, where he got involved in the construction business. He was married in 1888 and spent the next few years constructing homes in the Chicago area.

In 1897 the gold strike in the Yukon beckoned him and his spouse. They departed Chicago and headed north to the gold fields, but they did it the hard way. Rather than heading for the west coast, they took the long way via Edmonton, Alberta, the Canadian trail. They spent two full years on the trail, arriving in Dawson in February 1899.

Here they, too, found that all of the good ground was staked, so they mushed down the frozen Yukon River heading for Nome. They arrived in Nome in the spring of 1900 in time to do some beach sluicing and later some mining on Anvil Creek. In 1909 they decided to take their stake and head south to Washington where Abel took a job with the Yakima irrigation project. The news of a gold strike in the Shushana district fired them up again, and they headed north once more. They first stopped in Juneau for a year and by then found that the Shushana did not prove out to be what they expected. However, undaunted, they decided to head for Anchorage and seek their fortune in the construction of the new town.

Immediately upon their arrival, Abel was hired on to begin the construction of the first municipal building for the AEC, which at the time was financing schools and city buildings. After completion of the project, he took the job as foreman on Bridge Gang #3 ARR, stationed in Anchorage. He took an active interest in local politics and joined several civic groups and fraternal organizations. He was elected to the first City Council in 1921 and served one year. He stayed with the ARR until his death in 1927. He is buried in the Masonic Tract of Anchorage Memorial Park. His wife returned to the Chicago area after his death. She was typical of the Pioneer women of the day. They stuck with their spouses through thick and thin, hardships or no.

T. J. "TOM" FINNEGAN was another railroad construction man who arrived on the scene in 1915. He was born in Spokane, Washington in 1885 and graduated from Gonzaga University in 1909 with a degree in civil engineering. His true love, however, was baseball, and he played semi-pro ball around Spokane and Seattle before he accepted a job in Alaska with the AEC as division engineer in the Turnagain Arm district. He spent most of his time in Anchorage during 1917-18, and organized a local baseball team that won the Cook Inlet League Pennant in 1917.

World War I and the United States Army occupied all of his time until 1920. He returned to Anchorage and was employed by the Alaska Road Commission until his untimely death in 1938. He is buried in the Veterans section of Anchorage Memorial Park. It is unknown if Tom ever married and his only known relative was a brother who was a district judge in Nome.

R. O. "BOB" ALBRITTON was another appointee to the AEC and arrived in Anchorage in 1915 working with the engineering department. After completion of the road, he stayed with the engineering department as chief accountant. Little is known about where Bob came from prior to coming to Anchorage. He was married, and he and his wife had no children. When he retired in 1946, he was awarded a commendable service medal from the Department of Interior. He and his wife retired in Seattle, Washington where she passed away in 1955, and he died in 1962.

JOHN STEWART BAILEY first arrived in Seward with his parents in 1905. His father was in the construction business and engaged in business as a building contractor. The family returned to Seattle within a year where they took up permanent residency. "Stew," as he was known, was raised in Seattle and as a young man went to work for the Canadian Pacific Railway in Prince Rupert and Vancouver, British Columbia. Remembering his short time in Seward, Stew wanted to return, which he did in 1915. He went to work for the AEC in Anchorage in construction until 1917, when he went on the train crew as a fireman. He eventually became a locomotive engineer and remained as such until his death.

Stew was born June 7, 1897 in Seattle, Washington. He married in 1931 in Bellingham and had three stepchildren, Grace, Madeleine and James Bailey. He died at the young age of thirty-nine in 1936.

Another railroad construction man that came on the scene in 1915 was JOHN M. COLLINS, better known as "JACK." He spent time on the construction crew, laying track on Turnagain Arm. However, he preferred entrepreneurial activities over work with his hands. He opened a cigar store in 1917 and operated it until 1922 when he sold it to finance the purchase of the Crescent Hotel, located on the corner of 4th Avenue and C Street. Jack operated the Hotel, as well as being one of the investors in the Evan Jones Coal Company and in a private corporation that was trying to develop the oil properties at Cold Bay, adjacent to the Standard Oil prospect.

He was born in Canada in 1878 and died in Seattle in 1928, where he had gone for medical treatment. His wife disposed of his real estate holdings and never returned to Anchorage. It is believed that he is buried in the Seattle area.

WILLIAM ELLIOTT was born in Germany in 1852 and immigrated to America in 1890. He led a nomadic life traveling from state to state for many years until the gold fever hit him in 1898. He left for Alaska and went over Chilkoot Pass to Dawson and to the gold-laden Klondike River. He spent most of his time in Dawson and Fairbanks before coming to Anchorage in 1915 to work for the AEC in construction of the Railroad. After the construction phase was over, he stayed on as a telegrapher serving in Chickaloon, Talkeetna, Moose Creek and Girdwood.

In 1930 his health began to fail him, and he moved to Hot Springs, Arkansas where he stayed for a short period, then moved to St. Petersburg, Florida where he passed away in 1934. Here again is another stampeder and railroader who spent thirty years in the Territory leaving only a legacy of having been here.

LOUIS WANSTED was one of the first general contractors to operate in Anchorage in 1915. A native of Denmark, he was born in 1877 and immigrated to the United States in 1900.

After spending several years working construction around the west coast, he decided to meet the challenge of a new town being built on Cook Inlet in Alaska.

Upon arriving in Anchorage, he partnered up with an old friend, OLIVER DAHL, and they started their contracting business under the name of Dahl and Wansted. They built the original First National Bank building, the Frisco Café, Loussac Drug Store, J. Vic. Brown and Son jewelry store and Bagoy's first greenhouse. They had a carpenter and cabinet shop at 919 5th Avenue. Oliver Dahl built an apartment building on 4th Avenue approximately where the Captain Cook Hotel now stands then left the partnership to do some mining. Louis retired to Seattle because of failing health and died on November 20, 1952.

A true railroad construction man, P. F. REINHARDT arrived in Anchorage in 1915 at the behest of his granddaughter Mrs. Charley Diamond. He did some contracting with the AEC in right-of-way clearing and grading. When the townsite started construction and the town lots were selling, he decided to enter the real estate business. As far as anyone can determine, he was the first realtor in Anchorage, licensed or not. He spent all of his years prior to coming to Anchorage contracting with the Milwaukee Road, the Great Northern and the Oregon Short Line, however, he traded that vast experience for the real estate business.

P. F. was born April 22, 1852 in Lincoln County, North Carolina and was a direct descendant of General Peter Forney, an officer of the American Revolution who fought against General Cornwallis at the battle of Ramseurs Mill. He died in Anchorage in 1931 and is buried in the Catholic Tract, Anchorage Memorial Park Cemetery.

An early Anchorage couple, OLGA and HJALMAR SAARELA arrived in Anchorage in 1915 and located their home at the corner of 4th Avenue and Cordova Street. Hjalmar worked a short time for the Alaska Railroad and put in all of his spare time building his home and establishing a Finnish steam bath house. He had been a professional wrestler in the old country, and over the years in Anchorage he was retained as a jail guard and performed other duties when the Marshals and Police Departments needed assistance.

Hjalmar was born in Hollola, Finland in 1883 and immigrated to the United States in 1905. He first came to Alaska in 1910, taking a job at the A. J. Mine in Juneau and later at the Treadwell in Douglas. Olga born in 1895, also in Hollola, Finland, immigrated to the United States in 1914, and proceeded directly to Juneau where she and Hjalmar were married.

Hjalmar and Olga had one son, Leo, who was raised in Anchorage. He became an accomplished violinist, however, he graduated from the University of Alaska in Fairbanks with a degree in chemistry. He was in charge of the Territorial Assay Office until 1950, when he was appointed Commissioner of Mines for Alaska. He served in that capacity until 1952, when he was appointed regional mining supervisor for the United States Geological Survey for the leased lands of Alaska.

Hjalmar passed away in 1949, and Olga passed away in 1979. They are both buried in the Pioneer Tract in Anchorage Memorial Park. Son Leo passed away in Sequim, Washington in 1995.

———

One of Anchorage most memorable 4th Avenue businessmen, KONSTANTINOS PAPPAGEORGIOU was better known to all of the oldtimers as "Gus George." He was a true shoemaker or cobbler from the old country and would very proudly make you a pair of shoes if you so desired. Gus came to Anchorage in the fall of 1915 and soon established himself in the Hewitt Building on the corner of 4th Avenue and E Street. He was born in Greece in 1868 and immigrated to the United States in 1898.

Most Anchorage women had a fear of Gus, because he simply would not work on most women's shoes. If they were flimsy and what he considered cheap, he would hand them back and say "junk, no fix." Most women had to get their husbands to take their shoes in for repair, and the only way they succeeded in getting the work done was to talk about Gus's ability as a shoemaker and get him to talking about leather.

Gus ran a clean shop. His equipment was polished to a tee as was his bald head, sticking out of a green eyeshade. His wooden floor was oiled and polished and kept that way regardless of how muddy the streets were. There was one particular woman in town that Gus refused to give service to under any circumstance. She asked various people to take her shoes in and have them repaired, but Gus instinctively knew whom they belonged to and would state his favorite refusal, "cheap shoe."

When Emil Pfeil and Tom Bevers remodeled the building, they moved Gus around the corner facing E Street. He liked this location better as the summer sun was not blasting in, and he could keep his window shades open as he worked.

Gus died in 1959, and Anchorage lost one of its most colorful characters. He was a master of his trade and would not accept anything but perfection in his work. "New soles on most shoes make bum shoes, but new soles on fine shoes are like restoring a masterpiece." He is buried in Anchorage Memorial Park Cemetery.

———

George Jenkins

After completion of the Panama Canal, many of the "railroaders" that were contractors on that job started looking north to Anchorage and the construction of the Alaska Railroad. One of the first men to arrive at Ship Creek in 1915, GEORGE L. JENKINS had just completed a contract on the Panama Canal.

George was born in New Orleans, Louisiana in 1887 and as a young man began his career working on the railroad. When the Boer War started, George joined up and served for a short period of time. He

Mae Cunningham Jenkins

Harriet Jenkins

Florence Jenkins

enlisted in the United States Army at the beginning of the Spanish American War and served in the Philippines, attaining the rank of First Sergeant under Company Commander Captain John J. Pershing. After his discharge from the Army, he worked on the Panama Canal in the Railroad Division and had obtained the position of project trainmaster at the completion of the project. With all of this experience behind him, he headed to Alaska to join the ARR.

When WWI broke out George took leave from the ARR and re-enlisted in the Army. He was one of the first volunteers to arrive in France, whereupon he immediately looked up his old commanding officer, now General John J. Pershing. He was immediately commissioned a Second Lieutenant in the railroad department and served until the end of the war. After his discharge he returned to his job with the Railroad in Anchorage and served until his retirement in 1945.

In 1924 George met Miss MAE BELLE CUNNINGHAM, who came to Anchorage to take a position with the school district as commercial arts instructor at the Anchorage High School. They were married in 1925 and made their home at 7th Avenue and F Street, where they lived until they purchased the home of George Vaara in 1933, at the southeast corner of 7th Avenue and E Street. They had two daughters, Harriet, born in 1926 in Anchorage, and Florence, born in 1927 in Appleton, Minnesota.

In 1945 George retired, and he and Mae moved to Eugene, Oregon. Mae died in 1960, and George died in 1961. Daughter Florence Elizabeth Jenkins Oates died in 1991 in Seattle, Washington; Harriet Belle Jenkins Bailey died in 1992 in Seattle, Washington. A grandson, Richard Oates, resides in Auburn, Washington. A stipulation in George's will was the request to have his ashes scattered over Mt. McKinley, the mountain he came to love so well while passing by it during his years on the Railroad. His son-in-law, Fred Oates, complied with his wishes, and on February 14, 1962 he poured George's ashes into the slipstream of a plane at the 12,000 foot level above Muldrow Glacier.

One of the first Anchorage businessmen who started his business in a tent in the Ship Creek flats, CHRIS ECKMAN began selling furniture on a part time basis and gradually built the business up until it became one of the largest in Anchorage.

Chris was born in 1874 in Denmark and immigrated to the United States in 1895. He spent several years in North Dakota, working in the lumber business. In 1906 he moved west to Seattle, Washington where he was employed in the wholesale furniture business until 1913. For the next two years he was a salesman for the Dornbecker Furniture Manufacturing Company in Seattle.

During his years as a traveling salesman, he met LENORA HENDERSON in Vancouver, British Columbia, and in 1911 they were married in the same city. In 1915 they decided to come to Alaska and make their fortune in the furniture business. His first job was with the Alaska Railroad as a clerk and baggage man, which made him well-known along the railbelt and in Anchorage as well. This job promoted his business for him, and he moved to a larger building on 5th Avenue and K Street in 1918. He left his job with the ARR to devote full time to the furniture store. After the move to new quarters, Chris and Lenore found there was not enough business yet to pay for a larger inventory, so Chris went back to work for the ARR, and Lenora ran the business. In 1920 he purchased the building adjacent to the First National Bank at the corner of 4th Avenue and G Street. He finally left the ARR in 1924 and devoted full time to his Eckman's Furniture Store.

Chris Eckman, Mayor
1926-1927

Chris maintained an active interest in local civic affairs and community matters. He was elected to the City Council in 1923 and served as a councilman until 1926 when he was elected Mayor. He served one term as Mayor, and then again in 1933 he was elected to the City Council for another two-year term. He served his community well, not only as a Mayor and councilman, but also as an athlete. He was one of the organizers of the first baseball teams in Anchorage and was a valuable player for many years.

Chris died of a heart attack on January 21, 1937. Lenora maintained the store for a number of years, and then, as her health started to fail her, she sold the business to Helen and Fred Carlquist. She moved to Seattle in 1950 to be with her daughter, Mrs. Irma Irene Larsen. Lenora was born in Collinsville, Texas in 1874 and died in Tacoma, Washington in 1953. It is believed both she and Chris are buried in Tacoma, Washington.

———

WINFIELD ERVIN was born in Lebanon, Oregon in 1869 and arrived in Seward in 1909, where he was employed by the Brown and Hawkins Company. He later transferred to Knik and remained there until moving to Anchorage in 1915. THEORA and the family moved up from Bellingham, Washington in 1917 to join Winfield. He joined the Bank of Anchorage and was employed by them until 1922 when he and sev-

Winfield Ervin

Theora Ervin

First National Bank

eral investors chartered the First National Bank for the amount of fifty-five thousand dollars. The bank opened on January 30, 1922 at its present downtown location on the corner of 4th Avenue and G Street.

According to the history of the First Presbyterian Church, Mr. and Mrs. Winfield Ervin, Sr. were among fifty-one persons to sign a petition for a church organization. On January 14, 1917 the minister preached a text and then read the list of persons that were received into the membership of the church. Among those listed were Mr. and Mrs. Winfield Ervin, Sr., Winfield Ervin, Jr. and Martha and Wells Ervin.

Theora was recognized as the spiritual leader among all of the members. Among the organizations of the Church was the Friendly Aid Society, whose object was to aid the Church spiritually, socially and financially. It was here that she did outstanding work in promoting the precepts of this organization. Theora McNall was born in Bellingham, Washington, and there she met Winfield, who was a candy maker. They moved to Portland, Oregon for a period of time, and Winfield, Jr. and Martha were both born there. Upon leaving Portland they moved to Lewiston, Idaho where Wells was born.

Winfield and Theora had two sons and one daughter. Son Wells and spouse Doady had two children. Betty Lou Ervin Broderick lives in Anchorage, and Clayton lives in Wasilla. Daughter Martha Ervin Maxwell had no children. Son Winfield, Jr. married widow Velma Brown who had two sons, Jack Brown who lives in Anchorage and Chet Brown who passed away in 1999.

Theora died in 1957, and Winfield, Sr. died in 1961. Wells died in a plane crash with Hakon Christensen in 1956, and Winfield, Jr. died in Seattle in 1985.

Winfield Ervin, Jr.

Martha Ervin Maxwell

Wells Ervin

AUGUST SEABERG was born in Backefors, Dalsland, Sweden in 1881 and immigrated to the United States in 1909. He was working as a carpenter in Seattle, Washington when he met CHRISTINA AMELIA NELSON in 1912. She was born in Lysvick, Varmland, Sweden in 1885. They were married in Seattle in 1913. In 1915 Gus heeded the call from Ship Creek and, leaving Christina and newborn daughter Helen in Seattle, he sailed for the north country, arriving in Tent City the same year,

Christina and August Seaburg

He contracted with the AEC for a period of time installing railroad ties. They then hired him as foreman on the tie laying crew. Gus sent for Christina and Helen in 1916 when he was made stationmaster at Matanuska. His work later took him to stations both north and south on the railroad, supervising tie installations. He built the family home, which still remains at 4th and Eagle, where the four daughters were all raised.

Home at 4th and Eagle

Eldest daughter, Helen, married Linus McGee, and they had no children. Helen died in 1975 as a result of an automobile accident. Daughter Beryl married Steve Lindsey, and they had one son, Steve, who lives in Hawaii. Beryl died in 1987. Daughter Lillian died in 1936, and daughter Hazel Warwick still lives in the original family home.

Lillian Seaberg   Hazel Warwick   Helen McGee

THOMAS PETERKIN was born in Bobcaygeon, Ontario, Canada in 1882. He started his railroading career with the Canadian Pacific Railroad prior to moving to Anchorage in 1915. He was employed as a locomotive engineer with the ARR from 1916 until his retirement in 1944. He purchased a lot on the first town lot sale and later homesteaded east of town. Tom and Anna lived on the homestead until they purchased the East Side Dairy from the Suomela family in 1928. They operated the dairy until 1940 when it was sold to the Matanuska Valley Farmers Coop. Tom met and married ANNA PACKEBUSH in Edmonton, Alberta Canada in 1918. They had four sons, all of whom grew up and worked on the dairy along with Anna. Tom kept his job as engineer on the ARR and put in his time on the dairy while in town and off his railroad run. They subdivided the homestead and sold off

Peterkin Family

Homestead House

Cow Pasture, City Water Tower in the Background

Tom and Anna Peterkin

residential and commercial lots in 1945 and named it the Peterkin Addition. Tom and two of the sons took up placer mining at Marshall on the lower Yukon in 1946 and operated the mine until Tom's death in 1947.

Sons Thomas, Ernest, William and John have all since passed away. Ernest was a Navy pilot and was killed during WWII. Thomas operated a wholesale grocery business, Peterkin Distributing in Kenai, and his son Bob still operates it today. The Peterkin grandchildren number seven. Thomas had three children: Robert T., Shelly and Bonnie Lee Rogers. John had three children: Matthew, John, Jr. and Diana. William had two children: Maynard and Ernest. Both Tom and Anna are buried in the Masonic Tract, Anchorage Memorial Park.

JOHN J. LONGACRE was born in Nevada, Missouri in 1881. He received his basic education in home schools before he took up electrical engineering in St. Louis. In 1898 he moved to California where he engaged in electrical construction work until he heard of gold in the streets in the Klondike and headed north to Dawson in 1900. In 1902 he returned to California, but not for long. In 1905 he landed in Fairbanks and for three years was with the Tanana Electric Company and installed the first electric power plant at Chatanika.

EDYTH JENSEN came north from California at fifteen years of age to join her mother and stepfather on his gold claim in Dawson. Soon after the claim flooded out they moved to Cleary Creek just north of Fairbanks. Edyth was born in San Diego, California in 1888, and when she and John were married in Cleary in 1906 she was just eighteen years old.

John and Edyth Longacre

Original Cottage on 3rd Avenue

With the flash of an oil discovery in Katalla, John joined the Guggenheims as an electrical engineer from 1907 to 1909 and operated a general store on the side. In 1910 John and Edyth moved out to California where he worked as an engineer and also had some interest in oil development. In 1915 they heard of the new city and railroad construction in Anchorage and came north again. He was employed by the AEC, became the first chief electrician for the Alaska Railroad, and held that position until his retirement in 1943. He served on the first City Council of Anchorage and was an active Mason.

John J. Longacre   Dora Jane Dennis   Frances Lawson

John and Edyth raised a family of three children: Frances Longacre Lawson, Dora Jane Dennis, and John J., Jr. John, Sr. passed away in California in 1950, and Edyth passed away in Anchorage in 1983 at age ninety-five. Prior to her death she was the last living charter member of the Pioneers of Alaska Auxiliary #4 and the Eastern Star #8. She shared all of the rigors of the pioneer life with her husband in the boomtowns of Alaska and the Yukon, a true Alaska Pioneer woman.

The Longacre grandchildren number eleven. Frances had two children, Holly Glen Elston and Michael Elston living in Washington. Dora Jane had four children: Carol Ann Morrisson lives in Bremerton, Washington; Patricia Arlene Porter lives in Kenai; Victoria Husa lives in Kirkland, Washington; and son Carl Dennis, Jr. passed away in 1979. John, Jr. had five children: Kathleen Diane lives in Arvada, Colorado; John David, Paul Douglas, and Roy Lee live in Anchorage; and Kenneth Allan lives in Maui, Hawaii. John, Jr. passed away in 1986.

HERBERT HAZARD McCUTCHEON was born in Bayside, California in 1876. He first arrived in Nome in 1899 as a chief steward aboard a steamship. He left the ship that same year and tried his luck at mining on Dime Creek. After a few fruitless years of prospecting, he moved to the goldfields of Chitina in 1908, and there he met CLARA JOHANNA KRUEGER. She was born in Mapleton, Minnesota in 1890 and at the age of seventeen went to Cordova where she worked as a cook and waitress for the Copper River and Northwestern Railway,

In 1910 H. H. and Clara were the first couple to be married in the community of Chitina. Five years later they moved to Anchorage and joined the hundreds of new residents establishing businesses and working for the AEC and later the Alaska Railroad. They first lived in a tent in Tent City while H. H. was taking on contracts to clear right of way in the Birchwood section. He built a log cabin at 310 West 7th Avenue, which became their home for many years.

H. H. later became roadmaster of the Railroad and entered politics in 1931 when he was elected to the Territorial House of Representatives. He

Clara McCutcheon   Herbert McCutcheon

Stanley
McCutcheon

Stephen
McCutcheon

Legislature

became Speaker of the House in 1941 and then was elected to the Senate and served there from 1943 to 1945. H. H. was one of the first members to join the Anchorage Elks lodge and was Exalted Ruler in 1925. He was also elected President of the Pioneers Lodge, however, due to ill health, was unable to complete his term. His eldest son Steve was one of the signers of the Constitution of the State of Alaska in 1955.

H. H. passed away in 1945 and is buried in the Elks Tract, Anchorage Memorial Park. Clara passed away in 1986 and is buried in Angelus Memorial Park. Son Stanley passed away in 1975, and son Steve passed away in 1999. Third son, Jerome, born in 1931, still lives in Anchorage. Son Stanley and his spouse, the former Evelyn Bockoven, had two daughters: Cheryl Scotte McCutcheon Ramstad living in Chugiak, Alaska, and Shelle Jay McCutcheon Mosely living in Willow, Alaska.

CARL E. MARTIN arrived in Seward in 1909 and headed for the Cache Creek country in search of gold. Unsuccessful in his quest, he began freighting out of Knik and Susitna Station. In 1910, after the Iditarod trail was opened, Carl carried the first mail from Seward to Iditarod via dog team.

LUCILLE BLACK arrived in Knik in 1911 with her parents who were working a gold claim on Friday Creek. She and Carl met at Susitna Station while he was freighting into the Cache Creek country. They were married in 1917 at the home of old friend Oscar Gill. Carl and Lucille moved to Anchorage in 1918 from the homestead in Palmer.

The young couple lived a hard life, as Lucille accompanied Carl on the trail during those freighting years, sleeping out on spruce boughs and putting up with the rigors of the trail. After a short period of time they gave up the freighting and took out a homestead near Matanuska and were actively engaged in raising potatoes for the local Anchorage markets.

Carl and Lucille Martin

Martin Family

After moving to Anchorage, Carl was employed by the Anchorage Commercial Company as head of their mechanical department. He later was engaged privately in the plumbing business. He was a past Exalted Ruler of the Elks and served on the Anchorage City Council for eleven years. Carl and Lucille are both buried in the Elks Tract, Anchorage Memorial Park.

The Martins had three children. Carl, Jr. was lost in his plane while on a flight to the interior. Dorothy and her spouse had three children: Michael and Patrick Rogers of Anchorage, and Robert of Tampa, Florida. Bonnie and Don McGee had three children: Don Martin, John Scott, and Kellyjo, all of Anchorage.

Bonnie McGee

Dorothy Rogers

Carl Martin, Jr.

AUGUST NIEMI was born in Ylistaro, Vaasanlaani, Finland in 1871. He arrived in the United States in 1900 and settled in Houghton, Michigan. MARIA SOFIA MIKKOLA was born in Lahtaja, Finland in 1880 and arrived in Michigan with her parents in 1901. She met August that same year, and they were married in 1902. Soon after their second child was born, the family moved to Itabo, Cuba, where August was employed on the construction of the Panama Canal. Two more children were born in Cuba, and in the year 1910 the family moved to Alaska. They spent five years in Douglas, near Juneau, where August was employed at the Treadwell Mine.

In 1915 the family packed up and moved to the coal-mining town of Eska, on the Alaska Railroad branch line, which was in the area of where Sutton now is. The coal-mining district there was Evan Jones Coal Mine, which was independently owned by Oscar Anderson and others, and the Eska Mine, which was owned by the Alaska Railroad. August was employed by the Alaska Railroad at the Eska Mine and also operated a small general store and rooming house. The family had now increased to six children, and they were becoming of high school age.

However, there was no high school in Eska. In 1925 August and Maria sent the children to Anchorage to live and "batch" in their home until she could move from Eska in 1926. August followed in 1927, after disposing of his store.

Soon after their arrival in Anchorage, August opened a hardware store in 1928 at the corner of 4th Avenue and D Street and operated it successfully until his retirement, when he sold out to Art Engebreth. August passed away in 1945, and Maria passed away in 1947. They are both buried in Anchorage Memorial Park.

August Niemi

Maria Niemi

Niemi children: William, Hilma, Waino, Walter and Gertrude

Niemi Home

Helen Niemi

The six children of the August and Maria Niemi family produced eight grandchildren. William J. Niemi and Bernice Kingsbury had two daughters: Miriam Anne who died in 1993 and Celia Beth living in Federal Way, Washington. Daughter Hilma Josephine Niemi and Gus Saario had three daughters: Bertha Irene Saario Axtell who lives in Minden, Nevada; Doris June Saario who lives in Port Townsend, Washington; and Joanne Verla Saario Rantala who lives in Anchorage, Alaska. Waino A. Niemi and Verla Fay had two children. Waino Ray lives in Palmer, Alaska, and Mary Wyanne Niemi Plummer lives in Anchorage. Hilda Gertrude Niemi Kellner and Kenneth Kellner had one child, Kenneth Kennedy, Jr., living in Corona, California. Walter T. Niemi had never married, and Helen Elizabeth Niemi Carlquist had no children.

FRANK I. REED was born in Council Bluffs, Iowa in 1872 and was living in the area when the Spanish American War began. Along with many other men of his age Frank enlisted in the Army. After the war in 1900, the news of the Nome gold rush attracted him, and, with other stampeders, he arrived in Nome to seek his fortune working for the Solomon Dredging Company.

Frank Reed

Pauline Reed

Aboard the ship while traveling to Nome, he met a young lady named PAULINE HOVEY, who, with two of her sisters and her mother, was en-route to Nome to take over the operations of a store in which her mother had purchased an interest. Pauline was born in Munson, Ohio in 1883, and her family moved to the west coast, spending some time there prior to going to Nome. She and Frank were married in Seattle in 1904 and lived in Nome until 1912, when they moved to the Talkeetna area to establish a gold dredging operation on Cache Creek. Frank's mining activity on Cache creek brought him to Anchorage prior to the laying of track. He took one of the first dredges into the Talkeetna area, towing it from Seattle and up the Big Susitna as far as he could and then hauling it by horse train to the mine site.

Reed with President Harding

Frank had developed some business interests in the new town of Anchorage, one of which was the Anchorage Lumber Company, a logging and sawmill firm. The firm went defunct in a short time, and Frank received for his interest the original Anchorage Hotel located on 3rd Avenue and E Street. He sold out his interest in the Talkeetna dredge to his partners, moved into Anchorage, and immediately began to remodel the hotel. Pauline took a great interest in the hotel as co-proprietor with her husband and became the hostess to thousands of travelers who at one time or another were hotel guests.

Anchorage Hotel

Frank's next venture was the founding of the Anchorage Light and Power Company. He probably had more to do with the advancement of the city of Anchorage than any other individual, and it was with this enterprise that he was most well known. He, with six other investors of vision, secured the hydroelectric site at Eklutna Lake in 1922 and six years later financed and constructed the power company. This was the nucleus of the Municipal Light and Power Department of the city of Anchorage and was purchased by the City in 1944.

Reed Family

Frank sold the Anchorage Hotel in 1936 to D. W. Metzdorf. He then moved to California due to his failing eyesight and passed away in 1944, after selling the power company to the city of Anchorage.

Pauline passed away suddenly in Seattle in 1934. She had been prominent in the business, social and political world of Anchorage for many years, and was the National Republican Committee Woman for Alaska at the time of her passing. Frank, Sr. died in 1944. He and Pauline are buried in Acacia Cemetery in Seattle, Washington.

Frank and Pauline had two sons, Frank M. and Paul I. Frank M. and spouse Maxine had two children. Pauline Jarnet Reed Mackay lives on Mercer Island, Washington, and Frank, Jr. lives in Rancho Santa Fe, California. Paul and spouse Marie had two daughters. Nell Robison lives in McKinleyville, California, and Ann Paul lives in Reno, Nevada. Paul died in 1996 in Riverside, California.

Frank M. and Paul Reed

Judge Tom Price

Mrs. Lois Price

Lois Price Haverstock

THOMAS C. PRICE was born in the mining country of Grizzly Gulch, Montana, on April 14, 1874. When Tom was twenty his family moved to Juneau, Alaska, where his father was engaged in the mining business. In 1895 Tom met a young college student named LOIS EVANS who was vacationing in Juneau, and they were married that same year.

Tom took up the plumbing trade and ran a contracting business in Juneau for a number of years. His heart and soul, however, were in the law. He aspired to become an attorney and constantly studied the law through correspondence courses and reading the law with several well-known attorneys. In 1906, when their daughter was born, he had to concentrate more on the plumbing to keep bread on the table.

Tom and family moved to Cordova in 1913, where he continued the plumbing business and also continued his law studies. In June 1915 he journeyed to Valdez to take the bar examination and passed with flying colors. Shortly after his acceptance to the bar, the family moved to Anchorage where he set up his first law practice, but he kept the plumbing trade as his ace in the hole.

Having reasonable success with his law practice, Tom ran successfully for the Territorial Legislature in which he served from 1919 to 1923, then served in the Senate from 1923 to 1925. In 1926 Judge E. E. Ritchie appointed him as Commissioner of the Anchorage District. There is some confusion as to just what happened, but it turned out that Judge Thompson continued to hold that office until he resigned in 1934. Judge Hellenthal then appointed Tom Commissioner on October l, 1934, and he held that office until his death in 1944. Tom was a charter member of the Elks Lodge, Pioneers of Alaska and the Chamber of Commerce.

Dr. Haverstock and Lois

Haverstock Home in Seward

DR. ARTHUR D. HAVERSTOCK, well-known and respected surgeon, passed away in Monrovia, California in 1937. He was born and reared in Philadelphia, Pennsylvania and came to Anchorage in 1923 as a Captain in the Army Medical Corps. During WWI he made a notable record in the Army and was decorated for his work. He served both at the Walter Reed Hospital in New York and the Letterman General in San Francisco. Dr. Haverstock practiced in Anchorage until 1931 and then moved to Seward to become Chief Surgeon of the Seward General Hospital.

He was married to Lois Price, daughter of Tom and Lois Price, and maintained a close relationship with his in-laws. Dr. Haverstock is buried in the Seward Cemetery. It is unknown where the rest of the family is buried.

JOHN CASEY McDANNEL arrived in Anchorage in the spring of 1915. He was born in Knoxville, Tennessee in 1864, and as a young boy he left his home and headed west, stopping first in Kansas City, Missouri. He continued on to a mining camp in Cripple Creek, Colorado, and there he met NELLIE NEAL LAW-ING, who was later well-known in Alaska as Alaska Nellie. John Casey followed the gold trails in Nevada, and finally the rush to the Klondike in 1898 found him over the Chilkoot Pass and down to Dawson. In 1900 the Nome gold rush attracted him, but his luck was no better there than in Dawson. After leaving Nome, he returned to Nevada, where he again engaged in mining and also hotels. He was involved in the ownership of hotels in Tonopah, Columbia, Bullfrog and Goldfield, Nevada. In Goldfield he built the Casey Hotel, which was considered the largest and best in the state of Nevada at that time.

McDannel Family

Alaska and the north were in his blood, and in 1915 he heard of the new terminus of the Alaska Railroad being built in Anchorage. He headed north and found a job with the AEC in the commissary and mess hall. He later had the concession for the railroad dining cars and sleepers from Seward to Fairbanks until the Curry Hotel stopover was built. Undaunted, he opened the Twins Café in Anchorage, which name was later changed to the Merchants Café. He operated the restaurant in conjunction with the Twins Hotel at 931 4th Avenue. In 1923 John was asked to operate the railroad din-ing car for President Harding when he came to Anchorage and Nenana to drive the golden spike at the completion of the Railroad.

Twins Hotel

MARY DAVIS arrived in Juneau as a tourist in 1913. Instead of returning to Seattle, she stayed in Juneau and was employed as a housekeeper for Judge and Mrs. Jennings. In 1915 she embarked for Anchorage to work as a wait-ress with the AEC. It was here that she met Casey, and they were married in 1921. It was Mary's second marriage, and during her first marriage she gave birth to twin girls, Helen and Mary, the first set of twins to be born in the new town of Anchorage. After her marriage to Casey she gave birth to a son, John Casey, and another daughter, Lucy Wingfield McDannel. Mary was born in Tredegar, Wales in 1878, and she passed away in Anchorage in 1955. John Casey died in Anchorage in 1930. Both Mary and Casey are buried in the Moose Tract, Anchorage Memorial Park.

Home and Restaurant

John Casey and Twins

Helen Osborne, Mary Patterson, John McDannel and Lucy Whitehead

The marriage of Helen McDannel and Calvin Osborne produced five children: Thelma Lorraine lives in Sequim, Washington; Linda Lee Osborne Hood lives in Anchorage, Alaska; Calvin M. lives in Arizona; Merla M. Osborne Christiani lives in Eagle River, Alaska; and Charles M. lives in Medford, Oregon. The marriage of Mary McDannel and Pat Patterson produced three children: Michael George lives in Anchorage; Lindapat lives in Salem, Oregon; and Casey Ira lives in Vancouver, Washington. The marriage of John D. McDannel and Marie Barber produced three children: John D., Jr. lives in Livingston, New Jersey; Mary Christine died in 1970; and Deanne Marie McDannel Lasiter lives in Bellevue, Washington. Daughter Lucy married Gilbert Whitehead, and they had no children.

Isaac Koslosky

ISAAC KOSLOSKY was born in Warsaw, Poland in 1872 and arrived in the United States in 1887 when he was fifteen years old. He participated in the first stampede to the Klondike in 1897 and for two years prospected the Bonanza Creek. In 1901 he returned to Kansas City, Missouri where he married Miss LENA SCHINDLEMAN. Lena was a nineteen-year-old beauty who had come to the United States with her parents from Russia in 1898. The Koslosky's operated a clothing store in Kansas City until 1915, when they heard of the new town being built on upper Cook Inlet in Alaska.

Isaac and Lena packed up the four children and headed north, arriving in the spring of 1915 in Tent City where they first set up housekeeping. Isaac immediately opened a store and, with Lena at his side, sold clothing and dry goods. They ran a successful business for two years and then decided to move back to Kansas City in 1917.

Lena Koslosky

Leo Koslosky

Jan Koslosky

Harold Koslosky

Four years later they returned to Anchorage and established a store, a trading business and a fur buying business. A fifth child, Ralph, was born in 1921 in Anchorage, completing a family whose business lasted for over seventy years.

Ralph Koslosky   Gladys Kravetz

Isaac was instrumental in establishing the fur trade in Anchorage and was followed in the business by sons Leo and Ralph. Son Jan opened the first store in the new city of Palmer in 1935, and son Harold oversaw the operations of the Koslosky store, the Hub clothing store and Harold's Shoe Store. Daughter Gladys left Alaska soon after high school, lived in southern California for many years, and finally returned to Anchorage in 1975.

The Koslosky businesses were always family affairs, and Lena often proudly mentioned the fact that they operated a business for over fifty years without any setbacks that they could not overcome. She often stated, "I have seen the time when the poorest day in business involved only the sale of a twenty-five cent pair of gloves."

Anchorage Store, 1930

Isaac passed away in 1940, and Lena passed away in 1962. Both are buried in Anchorage Memorial Park, as is son Ralph. Harold is buried in Angelus Memorial Park in Anchorage. Jan is buried in the Palmer Cemetery, and Leo is buried in Seattle. Daughter Gladys Kravetz is living in a retirement community in Danville, California.

Palmer Store, 1946

The Koslosky grandchildren number twelve. Harold had two sons, Herbert who lives in Anchorage, and Howard who died in the Viet Nam War. Leo had two children now living in California. Jan had one son Jan, living in Seattle, and two daughters, Susan and Linda. Ralph had two sons, Mark and Larry, and one daughter Cheryl. Gladys had one son Bill Levine, living in Danville, California, and daughter Janet lives in Los Angeles.

WERNER OHLS was born in Turku, Finland in 1893 and arrived in the United States in 1909. After spending three years in Washington he first went to Nome in 1912, working as a miner, and thence to Ruby. While in Ruby he was known as the "Ruby Kid" for his dog-mushing prowess, and he participated in the Nome forty mile race. In 1915 he was hired by a wealthy Nome woman to take her to Seward. She had over twenty thousand dollars in gold to transport, which amounted to about one hundred pounds, and Ohls agreed to transport her via dogsled to Seward. This was about a two thousand mile trip due to the twists and turns of the trail, however he succeeded in

Ida and Werner Ohls and Son

Dairy Farm

Werner as
Marathon Runner

Victor Ohls

Andrew Ohls

Karl Ohls

Ellen Ohls

delivering his charge to Seward. He protected his load by hiding it in the bottom of the sled and surrounded the sled with his dogs each night.

He spent a short period of time in Anchorage in 1915 working on the Railroad and then moved to Hoquiam, Washington where he met and married IDA ELIZABETH FISKER in 1920. Ida was born in Vassa, Finland in 1883 and moved to the Washington area with her family a few years prior to meeting Werner. In 1921 they departed for Anchorage, where Werner again worked for the Alaska Railroad. While working for the Railroad he began acquiring cows to form a dairy herd.

In 1924 they homesteaded on the 21 Mile Loop Road and started a family dairy farm. It was located just off the end of the east-west runway where Elmendorf Air Force Base is now located. The family all were involved in developing the dairy, and Werner delivered milk before and after work at the Railroad. In the winter he delivered by dogsled.

Werner was a well-known marathon runner in Anchorage and won the 4th of July races for many years. He also ran the Mt. Marathon race in Seward, twice coming in second place. He trained his oldest son Andrew as a marathoner during his high school years, but the advent of WWII put an end to this endeavor. With the military establishment coming to Anchorage, the government needed land and acquired almost all of the homesteader property on Loop Road including the Ohls Dairy. In 1942 after the sale of the dairy, he and Ida moved to Hoquiam, Washington where they lived out their lives. Werner died in 1973, and Ida in 1975.

D. W. Stoddard   Esther Stoddard

DAYTON W. STODDARD was born in Hutchinson, Minnesota in 1878 and spent his youth there. His family moved to Portland, Oregon at the turn of the century. In 1913 he met and married ESTHER GRAHAM who was born in Elgin, Iowa in 1884. They were married in Vancouver, Washington where he was a Lieutenant in the

National Guard. He was transferred to Ft. Liscum near Valdez, Alaska in 1918, and Esther and their two daughters joined him there the following year. The family was then transferred to Seward where Dayton was stationed for a short time prior to coming to Anchorage in 1919 where he took his discharge from the National Guard.

Home on L Street

Dayton was employed by the AEC for a period of time and then operated an ice cream parlor from 1921 to 1923. He then took the job of city clerk for Anchorage until his death in 1933. Esther was an experienced telephone operator and was employed by the City until her retirement in 1956. She moved to Oregon that same year and lived there until she passed away in 1971. Dayton is buried in the Legion Tract, Anchorage Memorial Park.

Ice Cream Parlor

The four daughters of Esther and Dayton Stoddard produced ten grandchildren. Daughter Beth Marie Stoddard Allen had four children. Deborah Lee and Robert Dayton reside in Renton, Washington; Kim Marie Allen Stanton and Cynthia Kay Allen Rabe reside in Anchorage, Alaska. Daughter Vivian C. Stoddard Laurie had four children. Alison Esther Laurie Lewis resides in Wrangell, Alaska; Fay Irene Laurie Von Gimmingen resides in Anchorage, Alaska; Laurie Lee Laurie Richmond resides in Hillsboro, Oregon; and Robert Bruce, Jr. resides in Juneau, Alaska. Daughter Fay Mildred Stoddard Eskilson was widowed in 1987 and resides in Olympia, Washington. Daughter Dorothy June Stoddard Walling had two children, both currently living in Oregon, Robert Eskil in Springfield, and Dorothy Denise in Warrenton.

D. W. Stoddard in front of City Hall

Dayton and Esther Stoddard's daughter Vivian's husband was ROBERT B. LAURIE, one of the young latter-day Pioneers who came to Anchorage during the depression years. He was born in Vancouver, British Columbia in 1911, and entered the United States with his family in 1923. He was raised in the Salinas, California area and in 1934 at the age of twenty-three years ventured to the last frontier. He arrived in Seward in the summer of 1934 and obtained employment as a longshore-man for a short period of time before moving on to Anchorage. The winter of 1934-35 found him on a trapline at Little Indian Creek on the Chickaloon flats. He then tried his luck at prospecting on Resurrection Creek but was unsuccessful, so he moved on to Palmer in 1935. There he discovered his talents as a mechanic and started his career

The Stoddard Girls

with the Northern Commercial Caterpillar Department. He and Vivian Stoddard were married in 1940. Robert passed away in 1984, and Vivian still resides in Anchorage.

ANDREW LANDSTROM was born in Norbotten, Sweden in 1892. He arrived in the United States in 1910 and eight years later he landed in Nome to try his luck at gold mining. He took a job with the Pioneer Mining Company and then went into the mining business on his own for the next several years.

Andrew and Elizabeth Landstrom

Elizabeth Landstrom Johnson, 1980

In 1914 he met ELIZABETH JANSSON, who was born in Bengtsfors, Sweden in 1871. She immigrated to the United States in 1910, joined her brothers in Nome in 1912, and was employed as a cook at Andrew's camp. She and Andrew were married in 1914 and soon moved to Seattle, where they lived until 1917. They then returned to Alaska and settled in Anchorage that same year.

From 1918 until 1936 Andrew was employed by the Alaska Railroad. In the fall of 1936 he retired to take over the full time management of the Landstrom Apartments. Andrew and Elizabeth had purchased an office building in Chickaloon and moved it to Anchorage. They converted this to an eight-unit apartment house, which still stands on the northwest corner of 3rd Avenue and H Street. Elizabeth took over the management of the building after Andrews' death in 1943.

Landstrom Home

In 1960 Elizabeth married Victor Johnson, a long time friend of the family. In 1962 they were honored as King and Queen Regent of the Fur Rendezvous by the Pioneers of Alaska. Mr. Johnson passed away in 1972. Elizabeth lived to be one hundred one years of age, passing away in 1994. Both Elizabeth and Andrew are buried in the Elks Tract, Anchorage Memorial Park.

The children of the Landstrom family produced seven grandchildren. The union between eldest daughter, Evelyn, and Dr. Asa Martin united two pioneer

Jean Donatello

Franklin Landstrom

Evelyn Martin

Anchorage families and produced two children, a daughter Alice Clare, living in Coupeville, Washington, and John Thomas who lives in Anchorage. The marriage between daughter Jean Landstrom and Don Donatello produced five children. Elizabeth Ann Donatello Sherwood, Mary Jean Donatello Hinds, and Margaret Jo Donatello live in Anchorage. George Christopher died in 2000. Benjamin John lives in Seattle, Washington. Son Franklin Landstrom and his spouse Mary live in Anchorage.

One of the first and one of the largest Anchorage families that came on the scene in 1915 was the RASMUS PAUL INGEBRIT SIMONSON family. Rasmus emigrated from Stolmen, Norway in 1882 at the age of twenty-one. He had traveled from a rocky Norwegian island to the wheat fields of North Dakota, where he found work on the Bonanza Farm north of Fargo.

He returned to Stolmen in 1887 to marry his sweetheart ANNA MONSINA STENEVIK. Together they traveled back to North Dakota where they developed a farm, established a general store and began raising a family. The farm suffered from a wheat blight, black rust, which wiped out the wheat harvest for two consecutive years and placed the family of eleven in dire financial straits.

Rasmus, having heard stories from relatives about the wealth to be found in the gold fields of Alaska, set out in 1914 with eldest son Ingebrit to find their bonanza of gold in the frozen north. Anna remained behind with the eight other children and patiently awaited word of a gold strike. When 1915 rolled around, and still no word arrived from the north, she took matters into her own hands, packed up seven of the children—Jenny, twenty-eight; Kari Ann, twenty-two; Margaret, sixteen; Inger, twenty-one; Rasmus, fourteen; Selma, twelve; and Sol, eight--boarded a Northern Pacific Railway train and headed for Seattle. Daughter Agnes stayed behind to marry her beau Adolph Julius Johnson. The family ended their train trip in Seattle, and boarded the Alaska steamship *S.S. Mariposa* bound for Ship Creek and what was to become Anchorage.

Rasmus suddenly heard of the exodus from North Dakota by a chance reading of the passenger list published in the *Anchorage Times*. With the new family about to arrive, he purchased Lot 7, Block 31 on the northeast corner of 4th Avenue and L Street at the lot auction on July 10, 1915 for the amount of $280. Disaster struck when a smoldering fire destroyed all of the material to be used for construction of a home and forced the family to spend their first winter of 1915-16 in a tarpaper covered tent. After withstanding the winter, the

Simonson Family

following spring the family moved into a new home, which was a replica of the North Dakota farmhouses.

With very little gold mining being done in the Anchorage area, Rasmus decided to go into the plumbing business. He opened a shop near 4th Avenue and I Street, adjacent to Gill's garage, which is now the site of the Nesbitt Court House. He also homesteaded an area now known as the Simonson Subdivision, a residential area north of Northern Lights Boulevard, from McKenzie west to Nathanial Court.

It was not long before the Simonson children were getting married and were rearing the third generation of Simonsons. Rasmus "Ras" Simonson became an accountant and was employed by the Alaska Railroad for many years. He married Gladys Petty in 1935, and they had no children. Gladys passed away in 1981, and Ras in 1986. Solomon "Sol" Johan became a plumber in his father's business. He remained a bachelor all of his life. He passed away in 1978. Ingebrit "Brit" Sevrin became a plumbing contractor. He married Frances Hunter in 1927, and they had three children, Isabelle, Elizabeth and Margaret Ann Simonson. Frances passed away in 1971, and Brit in 1972. Agnes Helena Simonson, the daughter that stayed in North Dakota, married her farmer beau, Adolf Johnson, and parented three children, Cecil, Ardith and Eunice. Adolf passed away in 1944, and Agnes in 1953.

Johana "Jenny" Paulina, Kari Anna "Anna," Inger "Inga" Kristina, Petrikke Magrethe "Margaret" and Selma all married Anchorage men who had arrived here seeking their fortunes. They were businessmen, railroaders, miners, prospectors and airplane pilots. All started another generation of pioneer Anchorage families.

Kari Anna Simonson and James R. Campbell were married on November 20, l920. Jim had arrived in Anchorage in 1916 and soon established himself in business. He owned the Panhandle Club and Bar on 4th Avenue, which still stands in the same place today. He and Anna built a fine home on 6th Avenue between D and E Streets, where they raised two sons, Weldon, born in 1921, and Arthur Marvin, born in 1923. In 1941 Jim sold his interest in the Panhandle and the Annex after his long time partner, Jack Omelia, died. The family moved to California in 1943, and Jim died that same year in San Francisco. Anna passed away in 1973. Eldest son, Weldon, married Amelia Tschida in 1946, and they had three children. Weldon passed away in 1992 in Sequim, Washington. Marvin never married and is now retired in Aberdeen, Washington.

Ingeval Severin Thomasson arrived in Anchorage in the construction years of the Alaska Railroad, between l9l5 and 1920. He was employed as a telephone repairman and lineman, constructing and maintaining the telephone system. In 1920 he and Inga Simonson were married and took up housekeeping in their home on 4th Avenue and L Street, in the same area as the Simonson elders resided. This union produced three children, Phyllis, born in 1921, Inez, born in 1924, and Thomas, born in 1925. In 1950 Inga and Ingeval retired to Seattle, Washington. Ingeval passed away in 1956, and Inga in 1978. In 1943 Phyllis married William Redling, and in 1948 Inez married John Richards. The girls and their spouses left Anchorage and resided in South Carolina and California respectively. Thomas died in 2001.

Floyd Ingrim, a young miner, and Selma Simonson were married in 1926. The marriage produced two boys, Delmar, born in 1927 and William, born in 1928. After some years, Floyd was involved in a mining accident and went to California where he subsequently died. Selma had a teaching degree and had taught in Unga and Wasilla. She kept on with her teaching career after the death of Floyd.

In 1933 Selma met Bill Smith, a young miner, dog musher and railroader. William Anderson Smith arrived in Alaska in 1907. Born in England, he left home at the age of sixteen to pursue his fortunes in America. He first landed in Cordova, where he worked on the Copper River and Northwestern Railway as a laborer. From Cordova he went to Hope-Sunrise to try his luck in the pursuit of gold. He had a brief stint in the Army in WWI and then returned to Anchorage, where he hired on as an engine hostler and gradually made his way up to locomotive engineer. Bill and Selma were married in 1934, and a son Wallace was born of this union in 1937. Selma stayed active in public service causes. She served on the Anchorage School Board, as President of the Alaska Federation of Womens Clubs, the Eastern Star, Sons of Norway, and as a Grand Trustee of the Pioneers of Alaska. Bill retired from the ARR in the 1950's, but was not content to sit around. He went to work for the Lathrop Company who owned the 4th Avenue Theater. After a few years he became manager, then retired permanently. Selma retired from the city of Anchorage after nineteen years service.

Selma's and Floyd's son Delmar married Thelma Craig, and they had one daughter. Del retired from the City of Anchorage Water Utility. Son William married Delores Otter, and they had five sons. William presently operates Watcon of Alaska. Selma's and Bill's son Wallace married Beverly Stow, and they have three daughters and a son that passed away. Wallace retired from the Anchorage School District and presently is an adjunct instructor at the University of Alaska, Anchorage. Bill passed away in 1981; Selma passed away in 1984; and son Delmar passed away in 1989. All are buried in Anchorage Memorial Park Cemetery in the family plot.

In 1898 Will Bowker, at the age of eighteen, accompanied by his brother Way, landed in Skagway enroute to the Klondike gold fields. Leaving the Klondike, he prospected the Chandalar and Upper Koyukuk Rivers and was reasonably successful. At the time they had found the largest nugget on record, weighing one hundred twenty-eight ounces, which was displayed at the San Francisco Exposition of 1907.

In 1915 he arrived in Anchorage and here met Jenny Simonson. They were married in 1919 and had one daughter, Helen Patricia Bowker, known by all as "Patsy," born in 1920. In 1921 Will became involved in the Kanatak oil rush, which did not prove out. In 1923 he developed peritonitis from a ruptured appendix and passed away in Portland, Oregon. Jenny, unfortunately, contracted polio shortly after Will's death, and she and daughter Patsy moved into the family home at 4th Avenue and L Street.

In 1940 Patsy met and married a young miner from Idaho. Michael James, who came to Alaska seeking his fortune. This marriage produced two boys, Michael and Patrick. Michael was born in 1942, and Patrick in 1944. Patsy and Mike operated restaurants in Fairbanks for a number of years, and then, in Anchorage, opened the Kobuk Coffee Company and the Gold Pan Gift Shop, which still operate today.

Michael married Lynda Rae Allen in 1966 and had four natural children and one adopted daughter. Michael is a medical doctor practicing in Anchorage. Patrick married Carol Ann Scofield, and they have three children. Patrick is a practicing attorney in Anchorage. Johana Paulina Simonson Bowker passed away in 1950. Helen Patricia Bowker James passed away in 1990, and Floyd Francis James passed away in 1969. They are all buried in Anchorage Memorial Park in the Simonson family plot.

In 1915 a young boomer named Alf Nikolai Monsen arrived in Anchorage seeking his fortune. He had entered the United States in San Francisco in 1906 and worked around the Oakland/San Francisco area until the lure of Alaska brought him to Anchorage. He landed his first job as a woodcutter for the Alaska Railroad in Chickaloon and later worked as a locomotive fireman.

In 1919 he met a young lady named Petrikke "Margaret" Simonson, the daughter of the well-established Simonson family. Margaret was in the first graduating class of four students in Anchorage High School in 1918. She was working as a file clerk for the Railroad when she and Alf met. They were married in Anchorage in 1920 and took up residence in Chickaloon.

Alf and Margaret Monsen

The family left Chickaloon for Oakland, California in 1922 where eldest son Wesley was born. They returned to Anchorage that same summer. Alf worked summers in Chickaloon and spent winters in Oakland. He decided to learn how to fly, and in 1928 he received his license. In 1929 the second child Albert Monsen was born in Oakland, California.

Monsen Home in Anchorage

In 1930 Alf flew for the Pacific International Airways out of Anchorage, covering the bush routes. In 1933 Pan American World Airways absorbed PIA, and Alf became a captain for Pan American. The family moved to Seattle in 1937, and Alf flew the Seattle-Fairbanks-Juneau run until he was killed in a plane crash on Annette Island in 1947. Alf was rated as a Master Pilot and was the most experienced and oldest pilot in Pan American's Alaska Division.

Alf Monsen and Son Wes in Chickaloon

Albert Monsen, 1948

Wes Monsen, 1951

Alf Monsen on Air Field in Bethel

Wes followed his father's footsteps and flew for Pan American World Airways until his retirement. He now lives with his spouse Mary in Rocklin, California. He and Mary had six children. John Douglas and Lesley Marie Monsen Carpenter also live in Rocklin, California; Craig Alf died in 1958; Bruce Wesley died in 1973; Susan Ann Monsen Branden lives in Bethany, Connecticut; Lesley Marie Monsen Carpenter lives in Rocklin, California; and Christopher Joseph lives in Monument, Colorado. Albert was killed in a traffic accident in 1948.

Another tent town entrepreneur, JOHN SULTAN was a Greek emigrant who arrived in Ship Creek in 1915. He hired on with the ARR on the section crew in Anchorage until he could get himself established in the restaurant business. He was a chef by trade, and it was not long before he partnered with Bob Kuvara, and they opened the Royal Café in 1917. John was drafted for duty in the Army, and Bob remained and operated the café.

In 1919 John returned to take up where he left off and eventually bought out his partner. In 1922 the café was destroyed by fire. However, John was not one to give up. He built a new building, and opened the Anchorage Grill at 421 West 4th Avenue, which turned out to be the most popular restaurant in town.

In November 1935 he left on a visit to Greece and returned with a new bride. Her name was KRISULA VELLIOU, and she joined John in the operation of the Anchorage Grill. On December 20, 1936 John died of a heart attack the day following his first wedding anniversary, leaving his wife with a three-month-old son. His wife "Goldie," as she was nicknamed, married George Grames in 1937 and continued to operate the Anchorage Grill. After the death of George in 1951, she married John Tsakres in 1955 and in 1959 disposed of her interests in the Grill and spent her time developing real estate in Anchorage.

John Sultan was born in Levadia, Greece in 1891 and immigrated to the United States in 1911 to Washington. He spent three years in Vancouver, British Columbia prior to coming to Anchorage. Krisula Velliou "Goldie" Sultan Grames Tsakres passed away in 1995 at the age of eighty-seven. She and George Grames are buried in the Elks Tract, Anchorage Memorial Park. John Sultan is buried in Tract 3, Anchorage Memorial Park.

About the same time that John Sultan was opening his café, another entrepreneur was opening a jewelry store in Anchorage. FRED CARLQUIST had arrived in Seward in 1914 and walked to Anchorage in 1915. He spent a year homesteading in the Matanuska Valley and then moved back to Anchorage in 1916 to open his jewelry store. He was born in Minnesota in 1885 and his family later moved west to Washington. He married ANNA MAY MACGILLIVRAY in Auburn, Washington in 1913. She came up to join Fred in 1916 at the homestead in the Valley prior to moving to Anchorage. She had been in

Fred Carlquist

Helen Niemi Carlquist

failing health for some time and passed away in Seattle in 1923. In 1921 Fred's brother Frank had come to Anchorage and joined him in the operation of the jewelry store. Both of them were watchmakers, and the business was successful for many years.

In 1926 Fred married HELEN ELIZABETH NIEMI, a member of a pioneer Alaska family. They sold the jewelry store to Fred's brother Frank in 1936 and purchased Eckman Furniture store, which they operated for many years.

Helen was born in Calumet, Michigan in 1903 and came to Alaska with her parents in 1910, first landing in Douglas. The family moved to Anchorage in 1915 where Helen finished grade school and high school and was a member of the first graduating class in Anchorage High School. There were three girls and one boy in the class of 1919.

Fred was not in good health, so they moved to Puyallup, Washington where he passed away in 1953. Helen continued on in Anchorage, running several other businesses that she and Fred owned. She retired from active participation in 1962 and spent most of her time as a volunteer in her church and in the Christian youth organizations. She passed away in 1994 at the age of ninety-one in the Tacoma Lutheran Home.

———

FRANK E. CARLQUIST was born in Alexandria, Minnesota in 1884. He moved west to the Seattle area, where he worked as an optician and watchmaker. In 1914 he married MAY ACKROYD in Seattle. In 1921 Frank joined his brother Fred in the jewelry store in Anchorage, and May came up the following year. May and Frank had three children: Barbara Janet, born in 1916 and Doris Ruth, born in 1918, both in Leavenworth, Washington, and Donald Ackroyd, born in 1923 in Anchorage.

Frank Carlquist

May with the Children

May passed away in 1934 at an early age in Spokane, Washington. Frank continued the business until 1945 when he sold to Fred Axford. He passed away in 1979 in Sitka, Alaska.

Barbara married Harold Strandberg, a member of a well-known Alaska mining family, in 1938. They had three children: David Harold living in Prescott, Arizona, Douglas Frank living in Friday Harbor, Washington, and Steven Frederick living in San Francisco, California. Harold passed away in Green Valley, Arizona in 1995.

Doris Ruth Strandberg married Najeeb Halaby in 1945, and they had three children. Lisa, who married King Hussein of Jordan and became Queen Noor, lives in Amman, Jordan; Christian lives in Menlo Park, California; and Alexa lives in Algeria. Donald married in 1947 and had four children: Caren Carlquist Hackney and Chris Carlquist of New York City, Michael of Las Vegas, Nevada, and Mark of Los Gatos, California. Donald passed away in 1997 in Las Vegas, Nevada.

Donald Carlquist

Barbara Strandberg and Doris Halaby

WHATEVER HAPPENED TO MOOSEMEAT JOHN?

All of the Anchorage oldtimers knew "MOOSEMEAT" JOHN HEDBERG, but no one knows what happened to him. He was always a familiar figure in Anchorage and a regular on Fourth Avenue. No one really knows for sure when he came to the Cook Inlet area, but a good guess would be around 1895.

He was born in Sweden and, as a young man, entered the United States and traveled across the country, working as a logger and laborer. He found his way to Alaska, lured not by gold but by furs. He was a natural-born trapper and fisherman and made a good living at his calling. He was also a dog musher, and in his early years here he carried the mail to Sunrise, Hope and Knik. During the railroad construction years he cut piling and ties on Point Possession for the AEC. After the completion of the Railroad, John worked for H. J. Emard, who was opening a salmon cannery in Anchorage. John built two fish-traps for Emard at Nikiski number two.

In 1908 he married Anastasia Nutnaltna, and they settled on his homestead in the Nikiski area. John, in his later years, usually spent winters in Anchorage and kept his dory at Emards Cannery until spring. He had a cabin that he maintained on East 2nd Avenue and made daily trips uptown to shop at Lucky's Grocery and greet all who would stop and talk

In the spring of 1950 John had turned eighty-five years old and was living peacefully in Anchorage. He suddenly heard that someone was squatting on his homestead property. He immediately headed for Kenai and contacted Marshal Peterson to come with him and investigate. The Marshal was apparently unable to leave at that time, so John took his dory and went on alone. That was the last that anyone ever saw of him. Much speculation and rumor followed, but

Moosemeat John Hedberg in Center with Two Friends

it still remains a mystery today. One story that is probably true states that in his later years John never used a motor on his dory but always drifted with the tide and rowed. This caused many to feel that, at his age, he was overcome with fatigue and simply died. The boat then drifted out to sea with the tide and eventually sank in a storm.

U. A. LEGAULT, another of the 1915 boomers that came to Anchorage to make their fortune, reached the end of the trail in Girdwood on January 17, 1935. He arrived in Anchorage in September 1915 with one of the original survey crews and established permanent residency in Anchorage. In 1925 he married the former Mrs. Cora B. Westenbarger, a widow of another well-known early Anchorage Pioneer. Mr. LeGault was born in Bay City, Michigan in 1880 of French Canadian heritage. He spent the last seventeen years with the Alaska Railroad on the telegraph and telephone crew as a lineman and telephone repair man.

Esther and John Johnson

JOHN JOHNSON was born in Yettermark, Finland in 1892 and immigrated to the United States in 1909 at the age of seventeen. He first entered Alaska at Valdez, where he was employed as a hard rock miner for four years. In 1915 he moved to the tent city of Anchorage and, like most all of the new arrivals, was employed by the Alaska Railroad.

John with the Boys

ESTHER A. BLOOMQUIST was born in Seattle, Washington in 1893 and first landed in Valdez with her parents in 1912. It was there she first met John Johnson, and when the family moved to Anchorage in 1918 they met again and in that same year were married. John was employed as a carpenter for the ARR until his retirement in 1943. Esther was employed as secretary to attorney Leopold David, who later became Anchorage's first Mayor.

Russell Johnson

Forrest Johnson

The couple had two sons. Forrest, who lives in Seattle, married Gunvor Wikstrom, and they had three children: Lynn Irene Pratt lives in Cle-Elum, Washington; Judith Ann Osborne lives in Panama City, Florida; and Eric Forrest Johnson lives in Savannah, Georgia. Son Russell and spouse Nona Hall had two children. Gayle Justine Cowley lives in Yuba City, California, and David Wayne Johnson lives in Anchorage. Both John and Esther are buried in Anchorage Memorial Park. Esther passed away in 1950, and John in 1964.

HENRY "DAD" BAXTER was born in England in 1859. With his family he entered the United States in 1868 when he was nine years old. They originally settled in Detroit, Michigan, but kept moving west and finally settled in Spokane, Washington. He was employed by the First National Bank as a cashier until 1899, when he decided to head to Dawson. He arrived in Skagway that same year. There he met and married his wife LAURA LARSON who had a young son, Lyle W. Larson, by a former marriage.

The family proceeded over the Chilkoot to Lake Bennett, where they joined a group building a steamer to traverse the Lake and navigate Miles Canyon and the Whitehorse rapids enroute to Dawson. They lived in Dawson for a few years and then returned to Whitehorse in 1910 and finally went to Victoria, British Columbia, where Henry managed the Westhall Lumber Company until 1913. Hearing of the gold strike in Shushana, the family headed north again, but with no luck there they made their next move to Anchorage in 1915.

With a partner, Oliver LaDuke, Henry obtained the first coal contract with the AEC in 1916. He spent a fortune in trying to develop the Matanuska coal fields, to no avail. Reviewing his priorities, he moved the family back to Anchorage in 1916 and opened Baxter's Corner, a cigar store on the corner of 4th Avenue and E Street, where the Anchorage Hotel Annex now stands. He passed away in 1931, leaving the Cigar Store operations to his stepson Lyle and wife Laura.

Lyle operated the business and took an active interest in local affairs. He became Exalted Ruler of the Elks in 1924, and then held the position of secretary for almost ten years. He also served as secretary of the Chamber of Commerce and directed his efforts to the development of the City. When the United States entered WWI, Lyle was one of sixty men who hiked to Seward to enlist in the Army. Lyle passed away from a lingering illness in 1936, and he and his stepfather are buried in the Elks Tract, Anchorage Memorial Park.

————

IRVING LEONARD KIMBALL was born in Osceola. Pennsylvania in 1869 and as a young man moved westward to Oregon in search of his fortune. He shipped out on a cargo ship that was plying Alaska waters as far north as Nome. Before shipping out, he met a young lady who had moved to Oregon with her parents, and they became engaged. After four years at sea, he found his niche as a trader. He returned to Portland, and he and DELLA CARPENTER were married in 1901. The young couple left for Kodiak the following year with a load of trade goods and thus started their career as merchants and traders.

Della was born in Manson, Iowa in 1880. She spent her childhood on a farm, traveled with her family in a covered wagon to Oklahoma, and then moved on to Glenwood, Oregon. After her marriage to Irving, and following their jaunt to Kodiak, they moved on to Seward where they established the first trading post there.

Irving and Della Kimball

In 1908 the boomtown of LaTouche called them, and there they established another trading post until the Guggenheim copper operators found a richer lode in the Cordova area. In 1915 Irving and Della were looking for new territory, and the news of the construction of a new townsite and the Alaska Railroad attracted them to the tent city of the Alaska Engineering Commission. They put in a winning bid of $500 on Lot l, Block 51 in the new townsite and moved their tent operations "uptown." They built their store on this lot, and it still stands today as one of the city's first mercantile establishments. In 1921 Irving passed away, and Della operated the

Kimball's Store Front

Vera Kimball

Inside the Store

store by herself until daughter Decema Kimball Andresen joined her in partnership in 1950. Della was one of the organizers of the Anchorage Womans Club and was actively engaged in community affairs for many years.

Irving and Della had two daughters, Decema and Vera. Decema married Moritz Andresen (see following). Della passed away in 1958. Daughter Vera Castles passed away in 1986. Both Della and Irving are buried in Anchorage Memorial Park Cemetery.

MORITZ A. ANDRESEN arrived in Anchorage after a tour as a seaman on a whaling ship operating in the Aleutian Islands. He came ashore in Anchorage in 1921 and started his search for gold in the Cache Creek area. He moved back to Anchorage permanently after his sojourn in the mining district and took a job with the Brown and Hawkins Company. He moved from there to the Alaska Transfer Company and Berger Transportation Company.

In 1925 he met and married Decema Kimball, the daughter of the Pioneer Kimball family who operated Kimball's Dry Goods store at the corner of 5th Avenue and E Street. The original building still stands and is managed by Decema Kimball Andresen today. Decema was born in Seward, where her parents had a small store, on June 25, 1906. She graduated from Anchorage High School in 1923 in a class of eleven students. She learned to fly in 1950 at the age of forty-four and obtained a commercial license. However, she did no commercial flying. In 1962 she went on a polar bear hunt and successfully shot a record size bear out on the polar ice. She flew her own plane out on the ice into" tomorrow" across the international date line, shot the bear, and returned "today."

Moritz Andresen

Decema Andresen

Moritz joined the Anchorage Volunteer Fire Department and was the driver of the truck for many years. He served on the City Council from 1937 to 1944. Civic minded and volunteering his knowledge and assistance whenever needed, Moritz was a major player in the development years of Anchorage.

Moritz and
Decema Andresen

Decema with a Prize
Lettuce

Eloise and Carl
Andresen

Moritz on Fire Truck

Moritz and Decema had two boys, Carl and Alfred. Alfred never married and passed away in 1995. Carl married Eloise Beilefeld in 1965, and they raised three sons and one daughter, all living in Anchorage: Carl Robert, L. William, V. Richard and Kimball Rose. Moritz died in 1948 and is buried in the Masonic Tract, Anchorage Memorial Park.

JACOB B. "JAKE" GOTTSTEIN was born in Des Moines, Iowa in 1886. As a young man he was a traveling salesman covering the Fraser River country in British Columbia from 1907 to 1911. He retired a wealthy man in Prince Rupert, British Columbia at the age of twenty-five, traveled extensively in Europe, and returned broke in 1915. He heard of the construction of the Alaska Railroad on Cook Inlet and immediately set out to find his niche in the new development of Anchorage. He was prepared to start his own grocery business and first opened in a tent on Ship Creek flats. He began selling cigars and sundries to construction workers and miners along the railbelt and walked many miles where there was no track. He made as many as nine dogteam trips to Seward and back serving his customers.

Gottstein Warehouse

Jake built his first warehouse at 5th Avenue and D Street in Anchorage and later opened up at the corner of 4th Avenue and G Street, where the building still stands. He was one of the first wholesale grocers in Anchorage. The business survives today.

Anna Gottstein

J. B. Gottstein

Molly, Barnard and Anna
Gottstein

Barney Gottstein

Molly Oyer

ANNA JACOBS was born in Des Moines, Iowa in 1889, and, two years after graduating from the University of Minnesota in 1916, she went to Valdez as a schoolteacher. She spent two years in Valdez and then moved to Anchorage in 1919 where she met Jake. They were married in Anchorage in 1920. Anna was instrumental in starting the first PTA in the Anchorage School system and was renowned for her interest in education.

Jake retired from the business in 1945, leaving son Barney to take over the operations of the business. Jake and Anna retired to Seattle, Washington where Jake died in 1963, and Anna passed away in 1981.

Jake and Anna had two children: Molly Gottstein Oyer and Barnard J. Daughter Molly had four children: Katherine O. Cruze lives in Renton, Washington; Russell J. lives in Seattle, Washington; Steven L. lives in Dallas, Texas; and Gordon N. lives in Federal Way, Washington. Son Barnard had five children: Sandy Mintz, James, Robert, and David, all living in Anchorage; daughter Ruth Ann Faust lives in West Hartford, Connecticut.

FRED PARSONS and his brother JACK came to Alaska aboard a fur-sealing ship, landing in Nome about 1896. Their ship had just outrun the Coast Guard which had been chasing it because of a recent law outlawing the taking of fur seals. The ship was at sea when the law was passed, and the captain felt that they had a right to another harvest because they were at sea when the law was passed. Fred and Jack both jumped ship at Nome and joined the search for the elusive gold. Without great success in Nome, they proceeded to the Klondike via Skagway in 1898. They followed the stampeders first to Fairbanks, then Iditarod, and finally in 1914 settled on Tent City on Ship Creek, waiting for the AEC to start construction on the Alaska Railroad.

On July 19, 1915 the Parsons brothers purchased Lot l, Block 29 in the new Anchorage townsite, for the amount of $395. This lot is on the southwest corner of 3rd Avenue and H Street and is currently the parking lot for the State Court house.

JANE MCKILLOP was born in Glasgow, Scotland in 1881. She had already lived an exciting and varied life in Australia, South Africa, England and the United States before journeying to Alaska at the age of thirty-three. Her arrival on Tent City, Ship Creek in 1915 was the beginning of another adventure for her. She opened one of the first restaurants in the new city and named it the Three Sisters Café. During the construction of this restaurant she met Fred Parsons, whom she had hired to install the floor in her new establishment. She and Fred married in 1917 and, along with Fred's brother Jack, they built the Parsons Hotel two years later on the lot purchased by Fred and Jack. Fred and Jessie, which was the name she went by rather than Jane, operated the Parsons Hotel for many years. They enjoyed an excellent reputation for clean, comfortable and inexpensive rooms.

Jessie Parsons

Fred Parsons

Jessie was well-known as a storyteller and kept her customers entertained telling tales of old. She compiled the first *Alaska Sourdough Cookbook* to assist in a fund drive for the construction of Providence Hospital. She also presented the first fur style show in the first Anchorage Fur Rendezvous. She was a past President of the Womans Club and a charter member of the Pioneers of Alaska Auxiliary #4.

Parson's Hotel

Two children were born of the union of Jessie and Fred, a son Stanley and a daughter Linette. In 1931 their marriage dissolved, and, even though they were divorced, Fred kept taking his evening meals with his ex-wife and son and daughter. Their daughter never knew they were divorced until told by a friend. She always thought that one living in each end of the Hotel was so that they could keep an eye on what was going on.

Fred and Jessie kept their business partnership intact until 1942, when Fred sold his interest to Jessie and retired to Washington. One year after acquiring Fred's interest, Jessie sold out and left Alaska in

Linette Anderson
Parsons

Stanley Parsons

1959. Fred passed away in Los Angeles in 1944. Jessie spent the rest of her life in California, living with her daughter Linette Anderson. She passed away in 1973 at the age of ninety-two.

Daughter Linette Parsons Anderson had six sons: Gary, Jack, Gib, Logan, Jim and Stanley, all living in California. Son Stanley had three children: Terry of LaFayette, California, Kay Mertes of Sarasota, Florida, and Robert of Anchorage. Stanley died in 1988, and Linette passed away in 1998.

———

ROY LAURENCE LEE came to Anchorage in 1915 with his parents after a short sojourn in Cordova and Juneau. He was born in 1906 in San Pedro, California. His family left Alaska around 1920, and Roy returned in 1923. He worked for the Anchorage Times as a linotype operator and later as a shop foreman. He went into private business in 1939 and started the Alaska Stationers and Printing Company. He started a weekly newspaper in the same year and then discontinued it when WWII broke out. He died in 1957.

———

Among the early professional people who migrated to Alaska in 1915, ROBERT COOKE LOUDERMILCH was born in Upper Sandusky, Ohio in 1891. He spent his early life in Sandusky and on the west coast and first came to Alaska in 1912 with the United States Naval Coal Commission as their first aid man. After his tour with the Coal Commission he returned to Alaska in 1913 with the Alaska Engineering Commission, again as a first aid man. His mode of operation was to have a two-room log cabin about every fifty miles at the "head of steel." This cabin was both home for Robert and field hospital for the ARR. His means of transport was by dog team, horseback or railroad speeder when track was available.

———

In 1916 when the railroad was approaching Fairbanks, he enlisted in the United States Army and went to France as a medical corpsman. He participated in the battles of Meuse-Argonne, Verdun, and St. Mihiel. He was severely wounded at St. Mihiel and spent over a year in hospitals recovering.

In 1919-1920 he spent some time in Chicago, Illinois earning an embalmers certificate and meeting his future bride, MAE JANE ZIMA. Mae was born in Grand Haven, Michigan in 1890. In 1920 Mae was working for a Chicago food processing company and met Robert at an ice rink. They were both excellent skaters.

Robert returned to Alaska in 1921, and Mae came to meet him in Seward, where they were married. They returned to Anchorage, where he worked as a surgeon's assistant at the Railroad Hospital. In 1922-24 he started the Anchorage Funeral Parlors mortuary and also the Loudermilch Ambulance Service and the Anchorage Motor Company. His first hearse was horse drawn, and he did not acquire a motorcar hearse until 1926. Mae

Mae and R. C. Loudermilch

handled all of the paperwork for the funeral home and paid all of the bills. Robert was a good hunter and, like that of so many early Anchorage residents, his larder was always full of moose, ducks, rabbits and grouse. Mae was busy canning and preserving, taking care of the two children and helping with the business.

Loudermilch House at 528 2nd Avenue

As automobiles increased in number in Anchorage, it was difficult to obtain parts, repairs and winter storage. As a solution, Robert built the Anchorage Motor Company next door to the funeral home at 5th Avenue and D Street. He was able to machine parts as necessary and also to store autos for the winter. It was the norm then to store your car for the winter up on blocks.

While involved in many business ventures, Robert still had time for civic duties and community affairs. He was a volunteer fireman and a member of the City Council in 1927 and 1928. He had a tour as commander of both the American Legion and VFW. He moved through all of the chairs of the Elks and Masonic Lodges, and even managed the Anchorage City Band for several years.

Ruth Loudermilch and Marjorie LeClercq

Robert and Mae retired in 1944 and moved to Seattle, Idaho, California and Oregon. Robert died in Ashland, Oregon in 1959, and Mae passed away in Seattle in 1962. The union of Mae and Robert produced two children. Daughter Marjorie Mae Loudermilch LeClercq died in 1996 in Seattle, Washington. Son Robert Clyde Loudermilch and spouse Ruth Vandenburg had four children. Lynn Ellen lives in Merrimack, New Hampshire; Mark Gerard lives in Charlottesville, Virginia; Brian Robert lives in Nashua, New Hampshire; and Jane Bridget lives in Greenfield, Massachusetts. Robert and Ruth live in Scituate, Massachusetts.

Robert Clyde Loudermilch

Another young couple landed at Ship Creek in 1914 seeking their fortune in the newly developing community of Anchorage, Alaska. ASA T. and ALICE C. MARTIN set up housekeeping in Tent City immediately upon their arrival. Asa joined in the auction of town lots in 1915 and purchased Lot l, Block 36 for $208. He was employed by the Alaska Engineering Commission as a structural steel worker. He worked on the Nenana Bridge, the Hurricane Gulch Bridge and many others. They lived in Seward, Nenana and Fairbanks while Asa was employed by the AEC.

Asa T. Martin was born in Birmingham, Alabama in 1881 and was engaged in structural steel work. He met and married Alice Clare Walsh in Milwaukee, Wisconsin in 1914, prior to

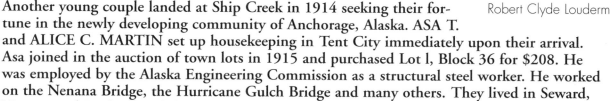

John and Asa Martin

Alice, John and Asa Martin

Asa with Delivery Truck

Step-and-a-Half Dairy Ranch House

Evelyn Landstrom and
Asa Martin

their coming to Alaska. Alice was born in Milwaukee in 1889 and lived there until her marriage to Asa.

A son, Asa Leon Martin, was born to them in 1919. They resided in their home at 4th Avenue and L Street until 1924, when they moved back to Milwaukee, Wisconsin. After six years in Milwaukee, they returned to Anchorage in 1930. They purchased thirty acres of land east of town opposite Merrill Field, and also took another two hundred forty acres under lease to start a dairy farm. Starting first with two cows, they built their herd from there.

Asa took great pride in his cows and his spotlessly clean dairy. Visitors were always welcome and invariably were invited into Alice's kitchen for a cool glass of milk. They named the Dairy the Step-and-a-Half Ranch, as it was only a step-and-a-half from downtown. Their motto was "the best milk you ever had."

The Martins sold the dairy in 1941, and Asa went back to work for the Alaska Railroad until his retirement in 1948. On April 2, 1949 both Asa and Alice were killed in a tragic accident on the Alaska Highway. They are both buried in Tract 14, Anchorage Memorial Park Cemetery.

In 1944 Dr. Asa L. Martin and Evelyn Landstrom, both members of Pioneer Anchorage families, were married. They had two children: John T. Martin born in 1950, and Alice C. Martin born in 1952. John still resides in Anchorage, and Alice lives in Coupeville, Washington. Dr. Asa L. Martin passed away in 1989, and Evelyn Landstrom Martin passed away in 1991. They are both buried in the Pioneer Tract, Anchorage Memorial Park Cemetery.

EDWARD BURTON and EVA MARY DUNBAR ALLENBAUGH left New Westminster, British Columbia on the steamer *S.S. Mariposa* in July of 1915 with their six

Eva Mary Dunbar
Allenbaugh

Edward Allenbaugh with James
and Bill

Allenbaugh Family

Ted Allenbaugh

children, heading to the tent town of Ship Creek. Edward had dreamed of establishing a fox farm in Anchorage; however, funds were not available for this enterprise, so he took a job with the Alaska Railroad, as almost all newly arrived people had to do. He had been a ranch foreman in Nevada, a cowboy in Montana, and a miner in British Columbia, and was a qualified and experienced jack-of-all-trades.

Their immediate task was to build a home, and, with the purchase of a lot at 711 M Street, they built a two-room log house with a sleeping loft for the children. In 1917 tragedy struck the family when son Eric James was killed by a train at the age of seventeen. In 1919 Edward was fighting a house fire and accidentally fell off the roof. He was permanently injured with brain damage and died in 1921 at a Portland, Oregon hospital.

Eva was left with five children and was the sole support of the family. She obtained employment with a local dry cleaners and tailor shop and kept the family going until the children were able to help provide income. In 1923 they purchased another house and had it moved to 711 M Street. The two remaining boys tore down the log house and sawed it up for firewood.

Eva and Edna Allenbaugh

Eva Dunbar was born in Fall River, Kansas in 1873 and died in 1958. Edward was born in Cassville, Missouri in 1876 and died in 1921. They were married October 18, 1896 in Cassville, Missouri. Their children were: Maude, born 1898 and died at age one; Eric James, born in 1899 and died in 1917; William Henry, born in 1903 and died in 1968; Edna Frances, born in 1907 and died in 1999; Eva Mary, born in 1912 and died in 1993; and her twin Edward Neil "Ted" who died in 1983. There are grandchildren living in Anchorage and in Washington.

Bill and Blanche Allenbaugh

JOHN B. "JACK" WADMAN came to Alaska in 1904 from Chicago, Illinois where he was born in 1876. He first landed in Ketchikan, and his interest in gold led him to Iditarod, Ruby, Chisana, and a brief interlude in Dawson in 1914.

He came to Anchorage in 1915 just shortly after the townsite was laid out. He opened a paint store on 4th Avenue near G Street and operated as a painting contractor and paper-hanger. Jack was a well-respected member of the community and was vitally interested in civic affairs. He was an honorary member of the Elks, a life member of the Pioneers, and a past President of the Pioneers. He had served four one-year terms on the City Council, in 1933, '34, '35 and then again in 1944. His support of the Alaska Crippled Children's Association was well known among his civic interests. Jack was forced to retire in 1935 due to failing health, and in 1949 he left Anchorage for the warmer weather of southern California. He passed away in October of 1950.

JOSEPH STAINO was born in Corgliano, Italy in 1887 and immigrated to the United States in 1906. He worked his way across America to the west coast doing manual labor with several different railroads. He first came to Cordova in 1915, but decided on the new town of Anchorage, and arrived here in late 1915. He obtained work with the Alaska Railroad in 1916, working on the section until his retirement in 1941. He passed away in 1969 in Yuma, Arizona and is buried in the Elks Tract, Anchorage Memorial Park.

GEORGE JEKOS left his home on the Island of Crete in 1910 and immigrated to the United States. He spent the next five years working around the Seattle and Tacoma, Washington area and arrived in Anchorage in 1915. He was greeted with open arms by the Greek community living in Anchorage. His career in Greece had been illustrious. His countrymen hailed him as a patriot and wrote his name in their history. He had taken part in the bloody Macedonia struggle for liberty that lasted for over four years. He had received a medal of high honor for bravery and courage in this bloody conflict. He was born in the village of Scheenai on the Island of Crete in 1887 and died in Anchorage in June 1916. He is buried in the Catholic Tract, Anchorage Memorial Park Cemetery.

ROBERT LEE MAXEY left Redding, California on April 24, 1915 for Alaska in search of gold. He sailed from Seattle on the *Northwestern*, arrived in Seward in May 1915, and came to Anchorage on May 26. He was employed as a track car repairman by the Alaska Railroad on the Anchorage section when the track was laid as far as Wasilla. He retired from the Railroad in 1945 and went south to California, where he passed away in 1969. Bob was born in Olagah, Oklahoma in 1893.

WILL A. JOHNSON was born in Algona, Iowa in 1873. His family moved west to Salem, Oregon that same year and remained there for fifteen years. They then moved to Bellingham, Washington where Will finished high school. He worked in mining in the west from California to Colorado.

He became interested in Alaska when he witnessed the unloading of seventeen boxes of raw gold in Seattle. In 1906 he left for Valdez, prospecting around Prince William Sound and the Copper River country. In 1909 he arrived in Cook Inlet and landed in Knik, working there until the Railroad survey crews arrived at Ship Creek. He served as a scout for the Alaska Engineering Commission when they surveyed the Railroad route, and in later years he was also a guide for a scientific party that preceded the establishment of the Matanuska Valley Colony. He staked considerable claims at Gold Creek and in 1911 freighted supplies up the Big Susitna by boat in the summer and by dogteam in the winter.

Will was well known for his poetry and contributed regularly to the *Anchorage Times* "Poet's Corner." He was a former President of the Pioneers of Alaska Anchorage Igloo, and later served as historian. He left Alaska in 1951, retiring to Bellingham, Washington. He passed away in 1957 and is buried in Bellingham.

———

DAVID ANDREW CHECKTESON was born in Christiania, Russia in 1886. He entered the United States in 1909 and proceeded to Nome, Alaska for a short stay. He then moved to Seward in 1910 where he worked for the Alaska Railroad at Kern Creek. In late summer of 1910 he worked for the Alaska Road Commission on the Valdez-Fairbanks Road and was stationed at Paxon. He returned to Seattle in 1914 and then came back to Anchorage in 1915, working for the Railroad until 1936. After another sojourn to the Fairbanks gold fields he returned to Anchorage in 1951 and was employed as a warehouseman for the ARR. It is unknown where he spent the rest of his years or in what year he passed away.

———

Another Anchorage Pioneer industrialist, HENRY J. EMARD first arrived in Skagway in 1898 on his way to the Klondike. He did not stay long as most of the good ground was taken, so he proceeded on to Ruby in 1908. Not having much luck in the gold fields, he moved on to Juneau, where he took on a job as engineer in the A. J. Mine in 1911.

Hearing of the new railroad being built from Seward to Fairbanks in 1915, he immediately moved into the tent city. First being employed by the AEC in communications, then subcontracting portions of the construction, he finally was the builder of the first telephone system in Anchorage. He contracted with the Kellogg Company for the latest switchboard equipment and had crews out cutting timber for poles and crossarms and getting the distribution system set up while he was waiting for the switchboard. It was operational in 1916 and had the first thirty customers on line that same year.

In 1927 he founded the Emard Packing Company and brought his cannery on line at the mouth of Ship Creek that same year. In his third year of operation he added another "line" and was successfully operating from May 25 each year until late August, packing king, sockeye and coho salmon. He had three tenders operating the inlet and also owned two fish traps. The *North Cape*, the *Henry J*, and the *Giant II* were his first boats. He later added the *Smith*, a converted WWI sub-chaser, and the *Helen T*. Henry J. Emard contributed to the economy of Anchorage and its youth each season by hiring high school boys and girls for the summer season, many of whom were working their way through college.

In 1936 he purchased the ocean dock from the Alaska Railroad, planning to use this as an addition to his plant. For years the ocean dock had been operated by W. W. Stoll and had also been a salmon packing cannery named the Farwest Packing Company and owned by the Gorman family. That first year the Emard plant packed over sixty thousand cases of salmon - a record year. Two lines operated twenty-four hours per day, and the young workers reaped a harvest in overtime work. With the demise of fish traps, stiffer regulations, and the advent of fast freezing and processing, Henry sold his interest in the cannery and retired to Seattle, Washington. He was a director of the First National Bank of Anchorage and also a stockholder of the Bank of Cordova. He passed away in Seattle in 1963.

Ed and Jenny Carlson

EDWARD CARLSON was born in Annenburg, Sweden in 1881. After immigrating to the United States, he spent some time in Colorado prior to coming to Valdez in 1907. After spending three years in the Valdez area, he returned to Colorado where he and JENNY VIKE were married. Jenny was born in Molde, Norway in 1892 and came to the United States with her parents.

Ed and Jenny and their children returned to Alaska in 1915, landing at the tent city on Ship Creek. They immediately bought two lots at auction, one in Block 37, Lot 10, for $280 and the other in Block 36, Lot 6 for $210. They built a log cabin home on Lot 6, Block 36, which was located on L Street between 4th and 5th Avenues.

Ed worked for the Alaska Railroad until 1927, when he and Jenny bought the Inlet Hotel, located at 4th Avenue and K Street. He and Jenny operated the Hotel until 1937, when they sold it and went into semi-retirement.

Jenny and Children

Ed and Jenny had three children. Son Robert was killed in a plane crash in 1936. Daughter Thelma married Earl Bell, and they had three children. Jesse lives in Anchorage; Jenny Earl lives in Palm Desert, California; and Rodney is now deceased. Daughter Ruth Carlson married Harold Libbey, and they had two children, Carl who lives in Anchorage, and Helen, now

Bob Carlson

Thelma Bell

Ruth Libbey

Inlet Hotel

deceased. Edward died in 1969, and Jenny died in 1970. They are both buried in Anchorage Memorial Park Cemetery as are son and daughter Robert Carlson and Ruth Libbey and grandson Rodney Bell.

In 1902 young SOL SILVERMAN arrived in Ketchikan to work for the Hadley Copper Mines. He was hired as an accountant, a metallurgist and an assayer. Born in Butte, Montana in 1870, Sol was well fitted for the pioneering days ahead of him, because as a young man he spent much time on the plains and in the mountains of Montana. His father had a general store, which gave him basic training in salesmanship. He later became a salesman for several wholesale distributors and covered a large territory on horseback, on foot or by horse and wagon. The deep snows of the coastal regions of Alaska were not new to him, and he took it all in stride at his new job.

In 1908 a young Norwegian girl he had known in Montana stepped off the boat in Ketchikan to become his bride. She was MARIE NELSON, who had come to the United States with her parents from Norway when she was eight years old.

The sudden death of Marie's relatives, killed by a snowslide in Washington, called them back to Seattle in 1910. A year later Sol went back to Alaska, this time to Lawing, and then Seward. Marie returned to Alaska in 1912 and joined Sol in Seward, where he was employed by the Brown and Hawkins Company. He was soon sent to the community of Knik on Cook Inlet to open a new store for the firm.

Further expansion by Brown and Hawkins soon found Sol and Marie in Anchorage to supervise the opening of a new store. In 1918 he left the mercantile business and went to work for the Alaska Railroad, known then as the AEC, as head of the stationery department, a job he held until 1933. He again switched jobs and became a night watchman for the ARR until his retirement in 1936. He was then offered a position as circulation manager of the Anchorage Daily Times, a position he fulfilled until his untimely death on March 17, 1942. Sol took on the job as secretary of the Masonic Lodge for the twenty years prior to his death.

Marie Silverman

In the meantime, Marie was very active in clubwork, the Eastern Star, the Pioneers of Alaska Auxiliary and the Sons of Norway, giving generously of her time to lodge functions and charitable work. She went to work for the Times after Sol's death, and when she retired in 1959 she was honored by the Times as their longest employee. During WWII Marie spent a great deal of time as a USO volunteer. She acted as a surrogate mother to many of the boys and developed friendships that lasted for many years after the War. In 1950 she was named "Queen Regent" of the Fur Rendezvous. She was also named Honorary Mother by the Job's Daughters and Temple Mother by the Pythian Sisters.

Marie was born May 9, 1878 in Norway and died in Anchorage on April 7, 1967. Both she and Sol are buried in the Masonic Tract, Anchorage Memorial Park Cemetery.

JACOBUS E. "JIM" VAN ZANTEN was born in Hillegon, Holland in 1888 and immigrated to Canada, where he followed his early training in Holland and worked as a cook in the railroad construction camps. He saved his money and sent for his sweetheart to come to Canada.

JOHANNA HELENA MATOT was born in Harlem, Holland in 1886 and at the age of twenty-five came to Canada to marry Jacobus. They were married in Lytton, British Columbia in 1911.

When the Canadian construction job was completed they moved to Seattle, where Jim worked as a chef in his uncle's restaurant in Ballard. He heard about the new construction of a railroad in Alaska and set out for the tent city on Ship Creek in 1914. He immediately went to work as a cook in the Chickaloon Navy Coal Mine and in the spring of 1915 sent for Johanna and first-born son Jack to join him at Chickaloon.

After the Navy shut down the mine operations, Jim moved into the Nelchina mining district, cooking in the mining camps. He had to leave his wife and three children in a cabin on the Chickaloon River while he worked on the Nelchina. The family spent a lonely winter chopping holes in the river ice for water, waiting for Jim to return. When he returned from the Nelchina they moved into Anchorage, and, tired of having to leave his family, he took a job locally as janitor in the Anchorage School and worked there until all of the children graduated from high school. During WWII he was chief steward for the Railroad and later returned to cooking for the Alaska Road Commission camps. Through all of this, Johanna kept busy as a homemaker, raised the four children through school age, and then joined Jim in the camps as his assistant. Jim and Johanna had four children and twenty-one grandchildren. Eldest of the family was Jack who had five children:

Johanna, Jim and Jack VanZanten

VanZanten Home in Anchorage

Van Zanten Family: Jack, Helen, Dorothy and Bertha

Jacqueline Avon Richardson lives in Juneau; David James and Thomas Lee live in Homer; Terry Joseph lives in Talkeetna; and Celia Beth passed away in 1971. Daughter Helen Van Zanten Gilbert had four children, all living in Washington. Larry Lee lives in Burien; Bruce R. lives in Tacoma; James Roy lives in Ballard; and Charles Allen lives in Seattle. Daughter Dorothy Van Zanten Jackson Secondi had three children. Mary Leone Jackson lives in Medical Lake, Washington; Rebecca Lynn Secondi is deceased; and David Eugene lives in Ellensburg, Washington. Daughter Bertha Van Zanten Porter had nine children. Morris Lee, Jr. lives in Washington; Ami Jo Radiske, Robert William, Bertha Karen Kivi, Coline Ann Kivi, and Anna Marie Johns all live in Nikiski; and Harold is deceased. Jim died in 1979, and Johanna died in 1980. They are both buried in Ellensburg, Washington.

NELS GUSTAV BYSTEDT was born in Stockholm, Sweden in 1867. He first came to Alaska aboard a whaling ship and spent his first winter of 1904 on the ship frozen in the Beaufort Sea ice. After his sailing days ended on the west coast, he returned to Alaska as a miner, first in Juneau, then Cordova in 1907, and to Valdez in 1913. In Valdez he met ANNA OTHILDA JOHNSON, who was born in Amaldasland, Sweden in 1882. They were married in Valdez in 1913, and together operated a small dairy farm.

Elizabeth Bystedt

James and Theodore Bystedt

Gustav and Anna moved up to Cook Inlet in 1916 and homesteaded in the Eagle River area out of Anchorage. Shortly after, Gus took a job with the Alaska Railroad at Matanuska as section foreman, and Anna cooked for the section crew.

In 1922 they moved to Anchorage and purchased a home on 4th Avenue and B Street. Gus worked his quartz claim and placer claims on Bird Creek, while Anna operated a small hand laundry out of their home.

Gus and Anna had four children. Anna Elizabeth Mathewson had one child, Robert Shernberg, who lives in Anchorage. James A. Bystedt and spouse had four children: Frederick James lives in San Leandro,

Gustav Bystedt

Peter Bystedt

Anna Bystedt   Anchorage Home   Cabin
and Laundry

California; Kenneth Peter lives in Anchorage; Richard Andrew is now deceased; and Gus Allen lives in Fairbanks. Son Peter was killed in an airplane accident in 1939. Son Theodore never married and died in 1947. Anna died in 1937, and Gus died in 1944. Both Anna and Gus and sons Peter and Theodore are buried in **Anchorage Memorial Park Cemetery.**

ANOTHER PIONEER ENTREPRENEUR THAT HELPED BUILD A CITY

OSCAR F. ANDERSON was born in Sagerskog, Sweden in 1883. He immigrated to the United States in 1903 at the age of twenty with two of his brothers. They first settled in Massachusetts where they were employed in a shoe factory and later with the Seth Thomas Clock Company.

In 1905 the three brothers decided to make a move from the east coast. The older brother chose to return to Sweden, and Oscar and his younger brother chose to move west to Seattle, Washington. In Seattle they lived in a boarding house owned by a Swedish woman named Elizabeth. They found very little work around Seattle and did odd jobs including work in a meatpacking house.

Oscar Anderson and Family

The 1906 earthquake and fire in San Francisco lured them south as there was plenty of work available in rebuilding the city. After a short period of time Oscar received a message from Elizabeth, and he decided to return to Seattle, where he and Elizabeth were married in the same year. A child Maurice was born in 1907, and two more children followed, another son in 1909 and a daughter in 1911.

In 1915 Oscar decided to head for the proposed new town of Anchorage and start life anew in Alaska. Leaving the family in Seattle, he proposed to buy some lots at auction and build a home, then send for the family.

He first arrived in Seward in March 1915 and set out over the old Dalton Trail, destination Ship Creek. He and seventeen other men slept on the floor of a small tent awaiting the public auction of land. His first job was cutting wood on what is now Government Hill. The AEC put an end to the woodcutting, and

Anderson Home

Oscar and a friend named Jensen opened a meat market in a tent on the flats. Oscar took the first boat he could get back to Seattle to purchase equipment for a cold storage plant and established the Ship Creek Meat Company in June 1915. He purchased a downtown lot and built his plant, completing it in the fall of 1915. The building still stands on 4th Avenue and is occupied by Stewarts Photo shop. The cold storage area with the heavy refrigerator doors is still in the rear of the building.

His next move was to build a home for the family, which he did with two carpenter friends, "Stucco" Johnson and Aaron Wickland. The original house has been restored and was relocated a short distance from where it was originally built. In the fall of 1916 Oscar brought the family up from Seattle, and they all settled into the new home, which was the first home built in the new Anchorage townsite.

Ship Creek Market

Oscar operated the Ship Creek Meat Market for many years, serving both retail and wholesale customers along the railbelt and upper Cook Inlet. In 1920 Oscar, along with Evan Jones, Ike Bayles, Art Shonbeck and two others, organized the Evan Jones Coal Company on Wishbone Hill, just north of Palmer. Oscar was president and general manager for twenty-two years, from 1922 to 1944. He was the last of the original developers and owned the mine until he sold out to Harry Hill in 1944. Oscar often said he "supplied food and fuel" to the residents of Anchorage, the real necessities.

Oscar, along with Art Shonbeck, Gus Gelles and Ike Bayles, also organized the first airline operation in Anchorage. It was known as the Anchorage Airways, and Russel Merrill was hired as the chief pilot. When Merrill was lost, Anchorage Airways closed down. Another business venture with Bayles and Loussac was the development of the Anchorage Times newspaper. They were the first and last stockholders until 1935. Oscar ventured into the oil drilling business in Yakutat, and held a financial interest in the A. J. Mine in Juneau. He also owned and operated a sawmill on Knights Island, cutting and milling ties for the Alaska Railroad. Oscar's life resembled that of Cap Lathrop. Both men led productive lives in Alaska. They were courageous, resourceful and rugged individuals who came and stayed to sow what other generations might reap.

Central Building, 3rd Avenue and G Street

Jonesville Mine

Very little is known of Oscar's first wife, Elizabeth, who was the mother of his children. They were divorced shortly after the children left school, and Mrs. Anderson moved back to

Oscar at Age 86

Oscar and Elizabeth Anderson

Seattle. Oscar married again to a woman he met on a trip to California with his friend Charley Frye of the Frye Meat Packing Company in Seattle. We only know her first name was Jean. This was a short-lived marriage and ended in divorce. Two years later they were remarried in Anchorage, and divorced again. Oscar then met Elizabeth Peterson, an English teacher who traveled to Anchorage to visit family and friends. She and Oscar were married in 1940.

ELIZABETH PETERSON was born in 1905 in Rock Springs, Wyoming. The family moved to Tono, Washington where her coal miner father found work. She attended Western Washington Teachers College and taught English in Everett and Dahlia, Washington. She presently is ninety-four years old and lives in Centralia, Washington. Oscar's son Maurice passed away in Montana, and son Vincent passed away in Seattle. At the time of this writing, his daughter Ruth Burgess lives in Seattle. Oscar passed away in Olympia, Washington in 1974 at the age of ninety-one. He is buried in the Pioneer Tract, Anchorage Memorial Park Cemetery.

PETER J. CAVANAUGH was born in Dubuque, Iowa in 1876. At the age of twenty-two, he joined the rush to the Klondike in 1898 and later to Nome in 1899. While in Nome he met Miss AGNES ROSS, who had come to Nome in 1900 with her parents from her birthplace, Mt. Pleasant, Pennsylvania. Her parents operated a small hotel and grocery store in Nome. In 1914 Peter and Agnes moved south to the Pacific Northwest until 1915, when they heard the call of the north again, this time to Sunrise, on Turnagain Arm. Peter was a driller and had done some work in the Crow Creek mining area. That same year they

moved to the tent city of Anchorage in time to purchase a lot at the second auction of the townsite. The family lived in a tent while Pete built a log cabin home in between working with the AEC and working on the bridge crews on Eska, Gold Creek, Hurricane and Nenana bridges. He finished his time with the Alaska Railroad in the maintenance shop in 1936, when he retired.

The marriage of Peter and Agnes produced four children. James was born in

Agnes Ross Cavanaugh

Peter J. Cavanaugh

1909 and died in 1982. Emmett C., born in 1911, had two children, Mary Ann and Warren, both living in Seattle. Catherine Cavanaugh Weimer had three children. Robert E. lives in Anchorage; Russell lives in Seattle, Washington; and Bonnie Tisler lives in Anchorage. Norman F. had four children: Patty and Kathleen Cavanaugh Holt live in Anchorage, Darrell lives in Wasilla, Peter lives in Eagle River. Peter Cavanaugh died in 1940, and Agnes passed away in 1952.

Norman Cavanaugh, Katy Weimer and Emmett Cavanaugh

VICTOR JOHNSON was born in Dalsland, Sweden in 1882 and immigrated to the United States in 1902. He arrived in Alaska in 1906, landing in Cordova to work on the construction of the Copper River Railroad. He later moved on to Fairbanks where he was employed by the Fairbanks Exploration Company. When construction started on the Alaska Railroad, he moved down to Anchorage and worked for the AEC. On a trip to Seattle, Washington he met Miss ELIN ELIZABETH MARTINSON, who was also born in Dalsland, Sweden and had entered the United States in 1909.

In 1916 Elin came to Anchorage to marry Vic, and the newlyweds immediately set about building a log cabin home, located approximately where the Sheraton Hotel is. Vic was steadily employed by the ARR as section foreman at various locations, including Cantwell, Curry and Moose Creek.

In 1930 Vic purchased a government house from the Chickaloon Navy site and moved it to Anchorage, rebuilding it at the corner of 4th Avenue and Barrow Street. When taking leave time from the ARR, Vic spent his time in Anchorage casting headstones and monuments for the Anchorage Cemetery, many of which are still standing today. In 1961 Vic was chosen as King Regent for the Fur Rendezvous, representing the Pioneers of Alaska Igloo #15.

Victor Johnson

Vic and Elin had three children. Donald V. and his spouse, Olive Grace, had one son, Donald Douglas, who lives in Anchorage. Elizabeth Johnson Gahnberg had two children: Kurt G. lives in Bothel, Washington, and Loren W. lives in Mill Creek, Washington. John M. Johnson and Beryl Johnston had two children: Christine Elin lives in Anchorage, and John Mark lives in Juneau. Elin Johnson passed away in 1952, and Victor died in 1972. Both are buried in Snoqualmie, Washington.

First Home

Elin Johnson

New Johnson Home

Elizabeth Johnson

John and Donald Johnson

H. M. LYNCH was another boomer who arrived on the Ship Creek flats in 1915. He was employed by the AEC and continued on with the ARR after the railroad construction was completed. He was one of the many single Pioneers who came to the blossoming city of Anchorage from elsewhere in Alaska. As far as can be determined, he resided in Juneau for many years prior to coming to tent city Anchorage. He was engaged in the real estate business from 1920 to 1930 when he moved to the Sitka Pioneers Home where he passed away in 1932. He was a past Grand President of the Pioneers of Alaska and is buried in the Sitka Pioneer Cemetery.

A 1915 arrival in Anchorage who was immediately put to work with the AEC, TOM KOVAK was originally from Yugoslavia and immigrated to the United States in 1910. He had gained experience in operating steam equipment in the mining camps of California. When he arrived in Anchorage he was put on as a steam shovel operator and put in continuous service for over thirty-five years. He retired to Seattle, Washington in 1951. His wife Bessie passed away in 1943 and is buried in the Pioneer Tract, Anchorage Memorial Park. Tom passed away in Seattle in 1971 and is buried in the Lakeview Cemetery.

J. H. McCALLIE, an early day Pioneer, practiced dentistry in Anchorage for many years, coming here during the early construction days in 1915-16. He set up his dental practice in Anchorage; however, he covered the upper Cook Inlet area from Knik to Kenai. He left Anchorage in 1929 and returned to his home state of Idaho. He passed away there in 1935 and is buried in the Moscow Cemetery.

DR. FRANK M. BOYLE, a prominent physician of early Anchorage, came here in 1915 during the construction days of the Railroad. He practiced medicine along the railbelt, traveling by dog team, by riverboat and packhorse prior to the completion of the Railroad. Before to coming to Anchorage he spent many years in Valdez. He moved to Seattle in 1921 due to failing health and died in Seattle in 1922.

BYRON C. ELMES, better known to his many friends as "JOE BUSH," was born in Oneta, New York in 1883. He came to what is now Anchorage in 1915 after spending three years on the Panama Canal Railway. He was first employed by the AEC as track inspector and later as track foreman. Upon completion of the Railroad, he became a locomotive engineer and later served as trainmaster and traveling engineer. He retired in 1943 and at that time held the position of Assistant Superintendent of Motor and Power Equipment.

After retirement he moved to Hollywood, California where he was employed in a defense plant. He left California just prior to the end of WWII, moving to Republic, Washington, where he and his wife purchased a small hotel. He died in Spokane, Washington in 1948.

Another Anchorage pioneer entrepreneur, who was one of Anchorage's foremost business and civic leaders, ARTHUR A. SHONBECK was born in Clayton, Wisconsin in 1878 and, as a young man, stampeded to Nome in the 1900 gold rush. Being unsuccessful in Nome, he headed for the gold fields of Fairbanks in 1906 and finally to the Iditarod in 1910. His mining interests in Iditarod were reasonably successful; however, he established a retail merchandise store in Flat as well. He operated there until 1915 when he moved to Ship Creek on upper Cook Inlet, preparing for the establishment of Anchorage.

Art established a retail merchandise business primarily selling produce from a farm he had established in the Matanuska Valley. In 1920 the labor temple building at the corner of 4th Avenue and H Street was destroyed by fire. Art purchased the property and rebuilt it into a three-story apartment house, named the Shonbeck Apartments. Everything was of the latest and most modern materials, and it was the showplace of rentals in Anchorage at the time. The ground floor was reserved for business. Art became the Ford dealer in 1929, selling Ford farm tractors and Ford cars. He was appointed the dealer for the Giant Powder Company, so he sold dynamite out of the back door, cabbages and cauliflower out of the front door, Ford cars at the order desks, and Standard Oil gasoline and other products out of the side door.

He, along with Gus Gelles, Oscar Anderson and other investors, started Anchorage Air Transport, the first airline in Anchorage. They hired Russel Merrill as their chief pilot, and had two airplanes, *Anchorage #1* and *Anchorage #2.*

Art was a charter member of the Chamber of Commerce. He served on the Anchorage City Council; he was appointed to the Board of Regents of the University of Alaska in Fairbanks, was a past President of the Pioneers of Alaska, Igloo #15, and was the Democratic National Committeeman for Alaska. He was instrumental in convincing the federal government to establish farming in the Matanuska Valley, where he proved, with his own farm, the viability of farming there.

Art and his wife Anna were married in Seattle in 1906 while he was out on a business trip from Fairbanks. Anna was one of the original members of the Christian Science Church in Anchorage, and was extremely active in the Church.

Art disposed of most of his business interests in the early forties and concentrated on his mining interest in the Ophir district, particularly on Gaines Creek. In the summer of 1945 he and his long time friend John Beaton were inspecting some mining property when the pickup they were in left the road at the Gaines Creek Bridge, and both were drowned. This was a huge loss to the community and to the Territory of Alaska, as the influence of these two men contributed much to the development of Alaska. They died in true Alaska Pioneer style, with their boots on.

Anna Shonbeck left Alaska and moved to California in 1947 and passed away in Pasadena in 1964. Her ashes were shipped to Anchorage, and she is buried with Arthur in a single grave in the Elks Tract, Anchorage Memorial Park.

The name SEIDENVERG is synonymous with KOSLOSKY, BAYLES and KENNEDY in early Anchorage. All four of these men and their families came to Anchorage in 1915 and opened men's clothing stores on 4th Avenue. Koslosky came from Dawson, Bayles came from Iditarod, Seidenverg came from Nome and Seattle, and Kennedy came from southeast Alaska. They all came with the same purpose in mind, to build a business and raise a family in the new city.

HARRY SEIDENVERG was born in Odessa, Russia and immigrated to the United States in 1902. Like so many other immigrants he wished to avoid the constant military service demands that were made on single men in much of Europe at the time. Harry went to Nome in 1906 where he first went into the clothing business. In 1909 he returned to Seattle where he met and married HATTIE KARNOFSKY that same year. Hattie was born in New York City and came to Seattle with her family at the turn of the century.

In 1915 Harry and Hattie packed up and moved to Anchorage where he immediately built and opened a men's clothing store located just west of where Stewarts Photo presently stands. The wife and children moved back to Seattle in 1938 for health reasons, and Harry operated the store until 1942, when he sold out to his brother LEO SEIDENVERG, who operated the store until it burned in 1946.

Harry and Hattie had two children. Son Louis, born in Anchorage in 1919, lives in Scottsdale, Arizona. Daughter Gladys Seidenverg Rubenstein was born in Anchorage in 1921. She presently lives in Seattle and has a son Mark Edward who lives in Corte Madera, California, and a daughter Fluff Seidenverg Anderson who resides in Seattle, Washington. Harry passed away in 1966 in California, and Hattie passed away in 1969 in Seattle, Washington.

The other half of the Seidenverg clan was Leo, who first went to Nome in 1900 where he established a general store and operated trading posts on the Siberian Coast. The Russian government confiscated his trading posts, and he filed claims against the Russian government for reparations. He eventually had an audience with Lenin, the Soviet Premier, and successfully settled his claim through the United States State Department. Leo passed away in Seattle in 1959.

One of the Klondike stampeders who finally settled in Anchorage in 1915, CHARLES WATSON was born in Des Moines, Iowa in 1868 and as a young man moved west to Oregon. When he heard the first cry of "Gold in the Klondike," he immediately quit his beat as a policeman on the Portland police force. He did not see his first gold camp until several years after he came over the Chilkoot. He found that there was an easier way to make money by starting a stage line and hauling freight over the winter trail from Whitehorse to Dawson.

Charley returned to Portland in 1900 where he met and married GRACE JOBSON, who had moved to Portland with her parents from Chicago where she was born in 1881. Shortly after their marriage, Charley got a job with the White Pass and Yukon Railway under construction from Skagway to Whitehorse. They moved to Skagway in 1902, and Charley was assigned to work with Michael J. Heney, the engineer who conceived of and built the Copper River Railroad into Kennecott. When the White Pass Railroad reached Lake Bennett, Charley went to work for Bob Lowe, a freighter, and started driving stage again from Whitehorse to Dawson. Grace was at his side on these trips and shared the hardships of the trail with him.

In 1905 they moved to Fairbanks intending to establish their home, but fate had other things in mind. Charley started hauling freight and passengers on the stage line over the Valdez trail into the Chitina country and the Nezina. Grace again was at his side on all of the treks into the Alaska wilderness, sharing board and lodging with miners and stampeders in roadhouses, tents and temporary camps.

The year 1915 saw them in the new town of Anchorage, just about the time that the tent squatters in the Ship Creek flats got the word to move out and settle in the new townsite. Here again Charley, with a partner Shorty Whinke, started up the Pioneer Express, and began moving the tent squatters up the hill on the south side of Ship Creek. With his teams of horses, he and Shorty figured prominently in the moving of the new residents and also in the clearing of the land for the new townsite.

Charley became a member of the Anchorage police force in later years and then became a United States Deputy Marshal under both Harry Staser and Frank Hoffman. Charley and Grace had one daughter, Gertrude Watson Kennedy, who taught school along the railbelt, in Matanuska, Talkeetna and Nenana. Gertrude was married to Dan Kennedy, co-owner of a men's clothing store. They had no children. Charley passed away in 1940, and Grace in 1966. Dan and Gertrude Kennedy are both buried in the Catholic Tract, Anchorage Memorial Park, and Charley and Grace are buried in the Elks Tract.

Another original stampeder who came to Anchorage in 1915, FRED WRIGHT was well known in various parts of Alaska, but especially in Anchorage, as a restaurateur. Fred was born in Boston in 1874 and moved west as a young man to Seattle, Washington. In 1897 he heard about the gold strikes in the Klondike and made his way north, but he ran out of money when he got as far as Juneau. He worked in a restaurant in Juneau until he replenished his bankroll and then proceeded on to Skagway and over the Chilkoot to Dawson. In 1899 after some luck in the Klondike, he headed for Nome and was one of the group of men who discovered the famous Topcock Beach, where a wealth of gold was found. He returned to Seattle and there, in his own words, he "cooperated with others in spending his northern gold."

After "various starts and breakdowns" as he put it, he married in Juneau, where a son was born. After two years in Juneau, the family headed north to Cleary Creek out of Fairbanks and spent four years mining the area. They again departed for Seattle and after a long trip to Europe returned to Alaska, this time to the tent city of Anchorage in 1915. They first arrived in Seward and came by dog-team from Seward to Anchorage. Fred obtained work as a chef working for Dick Dickinson and Dave Maheny in their new D and D Café. In the fall of 1915 Fred took over the operation of the café and moved it from Tent City to the location on 4th Avenue, between C and D Streets.

A fire leveled the café in 1921; however, Fred rebuilt better than ever and continued to operate until he sold out in 1935 to Dick Matthews and Martin Skinner. He always claimed he "first experienced the feeding game" in Juneau when he worked for room and board. The D and D was one of the oldest cafés in Anchorage and stood until the 1964 earthquake took out the entire block on the north side of 4th Avenue between C and D Streets. Fred always claimed that the success of his restaurant venture in Anchorage was due largely to his lifetime partner, John Olsen, also a Nome stampeder.

Fred and his wife retired somewhere in California. It is unknown where his building was taken by Mother Nature. Like so many others, the written word will be his memorial.

———

A neighbor and old stampeder friend of Fred Wright, CHRISTOPHER WOODHOUSE was born in England in 1883. Very little is known of his history prior to coming to the tent city of Anchorage in 1915 from Knik with his spouse MARY. They arrived in Knik in 1910 where Mary taught grade school and sold New York Life Insurance to supplement their income.

Chris worked for the AEC, and, when the headquarters of the ARR was completed, he worked in the foundry until he retired. One of the workers in the foundry with Chris was John Bagoy, who had come to Anchorage from Flat in 1921. Both of these men had the gold bug as well as three other prospecting partners, Charley Quinton, Mike Jacobs and Jake Knapp. All five took

Woodhouse at Kantishna

Splashdam for Sluiceway

Partners

time off from their employment and packed in sixty-five miles to the Kantishna where they did assessment work on their claims and prospected for the elusive yellow rock.

Mary Woodhouse was in failing health in 1949 and was sent to Portland, Oregon for special help. Chris also was hospitalized there for a short period of time but returned to Anchorage. Mary died shortly after he left in 1950. Chris was hit by a car and killed instantly three months later in Anchorage crossing the street at 4th Avenue and Gamble. Mary is buried in Portland, and Chris is buried in the Elks Tract, Anchorage Memorial Park.

Another one of Anchorage's first residents, GEORGE M. CAMPBELL arrived at the tent city in early 1915. During the formative years of Anchorage he was one of the most popular and successful businessmen in the city, heavily involved in real estate, construction, contracting, mining and accounting. He was quite active in civic affairs in the early years and was instrumental in developing the swimming beach at Lake Spenard, which another old-timer, Joe Spenard, discovered.

George was an avid baseball fan, and in 1919 he borrowed a team of horses from Cap Lathrop and cleared the stumps from the land where the original Mulcahy Park stood, at the southeast corner of 6th Avenue and C Street, where the downtown fire department is now. George was a charter member of the Bill's Club, which was the original name of the Elks, and also was the treasurer of the Pioneer Igloo #15. He maintained a huge collection of photographs, clippings and old newspapers recording the history of early Anchorage. George died in 1955 and is buried in the Elks Tract, Anchorage Memorial Park.

The man who cashed the first check written on the newly opened First National Bank of Anchorage, HARRY M. HAMILL was born in Dwight, Illinois in 1884 and at the age of thirty, in 1915, made his way to Alaska via Seward. He started work as a shipping clerk with the AEC and the ARR until 1922, when the First National bank opened its doors. He spent thirty-six years with the bank and retired as vice president, having served under Win Ervin, the first president, and retiring during the presidency of the Cuddy family.

While on a trip to Portland, Oregon in 1918, Harry and MILDRED IMMAC- ULETTA HENTHORN were married. Mildred had come to Seward in 1915, went to work for the AEC as a secretary, and in 1917 moved to Anchorage via dog team over the Dalton Trail. She was still employed with the ARR and met Harry

Mildred Hamill   Harry Hamill

First Home

Robert and Opal Hamill

Last Home: Cottage #23

after she moved to Anchorage. She was born in Denver, Colorado in 1890 and moved to the Portland area in 1912.

Mildred was an artist when she met Harry but had not kept up with her training. After their marriage and return to Anchorage, she started a secretarial school for young women, training them for work with the AEC and the forthcoming railroad. Not having any typewriters available, she made cardboard mock-ups of the keyboard to teach the students.

She studied life drawing at the Art Museum of Portland, Oregon in 1914, and in Anchorage she studied landscaping under Sydney Laurence. In 1924 she was in the third year class of the Art Institute of Chicago and took lessons in pastel portraits from Mr. Mark Tobey in Seattle, Washington. She had various exhibitions in Anchorage and in Seattle, mostly in landscapes. In 1944 she painted the only portrait of Sydney Laurence for which he sat. She was also well known for her paintings of children. Most of her paintings are held privately by many individuals in Alaska and Seattle. Her Alaskan landscape "Frosty Morning" won first and second choice at the art exhibit in Anchorage in 1945. She is listed in *Who's Who in American Art* and *Who's Who in American Women*.

Harry and Mildred had one son, Robert Magee, who wed Opal O'Merria Barton. This union produced three children. Barton Magee lives in Henderson, Texas. David Rayburn and Robert Glen live in Houston, Texas. After Harry passed away in 1958, Mildred moved to a retirement home in Seattle. In 1968 she became ill, and son Robert took her to Houston, Texas, where she passed away in 1970. Robert passed away in 1975 and is buried in Houston, Texas. Harry is buried in the Elks Tract, Anchorage Memorial Park. Mildred was cremated, and some ashes were scattered over Mt. Susitna and some buried with Harry.

One of the most prominent, well-known and well-respected women of her day in the entire Cook Inlet area, MARTHA "MOTHER" WHITE died on February 11, 1919 after a long illness. Her funeral and cortege were the largest ever held to that date. Her obituary covered almost a full page in the *Anchorage Daily Times* and told of the prowess, courage and generosity of this Pioneer woman. Rather than do a piecemeal sketch on her life and history, I am going to copy her obituary and comments verbatim as printed in the 1919 February 3, 11 and 13 issues of the *Anchorage Daily Times*.

The following historical sketch of the life of Mother White was given by Mrs. Christopher Woodhouse, Historian of the Pioneers of Alaska Auxiliary # 4.

Mrs. Martha Greer White passed to her reward February 2, 1919 after a long illness. She was born in Glasgow, Scotland, February 22, 1867. Her mother so loved America that when her eldest daughter was born on Washington's birthday, she named her Martha, after the pioneer mother of our country. At the age of 14 years, in company with her brother and sister, she landed in New York City, where she lived for some months with an aunt. Before the end of the year, she was married to a Mr. Grove. A son blessed this union in the person of Robert Grove (White) After this short marriage we find her in Patterson, New Jersey, where she had married a Mr. White. From Patterson she went to Texas accompanied by her son, where she was soon joined by Mr. White. After four years in the Lone Star State, the family next moved to the Pacific coast where they set tled on a homestead in Grays Harbor, Washington

During her trip to the states last year, Martha paid a visit to Grays Harbor and was given a very hearty welcome. This was especially due to the fact that her heroic deed of some years ago had not been forgotten. For unassisted Martha had rescued four English sailors from a watery grave, which was recognized by nothing less than the awarding of two gold medals: one by a special act of Congress, the other by the Chamber of Commerce of Portland, Oregon.

In May of 1894, Mr. and Mrs. White had come to Alaska and settled on the west side of Cook Inlet at the Indian village of Ladds Landing, or Shuitna as it was called. From a fur trading business which they had established, a nice little fortune had accumulated, which was later invested in mining property in Hope.

Of the four children born to Mr. and Mrs. White, only two survived, Robert Grove of Anchorage and Mrs. Frank Cotter of Seward, who was the first white child born on Cook Inlet. During the years she lived in Hope, Martha White's charity became known to every one, for legion are the recipients of her various deeds of kindness.

When the government was about to begin construction of the railroad, Martha was among the first arrivals. The restaurant and lodging house conducted by her in the old town were in great demand. As soon as the present lots were put on the auction block, she purchased the one on which the structure which bears her name was erected. That she endeared herself to the Anchorage pioneers and Alaskans in general goes without saying. Her interest in the welfare of the town in the various organiza-

White House Restaurant, 1916 (One of Two Women Pictured is Mother White)

tions, in Red Cross work, in a word, in whatever contributed to the assistance and comfort of her neighbors is too well known to all to need repetition here.

Mother White, as she is known certainly earned the name. She fulfilled the office of mother after a manner that might well be envied. As "Mother White" she still will adorn the pages of Alaska history. With her passing, the people had lost a dear friend, Anchorage a loyal citizen and all of us a noble example of charity.

Obituary, *ANCHORAGE TIMES*, February 3, 1919

MOTHER" WHITE was among the first white women to settle the Cook Inlet country, and a daughter, Mrs. Frank Cotter of Seward, was the first white child born in this partof Alaska. Mrs. White was an exceptional woman, possessing all of the best traits and characteristics of the Pioneer settler on the frontier. She was brave, yet tender; keen in business, yet generous to a fault. She ministered to the afflicted, cared for the sick, aided the needy, cheered the downhearted, gave good counsel to those who came to her for advice, and was indeed a "mother," during her long and useful life, to the inhabitants of this remote region.

The funeral services will be held under the auspices of the ladies Auxiliary of the local Igloo of Pioneers of Alaska, in obedience to the departed's last wish. Let the local busi ness be suspended; let the town en masse attend the last rites of this noble, beloved pioneer woman.

"Mother" White's honored name is indelibly written on the pages of Cook Inlet history. All stores and places of business are urged to close between the hours of 2 and 3 o'clock p.m.

Martha is buried in the Pioneers of Alaska Tract 10, Anchorage Memorial Park.

Few individuals have led a more vigorous life of adventure than one GERRIT "HEINIE" SNIDER, who arrived on the Alaska scene in 1910. This doughty Dutchman was born the

Heine and Alice Snider

son of a shoemaker in the fishing village of Monnikendam, Holland, on April 13, 1886. Heinie first exhibited that daring of adventure when he left home and ran away to sea at the age of fourteen. From 1900 to 1908 he sailed all over the world as a steward aboard many types of ships. He took two years off his sailing schedule to join the German Colonial Army to fight in the Boer War in South Africa, where he was twice wounded. Heinie returned to the sea before the end of the war, and, after another year at sea, he jumped ship in New York. From there he rode the rails to Spokane, Washington, where he had friends from the old country. He worked as a waiter at the Davenport Hotel in Spokane, shipped out on Alaska Steamship boats as a waiter, worked on the Yukon river boats, and prospected for gold in the Shushana district.

In 1915 he sent for his sweetheart in Holland, and they were married in Spokane, Washington that year. ALICE JACOBA ALDENBERG was born in Monnikendan, Holland in 1894, and she was twenty-one years old when she heeded Heinie's beck and call.

The year l916 found the young couple living with their first born child in a tent on the Ship Creek flats in the proposed site of Anchorage, sleeping on spruce boughs, with a sugar barrel as a baby's crib. Heinie worked odd jobs around the tent city, trying to save enough to build a decent home for his growing family. The family spent several years around the Anchorage and Wasilla areas. In 1925 he was able to purchase a three hundred twenty acre homestead on Lake Lucille in Wasilla. This proved to be the turning point in the Sniders' life, as they finally found a place they could call home.

Heinie worked for the Alaska Railroad as a section foreman. He was a miner, farmer, teamster, waiter, bull cook, fur farmer, laborer, truck driver and a watchman, a jack-of-all-trades and a true pioneer Alaskan. Heinie was always on the side of the "little" man, and his sympathies lay with those men who worked with their hands and used their backs. He ventured into politics, serving in the Territorial House of Representatives from 1947 through 1949, in the Senate from 1951 to 1955, and as a delegate to the Republican National Convention in Chicago in 1952.

Heinie served as Grand President of the Pioneers of Alaska in 1953. He and Alice donated five acres of land on their Lake Lucille homestead to the Pioneers Order to be used as a park and picnic ground; and in 1925 they donated the land for the Wasilla airport.

Heinie authored two books: *So was Alaska in* 196l and *l00 Alaska Stories* in 1966. Alice, the love of his life, was his inspiration. The dedication in *So was Alaska* was: "It is to my Alice, who provided the inspiration to put my thoughts into writing, and who has an abundance of all of the qualities and virtues so characteristic of our pioneer women, that I dedicate this book with love and gratitude."

The union of Heinie and Alice Snider produced four children, one son and three daughters. Son Lincoln Peter was killed while serving in the U. S. Navy in 1940. Eldest daughter Elizabeth

Marie Snider Betts

Lincoln "Pete" Snider

Pat and Al Hjellen

"Pat" Snider Hjellen had six children. Gerrit, Susan Hjellen Brown and Ida Hjellen McMahon live in Wasilla; Gilbert, Alice and Peter live in Anchorage. Daughter Anna Snider Short had four children: Joan Rogers and Laura Short live in Anchorage; Jim Rogers lives in Alameda, California; and Lyle lives in Hoonah, Alaska. Daughter Marie Snider Betts had three children: Wetzel and Wylie both live in Wasilla, and Billy is deceased. Heinie died in 1972 at the age of eighty-six. Alice died in 1986 at the age of ninety-two. Their ashes were scattered over Pioneer Park on Lake Lucille.

The first professionally trained artist to take up permanent residence in Alaska was the great impressionist SYDNEY M. LAURENCE. He was born in Brooklyn, New York, October 14, 1865. His father was reportedly Australian and his mother was English. His father's business address was 1 Wall Street in New York City, indicating a position of distinction in the business community. Sydney was reared with every advantage and every luxury. He attended Peekskill Military Academy and, at the age of seventeen, ran away to sea for four years, becoming first mate on the *Edmund Yates*. After returning to New York, he entered the National Academy of Design, a most celebrated art school. There he studied marine art under Edward Moran and figure painting under the celebrated Walter Sattersly. He became one of the world's greatest marine painters.

In 1889 Sydney married another art student, Miss Alexandrina Dupre. They lived in Cornwall and in Kent in England and were charter members of the St. Ives Club, hobnobbing with English society. At the age of twenty-four Sydney went to Paris, entering an arts college where he studied for five years. He won recognition in 1894 at the Paris Salon for a painting done at Cornwall on the English coast. Somewhere in this period Sydney fathered two sons, however it is unknown where they were born.

In 1898 he covered the Spanish American War for the *New York Herald* and in 1900 the South African War and the Boxer Rebellion in China as artist for the British publication *Black and White*. At end of 1900 he began his work as a professional photographer, and he began his adventure in Alaska.

Sydney Laurence and His
Model T

Sydney suddenly left England, his wife and family in 1901 or 1902 and supposedly arrived in Juneau in 1903 where he secured work as a photographer. He went to Valdez in 1904, prospecting for gold in the summer and doing odd jobs during the winter months. His earliest known Alaska painting was "Seldovia, Alaska," completed in 1912. It is in the Anchorage Museum of History and Art collection. He sketched Mt. McKinley in 1913 and completed "The Trapper" and another large painting in 1914. "The Trapper" is in the Cook Inlet Historical Society Collection and is displayed along with the six by twelve foot painting of Mt. McKinley in the Anchorage Museum of History and Art.

There are many unsubstantiated stories of Sydney Laurence and his travels in Alaska. Snippets of information are found regarding time he spent in the vicinity of Cordova, where he became acquainted with Jack and Nellie Brown, who were two of the first homesteaders in the Ship Creek flats. The story goes that he was on the trail when he fell through shell ice and became soaked with water in twenty-degrees-below weather. Nellie Brown's father found him in a vacant cabin and supposedly saved his life and kept his limbs from freezing. This started the long friendship between Sydney and Nellie Brown, who acquired a huge collection of his paintings during the years she and Jack spent in Anchorage.

Sydney opened a studio in Anchorage on 4th Avenue in 1915 as a photographer and water colorist. He moved into the Anchorage Hotel in 1920 and maintained his studio and living quarters there until 1930. By 1925 he began spending some winter months in Los Angeles, painting many Alaska subjects sketched the previous summer. In Los Angeles he met JEANNE KUNATH, a young French painter who was studying in Los Angeles, and after a short courtship they were married on May 8, 1928. In 1929 he painted another six by twelve foot Mt. McKinley in Los Angeles. Then, for a few years in the early thirties, he lived and painted in the New Washington Hotel in Seattle, Washington. Sydney returned to Anchorage with Jeanne in 1934.

Sydney was already thirty-eight years old when he first came to Alaska, and was sixty-two when he and Jeanne were married. As mentioned, very little is known about his early life, and many have speculated as to his Alaskan exploits, but we do know that he was an Alaskan treasure and that examples of his work are in many private and public collections.

Jeanne was born in Colmar, France in 1887 and studied art in her homeland from childhood. She was a nurse's aide on the front lines of Alsace during WWI and left for America in 1920. She met Sydney while studying at the Otis Art School in Los Angeles. After their marriage, the two artists spent summers hiking and sketching all over Alaska. Jeanne's career as an Alaskan artist started in 1928 while on their honeymoon. She identified and painted more than three hundred species of Alaskan flowers and specialized in detailing wild flowers on a black background. She wrote her first book, which contained one hundred thirty color plates of wildflowers, after twenty seasons of hiking around Alaska on collection trips that took her from Ketchikan to the Bering Sea, and on many trips to McKinley Park.

For years there was only one copy of her wildflower book as the plates were too expensive to reproduce, but in 1974 *An Album of Alaska Wildflowers* was finally published. Her second book, *My Life With Sydney Laurence*, recounting her life with Alaska's foremost impressionist, was also published in 1974.

Sydney died from heart failure in the hospital on September 12, 1940. He admitted himself the night before he died after telling friends that he would not be around after that day. He got a haircut

Jeanne Kunath Laurence

Laurence Monument

and a shave from his favorite barber the day before, and told friends that he was getting "prettied up to die." He also called a friend, who had ordered a picture for delivery next Christmas, and told him he had better get it today as tomorrow would be too late. Jeanne passed away on August 13, 1980, just four days before she was to be honored in Anchorage with the dedication of a wood mural carving on the west wall of the Sydney Laurence Auditorium.

Both Sydney and Jeanne are buried in the Pioneer Tract, Anchorage Memorial Park Cemetery. In 1999 the Cook Inlet Historical Society raised funds to place a new memorial monument at their gravesite. The Soroptimist Club placed a memorial bench at the gravesite in honor of Jeanne who was their oldest charter member at the time of her death.

All of the information given here on the Laurences was taken from Jeanne's book *My Life With Sydney Laurence*, the *Anchorage Times* obituaries and editorials, various newspaper clippings and articles written by Mr. R. L. Shalkop, former director of the Anchorage Museum of History and Art.

Jack and Carlotta Chisholm

JOHN JACK "J. J." CHISHOLM, a traveling salesman of some repute, was born in Dallas, Texas in 1881. He entered Alaska in 1894 with his father, who was an agent for West Coast Grocery Company. He went to Dawson for the B. M. Behrends Company, leaving Juneau and Skagway via the Dyea Trail with ninety tons of general merchandise in July of 1897. He returned to Juneau in 1899 and then went back to Dawson to mine and hopefully strike it rich. He was employed by Ames Mercantile Company and Sargent and Pinska in Dawson until 1904. He stampeded to Fairbanks in 1904 and became a partner with Frank Hall and later sold out to Hall in 1907. He left Fairbanks in 1907, making a seventeen-day trip by horseback to Valdez to catch the Alaska Steamship boat *Northwestern* to Seattle.

Chisholm and Krueger Families

In 1908 Jack returned to Alaska as an agent for West Coast Grocery Company of Tacoma, Washington, which he represented for thirty-one years, and later for the Washington Farmers Coop Association for sixteen years; the Pacific Bottlers Supply Company for fourteen years; the Puget Sound Butter and Egg Company for fifteen years; and for Kraft Foods Company for ten years. Jack set up his business headquarters in Anchorage in 1915. He traveled by dogteam, small plane, riverboat and on foot to take care of his customers in all parts of Alaska.

Jack had many experiences during his life traveling Alaska and his days in the Yukon and remembers his departure from Dawson with a twelve thousand dollar poke. He left Dawson with three companions over the Chilkoot when they met a stranger who talked them into taking a short cut. Jack's three

Joan and Jack Ray   Patricia Kreuger, 1941

companions did, but he stuck to the main trail. The three were all found dead and their gold gone. Jack could have been a victim also had he gone along with his friends.

In 1917 he and CARLOTTA QUINN were married. Carlotta was born in Los Angeles, California in 1885. She and her sister Mae Beattie became co-owners of the Parsons Hotel, located at the corner of 3rd Avenue and H Street. This marriage produced two children, Joan Quinn Chisholm Ray and Patricia Anne Chisholm Krueger. Joan had no children. Patricia Anne had a daughter by a marriage to Carl Garver, an Air Force pilot stationed in Anchorage in 1941. They were divorced in 1942. Daughter Karen Garver Cameron lives in Anchorage. Patricia and Rudy Krueger were married in 1948, and they had three sons: Kurt R. lives in Mt. Pleasant, South Carolina; Paul Quinn lives in Beaverton, Oregon; and John Chisholm lives in Las Vegas, Nevada.

John Jack Chisholm died in San Antonio, Texas in 1957, and Carlotta Chisholm died in Vallejo, California in 1965. Patricia Chisholm Krueger died in Portland, Oregon in 1985. Joan Chisholm Ray died in Anchorage in 2000. All of the Chisholm and Krueger families are interred in Acacia Memorial Park, Seattle, Washington, with the exception of Joan, who had her ashes scattered over Cook Inlet.

For the early arrivals, "Tent City" and "Ship Creek Flats" have been used interchangeably. Although Anchorage was not named until August 9, 1915, histories of most of these people read that they came to Anchorage in 1915, some prior to the time the town was named, and some after the naming of the community. The ones that say their arrival was to the Ship Creek Flats or Tent City obviously came prior to August 1915, and others that mention only Anchorage, we can assume arrived after August of that year.

The years 1915 and 1916 were busy ones. After the lot sales, buildings and homes started going up all over the townsite, and people were moving up the hill from the tent town in the Ship Creek Flats. The first signs of permanence were the construction of the post office, a movie theater, churches, hotels, restaurants, wooden sidewalks, a school, telephone lines, power lines and streetlights. A newspaper was started. Civic organizations were organized, such as the Chamber of Commerce and the Womans Club and fraternal organizations were also chartered.

We have covered the schools and made reference to various other establishments. Now we shall endeavor to give the history of the early established churches, the Womans Club and the fraternal groups that were organized in 1915 and 1916, and in some cases the history of the people that were the organizers.

In June 1915 a group of men held an informal meeting in Robarts Hall preparatory to organizing a local club of I.O.O.F., INTERNATIONAL ORDER OF ODD FELLOWS. The group consisted of A. J. Wendler, Alfred Benson, Charles Crawford and John D. Crawford.

In July 1915 a group of men organized the SOCIAL CLUB OF THE ELKS. This was the forerunner of the BENEVOLENT AND PROTECTIVE ORDER OF ELKS #1351. The original group of men were: A. J. Wendler, elected as chairman; F. A. Martin, secretary treasurer; and M. W. Diedrich, F. D. McCullough, and E. M. Culbertson, trustees. The first lodge building was a log edifice on 4th Avenue between F and G Streets, where the 4th Avenue Theater now stands. Their organizational meeting was held in the Inlet Soda Company building, and others in attendance and charter members were Chris Eckman, C. E. Rade, E. S. Reedy, J. Casey McDannel and F. G. Bartholf.

In July 1915 another group of men met in Robarts Hall to discuss organizing the FRATERNAL ORDER OF EAGLES, or the F.O.E. A. J. "Tony" Wendler was elected chairman; F. A. Martin was secretary treasurer; and Robert McIntosh, John Crawford and Frank Kartle were elected trustees. Others in attendance were Chris Eckman, Oscar Anderson, and E. J. Amundsen.

In September 1915 the ANCHORAGE WOMANS CLUB was formally organized. Officers chosen for the ensuing term were: President, Mrs. F. Mears; vice-president, Mrs. F. L. Shaw; corresponding secretary, Mrs. Tubby; recording secretary, Mrs. G. L. Jackson; and treasurer, Mrs. P. J. McDonald.

On June 8, 1916 the LOYAL ORDER OF MOOSE was organized at a meeting in Robarts Hall. Fred Martin was elected deputy district director, and governing members were Leopold David, Thomas C. Price, George H. Conklin and C. B. Peterson.

The MASONIC CLUB was organized in 1917 with fifty members in attendance. Mr. J. A. Moore was elected President, and Winfield Ervin was elected secretary. Their first order of business was to purchase two lots on 4th Avenue, on the southwest corner of E Street, which they still own today. The Masonic organizations that followed were Lodge #221 in February 1917, the Royal Arch #3 in February 1918, Knights Templar #2 in August 1920, the Shriners in August 1918, and Eastern Star in January 1918.

The PIONEERS OF ALASKA, IGLOO #15, was organized in January 1917, and the Auxiliary #4 was organized on March 27, 1919.

The AMERICAN LEGION JACK HENRY POST was organized in August 1919; the AMERICAN LEGION AUXILIARY was organized in August 1922; and the VETERANS OF FOREIGN WARS, DENALI POST #1685 was organized in July 1929.

THE CHAMBER OF COMMERCE was organized in 1915, and its first presidents were J. H. Smith and A. J. Wendler, holding the position jointly.

You will note that almost every organization had the name A. J. "Tony" Wendler as one of the organizers or a member. This is indicative of the character of Mr. Wendler. He was probably the most civic-minded person in Anchorage at the time.

THE FIRST CHURCHES

On September 14, 1915 ground was broken for the construction of the HOLY FAMILY CATHOLIC CHURCH. In early 1915 a group of about thirty Catholic men working and living in Anchorage petitioned the Bishop of Seattle asking that a priest be sent to Anchorage. The request was relayed to Fr. Crimont, who was the Prefect-Apostolic of Alaska, who in turn requested Fr. John VanderPol, a Jesuit priest then in Valdez, to go to Ship Creek and determine the need. Fr. VanderPol was unable to comply and sent Fr. William Shepherd to check out the reports for a Catholic Church. He spent two weeks in Anchorage and held mass on evenings and Sundays in Robarts Hall for a group of about thirty to forty men and women. Upon Fr. Shepherd's reporting back to Valdez, Fr. VanderPol authorized an old friend, A. J. "Tony" Wendler, to purchase two lots at the July auction. The lots on the southwest corner of 6th and H Street were purchased for $175, and construction was to begin immediately in September.

Fr. VanderPol designed a twenty-four foot by forty-eight foot simple design church, of wood frame construction, with an external veneer of ornamental cement blocks. The target cost was fourteen hundred dollars. This was the first church edifice completed in Anchorage at the time, and Fr. Shepherd held the first masses in November 1915. Several additions were made to expand the church to meet demand. An extension of the front brought the church to the edge of the sidewalk and increased the number of pews from three to twelve. It also added a small choir loft and bell tower. The following season saw the addition of the rectory and the priest quarters. These were directly connected to the church by a hallway to the altar. The Sunday collections that year averaged ten dollars to twelve dollars per week.

In 1919 there were twenty-four Catholic children in Anchorage representing approximately ten families. Even with the small attendance, there was a Sunday School.

Holy Family, 1916

Holy Family Cathedral, 2000

After four years Fr. Shepherd was transferred to Ketchikan and was replaced by Fr. Aloysius Markham. Fr. Markham acquired the two cemetery tracts, which are now owned by the Catholic Archdiocese, for the amount of ten dollars. In 1929 Fr. Markham left Anchorage, and Fr. Eline came down from Fairbanks to fill in until the arrival of Fr. Turnell, who was seventy-two years old when he began his service in Anchorage. Holy Week collections came to sixty-two dollars ninety cents on Easter Sunday, and Fr. Turnell was ecstatic. He was now able to put a bathroom in the rectory.

Illness plagued Fr. Turnell, and Fr. George Woodley filled in for him during the years 1928 to 1930. Fr. Woodley then took leave to go to flying school in the east, and Fr. Godfrey Dane took over as parish priest. Fr. Woodley returned in 1931, but was killed in a hunting accident the same year. Fr. Dane then became the permanent priest. During his time another addition was made to the rear of the church to be used as a parish hall. Ill health also plagued Fr. Dane, and he left Anchorage in 1933.

In 1935 Fr. Dermot O'Flanagan arrived and stayed for eighteen years. He was instrumental in organizing the drive to build the Cathedral as well as the Providence Hospital. Fr. "O," as he was called, was the best remembered priest in the early history of Anchorage. He was trained as a Jesuit, however he did not continue as such, but became a diocesan priest. He was appointed Bishop of Juneau in 1951, and passed away in 1972. He is buried in the Catholic Section of Angelus Memorial Park.

Some of the early members that were instrumental in the development of the church were: Mary Costello, Mrs. Dick Lucason, W. J. Boudreau, L. J. Seeley, Joseph Diamond, Ray C. Larson, George Colwell, Miriam Dickey, Wanda Gelles, Joe Bell, Sharon Baldwin and Frank Hoffman.

Episcopal Church, 1920

The first services held by the ALL SAINTS EPISCOPAL CHURCH were in the log Social Hall on Government Hill and were led by the Reverend Edward W. Moloney of Valdez, on July 10, 1915. The Reverend Moloney represented the Episcopal Mission and was sent to the new townsite of Anchorage to look into the establishment of a church.

On August 15, 1915 the Reverend Moloney and several local churchmen purchased two lots. Bishop Rowe later determined that the best location for the church would be overlooking the Inlet where it would be the first landmark viewed by those arriving in Anchorage. Consequently, the two lots purchased earlier were exchanged for a lot on the northeast corner of 3rd Avenue and K Street. In the spring of 1917 a church building was constructed which served as a church, parish hall and living quarters for the new priest in charge, Rev. E. W. Hughes. A Ladies Guild was organized that same year. Mrs. George Campbell was elected President and Mrs. James Watts was elected secretary.

In May 1920 Bishop Rowe determined that the church should be moved, as its 3rd Avenue and K Street location was not the most desirable. The building was then moved to its new location at the southeast corner of 5th Avenue and F Street. It remained at this location until 1951.

Church at 8th and F Street, 2000

In 1922 the Rev. Burdette Lansdowne replaced Rev. Hughes as the parish priest, and Rev. William A. Thomas replaced him in 1925. In 1927 the parish was without a priest for three years, and Bishop Rowe traveled to Anchorage, holding services on an unscheduled basis. The Rev. W. R. MacPherson served the parish from January 1930 until June 1933 when he was replaced by the Rev. Warren Fenn. Rev. Fenn's ministry lasted for seventeen years. The Rev. Fenn began his parish term with only eleven persons in the congregation. However, his great contributions produced steady growth of the congregation. As a result, for his important role in the growth of the Church, he was memorialized by the parishioners who named the parish hall Fenn Hall. Rev. Fenn was a well-loved member of the Anchorage community for many years. He was a volunteer fireman and organized the Anchorage Tennis Club. His work with the youth in the community was well known. Rev. Fenn passed away in St. Judes Nursing Home in Sandy, Oregon, February 14, 1974.

Father Fenn

THE FIRST PRESBYTERIAN CHURCH OF ANCHORAGE was started in October 1915. Reverend James L. McBride, who was the minister in Cordova, worked his way over to Anchorage as a cook on a small boat in May 1915 to investigate the possibility of building a church in the new town. His recommendation to the Board of Missions in New York allotted him $800 to purchase Lots 11 and 12 of Block 41, which is the northwest corner of 5th Avenue and F Street where Key Bank now stands.

In October 1915 Reverend McBride returned to take up his work of building a church. The first clapboard building was divided into an assembly room measuring twenty-four feet by thirty feet and two small rooms for the missionary living quarters. The cost was eight hundred one dollars, twenty-eight cents. Twenty-four people attended the first Sunday of services. It soon became evident that

Presbyterian Church, 1916

First Presbyterian Church on 10th Street, 2000

larger quarters would be needed, and in March 1916 the old building was sold, and construction of a new building began immediately. The new building was completed in July 1916 at a total cost of five thousand dollars. With the rapid growth of the community, a manse was constructed at the same time at a cost of five thousand five hundred dollars.

The actual organization of the church did not occur until January 14, 1917. The people decided that the name of the church should be the First Presbyterian Church of Anchorage Alaska, and the election of elders followed the dedication.

The Sunday school was organized the second Sunday in December 1915 in the first small building, with seven in attendance. This number soon increased to fifty. Mrs. Charles Palmer was the first regularly appointed Superintendent of the Sunday School, and Mrs. Ralph Moyer was the organist and primary teacher.

The first Christian Endeavor Society was organized in July 1917, with Miss Marian Albertson as President. However, she was replaced by Mr. O. A. Konyor when she left the community. The Christian Endeavor group was popular in the community, putting on plays and skits. Some of the participants were Lois Price, Gladys Lewis, Martha Ervin, Selma Simonson, and John Cook.

The Friendly Aid Society was organized while the Church was still using the old building. Its object was to "aid the church spiritually, socially, and financially." Mrs. Winfield Ervin was outstanding in the work of this organization. In 1917 Mr. Frank O. Berry was President of the Friendly Aid Society, and Mrs. Glen Jones served as Chairman of the Ways and Means Committee.

McBride's church became a community center, and he won the respect of the entire community. The pastors that followed Rev. McBride were C. M. Brown, 1917-1918, H. M. Course, 1918-1919, John L. Hughes, 1918-1920, Wallace Marple, 1920-1925, John E. Youel, 1925-1928 and Emil Winterberger, 1928-1935. All information given here was from church archives and the *Anchorage Daily Times*.

Students of CHRISTIAN SCIENCE began holding informal meetings in private homes in early 1916, and on July 24, 1916, the group purchased Lot 12, Block 14, the northwest corner of 3rd Avenue and H Street. A down payment of one hundred seven dollars seventy-five cents was collected at a meeting held in September 1916 at the home of Mrs. Frances McCain. Three more payments were made before the October meeting at the home of Mrs. Nina Brown, and the property deed was ordered. Plans were already laid for the construction of the church edifice, and in November 1916 the first service was held in the new church. The cost of the building was not to exceed one thousand dollars. While the church was under construction, the services were held in the Empress Theater, at a cost of twenty dollars per meeting. The theater owner, Cap Lathrop, however, often returned this fee, in the form of a contribution.

First Christian Science Church, 1916, Corner of 3rd Avenue and H Street

Formal organization of the group was completed on July 27, 1917, with the election of the following officers: first reader, Nina Brown; second reader, Anna Shonbeck; board president, Mr. Frank Knight; clerk treasurer, Isabel Christenson; librarian, Sigurd Gilbertson; Sunday school superintendent, Isabel Christenson; and directors, Luella Marshall, Frances McCain and Mrs. Schultz.

The charter members of the organization were: Anna Shonbeck, Frances McCain, Frank Knight, Waldemar Engberg, Wylie McDuff, Casey McDannel, Adelle Weber, Jessie Noble, Pauline Anderson and Mrs. William B. Clayton.

Christian Science Church, 2000, 1347 L Street

The group was officially recognized as a Christian Science Society by the Mother Church, the First Church of Christ Scientist in Boston, Massachusetts, in January 1918. The group was small, and many male members were frequently called out of town. This left the task of cutting and sawing wood for the furnace and maintenance of the building to the ladies. All information given here was from local church members.

THOMAS K. ORR was born in Boston, Massachusetts on July 5, 1870. The pioneer spirit entered Thomas's life early, and at the age of fourteen he left home to make his way in New York City. He followed the sea for several years, calling on every major seaport on the eastern seaboard, until 1890 when he moved west to South Dakota. There he opened a restaurant and was very successful until a disastrous fire destroyed everything he had. In 1894 he continued his trek to the west coast and went back to sea again, this time on the Pacific Ocean side.

In 1898 Tom joined the stampeders to Dawson and the Klondike. Being somewhat unsuccessful in that adventure, he departed for Nome in 1900, seeking his fortune in gold. In 1901 he departed Nome for San Francisco where he was employed as a cook in the officers' mess at the Presidio. After his tour at the Presidio, he went into private business as a restauranteur again until 1903 when he sold out to return to Alaska with the Alaska Central Railroad in Seward. After a year he bummed around Alaska working as a miner, cook and roadhouse operator.

In 1910 Tom decided to return to Boston to visit his relatives but found that most of them had passed on, so in 1914 he again returned to Alaska for a short stay. He then moved to Seattle, where he entered the bakery business. There he met and married MARY KISHPAUGH, and together they came to Alaska, landing in Anchorage in June 1916. Tom was then employed with the Alaska Railroad in Anchorage and held high office in the I.O.O.F. and in the Moose Lodge.

Mary Kishpaugh Orr was born in Tecumseh County, Michigan, November 27, 1875. She had been active in Pioneer Lodge circles and the Episcopal Church. Thomas passed away in Anchorage in September 1937, and Mary died in May 1945. They are both buried in the old Odd Fellows Tract, Anchorage Memorial Park.

———

Miss ANNA MCRAE arrived in Anchorage in April 1916 to work for the AEC as a stenographer. She eventually worked her way up into the general accounting office and became the highest paid female employee on the Railroad. She was born in Middle River, Nova Scotia in 1883 and moved to Anchorage from Vancouver, British Columbia in 1916. In later years she was the first bookkeeper to work for the Anchorage Times. Anna and her brother-in-law built the Strathlorne Apartments, formerly located on 5th Avenue adjacent to the Key Bank at 601 5th Avenue. At the time this structure was built, it was one of the City's largest apartment buildings. Anna died in 1941 and is buried in the Pioneer Tract, Anchorage Memorial Park Cemetery.

———

Charley Odermat

One of the first Pioneer restaurant operators to arrive in Anchorage in 1916, CHARLES ODERMAT was born in Austria in 1885 and came to Anchorage to work for Charles Cameron, owner of Camerons Café. Charley, as he was known, was not only a cook, but also a professional baker by trade. In 1930 he bought the Star Café located on 4th Avenue, adjacent to C Street. In 1936 he bought the corner lot on 4th and C from Henry Pope, who in turn had bought it from L. O. Nyberg. It was the first lot sold at the first auction on July 10, 1915.

The Hunter Bar and the Rex Barber Shop occupied the corner lot, with the Star Bakery and Restaurant occupying the second lot. It was Charley's intent to expand his restaurant; however, that never came to pass. In 1939 Charley sold the café to Tony Craviolini and took a long vacation, intending to return and assist Tony in the café business. Charley passed away in June 1961 and is buried in Angelus Memorial Park.

———

Early hotel operators in Anchorage, TOM WINN and his wife operated the Winn Hotel, located on the southeast corner of 4th Avenue and B Street. The structure still stands at this writing, although it was partially destroyed by fire. It is unknown where Tom came from, other than he had been in Cordova for some time working for the Copper River Railroad. When he moved to Anchorage he went to work for the ARR as a steam shovel operator and stayed for over twenty years. He retired to Oregon and passed away in Eugene, Oregon in 1943 at the age of sixty-two.

ROBERT "BOB" GRAHAM was another Alaska Pioneer who arrived in Anchorage in 1916. Bob was born in Ireland at Bellamina, County Derry in 1858. At the age of twenty-five he went to Australia, where he spent the next twelve years. He arrived in Vancouver, British Columbia after leaving Australia and spent two years there prior to joining the gold rush to the Klondike. He joined the stampede to Dawson and the Klondike in 1898, navigating the Chilkoot with the thousands of other stampeders.

Bob left Dawson with less than what he came there with and spent the next seventeen years in Fairbanks, Circle City and Shushana. Prior to moving to Seward he freighted with a dog team between Seward and Anchorage until 1916, when he settled permanently in Anchorage. He operated a transfer and freight business as well as a small hog farm at what is now 13th Avenue and C Street. He passed away in November 1944 and is buried in the Pioneer Tract, Anchorage Memorial Park Cemetery.

HOWARD and ROMA SCOTT were a young couple who also came to Anchorage in 1916. Arriving in Skagway in 1898, they spent a year there before moving on to Dawson. They spent the next seventeen years in Dawson and vicinity prior to coming to Anchorage. Howard was employed by the Alaska Railroad until his death in 1942. Roma remained in Anchorage until she moved to Gilroy, California in 1950, where she passed away in 1961 at the age of ninety-four. Roma was well known in local bowling circles, as she was winning tournaments and trophies well into her eighties. They are both buried in the Elks Tract, Anchorage Memorial Park Cemetery.

DAVE ENGLUND was a Pioneer prospector and miner who was no stranger to the mining business before he came to Alaska. He was known as one of the "Widow Boys" during the early days of the Coeur D'Alene, Idaho gold strike in 1883. The title was derived from the gold claim of that name staked by a man named Pritchard, who was the first to discover the mining district of Coeur D'Alene. Dave Englund and two friends relocated the property, and this began one of the greatest lawsuits in mining history, with the legal battle lasting for seven years. After all of this time the claim was worked out by Englund and partners, and every dime taken out of the claim went for the cost of fighting it in court.

Dave left the Idaho country and joined the stampede to Dawson in 1897, where he made a good stake on Bonanza Creek. After leaving Dawson he went to Nome in 1900 and did well there. He went from Nome to Ophir Creek in the Council area where he was also successful. He next went to Fairbanks, Circle and finally Iditarod, where he continued his success.

The year 1916 found him in Anchorage, and then in Wasilla, where he took up a homestead, doing some mining in the Willow Creek district until his death in 1925. No one really knew where Dave came from, but rumor had it that he was born in Idaho in 1851. He had worked virtually every major gold strike in the Yukon and Alaska, and was reasonably successful in all of them. He is buried in the Pioneer Tract, Anchorage Memorial Park Cemetery.

WILLIAM C. and ANNIE CUNNINGHAM also arrived in Anchorage in 1916. William was first employed by A. A. Shonbeck for a few years, then moved over to the Alaska Road Commission, working in the main office in Anchorage. William was born in Fielding, New Zealand in 1881 and immigrated to the United States about 1910. It is unknown where Annie was born. She was well known throughout the community for her garden and flowers. Her log home at 1016 6th Avenue was a showplace on many garden tours.

William passed away in 1949, and Annie died in 1955. They are both buried in Tract 14, Anchorage Memorial Park Cemetery. They had one child, George W., who settled in Klamath Falls, Oregon after WWII, and, as far as it is known, he had no children.

———

Another 1916 arrival in Anchorage, P. H. STAFFORD had joined the stampede to the Klondike in 1898 and was somewhat successful. He joined the rushes to Nome, Fairbanks and the Shushana, mining and prospecting claims in each area. By the time he came to Anchorage he had lost the mining bug. He started acquiring property in land and houses and was well known as a real estate developer and investor. Stafford was a native of New York State, and, as far as it is known, he was never married and had no known relatives. He was born in 1848 and died in 1933. He is buried in the Catholic Tract of Anchorage Memorial Park Cemetery.

———

A well-known early Anchorage resident, one of the few who did not seek the elusive gold dust, arrived in Anchorage in 1916. His name was ARTHUR LARUE, and he was born in Quebec, Canada in 1879. Shortly after his arrival in Anchorage he took up a homestead in what is now known as the Spenard area. He acquired four horses and went into the wood cutting business with the wood supplied by the trees on his homestead. He also did fur trading with many of the native trappers in the area. Art used his horses for hauling wood and furs, in the winter on a double ender bobsled, and in the summer with a wagon. During slack times in the winter, he plowed the sidewalks and the streets for the City, using homemade "V" plows, one small one pulled by one horse to clear sidewalks and a larger one pulled by two horses to clear the streets. The youngsters in town loved to ride on the plows, and Art allowed them to do so, as the additional weight made a deeper cut and did a better job. Art passed away in January 1951 and is buried in the Catholic Tract, Anchorage Memorial Park Cemetery.

———

ARTHUR BURGESS CUMMINGS was born in White Rock, Michigan in 1883. He came to Alaska in 1916 and entered the employ of the Alaska Railroad. He was appointed manager of the Curry Hotel in 1922 and served in that capacity until 1936, when he, along with Dewey Metzdorf, purchased an interest in the Anchorage Hotel. He retired in 1940 from the hotel business and moved to the States. He returned in 1943 at the request of Colonel Otto F. Ohlson, manager of the ARR, to take over the management of the McKinley Park Hotel when it was used for military R & R.

A. B., as he was known, was a close friend of Sydney Laurence and had an exceptional collection of Laurence paintings, as well as one of ivory and artifacts that he had collected over the years. He was a confirmed bachelor. He passed away October 9, 1944 at the McKinley Park Hotel. He is buried in the Elks Tract, Anchorage Memorial Park Cemetery.

PAUL BERAN was a 1916 arrival in Anchorage via the Alaska Military Cable and Telegraph System. He was born in Vienna, Austria in 1885 and came to Alaska in the military service. He served in the Army continuously from 1909 to 1919. The Alaska Communication System replaced the original Cable and Telegraph System in 1918. Shortly thereafter Paul was discharged and entered the employ of the Alaska Railroad in the accounting department, after receiving his naturalization papers in Valdez in 1919. In October 1943 he was appointed manager of the Curry Hotel for the ARR. While on fishing trip near the Hotel in July 1944, he suddenly collapsed and died of a heart attack. He is buried in the Elks Tract, Anchorage Memorial Park Cemetery.

JOE SPENARD was a well-known name in Anchorage in 1916, as well as in 2000. Born in the province of Ottawa, Canada in 1879, Joe Spenard landed in Valdez in 1910. He first entered business as a stockbroker and listed his business title as vice-president of the Alaska Securities Company. This business evidently did not flourish, and Joe then opened a second hand store. When business was slow, he reportedly loaded up a handcart and pushed it up and down the streets of Valdez, showing off his wares. This pushcart eventually blossomed into a full-scale transfer business in 1913, and he called it the City Express.

In 1916 Joe rushed to the new city on Cook Inlet and immediately opened a branch of the City Express. He eventually closed out his Valdez business and settled in Anchorage. Joe bought an REO truck and started his express business in Anchorage. He painted the truck yellow and sometimes wore a yellow suit to match. He wore a chauffeur cap with a brass shield with the name "Express" on it.

Joe was a happy, fun-loving genial person, and he loved kids. He would often load up his truck with kids and take them for a ride through the streets of town, wearing his yellow suit and plug hat and driving the yellow truck. He wrote poetry and plastered it on his truck and in his newspaper ads, for example: "Of all the cars both big and small, the yellow car just beats them all. Complete satisfaction, nothing less, is given by the City Express."

In the summer of 1916 Joe became interested in Jeter Lake. The *Anchorage Times* reported in July that he had taken up a homestead of one hundred sixty acres, which

Swimming in Lake Spenard

Joe Spenard

included the lake. The lake was presumably named Jeter Lake after Tom Jeter, the early homesteader on Ship Creek and the man who located the coal claims on the famous Anthracite Ridge of the Matanuska Valley.

Joe immediately began clearing land and building a bathhouse and dock for swimmers, as well as a dance pavilion. He, of course, named the lake Spenard after himself, and the place became immediately popular with picnickers and young people, who enjoyed the swimming and dancing. Access was from the railroad crossing to the lakeshore, as there was no road from Chester Creek to the railroad crossing until a corduroy road was built in 1917. He was on the road to success with his recreational development when disaster struck in 1917. Fire destroyed all of his buildings, including the dance pavilion. He lost his investment, as he had no insurance, so he went back to the trucking business. His luck did not change when, shortly after the fire, he broke his leg. The leg was not healing, so he sold his truck and, with his wife Edith, left for California. He intended to return in the spring, but he never did. He settled in Sacramento, California, and operated a hardware store until his death in 1934. (The Spenard story was taken from the *Anchorage Times*, 6/22/1960, *Alaska Sportsman Magazine*, February 1958, article by Bob De Armond, and *Anchorage Daily Times*, July 12, 1916.)

One day in March 1916 a twenty-two-year-old young man arrived in Seward to begin a life of adventure in Alaska. His name was LEON WILLIAM HARTLEY, born in Galesburg, Illinois, August 29, 1893. Like so many others moving into the new town of Anchorage, he set out from Seward on the train as far as Lawing, which was the end of the line. Nellie Neal Lawing ran a roadhouse there and charged two dollars for a spot on the floor to put down your blankets. This was too high of a price to pay for a night's lodging, so L. W., as he was called, made himself a bed of spruce boughs and slept out under the stars, which was a common practice among both men and women travelers in those days. With two friends, L. W. bought a sled and "necked" it from Lawing to Indian, then over the pass and down Ship Creek to the town of Anchorage. He found work with the ARR as a carpenter and muleskinner, and spent the first winter in a "remote" cabin at what is now 3rd Avenue and B Street.

He prospected for coal in the Moose Creek area and found a few small veins, which he dug and hauled to the railhead by horse and bobsled. That same year his high school sweetheart, RUTH MARIAN ENGLISH, arrived from Seattle, and they were married. Ruth was born in Carrol, Iowa and came north for the sole purpose of marrying L. W. They spent their first winter in a small cabin near Moose Creek and his coal diggings. He moved out of the coal business and returned to Anchorage where he was employed by the Brown and Hawkins mercantile company.

In March 1924, along with his partner Neil Wanamaker, L. W. purchased the C. W. Bolte Hardware Store in Anchorage for a reported price of sixty thousand dollars. This was purportedly the largest business deal to that date in Anchorage. The store was later sold to the Anchorage Commercial Company, which later evolved into the Northern Commercial Company. The N.C. Company became Anchorage's first department store, handling clothing, hardware, groceries and sundries as well as being agents for the Caterpillar Tractor Company.

Later the N.C. Company sold off all of its interests with the exception of the Caterpillar division, which still operates to this day. The Nordstrom department stores of Seattle purchased the clothing and general merchandise portion and incorporated it into their operation.

L. W. and family moved to Fairbanks in 1927 where he operated a furniture store. He returned to Anchorage in 1928 and in 1929 operated a salmon cannery and fish trap near Point Possession. A year later he and partner Pete Wolden operated the City Transfer, a trucking business which transported mining equipment to the Willow Creek mining district prior to the road completion between Anchorage and Palmer. When the highway was completed in 1936, they continued their trucking business for a number of years out of Anchorage.

L. W. took a swing at placer mining in the Ophir district until WWII put an end to it. He then moved the family to Kenai, where he owned and operated a trading post from 1941 to 1945. The family then moved back to Palmer, where L. W. purchased the old Jimmy St. Clair Resort on Finger Lake.

During his lifetime in Alaska L. W. was shipwrecked three times while traveling between Alaska and Seattle on the Alaska Steamship vessels *Alameda*, *Victoria* and *Yukon*.

L. W. and Ruth had three children. Lee, the eldest, had three daughters, Clare Hartley, Signe Wellman and Brenda Valley, all of whom live in Palmer. Son James, now deceased, had four children. James, Catherine Schwartz, and Joan all live in Palmer, and Karen Bieleford lives in Kenai. Son Robert had three children. Kirk Hartley and Helen Hulbert live in Palmer, and Roberta Swick lives in Seldovia. L.W. died at the age of ninety-three in the Pioneer Home at Palmer, and Ruth passed away at the age of eighty-eight in the Palmer Pioneer Home. Both are buried in the Butte Cemetery.

JOHN JOSEPH MEYER was born in St. Gallen, Switzerland in 1873. He came through the portals of Ellis Island in 1890 along with thousands of others seeking their fortunes in the United States. He roamed around the east coast of the United States seeking success and worked as a baker apprentice, eventually learning the trade. In 1899 he heard of the great gold rush to the Yukon and departed for Alaska and the Klondike. He never struck gold in Dawson, so he headed for Nome in 1900 to seek his fortune there.

Not finding gold in either place, John decided to open a bakery and mine the miners rather than digging in the ground. He opened his first bakery named the Anvil, after the Anvil Creek mining area, and the other bakery he opened in Nome and called it the North Pole Bakery. His business flourished, as he was a master baker, and his baked goods were in great demand by the townsfolk as well as by the miners out in the creeks.

John Meyer

Katherine with Grandchildren

John met KATHERINE HENDRICKSON in Nome, where she had gone to visit a sister who was married to a miner. She was born in Vaasa, Finland in 1889 and entered the United States via Ellis Island in 1906, the same year she went to Nome. They were married in 1911, and this union bore two children, Evelyn born in 1912 and John born in 1913.

The family decided to leave Nome for the warmer climate of California and settled in San Francisco in 1914 where John again was in the bakery business. In the summer of 1915 the Panama Pacific Exhibition was held in San Francisco celebrating the opening of the Panama Canal. John went into partnership with a young man named Alan Lockheed, who had built a two-seater hydroplane. They sold sightseeing trips over San Francisco, one passenger at a time. Alan was fascinated with flying and eventually became the president of the Lockheed Aircraft Corporation, one of the three largest aircraft manufacturers in the world.

Evelyn Meyer Ruttan

In the summer of 1916 the Meyer family moved to the new town of Anchorage, where John and Katherine started another North Pole Bakery on 4th Avenue, between D and E Streets, and what a bakery it was! It prospered until 1922 when it burned down. However, John did not hesitate to rebuild immediately. The new building remained until it went down in the 1964 earthquake. John Meyer earned the reputation of being probably the finest baker ever to operate in Anchorage. His napoleons, cream puffs and bread were unbeatable, as were his pies and cakes. He had six marble topped tables in the bakery with four chairs at each. Besides his pastries, he had a short menu of ham, cheese, tuna salad, chicken salad, roast beef and peanut butter and jelly sandwiches made with the freshest bread you have ever tasted. The drinks available were coffee, tea, milk, chocolate and water. The place was constantly full, and the lunch crowd from the railroad offices and downtown businessmen were his best customers. Katherine worked side by side with John in the bakery waiting on customers and waiting on tables.

Charles Ruttan

In the late thirties John became a director of the First National Bank of Anchorage, and in 1940 he and Katherine decided to retire to San Francisco. John died in 1952 at the age of seventy-nine, and Katherine passed away in 1978 at the age of eighty-nine. They are both buried in the San Francisco area.

Daughter Evelyn married Charles Ruttan in 1933, and they had two sons, Charles Jr., who lives in Vancouver, British Columbia, and John, who lives in Lantzville, British Columbia. Charles Ruttan and his partners Jack Waterworth and Steve Mills arrived in Anchorage with an airplane to start a flying school. This was the beginning of Alaska Airlines, however that is another story and is taken up in later chapters. Son John, Jr. developed schizophrenia and spent the rest of his days in San Francisco.

OSCAR S. GILL was born in St. Lawrence, Pennsylvania April 3, 1880. As a young man, after his mother's death, he moved to Portsmouth, Iowa to be near his aunt. In September 1902 he worked in Portsmouth as a mail carrier for a few years. During this period he met EMMA DOHRMANN, a local girl who was born in 1883 in Portsmouth. They were married in Council Bluffs, Iowa in 1905. The couple traveled west to Washington, settling in Anacortes where their first son, Victor, was born.

Oscar Gill

In 1907 Oscar, Emma and Victor headed north to Alaska upon hearing of the new town of Seward and opportunities that existed on the new frontier. Oscar landed a job with the Seward Light and Power Company owned by Sam Graef. Their second son William was born in Seward in 1907. Oscar's mechanical abilities kept him steadily employed. He next moved the family to Susitna Station, thirty miles up the Susitna River from its mouth in Cook Inlet. There he operated a sawmill and supplied cut lumber to the town of Susitna Station, McDougal, Talkeetna and Tyonek. Their youngest son Phillip, was born there in 1910. Two years later they moved back to Seward where, in 1912, their fourth child, Louise, was born.

Oscar kept taking on jobs that could possibly lead to better things. He held a mail contract with the Alaska Commercial Company carrying the mail from Seward to Knik and Iditarod during the winter months; he worked as engineer on the boat *Sea Lion*, built and owned by Jack Bartels, operating from Tyonek, to Knik, Sunrise and Hope. The family moved to Knik in about 1913-14, and there Oscar built a two-story home and operated a boat, lightering passengers and materials from ships anchored offshore.

Emma Gill

The tent city on Ship Creek flats was starting to blossom with the advent of the first survey crews entering the scene and the promise of the railroad to be built. The year 1915 saw several thousand squatters on Ship Creek flats. The same year the new townsite was surveyed and Tent City had to move up the hill on the south side of Ship Creek. In 1916 Oscar purchased a lot on 9th Avenue between I and K Streets and proceeded to move his Knik home to Anchorage via barge. He spent the years from 1917 to 1923 working as engineer on boats of the "mosquito" fleet and as a machinist with the AEC constructing the railroad.

Victor, William, Louise and
Phillip Gill

In 1923 Oscar bought Lot 7 in Block 29 and opened a garage and shop. He was now firmly established in the new city of Anchorage, and his interest in civic affairs brought him into the political arena. He served three years on the school board beginning in 1925; he was elected to the City Council for three terms, from 1929 to 1931; he was elected Mayor in 1932 and then again in 1934 and 1935. During his tenure on the Council, he was the driving force behind the purchase of the Light and Power Company, owned by the ARR, which proved to be a boon to the City. During his last term as Mayor he favored the construction of the new City Hall and was instrumental in securing the funds for it. His sense of civic duty led him to run for the Territorial Legislature, and he served two terms in the house, one term as speaker. Not only did Oscar serve the public in many ways, but he also was an ardent member of the Elks Lodge and served as Exalted Ruler in 1933.

During all of this, his wife Emma was busily raising the family and tending her yard and garden. The union of Oscar and Emma produced four children, and they in turn produced twelve grandchildren. Son Victor married Sidonia Martens of Persia, Iowa, and this union produced four children, Larry, Russell, Gregory and Christine, who all live in Anchorage. William married Evaline George, and they had two children, Mary and Robert, who live in Southern California. Phillip married Vernita Herron, and they had two children, Gerard and Jenny, who live in California. Louise married John Moore, a local bush pilot, and they had four children, Joan, Roy, Max and Suzanne, all living in Washington.

Oscar passed away at the age of sixty-seven from a heart attack while addressing the Elks lodge on November 18, 1947. Emma passed away on March 30, 1974. They are both buried in the Elks Tract, Anchorage Memorial Park.

Charles Cameron, Sr.

CHARLES CAMERON was born in Gray County, Province of Ontario, Canada, on December 29, 1871. When he was a young child his parents moved across the border to Bordeaux, North Dakota. He spent his youth traveling and working in mining towns of Montana, Idaho and Nevada. He was interested in learning the chef's trade and was getting his experience in the mining camps. He was working as a cook in Tonopah, Nevada in 1908 when he heard of the gold strikes in the Valdez district. He forthwith went to Valdez; however, he did not remain there long and returned to his native Canada. In 1911 he met ELLEN "NELL" BOWLES, who was born in Berkshire, England in 1884. They were married in Regina, Saskatchewan in 1912.

In 1916, again hearing the call of the north, Charles and Nell departed for the new town of Anchorage, which was being rapidly built into a thriving community. Shortly after his arrival in Anchorage, he opened Camerons Café, which eventually became the Anchorage Grill. In 1919 a son Charles was born, and in the same year they took a trip south. They stopped over in Seward waiting for the steamer and were impressed with the community. Upon their return they sold the restaurant in Anchorage and moved to Seward, where he opened another Camerons Café in 1922, which was formerly the Seward Grill. They then sold their café in Seward and departed for California. They returned in 1924, and Charles operated the former Camerons café in Anchorage until 1929. The family then left for Merced, California but returned again in 1934 to Seward, where Charles operated the Camerons Café until his death.

Thelma and Charles
Cameron, Jr.

Ellen Cameron

Charles died in 1938 in Seward, and after his death Nell moved to Anchorage where she operated a rooming house called the Central Hotel (formerly owned by Frank Johanson) on the corner of 5th Avenue and I Street. In 1953 she returned to Seward and was spending the winter on Kenai Lake with her friend Esther Deegan. While driving between Moose Pass and the lake, Nell was killed when their automobile overturned.

Central Hotel

Charles, Jr. had one child, Lawrence, by his first marriage.
Charles, Jr. passed away in Escondido, California in 1997, and his son Larry passed away in the same year. Charles' widow, the former Thelma Huff, passed away in 2000 in Escondido, California. Charles, Sr. and Nell are buried in the Seward Cemetery. Charles, Jr., Thelma and son Larry are buried in Escondido, California.

———

FREDERICK BROADWELL arrived in Seward on June 10, 1916. He proceeded to Anchorage in July 1916 and made his home in Seward and Anchorage for over forty years. He was a painter by trade, however his first love was chasing the elusive gold dust. Prior to his coming to Anchorage, he prospected in Nevada from 1903 to 1915. When he arrived in Alaska, his first prospect was in the Cache Creek-Talkeetna area, and later he prospected on the Kenai Peninsula. He was born in Gainesville, Texas in 1878 and died in Anchorage in 1967. He is buried in the Elks Tract, Anchorage Memorial Park Cemetery.

JOHN GARSON ODEN was born in Mandal, Norway in 1888. He arrived on the Anchorage scene in 1916 and began working for Cap Lathrop. John later practiced his trade as a skilled carpenter and masonry contractor. He was well-known for his hobby as a musician and violin-maker, however his skill as a cement mason kept him busy making tombstones and monuments. He maintained an inventory of figures and vases in his back yard and cast a good share of the tombstones and markers in the Anchorage Memorial Park Cemetery, many of which are still intact. John passed away in Seattle, Washington in 1958 and is buried there.

JACK CHOVIN arrived in Anchorage in 1917 and opened an electrical shop on 4th Avenue between E and F Streets. This was one of the first electrical stores in Anchorage, and Jack sold appliances as well as doing service work. He served one term on the City Council and was elected Exalted Ruler of the Elks Lodge for one term. Due to ill health of family members, Jack sold his business to Bob Watson in 1932 and moved to Seattle, Washington. He passed away in 1942 in Seattle and is buried there.

DANIEL S. DAXON was born in Moline, Illinois in 1887. He came to Anchorage in 1916 and was employed with the AEC in the construction of the Railroad. Prior to his coming to Anchorage, he was employed as a locomotive engineer with the Great Northern Railroad. In 1917 he was put on as an engineer on the ARR and served for 32 years. He retired to Moline, Illinois in 1946 and passed away there on November 27, 1979.

HARRY CRIBB spent half of his life in the north. Born in Cowes, Isle of Wight, England, he came to the United States as a young man and was naturalized an American citizen in Astoria, Oregon in 1894. He was the son of a British naval officer and followed the sea for many years. He traveled to ports all over the world, and, while following the sea, he learned his trade as a ship's carpenter.

In 1897 Harry went to the Klondike and was one of the first to mush over the Chilkoot Pass. He established himself in Dawson as a carpenter and builder. Many of the buildings he built are still standing in that city. Successful in his new enterprise as a builder, he returned to Astoria, Oregon and married the girl he had met there in 1894. The newlyweds departed for Alaska in 1898, and for the second time Harry crossed the Chilkoot. After spending three years in Dawson, Harry and Frances moved to Fairbanks where they spent the next fifteen years. Harry had established a reputation as a master builder in Fairbanks and was well respected in the community.

In 1916 they moved down to Anchorage, where Harry again established himself as a general contractor going under the name of Cribb Construction Company. He built many of the commercial buildings in Anchorage and a number of private homes and apartments. His charity work, known only to his closest friends, included all new pews and a new floor for the All Saints Church.

In 1935 Frances Cribb passed away after a long illness. She had been associated with the Anchorage Womans Club for over twenty years and was an outstanding officer and worker. She was past President and Director of the Alaska Federation of Womens Clubs and, being an able and talented writer, she contributed many magazine articles on behalf of the club.

Harry Cribb passed away February 25, l938 and is buried next to his wife in the Pioneer Tract of Anchorage Memorial Park. The Cribbs left a legacy in Anchorage for charitable giving and philanthropy. Harry left five thousand dollars to the Pioneer Igloo and the remainder of his estate to his sister until her death, with the remaining assets going to the Pioneers after her death. He also set up provisions for some young man or men to take over the lumber and contracting business on easy terms, and for his shop, tools, real property, etc., to be sold to this young man or men for the amount of six thousand dollars. He further willed that one thousand dollars be invested in bonds for the purpose of generating income to be used to maintain the gravesites of Frances and Harry.

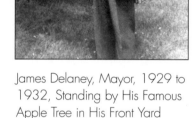

———

JAMES J. DELANEY came to Anchorage in 1916 from his native Ireland. After spending two years in Holyoke, Massachusetts, Delaney came directly to Anchorage and was immediately employed by the Alaska Engineering Commission. After the Railroad was constructed, he continued on with the ARR and retired in 1957 from his position as real estate and contract officer.

James Delaney, Mayor, 1929 to 1932, Standing by His Famous Apple Tree in His Front Yard

In 1929 Delaney was elected as Anchorage's seventh Mayor and served the community well during this trying year. He was so well thought of that he was again elected Mayor in 1930 and 1931. Even though he preferred not to run, he did so because there was no one else offering to do the job, and he was persuaded by his constituents to run again. Besides his civic duties, J. J. was elected Exalted Ruler of the Elks Lodge for one term.

J. J. left his legacy when the Delaney Park Strip was named in his honor. He was known for his calm demeanor and steady influence in bringing about cooperation between the City, the Alaska Railroad and the Chamber of Commerce, all for the benefit of the city of Anchorage.

J. J. and his wife Nancy had three children, two daughters and one son. Son James, Jr. lives in Anchorage, one daughter lives in Ketchikan, and one lives in Utah. J. J. and Nancy are buried in the Catholic Tract, Anchorage Memorial Park Cemetery. J. J. was born in 1896 and died in 1970. Nancy was born in 1896 and died in 1986.

James Delaney

Second Mayor,
Michael Joseph
Conroy, 1923-1924

The second Mayor of Anchorage was MICHAEL JOSEPH CONROY, who was born in the village of Ballyconneeley, four miles west of Clifden, County Galway, Ireland, on September 20, 1874. In 1880 his family immigrated to the United States and settled in Manchester, New Hampshire. Joe was educated in New Hampshire schools and was employed by the Boston and Maine Railroad until 1904 when he visited San Francisco and Los Angeles. In 1905 he went to Seward with John Ballaine to help in the development of the Alaska Central Railroad. From Seward he moved to Cordova in 1908, then back to Seward and then to Knik in 1909. He followed the mining game from the time he arrived in Alaska and had interests in the Willow Creek Mining District.

In 1913 Joe was admitted as a lawyer to the Alaska Bar at Valdez. He served as United States Commissioner in the Seward-Kenai precinct from 1913 to 1916. In June 1916 he moved to Anchorage and was first hired as clerk-treasurer and tax assessor for the City, and in 1918 he was appointed chairman of Draft Board #10.

Joe was elected Mayor of Anchorage in 1923 and served two years before resigning in 1924. Anchorage was suffering hard times. The ARR was operating, however its future was unsure; the United States Army establishment was gone; and the Navy had ceased operations in the Chickaloon coalfields. In order to conserve and save the town the cost of maintaining an office, Joe resigned as Mayor. His personal sacrifices, dedication, conservatism, proven methods of economy, and position against wasteful expenditures served the community well.

While in Seward in 1915, Joe married NELLIE RUSHTON MUSCOTT. She was born in Simpson, Kansas in 1876. She was a registered nurse by profession and received her education at a Denver hospital. In 1912 she joined the Bureau of Indian Affairs and taught school and nursed in Kake, Alaska for two years. In the summer of 1914 she went to Seward and worked for Dr. J. H. Romig, and there she met Michael Joseph Conroy.

Nellie died on September 5, 1946, and Joe passed on in November 1958. They are both buried in Anchorage Memorial Park Cemetery.

One of Anchorage's early philanthropists and a two term Mayor in 1947 and 1948, ZACHARY JOSHUA LOUSSAC was a Russian Jew, born in Moscow, Russia on July 13, 1883. He entered Germany in 1899, escaping Russia, where he was active in student socialist activities, which activity was frowned upon in Czarist Russia. Prior to escaping from Russia he had obtained a B.S. degree from the University of Moscow in 1899.

Zack had an uncle in the United States who sent him the fare for a ticket to New York. He obtained work in a drug store there. However, reading about the gold strike in the Klondike, he decided to venture to Alaska. He ran out of money by the time he got to Montana but was fortunate to obtain work in a local drugstore and after six months raised enough money to return to New York.

Zack entered Columbia School of Pharmacy and graduated in 1904 with a B.S. in pharmacy. He also studied law for one year at NYU. After graduation and a few years of work, he again headed for Alaska in search of gold. He stopped off in Seattle, Washington where he practiced pharmacy until 1907, when he heard of a position in Haines and jumped at the chance finally to get to Alaska. He stayed in Haines only nine months and then returned to Seattle.

In 1909-10 Zack heard of the gold strike in Iditarod and immediately departed for the gold fields. With a partner he opened a drug store, and they were doing well when a fire destroyed the store. They rebuilt the store with borrowed capital; however, about that time the boom period had ended for Iditarod, and the business failed after two-and-one-half years.

Returning south, Zack went to San Francisco, where he again obtained work as a pharmacist. In 1913 he heard that Juneau needed a pharmacist, and Zack was on his way. He spent three years in Juneau and operated two successful drug stores. Then in 1916 the boomtown of Anchorage beckoned him. He sold his interests in Juneau and moved to Anchorage where he remained for the next twenty seven years

Zack opened his first Anchorage store on 4th Avenue between D and E Streets. This venture was very successful. He operated a second store in the new Anchorage Hotel Annex, which was built on the corner of 4th Avenue and E Street in 1936 and still stands there today. He sold this store to Bill Abel and Bill Dahms, two pharmacists who were former employees.

In 1943 he decided to retire and devote his time to civic activities. He served with the Rotary Club, the Chamber of Commerce, and chaired the war bond drives. In 1947 he was elected Mayor and served until 1953. It has been said that he used his power as Mayor to knock out gambling in the city. This was ironic to the oldtimers who knew him as he, Harold Koslosky, Chris Poulson and George Kennedy were reputedly the best poker players in town.

In 1946 Zack used half of his wealth to establish the Loussac Foundation, which was to be used for social, scientific and cultural activities in Anchorage. Income from the foundation built the original Loussac Library, which was located at 5th Avenue and F Street, and aided the Alaska Methodist University, Sheldon Jackson College in Sitka and the Kings Lake Boys' Camp. The Loussac Sogn building and Loussac Apartments were a large part of the foundation income.

Z. J. Loussac

In 1948 Zack married for the first time. Ada was operating the Colonial Shop, a woman's ready-to-wear store in the Loussac building, and she and Zack had become old friends. Zack died in Seattle in 1965, and Ada died in Seattle in 1980. They are both buried in the Elks Tract at Angelus Memorial Park. (For the most part, this history of Loussac was taken from the *Anchorage Times* Obituary and Library archives.)

WHO WAS RUSSIAN JACK?
(This article was written in part by Bruce Merrill and is printed with his permission.)

It is the story of a famous or infamous man, homesteader, moonshiner and murderer. He was a convicted felon who had a street named after him, a major city park, an animal hospital, a branch bank, an apartment complex, a post office and an elementary school. How many Alaskans have left a legacy like this?

JACOB MARUNENKO was born in the Ukrainian village of Parevka in 1883. He was married at the age of twenty-four; he had a daughter in 1909 and a son born in 1912. He left his homeland and his family and made his way to Canada and finally to the west coast. According to the files of the National Archives, he traveled via Canadian Pacific Railway into the United States in May of 1915, entering at the border town of Blaine, Washington.

Jack next showed up in Anchorage in 1916 under the name of Jack Marchin, which name he adopted and went by for the rest of his life. He was listed as the proprietor of the original Montana Pool Room, located at 4th Avenue and E Street in 1920. He eventually either disposed of or lost the Pool Room, as in the early thirties he was cutting and selling wood, as well as operating a still at his cabin east of town. The location of that cabin is what is now Russian Jack Springs Park.

In 1938 Jack attended a drinking party and became involved with a cab driver name Milton Hamilton. The fight ended in Jack's shooting Hamilton in the head, killing him instantly. Jack claimed self-defense as he was beaten severely by Hamilton. In the ensuing trial, he was convicted of manslaughter and received two and one half years at McNeil Island in the State of Washington.

He was either paroled or served his time, as in the early forties he returned to Anchorage. If he was employed, it is unknown what his employment was. As far as can be determined, he lived on a small income, and in about 1962 he moved to California in the company of an unknown female. He lived out his days in the small town of Arvin, California, located in Tehachapi Pass east of Bakersfield. He died there in 1971, at the age of eighty-eight, and lies in an unmarked grave. What happened to the mysterious woman, no one knows.

Parts of this writing were taken from the *Anchorage Times*, Bruce Merrell article, local residents and personal knowledge.

––––––

One of the first hardware merchants in Anchorage in 1916, CARL W. BOLTE founded and operated Bolte Hardware from 1916 until he sold his business to L. W. Hartley and Neil Wanamaker in 1924 because of his ill health. His store was located on 4th Avenue between C and D Streets. He maintained an inventory of hundreds of items, and his motto was, "The store that has what you want when you want it." Hartley and Wanamaker eventually sold out to the Anchorage Commercial Company, which business eventually evolved into the Northern Commercial Company.

As far as can be determined, Carl never married. He passed away in Anchorage at the age of fifty-nine in the year 1929. He was presumably born in Chicago in 1879. His only known relative was a niece who formerly lived in Anchorage. She had his remains shipped to Manteca, California, and he is presumably buried there.

Another Pioneer of the north, J. J. "BIG JIM" SHERLOCK arrived on the Anchorage scene in 1916 in time to take on several clearing and grading contracts with the AEC in constructing the Railroad. He successfully held over fifteen contracts from early 1916 through 1919. He operated practically the length of the Railroad, from Anchorage both north as far as Curry and south as far as Portage.

Jim Sherlock

Jim first entered Alaska in the gold rush to the Klondike in 1898. He prospected and mined on Hunker Creek, a tributary of the Klondike River. There he met John Bagoy and Bill Taylor, both former prospectors. He proceeded to Fairbanks in 1906 and down to Iditarod in 1910. His final move was to Anchorage from Iditarod, and, like so many others, it turned out to be his final resting place. "Big Jim" was six feet five inches tall and weighed two hundred eighty-five pounds, a bear of a man. It was said he ran his crew with an iron hand and left no doubt as to who was boss. Jim died in Anchorage in August 1933 and is buried in the Pioneer Tract, Anchorage Memorial Park Cemetery.

JOHN TODD CUNNINGHAM was born in Grand Island, Nebraska in 1888. He moved to Anchorage in 1916 to take up the position of chief clerk of the Alaska Railroad. Upon arriving in Seward, he rode the train until it ran out of track and hiked the remaining eighty-five miles behind a freight sled over Indian Pass.

In 1918 he was made trainmaster and served in that position until 1923 when he was promoted to superintendent of

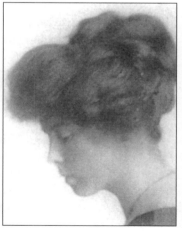

J. T. Cunningham, Jr.   Dorothy Dublirer   Eva Cunningham   John Todd Cunningham

partransportation. In 1948 he was made assistant general manager and retired the following year to California. Upon his retiring from the ARR, J. T. was awarded the Distinguished Service Award by the United States Department of the Interior.

First Home on Government Hill

Last Home on Second Avenue

EVA LOCKHART came to Valdez in 1901 with her mother B. Belle Lockhart and moved to Anchorage in 1916. She met J. T. that same year, and they were married in 1917. J. T. and Eva had two children, John Todd, Jr. and Dorothy Cunningham Dublirer. Son John Todd had no children. Daughter Dorothy had three children, all currently living in California. Jeffrey Gibley lives in Sacramento, Carol Gibley Addy lives in Carmichael, and Susan Hirzy lives in Davis.

Harry and Katsuyo Kimura

YUSUKE "HARRY" KIMURA was born in Nagasaki, Japan in 1880. He left home at the age of thirteen and traveled around Japan and China learning the cooking trade. He was hired on as a cook on the U.S.S. Arizona and prepared meals for President Teddy Roosevelt who was on board. Roosevelt was so impressed with Harry's cooking that he gave him a letter stating he could stay in the United States as long as he wished. He entered the United States in San Francisco just before the fire of 1906, and for the next ten years he followed the mining camps and logging camps on the west coast, always as a cook.

At age thirty-five Harry was working in Seattle and decided it was time to take a bride. He sent home requesting the hand of a pretty girl he remembered in his hometown. He met his bride-to-be at the boat in Seattle; however, it was not the girl he requested. It was her sister. The other girl was already married, so the parents sent the sister instead. **KATSUYO YAMASAKI** and Harry were married in 1913.

Chop Suey House

In 1916 with two sons, Frank and George, Harry and Katsuyo departed for the new town of Anchorage, Alaska. The couple took over a small hand laundry from a relative and named it the H and K Hand Laundry. It was located adjacent to the northeast corner of 5th Avenue and C Street. They also started a small restaurant called the Chop Suey House next door on the same corner. Harry operated the Chop Suey House, and Katsuyo ran the laundry.

H and K Laundry

Delivery Crew for Snow White Laundry

During WWI business was slow, and Harry and family moved back to Seattle seeking a better living. The depression years in Seattle were worse than in Anchorage, and they had to send their children, Frank, George, Louise and William, back to Japan to live with their relatives. It was five years later before all of the family was reunited in Anchorage. They went back into business with the H and K Laundry and the Chop Suey House in the same location. The family had increased with the youngest son Sam born in 1928. As the family grew, each member had his job to do in the laundry and in the restaurant.

WWII and Pearl Harbor changed their lives, when they were interred in a camp in Idaho. The family nearly lost everything they had during the war period. When they returned to Anchorage, Harry raised enough money to pay back taxes and get a new start.

Nikko Gardens

The laundry expanded into a full-fledged laundry and cleaners called the Snow White Laundry and Cleaners. It was the largest one in Anchorage and was highly successful. George and Frank operated the laundry until Frank's death in 1951. Son Bill and "Grandma" Kimura opened the Golden Pheasant Café on D Street between 4th and 5th Avenues. It was famous for Grandma Kimura's tempura prawns. Son Sam opened a photography studio but decided to go to photography school in New York and did not return for twenty years. George opened the Nikko Garden restaurant on Spenard Road where McDonalds now stands. It was the finest Oriental restaurant in town until it burned down in 1979. The Golden Pheasant closed, and Bill went to work in the laundry, as did daughter Louise.

Snow White, 1951

The laundry was sold, and the family went their individual ways. Bill was a fine artist, and his paintings are still in demand today. Sam returned to Anchorage and became an instructor, teaching photography at the University of Alaska, and his wife Joan taught art. George retired to Hawaii, and Louise remained a housewife in Anchorage. Katsuyo became an unpaid good will ambassador to Oriental visitors. Four years prior to her death she was awarded the Zuiho Sho, the sixth order of Sacred Treasure, by the Emperor of Japan for her outstanding service fostering good relations between the nations.

Harry died in 1957, and Katsuyo passed away in 1975 while visiting Hawaii. They are both buried in Anchorage Memorial Park Cemetery along with sons Frank, George, Bill and Sam.

Frank Kimura

Sam and Bill Kimura,
Louise Wood and
George Kimura

Son Frank and spouse Yuki had three children. Jeanne Kimura Mercer, Linda, and David reside in Seattle, Washington. Son George and spouse Kazue had two sons and one daughter. Their son Ronald died. Kathy Tuttle and Roger live in Anchorage. Daughter Louise Sawada Wood and spouse George had two sons. Steve Sawada lives in Salt Lake City, Utah, and Michael Sawada lives in Anchorage. Son William Kimura and spouse Minnie had four children. Christofer passed away in 1984, and Kerry, John, and Patricia Ann Tyson live in Anchorage. Son Sam Kimura and spouse Joan had two children. Carey resides in Anchorage, and Steven resides in Gig Harbor, Washington.

Frank and Lillie Berry

1918 Tent Home

1920 Home

FRANK O. BERRY was born in 1888 in Stillwater, Minnesota. He studied electrical engineering at Washington State University in Pullman, Washington. LILLIE BURBANK was born in St. John, Washington. She and Frank were married in Spokane, Washington in 1908. In 1916 Frank came to Anchorage and was employed as an electrician with the Alaska Engineering Commission. He installed the first generator and switchboard for the power plant and also installed the first telephone exchange in Anchorage. In 1917 Lillie arrived in Anchorage with her parents to join Frank. He stayed with the AEC and the ARR for five years. When the city of Anchorage took over the electrical and telephone system from the AEC, Frank was hired on as the city electrician.

Frank and Lillie lived in a tent for a year while they were building their first home on 8th Avenue and E Street in 1918. They left Alaska in 1928 and returned in 1936, when Frank again worked for the city of Anchorage until 1942. During that year he went to work for the Civil Aeronautics Administration until his retirement in 1956. Lillie meanwhile kept herself busy being involved in the Anchorage Womans Club and the Presbyterian Church, working at the Railroad Hospital, and doing part time dressmaking and tailoring for local boutiques.

Frank passed away in 1962, and Lillie died in 1973. They are both buried in the Masonic Tract, Anchorage Memorial Park Cemetery. They had one son, Frank E. Berry, and he and his spouse Betty Heverling Berry had four children. Frankie Michele Klingbeil and Dennis L. live in Anchorage; Janis K. Chapman lives in San Bruno, California; and David D. lives in Philadelphia, Pennsylvania.

Walter Burbank, Lillie's father, died in 1919 at the age of eighty-three. Lillie's mother, Catherine Elizabeth, then married JOHN E. O'NEILL in 1921. John was a steam shovel operator for the ARR and came to Anchorage in 1918. He was employed by the AEC

1932 Home

until 1928, when he and Catherine moved south only to return again in 1936. John passed away in 1944, and Catherine died in 1959 at the age of ninety-three. Catherine was born in Stockton, California, and John was born in 1873 in Mineola, New York. John O'Neill, Henry Burbank and Catherine Burbank O'Neill are all buried in the Masonic Tract of Anchorage Memorial Park Cemetery.

Frank E. Berry

People were still coming to Anchorage in droves in 1917. Almost all were being employed by the AEC in Anchorage or somewhere along the line between Anchorage and Seward and Fairbanks. Many were in private business, and new businesses opened almost daily. The service industry was booming, with restaurants, rooming houses, clothing stores, grocers, etc. on almost every corner.

JOHN WIRUM was one of these 1916-1917 arrivals. His first job was with the AEC building snow sheds on the rail line between Anchorage and Seward. John was born in Norway in 1887, and during his teen years he attended carpentry school in Norway and was considered a master carpenter. He first came to the United States via Canada and spent his early years working the logging camps and sawmill operations in Washington and British Columbia as well as lumber yards and boat yards on the waterways of the Seattle area.

Sigrid and John Wirum

After serving in the Army during WWI, John again worked for the AEC, this time, however, as a contractor building new homes on Government Hill and on 2nd Avenue downtown. He and a partner built one-story bungalows for seven hundred fifty dollars labor, and one-and-one-half-story houses for twelve hundred dollars labor, which prices included the excavation and basements. Many of these homes still exist on Government Hill and on 2nd and 3rd Avenues downtown.

John worked on several commercial buildings including the Masonic Temple on 4th Avenue and Teelands General Store in Wasilla. He was well known for his fine finish carpentry and

Harold and Marylou Wirum

John Wirum with Grandkids

First Home, 1920s

Second Home, 1932

Third Home, 1937

Wirum Friends and Neighbors

cabinetwork and also held an excellent reputation as a house builder. He eventually went to work for the Alaska Railroad full time as a cabinetmaker and millwright and retired from the ARR in 1949 as shop foreman.

SIGRID MARIE CARLSON was born in Sweden in 1888 and came to America at the age of eighteen in 1906. The steamship landed in Halifax, Canada, and Sigrid traveled directly by rail to Seattle, Washington. During her early years she worked as a cook for private families in Seattle and Spokane, Washington and in San Francisco and Santa Monica, California.

Sigrid came to Anchorage to work as a cook for the Railroad Hospital. She met John Wirum, and they were married in Seward in 1925. They made their home in Anchorage until Sigrid passed away in 1957. John began spending winters in Long Beach, California, after Sigrid died. He passed away in Seattle in 1971.

John and Sigrid had one child, Harold, who more or less followed his father's footsteps as a builder. Harold however became an architect, designing the homes and buildings rather than constructing them. In 1962 Harold and Mary Lou Payne were married, and they raised three children. Andrea lives in Orinda, California, and Jay and John both reside in Anchorage.

CHARLES L. CADWALLADER arrived in Anchorage in 1917 from Indiana, seeking his fortune like so many others. He engaged in various businesses, but his main business was owning a roadhouse in Wasilla. He moved to the Wasilla area in 1929 and remained there until his death in 1972. He was born in Taft, Indiana in 1885. His spouse, ALEXA, was born in Wayzata, Minnesota, in 1887 and came to the Anchorage area in 1919.

Charles' first adventure in Alaska was "mushing" the Iditarod trail on foot from Knik to Iditarod. With two experienced travelers, Dave Brown and Tom Riswald, Charles made it to Iditarod from Knik in sixteen days. He stayed in Iditarod for two years, employed by the Riley Investment Company, which was operating a dredge on Flat Creek and on Discovery. He returned to Anchorage in January 1919 over the same Iditarod trails. This time his trip took twenty-two days.

Charles and Alexa had two daughters, Jane Cadwallader Browne and Mary Cadwallader Bergman. The children of Jane and Neil Browne live in the Wasilla area; the children of Mary and Ray Bergman live in the Wasilla-Anchorage area.

Another Klondike stampeder who arrived in Anchorage in 1917, SAM TANSY first landed in Skagway in 1898 and went over the Chilkoot to Dawson. He spent five years working claims and prospecting various creeks without much success. He moved on to Fairbanks in 1903 and spent the next fourteen years there working the mines. He was engaged in several small businesses as well. He moved down to Nenana in 1915 and worked for the AEC in that division prior to coming to Anchorage in 1917. Sam was born in Worthington, Indiana, in 1870 and died in Cordova in 1941. He is buried in the Elks Tract in Anchorage Memorial Park.

PINKNEY MONROE MCMAHILL was born December 16, 1847 in Galesburg, Illinois. He ran away from home at the age of fourteen and enlisted in the Union Army of the Republic during the Civil War. He tried enlisting in his home state; however, he was refused because of his age. He then traveled to Kansas where he became acquainted with a Captain Anthony. The Captain was impressed with the courage of the lad and allowed him to enlist in his company. He took part in the Western Army, which operated as guerillas most of the time. He was seriously wounded and almost lost a leg; fortunately, he recovered.

Pinkney became acquainted with Susan B. Anthony, who was the founder of the National Womens Suffrage Association and was also the sister of his Captain in the Northern Army. He attended a speech by her while traveling on a Mississippi River boat and was taken with the fact that she was a dynamic speaker and the first woman he had ever heard speak publicly.

McMahill went to California in 1872 and mined on the Mother Lode for the next thirty-one years. In 1903 he stampeded to Nome and a year later returned to California and then to Washington. He married in 1903; however, nothing is known of his wife. He returned to Alaska in 1913 and took part in the rush to Nelchina. With no luck there he moved to Knik in 1914 and then back to Washington. He and his family came to Anchorage in 1917 and went into the hotel business. They bought the Inlet Hotel, which was formerly the Crist House, and operated it until 1920. Pinkney then bought the McMahill Apartments on the corner of 5th Avenue and G Street and operated them until his death in 1936.

The McMahills had two children, a son Edward and a daughter Mildred. Mildred died in 1924 and was buried with her father in the Legion Tract in Anchorage Memorial Park Cemetery. It is unknown where Edward and Mrs. McMahill moved after Pinkney passed away. McMahill was one of the few members of the Grand Army of the Republic who lived in Anchorage and prior to his death was made an honorary member of the Pioneers of Alaska, Igloo #15.

ED BERUTTO arrived in Anchorage in 1917 after spending several years in the United States Army. He was born in Triono, Italy, in 1885 and was trained as a musician in his youth. He gave instruction on trombone, piccolo, trumpet and accordion. He was adept at playing all four of these instruments. In 1936 Ed was appointed bandmaster for the city of Anchorage at a stipend of fifty dollars per month. LUCY BERUTTO arrived in Anchorage in 1915, after spending two years in Juneau. She was a native of California and was born there in 1885. Both Ed and Lucy are buried in Anchorage Memorial Park in the Catholic Tract.

HENRY EASTERLY, another stampeder of the gold rush days, arrived in Anchorage in 1917. He was born in Carbondale, Illinois, in 1864. He first landed in Alaska in Juneau in 1896 and in the following year joined the rush to the Klondike. He floated the Yukon on a raft and, rather than going to Dawson, he and one of his partners joined the rush to the Forty-Mile. After two years he left the Forty-Mile country and returned to Juneau for a short stay. He left Juneau for Washington, then Idaho and finally Oregon. He returned to Alaska in 1915, going directly to Nenana, and worked for the AEC. In 1917 he moved down to Anchorage and remained here until his retirement in 1934, when he moved to Seattle, Washington.

Henry homesteaded one hundred and thirty acres on Spenard road, beginning at Romig Hill. He farmed on his homestead, called the "Moosehorn Ranch," for almost seventeen years. A well-known and respected figure on the Anchorage scene for many years, Henry passed away in Seattle on December 4, 1935 and is buried in the Seattle area.

One of Anchorage's best-known businessmen, DENNIS HEWITT came here in 1917. Denny was born in Kingston, Wisconsin in 1890. He came to Anchorage to work as a machinist for the AEC and the Alaska Railroad. He was employed with the Railroad until 1925 when he and Bob Bragaw opened Hewitts Photo Shop on the northeast corner of 4th Avenue and E Street. He bought out Bob after a year and operated as Hewitts Corner for many more years. It was a meeting place for townspeople, railroaders, and businessmen. He had a small lunch counter, a full soda fountain, a cigar and cigarette counter and a candy counter. He sold school supplies, notions, newspapers and photographic materials and equipment. He maintained a portrait studio in his balcony and displayed dozens of Sydney Laurence paintings as well.

Denny was an ardent duck hunter. He never missed an opening day on the flats, with Nick Gaikema and the *Sea Lion* and six other local hunters. His golden retriever was exceptionally trained and spent his off-time in the store welcoming customers.

Civic minded, Denny gave much of his time to public service. He served as Exalted Ruler of the Elks in 1927. He also served on the City Council for three years, from 1936 through 1938.

Denny invested in real estate and other businesses in Anchorage. He had great faith in the growth of the city. He owned several store buildings on 4th Avenue and was also an investor in Alaska Sales and Service along with Max Kirkpatrick and Jack Clawson. The group bought out Mrs. Nanelee Wells in 1944. She was the widow of Cecil Wells and owner of the Wells Garage, the early day GMC automobile dealer in Anchorage. Alaska Sales and Service still exists today as a General Motors dealer, located on East 5th Avenue adjacent to Merrill Field.

Denny sold his store at the outbreak of WWII and retired to Seattle, due to ill health, The store was purchased by Francis Bowden and Lou Liston who converted it into a drug store. Hewitts Drug still is in Anchorage, with two locations, one on Northern Lights Boulevard and the other in the Northway Mall.

Denny passed away in June 1952 and is buried in Seattle's Calvary Cemetery. His spouse Freda married again to a Mr. Hunke. They moved to the midwest, where Freda passed away in 1999. Prior to her death she left a group of Sydney Laurence paintings (valued at over one-half million dollars) to the Anchorage Museum of History and Art. This was one of the major private collections of Laurence's work and had hung in Denny's gallery in the old store.

———

Two of the first hotel owners in Anchorage in 1917 were DAISY and FRED GITCHELL. Daisy came to Anchorage from Nome where she had operated a restaurant. When she arrived here she again went into the food business and operated a luncheonette. In 1919 she and Fred Gitchell were married. Two years later they built the Gitchell Hotel, which was a well-known landmark in Anchorage, located at the northeast corner of 4th Avenue and F Street. The following year they added a restaurant to the premises and for many years served the traveling public.

Fred operated the hotel end of the business, and Daisy ran the restaurant and did most of the cooking. She suffered a stroke in 1948, which kept her from being active in the business after that time. She did, however, spend her days in the lobby of the hotel and was a familiar figure greeting friends passing by. Daisy died in 1951, and Fred died in 1954. They are both buried in the Elks Tract, Anchorage Memorial Park.

———

Another Anchorage merchant, FREDERICK SCHODDE came to Anchorage in 1917, after spending two years in Juneau and Kanatak. He opened the Green Front Store in Kanatak in 1916 just after he and MARIE BUELER were married. After arriving in Anchorage they opened a bakery but sold it within a year. They then opened the Green Front Store at the northwest corner of 4th Avenue and C Street. The store served as their home for many years while they were developing their business. They sold candy, ice cream, newspapers, notions, school supplies and gift items. They also operated one of the few gasoline stations in town, with two hand-operated pumps on the sidewalk in front of the store.

Marie was born in Zurich, Switzerland in 1891, and Fred was born in Germany in 1890. He immigrated to the United States with his parents in 1895. The

Schodde Family

Fred and Marie Schodde

Original Store

Anchorage Store

Home on 5th Avenue and C Street

Toni Peterson

Virginia Davey

Schoddes were one of the first families to import an automobile into Anchorage, and Marie was the first woman to obtain a driver's license. She drove until she was eighty years old. She served two terms on the local school board and was active in civic affairs.

Marie and Fred had two daughters. Antoinette Schodde married Raymond I. Peterson, and they had four children: Charles and Raymond F. of Anchorage, Mrs. Fred Pierce of Aptos, California, and Mrs. Michael Willings of Fairbanks. Virginia Schodde Davey passed away in 1947 and had no children. Fred passed away in 1949, and Marie died in 1977. They are both buried in the Elks Tract, Anchorage Memorial Park.

EDWARD GUY "RED" BARBER first landed in southeast Alaska in 1892. He was born in Pentwater, Michigan in 1875 to William G. and Frances Beard Barber, who were part owners of the Diamond Match Company. His mother passed away when he was quite young, and he was raised by his father. In his youth he was sent to Paris, France, where he studied at the Sorbonne to be a chef.

Fanni and Red Barber

Red with Fox Pelts

After his father's death, Red sold his estate interest to his brothers and set out for the western United States. He landed in southeast Alaska in 1892 and associated himself with the Goldstein family, with whom he did some mining and prospecting. When the 1898 rush to the Yukon started, he and partner Frank Lows set up a business freighting potatoes over the Chilkoot Pass and evidently were reasonably successful.

Barber Family

Red moved to Valdez after the construction of the White Pass Railway and opened a restaurant. There he met FANNI PARNU, who was born in Finland in 1889. She immigrated to the United States in the company of her aunt, Alexandria Pahkala Lows, who was related to Frank Lows, Red's former partner. Fanni and Alexandria spent a short time in Minnesota and then moved to Douglas, Alaska. After a short time in the Juneau-Douglas area, they moved to Valdez, where Fanni worked for restauranteur Red Barber baking pies.

Fanni and Red were married in Valdez in 1909. That same year they moved south to Ontario, Oregon, where eldest son, Edward G. Barber, was born in 1910. The family returned to Valdez the following year where the youngest son, William Francis, was born in 1912. During this period, Red owned and operated two restaurants in Valdez, both of which burned to the ground in the ensuing years.

Home in 1918

Red then worked for the Alaska Road Commission in the survey of the Matanuska Valley in 1914, for the United States Geological party, for the A. J. Mine in Juneau, and for the Merchants Café in Valdez. The family moved to Anchorage in 1917 where Red went to work for long time friend Fred Wright, who owned the D and D Café in Anchorage.

He eventually bought Lot 2, Block 26 of the original residential auction and started to develop a fox farm. The location is approximately what is now 5th Avenue and Gambell. Red worked for the AEC and the ARR while establishing his fox farm, and Fanni maintained her large garden, tended her strawberry patch, and raised her family.

Bill in 1934

Red was an ardent hunter. During a moose-hunting trip near Otter Lake he collapsed from a heart attack and passed away on September l, 1934. Fanni remarried in 1939 to Mike Soine, an old family friend. Mike died in 1957, and Fanni passed away in the Palmer Pioneer Home in 1975. Red, Fanni and Mike Soine are all buried in Tract 4, Anchorage Memorial Park Cemetery.

Eldest son Edward married Janet Borges, a member of another Pioneer Anchorage

Home in 1937

Ed on the Duck Flats

family, and this union produced three children: Edward G., Jr., Hugh Francis and Richard Lee all live in Anchorage. Son William married Marjorie Dane, a nurse with the BIA, and they had one son, William F. "Skip," who lives in Anchorage. Edward passed away in 1982, and William died in 1992.

HENRY MATHIAS FRANKLIN FITCH BAYER, more commonly known as Frank Bayer, was a stampeder to Nome in the year 1905. He was born in Denver, Colorado on February 19, 1882. Being raised in the mining country of Colorado, he had mining in his blood. In

Frank Bayer

Mabel Bayer

1904 he lived in Seattle, Washington, and there he met and married MABEL LINNA FERN HADFIELD, who was born in Flandreau, South Dakota in 1886. When Frank left for Nome, Mabel stayed behind in Seattle awaiting his return in the fall. He worked a claim on 19 above Discovery on Ophir Creek the summer of 1905 and returned to Seattle that fall. In the year 1906 the lure of gold brought him to Fairbanks, via the Valdez Trail, where he took a lay on a claim 8 above Discovery on Cleary Creek.

Frank Bayer and Family

Frank moved then with Mabel to Juneau where he was employed by the A. J. Mine as ore sampler and assayer. In 1911 they moved to Knik, where Frank was employed by Milo Kelly at the Fern Mine in the Willow Creek district, again as assayer and millman. Mabel resided in Knik during this period, and their first-born son, Lawrence D., was the first white child born in Knik, August 28, 1913.

Home on 8th Avenue and M Street

Home on L Street

The family moved to Anchorage in 1917, and Frank began his career with the ARR as a "gandy dancer" on the section crew and ultimately worked his way up to chief clerk of the mechanical department in which position he remained until his retirement in 1944. Frank was a life member of the Elks Lodge and an ardent supporter. He was Exalted Ruler in 1937 and in 1963 was Elk of the Year.

Frank and Mabel had four children. Daughter Ida May Carol Bayer Hurst was born in Seattle in 1905 and passed away in 1992. Son Lawrence

Donald was born in Knik in 1909 and died in Santa Monica, California in 1984. He had two children. Randy lives in Fairbanks, and Renee lives in Tacoma, Washington. Son Benjamin Kenneth was born in Nelson, British Columbia in 1907 and died in Woodburn, Oregon in 1993. He had four children: Robert K. lives in Centralia, Washington; Theodore A. and Leroy Allen live in Kent, Washington; and Linda Bayer McCloud lives in Seattle, Washington. Daughter Alice Dora Bayer Beitel was born in Seattle, Washington and still lives there. Frank died in Anchorage in 1964 and is buried in the Elks Tract, Anchorage Memorial Park. Mabel died in Auburn, Washington, in 1968 and is presumably buried there.

———

WILLIAM ENATTI came to Douglas, Alaska in 1911 and was employed with the Treadwell Mine and the A. J. Mine in Juneau. He came to Alaska just two years after he emigrated from Oulu, Finland, where he was born in 1886. In 1912 he and EMMA WIRKKALA were married in Juneau. Emma was born in Kaustinen, Finland in 1882 and immigrated to the United States in 1911. The year 1917 found them in Anchorage and then in the Jonesville-Eska coal mining area of the Matanuska Valley.

The family moved back to Anchorage after a short time, and William was employed by the ARR as a carpenter until his retirement in 1949. In his retirement, he was self-employed as a carpenter doing work for local residents. At the time of his death he was the oldest member of the Moose Lodge, having joined in 1914.

William and Emma had two daughters. Helve was a teacher and never married. She passed away in 1978. Sigrid married George Karabelnikoff, and this union produced three sons. F. Lee, Don G. and Ken W. all reside in Anchorage. William passed away in 1957, and Emma died in 1970. William, Emma and Helve are all buried in the Pioneer Tract, Anchorage Memorial Park Cemetery.

Enatti Family

William and Emma Enatti

Sigrid Karabelnikoff

Helve Enatti

Home on L Street

Cabin in Jonesville

Alma Anderson

Anton Anderson

Anderson Family

In 1917 a man arrived in Anchorage who was destined to leave his mark not only in Anchorage, but in Alaska. He was ANTON ANDERSON, a New Zealand immigrant who was born in Upper Moonlight, New Zealand in 1892 of a Swedish father and an Irish mother. He worked at gold mining with his father in his hometown of Upper Moonlight and was educated there.

In 1914 he and his brother entered the United States and went to work as surveyors in Hoquiam, Washington. He took his engineer examinations at Seattle University and passed with flying colors. Anton arrived in Anchorage in 1917 to work for the AEC. He surveyed and engineered much of the railroad line and the original townsite of Anchorage. He was location engineer for the Matanuska Colonization Project and principal engineer for the United States Army in Alaska during WWII. He participated in the construction of the Eklutna hydro-electric project. His crowning touch was as chief engineer for the Whittier Tunnel project, which was named and dedicated in his honor in 1976. He was called "Mr. Alaska Railroad" and often said: "I think I walked over more of Alaska than any man since Alfred Brooks." [Brooks was the explorer for whom the Brooks Range is named.]

Whittier Tunnel Portal

Anton was active in Anchorage public service. He served on the City Council, was Chairman of the Public Utilities Commission, and was appointed to fill out the term of Mayor Hinchey in 1956. He was elected the following year as Mayor, however, was forced to resign early due to ill health.

Anton and ALMA MENGE were married in Williston, North Dakota in 1927. Alma was an honored artist and was listed in *Who's Who in American Art* in 1957. The marriage produced three daughters. Jean Anderson Graves had four children. Eric B. and Gary Anton live in Ester, Alaska; Kathleen Graves Moore lives in Kenai; and Sheila Graves Pennell lives in Bellingham, Washington. Daughter Patricia Menge Anderson had three children. Anton J. lives in Issaquah, Washington; Dan Christian lives in Lynwood, Washington; and Tracy Jean is deceased. Daughter Shelby Menge Argen had one daughter, Jennifer Anne, living in Seattle, Washington. Anton passed away in Mt. Vernon, Washington in 1960, and Alma died in 1972. They are both buried in Hoquiam, Washington.

Jean Graves

Patricia Anderson

Shelby Argen

Another Yukon stampeder who found his way to Anchorage in 1917, OSCAR TRYCK was born in Sweden in 1879 and immigrated to the United States with his parents in 1881. He was raised in the depressed iron ore area of Michigan and, with a brother, departed the iron mines and headed west. The lure of gold brought them to Skagway in 1903 where they hiked the White Pass, built a scow on Lake Bennett, and floated the Yukon to Dawson where they found work in the mines. They moved down-river to Rampart and Tanana working as woodcutters and freighters. Oscar began freighting with horses out of Fairbanks and on the Richardson Trail in 1906. In 1911 the strike in Ruby called Oscar, and, with his team of four draft horses, he boarded a vessel to Ruby. He took over the job of pioneering the road out to the mines from Ruby.

The winter of 1914 found Oscar back in Iron Mountain, Michigan, where he returned to marry his boyhood sweetheart, who had been waiting for him for ten years. LILLIAN BLANCHE TIPPING and Oscar were married that same year, returned to Fairbanks via Valdez, and waited for the spring breakup on the river to get to Ruby. Oscar mined on Trail Creek until it played out, and in 1917 they moved to Knik, where he was employed by the Independence Mine.

Oscar Tryck

Lillian Tryck

They built their home in Knik, and Oscar freighted to the mines until the railroad arrived in Wasilla, and they moved there from Knik. Oscar remained in Wasilla working for the Alaska Road Commission under the Anchorage district until his retirement. Blanche was active in school and community projects in Wasilla until her death in 1936. Oscar passed away in 1964. Both he and Blanche are buried in Anchorage Memorial Park Cemetery Tract 4.

Tryck Home

Road Camp

William Tryck

Charles Tryck

The marriage of Oscar and Blanche produced two sons, William born in Ruby and Charles born in Wasilla. Charles married Molly Chamberlin, and they had five children. Keith Eric, Douglas Allan, James Warren, Kathryn and Suzanne all reside in Anchorage. Son William had three children. William lives in Texas; Donna lives in California; and Lucinda Tryck Teitzel lives in Anchorage.

JOHN HUGO ERICKSON was born in Stockholm, Sweden in 1885. At the age of sixteen he signed on to the crew of a sailing vessel and rounded Cape Horn bound for the United States. He arrived in Valdez in 1912 and was engaged in mining. In 1917 he moved to Anchorage and was employed with the H. J. Emard Packing Company. He entered the service of the Alaska Railroad in the telephone and telegraph department. He became foreman of the department and served with the ARR until his death in 1934.

INGEBORG HAGGKVIST HENDRICKSON was born in Rockland, Michigan in 1888. With her friends the Bloomquists she came to Valdez in 1913. She made a visit to Seattle in 1914, and during her return to Valdez aboard the *Admiral Sampson* the ship was rammed by the *Princess Victoria*. It was an experience she never forgot.

The marriage of Ingeborg and John produced four children. Daughter Ebba Erickson Montgomery had two children: Julie K. Grinder, who lives in Anchorage, and Marilyn Jo Odom, who lives in Asotin, Washington. Daughter Alva Davey had four children: Linnea Zoe Sledge lives at Big Lake; Bonnie Jean Pischke lives in Spokane, Washington; Cheryl Edith James lives in Cooper Landing; and Linda Marie Ball lives in Harrison, Iowa. Third child, John Leonard and his wife Betty had one

John and Ingeborg Erickson

Erickson Home

John at Switchboard

Edith Colley
John Erickson
Alva Davey
Ebba Montgomery

daughter, Deborah Lee, who lives in Anchorage. John died in 1975. Fourth child, Edith Colley lives in Port Townsend, Washington. She had two children, Randy and Shiela. John passed away in 1934, and Ingeborg died in 1949. They are both buried in the Masonic Tract, Anchorage Memorial Park Cemetery.

OSCAR MILLER was born in Stettin, Germany in 1884. When he was thirteen years old he stowed away on a Norwegian sailing ship. He was subsequently found out, and a sympathetic captain and crew fed him and put him to work. In 1908 he left the ship when it docked in Seattle, Washington. He made his way to Alaska, first landing in Seward, and then on to Sunrise, Hope, Flat, Ruby and Iditarod.

Oscar returned to Knik where he obtained employment at the gold bullion mine. While working there he met two brothers, Charles and Ray Ketchum, and they became very good friends. The three of them together built a log cabin in Knik, which was a place for them to stay when they were not working.

Marie and Dorothy (rear right) Miller
Dorothy Miller
Oscar Miller

MARIE AUGUSTA KETCHAM was born in Red Lodge, Montana in 1891. She was raised in Red Lodge, and at the age of nineteen she married Charlie Steele. In 1912 Charley Steele died, and Mary was left a widow with a daughter, Dorothy. Times were hard in Montana, and her two brothers who were working in Knik sent ninety dollars for her to come to Knik to seek employment. She found employment as a cook and chamber maid in the roadhouse owned by Mary Morrisson. She had to leave her daughter Dorothy with relatives in Bridger, Montana, and it wasn't until the spring of 1916 that she was able to save enough money to send for her daughter.

In Knik Marie met Oscar Miller, the friend of her two brothers. Marie moved to Anchorage later in 1916 and had saved enough money to purchase a two-room tarpaper shack on a lot on 9th Avenue. She and Oscar Miller were married that same year in Anchorage. Judge Leopold David, later to become Anchorage's first Mayor, performed the marriage.

Oscar obtained work as a longshoreman, and Marie worked as a chambermaid at the Crescent Hotel and as a cook in Gitchell's Café. The following year the family moved to Eska, and Oscar worked in the power plant until the mine closed down. They moved back to Anchorage in 1917 where Oscar was hired by the ARR as a power plant engineer. He later owned a fox farm near what is now 8th Avenue and Gambell. The bottom fell out of the fur business in the twenties, and he then obtained employment with the city of Anchorage, and eventually became superintendent of streets, water and sewer. He held this position for thirty years until his death in 1949. Marie passed away in 1994 at the age of one hundred three. Both she and Oscar are buried in the Elks Tract, Anchorage Memorial Park Cemetery.

The first marriage of Marie Ketcham and Charles Steele bore one daughter, Dorothy, who in 1930 married Edward Johnson. They had one son, Edward M., who was born in Anchorage and still resides here. Dorothy resides in the Pioneer Home.

EDWARD J. STIER was born in San Joaquin County, California in 1860 of prominent California pioneers who settled there during the 1849 gold rush. Ed came to Alaska in 1913 and was for many years clerk of the Court for Judge Wickersham in Fairbanks. He later left the court system, moved down to Anchorage, and continued with the ARR until he retired in 1930. He passed away in Anchorage in July of 1934.

WALTER R. EUBANK was born in Winchester, Kentucky in 1869. He and his wife came north together in the great gold rush of 1898 to the Klondike gold fields. After spending several years in Dawson, they went south to Juneau where he went into the logging business and expanded into Sitka. They left Sitka and moved to Anchorage in 1918 where he was employed by the AEC and the ARR as a powder man, then as pile driver engineer, and later as yard hostler. In 1925 he was promoted to coal station operator at Willow. Walter passed away on May 6, 1934 and is buried in the Catholic Tract, Anchorage Memorial Park.

W. E. "BILLY" AUSTIN was born in Winters, California in 1882. He came to Valdez in 1900 with his parents, who were operators of a hotel there. Billy went to work in the mines until he heard of the gold strikes in Sunrise and Hope on Cook Inlet. Having no luck with mining, he acquired a boat and began operations hauling freight and passengers between Hope, Sunrise, Susitna Station, Knik and eventually Ship Creek and Anchorage in 1918. He was a familiar figure on the streets of Anchorage, spending time here between trips on the Inlet. He would usually winter in Hope and occasionally in Anchorage. Billy stayed active in his boating business and obtained a mail contract from the Post Office in later years. In 1962, due to failing health, he moved to White Salmon, Washington. He passed away there in 1963.

JOHN HORATIO CRAWFORD was born in Grenville, Quebec, Canada in 1879. He was a veteran of the Boer War and immigrated to the United States in 1910. In 1911 he met and married NELLIE MAY HEILMAN, who was born in Washougal, Washington in 1892.

Jack and Nellie came to Anchorage in 1918 and moved into a newly built log cabin. Jack had obtained work as a crane engineer with the ARR and continued with them until he retired in 1951. Nellie, who was a long-time employee of Providence Hospital, retired in 1949.

Bertha Meier

Nellie and Jack Crawford

Nellie and Jack had two children, Bertha Crawford Meier and Leroy. Nellie died in 1957 and is buried in Anchorage Memorial Park Cemetery. Jack died in 1964, and his place of burial is unknown.

Crawford Home

Leroy Crawford

Crawford Family

Harry Mikami

Flora Mikami

Mine Mikami   George Mikami

GEORGE MIKAMI was born in Tokyo, Japan in 1864 and immigrated to the United States in 1885, landing in San Francisco, California. In 1910 he returned to Japan to marry MINE MORIOKA, who was born in Tokyo in 1884. Together they returned to the United States in 1911. With two of their children, they arrived in Seward in 1915. They spent the next two years in Seward, where two more children were born. In 1918 the family moved to Anchorage, and here George opened a tailor shop on 4th Avenue between C and B Streets. The children all did their part in the family business, both George and Mine doing the heavy alterations and tailoring.

Alice Mikami   Mary Mikami

George and Mine had three daughters and one son. Daughter Mary Mikami Rouse had two children. Peter lives in Washington, D.C., and David Alexander lives in Narberth, Pennsylvania. Daughter Alice Mikami Snodgrass had one child, John Roland, who lives in Palmer. Daughter Flora Mikami Newcomb had two children: Simon John, who lives in Tsawwassen, British Columbia, and George Anthony, who lives in Richmond British Columbia. Son Harry Mikami had no children.

HORACE WILLARD NAGLEY was born April 5, 1875, in Utsaladdy Camano Island, Washington Territory, the second of thirteen children. He first arrived in upper Cook Inlet in the town of Seldovia on June 6, 1905, when he traveled to Alaska on the steamer *Bertha*, then owned by the Alaska Commercial Company. He later worked as purser traveling the Inlet on the steamer *Neptune* in the summer months and spending the winters in Seattle.

In 1907 he returned to Susitna Station with a stock of goods with the intent of starting a trading post with two partners, Litchfield and Churchill. After about a year the partners sold out to the

Alaska Commercial Company. However, Nagley saw continuing opportunity in the area and was determined to remain in business. He purchased a new site in Susitna Station from Chief "Big" Ivan and his wife Katherina on June 10, 1908, and began business as H. W. Nagley, General Merchandise. During his early years at Susitna he often traveled to Tent City to purchase supplies, and in 1915 he bid on two lots located at the southwest corner of 5th Avenue and B Street for the price of $395 and $245. In 1915 he opened a branch trading post in McDougal and in 1916 a third store in a tent in Talkeetna. With the forthcoming railroad, Talkeetna was taking on the appearance of a boomtown, while Susitna and McDougal were losing population.

At Susitna Station, 1918

In 1917 Nagley was able to acquire his original location when he purchased the assets of the Susitna Trading Company from investors Edward McNally, William Maitland and A. A. Shonbeck, who had bought the assets of the Alaska Commercial Company some months previously. H. W. Nagley was now the only trading outfit in the area. The Susitna stores became short-lived as the Railroad went via Talkeetna, so all efforts were then concentrated in operating the Talkeetna store.

During the 1920's Nagley acquired gold claims on Dollar Creek, Falls Creek and Short Creek in the Cache Creek Mining District. He held these claims for many years and leased the ground to various miners. Many of the miners became trappers in the winter months and brought in their furs to the store to receive store credit for exchange when the mining season started once again. In 1921 Nagley was appointed U. S. Commissioner, Probate Judge, ex-officio Justice of the Peace, coroner and recorder for the Talkeetna Precinct, serving until 1934. He was appointed postmaster in 1927 and served until 1947. He had already seen service as the first postmaster in Susitna in 1907.

JESSAMINE ELIZABETH MILLIKAN was born March 23, 1872 in Thorntown, Indiana, one of four children. She attended Purdue University during 1891-92 and completed her teacher training in two years at the Indiana Kindergarten and Primary Normal Schools in Indianapolis. She taught school in Ponce, Puerto Rico for two years, and in 1909 she applied for a position to teach in the United States Public Schools in Alaska at Hoonah for a stipend of ninety dollars per month. In 1911 she taught summer school at Chignik and in the fall received a contract to teach at Susitna Station. It was there she met her future husband, and in July of l912 she married H. W. Nagley.

Jessamine, Willard, Jr. and Horace Nagley in Talkeetna, 1941

Anchorage Home

In 1913 Jessamine stopped teaching and began assisting her husband in the general store. When the branch store was opened in Talkeetna in 1916, they began spending more time at Talkeetna than at Susitna and eventually built a log store building on "Nagley" Street on the original townsite. In 1913 she lost her first child during childbirth, and in March 1918 she gave birth to a son in the Railroad Hospital in Anchorage, after traveling from Talkeetna by dog team. "The Railroad Doctor," J. B. Beeson, was the attending physician. In 1921 the family built a new log home on Main Street. Jessamine taught her son at home using the Calvert system since there were no schools in Talkeetna.

Willard Nagley, Jr.

In 1926 Anchorage with its elementary school beckoned the family, and Jessamine took an apartment in the Anchorage Hotel so that their young son could attend the third grade. Later they purchased a home at 414 L Street and resided here during the winter months and in Talkeetna during the summer until 1936 when Willard, Jr. graduated from high school.

Over the years many investment opportunities presented themselves to Mr. and Mrs. Nagley, and they eventually became investors in the original Westward Hotel, which evolved into the present Hilton Hotel. In 1946 Mr. Nagley sold the Talkeetna store to Donald G. Barrett of the Barrett & Kennedy Trading Company and in 1950 retired from the operations of the mining claims as well. They spent their time traveling throughout the south 48 in the winters and lived in their Talkeetna home during the summer.

On December 5, 1955 Jessamine passed away in Palo Alto, California, and H. W., Sr. died June 8, 1966 in Seattle, Washington. They are both buried in the Elks Tract, Anchorage Memorial Park Cemetery. Their son H. W. Nagley II married Sarah B. Edmunds in 1956. They had one son, H. W. Nagley III, who lives in Washington. Sarah passed away in l979. H. W. "Willard" Nagley II lives in Kirkland, Washington.

———

ANNA ASHTON was born in Canton, Ohio in 1880. She first arrived in Alaska at Nome with her husband Wright and Daughter Catherine in 1900. Wright Ashton passed awa in Nome, and in 1915 mother and daughter made the long boat trip from Nome to Seward and thence to Anchorage. Anna first opened a small grocery store at 4th Avenue and I Street, and in 1916 she opened a ladies ready-to-wear, named Ashtons Ladies Apparel, near 4th Avenue

Nome, 1908

Nome, Snowgoose Railroad

Harry Schultz

and D Street. Mother and daughter operated the store in Anchorage until 1930 and also maintained a store in Seward from 1920 - 1927.

Anna built the Ashton Apartments on the property near 4th Avenue and I Street and lived there until her death in 1945. Daughter Catherine married HARRY SCHULTZ in 1916, and a son, William, was born in 1917. Harry had mined in the interior prior to becoming a United States Deputy Marshal in Anchorage and Valdez. Catherine and Harry divorced after several years. Harry J. Schultz was born in Beatrice, Nebraska in 1886 and passed away in 1983.

EDWARD FRANK BITTNER was born in February 23, l894 in Portland, Oregon. He arrived in Skagway in 1898 with his parents, enroute to the Klondike gold fields. His father mined in other locations including Nome and Chisana. Ed came to Anchorage after WWI and went to work for the Alaska Railroad until he retired. In 1927 he and Catherine Ashton Schultz were married, and Edward adopted Catherine's son, William.
Edward Bittner passed away in 1954.
Catherine Ashton Schultz Bittner was
born in Massillon, Ohio in 1899 and died
in Seattle, Washington in 1981.

Son William Bittner married Elladean
Hays, and they had three children.
Daughter Catherine Ann married Senator
Ten Stevens and resides in Washington,
D.C. and Girdwood, Alaska. Son William
Hays married Michelle Stone, and they
live in Anchorage. Daughter Judith Ellen
lives in Anchorage. William Bittner died
in 1989 in Arizona.

William Bittner

Ed and Catherine Bittner

ROBERT S. BRAGAW, SR. was born in New London, Connecticut on October l, 1851. He was educated in the public schools of his state, and his first occupation was in the wholesale grocery business in New York City. At the age of twenty-three he moved west to Denver and engaged in mining and real estate. In 1883 he moved to Coeur d'Alene, Idaho and started his official career as recorder of Kootenai County, serving in that capacity until 1890. That same year he was elected clerk of the District Court, ex-officio county auditor, and clerk of the County Commissioners, holding those offices until 1899. In that year he was appointed supervisor of the Priest River Forest Preserve and served in that office until 1904 when he became state auditor.

Mr. Bragaw was a direct descendant of the family of Bourgon Brouchard and his wife Catherine LeFebre, French Huguenots from Manheim on the Rhine, who landed on Manhattan Island, New York in 1676. They bought an estate in old Nassau and there established the family whose members are now variously known as Bragau, Bragaw and Brokaw.

He had married in 1885, and apparently he and his spouse became estranged some time during his stay in Idaho. In 1906 Mr. Bragaw moved to Spokane, Washington with his son Robert S., Jr., where he again engaged in the real estate business. He then moved on to Los Angeles and finally to Anchorage in 1917 where he resided until his death. During his years in Anchorage he served as deputy director of the court for a number of years. Mr. Bragaw died in Anchorage on February 18, 1928, and his wife passed away in Seattle on May 7, 1928. They are both buried in the Masonic Tract, Anchorage Memorial Park Cemetery.

ROBERT S. BRAGAW, JR. was born in Rathdrum, Iowa on May 2, 1889. In 1912 he married EVELYN JOHNSON in Spokane, Washington. He established a photography and gift shop in Anchorage on the corner of 4th Avenue and E Street which he sold to Denny Hewitt, who operated the business until Hewitt retired after WWII, when it was again sold and became Hewitts Drug Store, which still operates under the same name in Spenard.

Bob Bragaw was a civic leader during the early Anchorage years. He was a territorial senator from 1931 to 1935, city clerk and treasurer from l935 to 1944, and assistant manager of Anchorage Light and Power Company. He was one of the original organizers of the Alaska Guides, along with Gus Gelles and Andy Simons, which brought in big game hunters from

Robert and Myrtle Bragaw

Fish Trap Near Kasilof

all over the world. He was President the All-Alaska Chamber of Commerce in 1941. He has a Mountain View Street named in his honor. In 1944 Bob and Evelyn left Anchorage due to her ill health. They settled in Sumner, Washington, and Evelyn died there in 1949.

Eklutna School, 1930

In 1951 Bob and MYRTLE EVERETT were married on Whidbey Island, Washington. Myrtle was the widow of EDWIN L. EVERETT, who passed away in 1939. The Everetts had operated a mink farm in Anchorage, located around 10th Avenue and P Street. Myrtle was born in Kansas City, Missouri in 1888. She and Edwin came to Alaska in 1922. Evelyn taught school at the Tyonek reservation school and also at the Eklutna school. They later purchased a salmon trap site at Trading Bay and operated it seasonally until Edwin became ill, and they gave up the site.

Bob and Myrtle lived on Whidbey Island, Washington, where they owned and operated the Coupeville Realty Company until 1963 when ill health forced Bob to retire. He died in Mt. Vernon, Washington in 1969. Myrtle passed away in Mt. Vernon, Washington in 1973. They are both buried in Evergreen-Washelli Mausoleum in Seattle, Washington.

WILLIAM GORDON came to Alaska in 1897 and was identified with most of the mining camps from Nome to Fairbanks to Iditarod. He arrived in Anchorage in 1916 and was employed by the AEC and later the Alaska Railroad in the mechanical department. He was born in 1866 in North Carolina, and his family moved west into Montana and California in later years. He died in 1930 and is buried in the Masonic Tract, Anchorage Memorial Park.

WILLIAM T. DORWIN was born in Ruby Washington in 1891. He was raised in Washington and came to Anchorage in 1916. He was employed with the AEC and later the Railroad. In 1919 he and his spouse JOSIE developed a mink farm near Montana Station on the Railroad. He later sold his mink farm and was re-employed by the Alaska Railroad in the mechanical department in 1921. In 1928 he moved his family to Snohomish, Washington and passed away there in 1931.

WILLIAM B. CLAYTON arrived in Anchorage in the fall of 1916. Prior to coming to Anchorage, he was connected with several musical organizations on the west coast. He was the manager for the well known Victor Herbert Band and librarian for the Gilmore Band. During his musical career William was instrumental in organizing the Clayton-Priest Musical Company, which introduced the Chicago Grand Opera Company to the west coast. He also held the distinction of being the past Grand Master of the St. Cecelia Lodge #568 of New York City. His affiliation with the local Masonic Lodge was very well known, and he devoted all of his spare time to the organization. He died on October 8, 1920 and is buried in the Masonic Tract, Anchorage Memorial Park.

Harry and Elsie Hill

Hill Family, Donald, Harry, Sylvia and Granddaughter

HARRY J. HILL was born in Wainfleet, England in 1905. He immigrated to Alaska in 1919 where he joined his widowed mother, Sylvia Ringstad. His mother moved to Fairbanks in 1920, and Harry remained in Anchorage, being employed by the Alaska Railroad doing various jobs until 1923, when he went to work for the colorful Cap Lathrop as timekeeper at the Suntrana Coal Mine in Healy.

In 1928 Harry met ELSIE EDMISTON, a young schoolteacher who was teaching at the Healy School in Suntrana. Elsie was born in Glasgow, Scotland in 1907, and her family immigrated to Canada in 1910 and to Alaska in 1915.

In 1934 Lathrop sent the young entrepreneur to Anchorage, where he managed the 4th Avenue Building and the Empress Theater. In 1944 the coalfields again beckoned him, and he left the Lathrop organization and formed a partnership with Oscar Anderson to manage the Evan Jones Coal Mine in the Matanuska Valley. This operation was one of the two major coal producers in the valley, and its primary customer was the military establishment in Anchorage.

In 1951 Harry sold his interest in the Evan Jones Mine and rejoined the Lathrop organization. He was named one of the executors of Lathrop's will, and with the death of Cap Lathrop in 1950 he became involved with all operations of the Lathrop Company. The Lathrop holdings in 1950 included five movie theaters, two radio stations and two television stations in Anchorage and Fairbanks. The TV and radio stations in Fairbanks operated under the call letters of KFAR, and the Anchorage stations operated under the KENI call letters. Shortly after Hill took over chairmanship of the Lathrop Company, a group of employees headed by Alvin Bramstedt purchased the TV and radio stations.

Elsie and Harry Hill, 1970

In the 1960's the Lathrop Company became involved in the construction of several major building projects in Anchorage. The firm constructed the RCA building in 1960 and in 1962 built the largest privately owned building in the City, the Hill Building, which is now the City Hall at the corner of 6th Avenue and G Street. The same year the company built the Alaska Mutual Savings Bank building at the corner of 5th Avenue and F Street and in 1963 acquired the Cordova Building. Throughout the sixties the firm continued to build theaters in Anchorage and Fairbanks. In 1969 a

Hill Building

3rd Avenue Home

Donald Hill

national firm based in Florida, Mometco Enterprises, Inc., merged
the Lathrop Company into their own, and Harry became
Chairman of the Board of Mometco Enterprises.

Harry passed away in 1973, and son Donald passed away in 1992. Elsie Hill still resides in
Anchorage. Son Donald married and had three children. Harry lives at Big Lake, and Sue
Hill Bergstrom and Dona Hill live in Anchorage.

CLIFFORD E. SMITH was born in Columbus, Ohio in 1900 and came to Anchorage in
August 1919. He began his career with the Alaska Railroad in 1921 as a checker in the
freight house and worked his way up to clerk and then to cashier. He entered the auditing
department in 1931. After several years in the auditing department he returned to the claims
department then back to the auditing department in 1948.

"Smitty," as he was called, was an ardent member of the Anchorage Elks. He was awarded his
sixty-year pin in 1979 and was a past Exalted Ruler in addition to being a life member for
over thirty years. In 1963 Smitty was chosen King Regent of the Fur Rendezvous representing the Pioneers of Alaska. Smitty was killed in an auto-pedestrian accident in 1982. He is
buried in the Masonic Tract, Anchorage Memorial Park Cemetery.

HERMAN JOHNSON was born in Sweden in October 23, 1889. He entered the United States
in January 1911 and went directly to San Francisco, where he was employed as a cabinetmaker
and carpenter. In April 1919 he left California and headed to Alaska, first landing in Cordova,
where he worked for three months. He then departed for Seward and obtained employment with
the AEC, building snow sheds at Spencer Glacier. He spent some time working in and out of
Anchorage in 1920 and 1921 and then headed for the oil boomtown of Kanatak. One year later
he moved back to Seward, Fairbanks and then again to Anchorage in 1923.

In 1938 he bought the estate of the Harry Cribb carpenter shop and contracting business.
He operated the business, constructing homes, store buildings and apartment houses
throughout the City. He maintained a high standard of workmanship and kept up the legacy

left by Harry Cribb. Herman died of a heart attack in June 1956 while on a fishing trip to the Anchor River. He is buried in the Pioneer Tract, Anchorage Memorial Park Cemetery.

Tom Bevers

One of Anchorage's best friends and civic leaders, THOMAS S. BEVERS was born in South Boston, Virginia on March 30, 1889. He arrived in Anchorage in 1919 and first worked for the Alaska Railroad at various jobs. He was the first chief of the Volunteer Fire Department, a post he held for over twenty years.

Tom had great faith in the future of Anchorage and was one of its greatest boosters. He was instrumental in the development of the Fur Rendezvous and traveled throughout Alaska touting Anchorage and the Rendezvous. He served on the City Council for several terms. He was on the airport committee and was responsible for the early development of Merrill Field. He took such an interest in the airport that he actually maintained the runway by himself as a volunteer, clearing snow and keeping the runway clear of debris.

Tom had a great interest in real estate and owned and started development of the property bordering 9th Avenue and Cordova east to Gambell and south to 15th. It was aptly named the Bevers Subdivision and later became known as the Bevers and Pfeil Subdivision, when Emil Pfeil became associated with him in the real estate venture. The Hewitt building on the corner of 4th Avenue and E Street was owned by Tom and Emil and was remodeled into an apartment building on the upper floor and commercial space on the ground floor. It was renamed the Bevers and Pfeil Apartments. The downstairs housed Hewitts Photo owned by Denny Hewitt, the Cheechako Tavern owned by Walt Grohnert, the Cheechako Café owned by John Balios, and the Gus George shoe repair shop.

Tom was considered the "official greeter" in Anchorage, always taking the time to show off the City to visitors and dignitaries. He was forever willing to serve on committees for the benefit of the community.

While on a duck hunting trip on October 4, 1944, Tom was stricken with a fatal heart attack. Although his body was supposedly shipped to his native home in Virginia for burial, cemetery records show him as being buried in the Masonic Tract, Anchorage Memorial Park Cemetery.

ARTHUR FRODENBURG arrived in Anchorage in 1919. He was born in Duluth, Minnesota in 1900 and made his way to Anchorage, finding work with the Alaska Railroad. He married Sally Roop, who had come to Anchorage with a brother in 1920, in Anchorage, and together they opened Sally's Sweet Shop on 4th Avenue between G and F Streets. This was the predecessor to Richmonds. In the thirties they moved up to the Matanuska Valley and also to the Independence Mine. Art and Sally left Alaska and moved to Tahoe City, California, where Sally passed away in 1952. She was born in Warrensburg, Missouri in 1899. Art passed away in 1969 in Bowling Green, Ohio.

CARL ARTHUR "MOOSE" JOHNSON arrived on the Anchorage scene in August 1919 to work for the AEC and the Alaska Railroad as a cook. He was born in Des Moines, Iowa, May 14, 1883, of a pioneering family. His parents pioneered western Oklahoma and southern Kansas in a covered wagon when that part of the country was free range land. While his parents stayed in the midwest and participated in the development of great farmlands, Carl came to Alaska to join the mining stampedes.

Carl spent a great deal of his time prospecting and mining in the Chulitna area and working on and off with the Railroad as a cook and sometime section foreman. He maintained a huge circle of friends and could often be found at the Schodde Green Front Store when he was visiting in town. He received his nickname because of his great prowess on the trail, simulating a moose in strength and endurance. He also used the name permanently to prevent mix-ups in the mail, as there were two other C. A. Johnsons in Anchorage at the time. Moose passed away on November 2, 1942. He is buried in the Pioneer Tract, Anchorage Memorial Park Cemetery.

CHARLES EDWARD OLSON was born in Kalmar, Sweden in 1878. At the age of nineteen he immigrated to the United States and immediately enlisted in the Revenue Cutter Service, which was the forerunner of the United States Coast Guard. He served aboard the cutter *Manning* in Alaska, and after a four year hitch he joined the gold stampede to Nome in 1901. He mined around Nome for some time and then moved on to the gold strike in the Iditarod in 1910.

Matilda Olson

Charles Olson

In 1911 Charley was visiting in Chicago, and there he met MATILDA KARLSON. Matilda was born in Orebro, Sweden in 1881 and came to the United States with her parents in 1900. Charley was a successful miner in the Takotna mining district and held several claims on the well-known Gaines Creek. In 1912 Charley sent for Matilda, and they were married in Takotna the same year.

They continued to mine on Gaines Creek until 1919 when they moved to Anchorage. Charley suffered with arthritis and could no longer work in the placer operations. After their arrival in Anchorage, Matilda opened a small cafeteria to serve the workers in the railyards. They also maintained a large garden at their Anchorage home and raised fresh produce, selling it to the local stores.

Gaines Creek

Olson Wedding

Second Home

Ruby Olson Mathews

Charley and Matilda had one daughter, Ruby. She and Raymond Mathews were married in Fairbanks, and this union produced two daughters. Jane Ruby Mathews Swain resides in Homer. Shirley Ann resides in Anchorage. Charley passed away in 1932, and Matilda died in 1965. Raymond Mathews passed away in 1961. Ruby Olson Mathews presently resides in the Anchorage Pioneer Home. Charley and Matilda are both buried in Anchorage Memorial Park Cemetery.

FRED HOWE was born in Springfield, Illinois in 1870. He came to Alaska in 1897, first arriving in Nome where he spent several years mining. He moved on to Valdez in later years, prospecting in the Shushana district. His next move was to Sunrise on Cook Inlet doing prospecting in and around Hope. When the AEC started work on the Alaska Railroad, he joined the construction crews and remained as a bridge foreman until his retirement in 1936.

ELLEN PUKKILA STOLT was born in Finland in 1880. She and her spouse immigrated to the United States and settled in Boston, Massachusetts, and there their first child, William Stolt, was born in 1900. Her husband died the following year in 1901, and she stayed on in Boston working as a cook and baker. In 1909 she remarried and moved to Juneau, where second son Paul was born.

Fred and Ellen Howe

Howe Home on 4th Avenue

In 1917 the family moved to Anchorage, and in 1918 Ellen and her second husband were divorced. Ellen went to work for the Alaska Railroad in 1920, working as a cook on the bridge crew, of which Fred Howe was the foreman. In 1921 she and Fred were married, and she set up housekeeping at their home in Anchorage.

Here again, we have the joining of two Pioneer Anchorage families. William Stolt and Lillian Rivers were married in

Anchorage in 1929. Bill and Lillian started on a long career in Anchorage as business partners in Stolt Electric Supply. Bill was a graduate electrical engineer, and Lily had a degree in business administration. Together they operated an electrical contracting business and gift shop for many years.

Bill served three terms as Mayor of Anchorage during WWII and two years on the City Council. The marriage of Bill and Lily produced three children. Sons William Edwin and Wayne Allen both live in Anchorage, and daughter Elaine Stolt Waters lives in Arizona.

Fred Howe died in 1943, and Ellen passed away in l962. They are both buried in Anchorage Memorial Park Cemetery. Bill turned one hundred years of age in the year 2000 and died the following year, 2001. Lily resides in the Anchorage Pioneer Home.

Paul Howe

Bill Stolt

Bill and Lily Stolt

ADELINE and WILLIAM HUGEL were a true Pioneer Alaska couple. The history on this couple is rather sketchy; however, they left their mark in Alaska, and, even though information is scarce, I will relate what is available.

Adeline was born in Sweden in 1868. She and Ed, as William was known, were married and living in Seattle when the news broke of the great gold strike in the Klondike. They joined the thousands of stampeders heading for the gold fields and landed in Skagway in 1899.

From the time they arrived in Skagway they became real pioneers in that they never hesitated to do their part in driving a team of dogs, taking their turn at the paddle, driving a team of horses or taking their turn at the tow rope pulling a boat. They arrived in Dawson too late to stake good ground, so Adeline and Ed and her sister and sister-in-law and a few others started out for the headwaters of the Koyukuk River via the Chandalar River and across a divide to their destination where it was rumored a fabulously rich gold strike had been made.

This was a trip to test the mettle of strong men, let alone several women. The trip, however, was made, and, much to their disappointment, the gold strike turned out to be just a glorified rumor. There was very little grub left, and even less in the barren country they were in, so they decided to head back to Dawson. They hiked over the divide in the Brooks Range to the Chandalar River where they built a log raft and floated down to the mouth of the river where it joined the Yukon. At this point they flagged a steamer heading up river to Dawson, where they landed hungry and tired.

They left Dawson in 1914 and spent some time in Tenakee Hot Springs in Southeast Alaska. From there, in 1915, they came to Anchorage and resided here until their deaths. Ed worked for the AEC and the Alaska Railroad as a carpenter. Adeline died in 1934, and Ed died in 1936. They are both buried in the Pioneer Tract of Anchorage Memorial Park Cemetery. Ed was born in 1865, however it is unknown where. No information was available that told of their early life prior to coming to Alaska, nor is there any information available on how they spent their years in Anchorage.

———

Prohibition was in effect during these years and it kept the United States Marshals busy enforcing the laws. The "Pro-Hi's" as they were called simply could not keep up with the hidden stills, mostly out on the Loop Road, locally, and on Fire Island and on McKenzie Point. The lower Inlet was also rife with bootleggers. One man, a former Anchorage deputy, JIM HILL, who was stationed in Seldovia, was shot in the back in cold blood.

Jim was forty years old and was a former employee of the Alaska Railroad on the T and T Gang (telephone and telegraph). He arrived in Anchorage shortly after WWI. He had served overseas with Colonel Mears' 31st Engineers and came to Anchorage at the behest of the Colonel. He received his appointment as United States Deputy Marshal for Seldovia in 1922, and he and his family took residence in Seldovia at that time.

Jim was investigating a bootlegging suspect named Jacobsen and was attacked and bitten by Jacobsen's dog. Hill was trying to shoot the dog when Jacobsen's friend William Brooks came up behind him and shot him in the back. Brooks then went into the house and shot himself. Jim Hill is buried in the Elks Tract, Anchorage Memorial Park.

———

On February 20, 1921, just two years prior to the shooting of Marshal Hill, Chief of Police JACK STURGUS was found shot to death in the alley in the rear of the Anchorage Drug Store. Evidence showed that some sort of altercation took place at the scene and that Jack was disarmed and shot with his own revolver.

Jack was born December 24, 1861 in Mansfield, Ohio. He came west and lived for many years in Montana where he acted as a peace officer and later in Everett, Washington, working in the same capacity. He came to Anchorage in 1916 after participating in the Shushana gold rush in 1913 and was employed as special United States Deputy until his appointment as Anchorage Chief of Police. He is buried in the Elks Tract, Anchorage Memorial Park Cemetery.

———

More old timers have left their mark one way or another in Anchorage, not politically, socially or financially, but just by being here and maybe building their home here, or opening a store, or cutting the brush on C Street hill, or grading 4th Avenue, or digging the sewer and water lines, or installing the telephone poles and wire, all of which was necessary to develop a community. Many lived and died here, and their only legacy is a granite marker in the Cemetery that says, "I was here."

One of the old timers was FRANK W. REDWOOD, who was born in New Zealand and landed in Alaska in 1900. He first went to Nome and participated in the mining game for several years prior to coming to Anchorage in 1915. In 1916 Frank built the Crescent Hotel on the southeast corner of 4th Avenue and C Street. He operated it for over ten years and then sold the hotel to Jack Collins in 1926. It was later sold to Harry Lane, who renamed it the Lane Hotel. Frank was living on A. A. Shonbeck's ranch in Palmer and passed away in the Palmer hospital in 1939. He is buried in the Elks Tract in an unmarked grave in Anchorage Memorial Park.

P. O. SUNDBERG was another early entrepreneur who arrived on the Alaska scene in 1894. He was widely known throughout all of Alaska, from the Juneau mines to Shushana to Iditarod, Fairbanks and Valdez. He arrived in Anchorage in the spring of 1915 and immediately set up shop in the grocery business. He opened and operated the co-op store on 4th Avenue and D Street and another on 4th Avenue and H Street. He eventually combined both stores into one at the 4th and D site. He was born in 1860 and passed away in Anchorage in 1924. He is buried in an unmarked grave in Tract 12, Anchorage Memorial Park.

MARY WEVER was Anchorage's first librarian and served the community for over twenty-two years. Mary was born on a ranch in California in 1876. Nothing is known of her early life, other than she was living in Seattle, Washington when she met attorney Robert L. Wever. They were married in Seattle in 1917 and two years later moved to Seward, where Mr. Wever accepted employment doing clerical work for the AEC and the Alaska Railroad. In 1922 Robert was transferred to Anchorage with the Railroad, and they remained here for the rest of their lives.

Mary started the first library in this city in 1923. She started out by loaning books to people without charge, and her collection was made possible through donations. When the public library was opened in 1925, Mary was made librarian and served in that capacity until 1944. Robert passed away in 1940, and Mary died in 1945. They are both buried in the Masonic Tract in Anchorage Memorial Park Cemetery.

Prior to coming to Anchorage OSCAR BERGMAN was engaged in mining in various places throughout the Territory. In 1913 he and JENNY LIND were married in Tanana. They moved to Anchorage in 1916 where Oscar was employed by the AEC as section foreman on the early railroad construction. They later moved to Wasilla where Oscar continued to hold the position of section foreman. Jenny passed away in February 1938, and Oscar died in April of the same year. They had five children, however very little is known of their whereabouts. Both Oscar and Jenny are buried in the Masonic Tract, Anchorage Memorial Park Cemetery.

NELS T. GILBERTSON was born in Ada, Minnesota in 1887. Nels joined the Alaska Railroad in 1919 and was employed by the Railroad for almost twenty years. He initially came to the Anchorage area in 1917 and worked on various construction projects with private contractors before joining the ARR. He passed away in November of 1936 and is buried in the Elks Tract, Anchorage Memorial Park Cemetery.

MAURICE L. SHARP was born in Indiana in 1898 and came to Anchorage in 1919 to work for the AEC as a chemist. He retired to Ft. Wayne, Indiana after twenty-five years with the ARR. He was a WWI veteran and was the first Commander of the Alaska Post Consolidated of the American Legion and president of the first Anchorage Camera Club. As an entertainer, Maurice was among the first to perform on the Ice Worm Amateur Radio program on KFQD in the early days of Anchorage radio, along with Bert Wennerstrom and his group. Maurice was killed in an auto accident in Ft. Wayne, Indiana in 1950 and is presumably buried there.

HARRY I. STASER was born in Newburg, Indiana in 1891. Harry entered Canada via Haines, Alaska on his way to Dawson in 1908. A young man still in his teens, he was determined to reach the gold fields of the Klondike. After his arrival in Dawson City, he met a man named Stevenson, and together they took a freighting contract to deliver supplies via dog team to the mounted police station on Herschel Island.

The following year Harry returned to Indiana for a short period then returned to Alaska via Valdez. He hiked the Valdez trail to Fairbanks, and it was there that he met BARBARA dePENCIER. Barbara was born in Colfax, Washington and had come to Dawson with her mother in 1899. During their sojourn in Dawson, Barbara and her mother, Jane, opened a small ladies ready-to-wear shop. The big rush was petering out in Dawson, so Barbara and her mother moved down-river to Fairbanks in 1903.

While in Fairbanks Barbara married a riverboat captain named Green, and they moved down to Iditarod during the 1910 rush. Here a daughter, Jean, was born in 1912, and shortly thereafter they returned to Fairbanks where the marriage between Green and Barbara was annulled.

Harry Staser

Barbara Staser

Harry again met Barbara, and they were married in Reno, Nevada in 1916. World War I was going strong, and the United States was becoming more involved. So, Harry and Barbara moved to Ft. Lewis, Washington, where Harry joined the Army. He served overseas with the 13th Infantry Division as a First Sergeant in a heavy machine gun company.

After WWI the couple moved to the new city of Anchorage in 1919. Harry was hired on as superintendent of the railroad material yard that same year.

He then built a log cabin at the corner of
7th Avenue and D Street to accommodate
his family, now composed of daughter
Jean and two sons born in Anchorage. In
1923 he left the employ of the Railroad
and was appointed Deputy United States
Marshal for Anchorage, serving in that
capacity until 1933. In 1926 Harry
acquired a hard rock gold prospect named
the Monarch Mine on Crow Creek adjacent to
Girdwood and began mining operations there.

U.S. Marshal Office and
Jail

Home, 7th Avenue and D
Street

In 1935 Barbara, son Bruce and son Beverly were
involved in a serious auto accident, which left Barbara
paralyzed. Harry suffered a massive heart attack at the
mine and died in 1940. Barbara passed away in 1952.
Harry is buried in the Masonic Tract, Anchorage
Memorial Park. Barbara is buried in Los Angeles.

Jeanne Staser

Beverly
Staser

Bruce Staser

Son Beverly and spouse had three children. Gail Lynn lives in Oak Harbor, Washington;
Gregory John and Barry Dwight live in Anchorage. Son Bruce had three children. Merry Ann
lives in Oak Harbor, Washington; Jeffrey Bruce lives in Alexandria, Virginia; and John R.
lives in Anchorage, Alaska.

EDWARD A. RASMUSON was born in Copenhagen, Denmark, April 15, 1882. He
came to the United States at the age of nineteen and was naturalized in Minneapolis,
Minnesota. He enrolled in the Minehaha Academy in Minneapolis, and after graduation
he accepted the position of assistant Swedish Covenant missionary of Yakutat, Alaska. It
was in Yakutat he met JENNY OLSEN, who was born in Varmland, Sweden in 1880. She
was a Christian education worker in
Yakutat, and she and Edward were
married in 1905. Edward took charge
as a missionary after their marriage.

They left Alaska in 1912, visited
Sweden, and upon their return went to
Minneapolis where Edward invested his
savings to purchase a block of homes,
which he sold to finance the study of
law. After Edward passed the Minnesota
bar, they moved to Juneau where he
studied under District Judge Jennings.
They then moved to Skagway where he

Edward A. Rasmuson

Jenny Rasmuson

Rasmuson Family

Elmer Rasmuson

Bank of Alaska, 1916

Evangeline Atwood

was appointed United States Commissioner. When the Bank of Alaska was organized, he became the corporate attorney, and in 1917 he was named the bank President.

In addition to operating branches in Anchorage, Skagway, Cordova and Wrangell, Edward established the First National Bank of Ketchikan. In the 1930's the Cordova branch became independent, and the Wrangell bank was separated from the Bank of Alaska. Edward became President of that bank upon his retirement.

Edward served as Swedish consul for many years and was knighted by the King of Sweden in 1937. He also served as the Republican National Committeeman for Alaska for sixteen years. Edward died in 1949 in Minneapolis, and Jenny died in 1966. Jenny is buried in the Pioneer Tract, Anchorage Memorial Park Cemetery, and Edward is buried in Minneapolis, Minnesota.

The marriage of Edward and Jenny produced two children: Evangeline Rasmuson Atwood, born in Sitka and passed away in 1987, and Elmer E. Rasmuson, born in Yakutat. Son Elmer E. Rasmuson and spouse Lile Rasmuson had three children. Edward B. lives in Anchorage; Lile Muchmore Gibbons lives in Greewich, Connecticut; and Judy Ann lives in Clinton, Connecticut. Daughter Evangeline Rasmuson Atwood had two daughters: Marilyn Atwood Odom who passed away, and Elaine Atwood who resides in Anchorage.

WILLIAM DAVID MCKINNEY was born February 7, 1901 in Sulphur Wells, Kentucky. He left home at an early age and joined the United States Army. While in the service, he punched his sergeant in the nose and was given the choice of a dishonorable discharge or service in Alaska. He chose Alaska. He first arrived in Chilkoot barracks, Haines, Alaska in 1918. Bill, as he was known, was a bugler and was soon transferred to Anchorage where the military detachment was in need of one.

In Anchorage he met ALICE LOFTQUIST. Alice had come to Anchorage with her parents in 1915 from her birthplace of Portland, Oregon. Alice's father, CARL LOFTQUIST, built the first rooming house in Anchorage, called the Kenai Hotel. It was located on the north side of 4th Avenue between B and C Streets. Mrs. Loftquist operated the hotel while Carl plied his trade as plumber. Mrs. Loftquist passed away in 1929, and Carl passed away in Portland, Oregon a short time later. He is buried in Portland, Oregon, and Mrs. Loftquist is buried in Tract 3, Anchorage Memorial Park Cemetery.

Bill and Alice were married in Anchorage in 1920 and were one of two couples married in Anchorage that year. In 1970 they received recognition from the Mayor as part of the commemoration of the 50th Anniversary of Anchorage. The couple lived in various locations prior to owning their own home. In 1929 Bill acquired a new truck and, with partner Jerry Sigmund, started the Federal Transfer Company, doing general hauling including coal and wood.

For a period of time Bill worked for the Alaska Railroad at Moose Creek and Girdwood. He next located on the McCain Ranch, located on Spenard Road near Deadmans Curve, and tried a hand at raising turkeys, which was unsuccessful because a loose dog killed all of the birds. In the meanwhile his family kept growing, and he needed steady employment. He was offered a job with the Railroad again, this time in the mechanical department shops. He then worked as relief man in the fire department and in a matter of years worked his way up to being Railroad fire chief.

In 1934 Bill acquired a homestead at Fireweed Lane that ran from Arctic Boulevard to B Street. A cabin on the homestead became their new home, and they constantly kept improving the home and property. He became active over the years in helping to develop the Spenard Volunteer Fire Department. He was

Amelia Loftquist

Carl Loftquist

Homestead Home

Kenai Hotel

Bugler, W. D. McKinney, Sr.

Alice and Wiliam McKinney, Sr.

McKinney Family

Latest Home

elected to the board of the first Anchorage Independent School District.

Bill retired from the Railroad in 1952 after twenty-seven years of government service. Not one to remain idle, he started a landscaping business and operated it for ten years. In 1962 he sold out his business, and he and Alice moved to Forest Grove, Oregon. Alice died in 1971 in Oregon, and soon after her death Bill moved to Scottsburg, Indiana to be with his widowed sisters. He passed away in the Veterans Hospital in Portland, Oregon in 1995 at the age of ninety-five.

Bill and Alice had five children and fifteen grandchildren. Son William, Jr. and spouse Thelma had seven children. Mary Cooper lives in Palmer; William III, Michael, Mark, Brian, Richard and Daniel all live in Anchorage. Daughter Eva and spouse Ed Snyder had three children. Thomas III, William and John all live in Anchorage. Eva passed away in 1980. Daughter Clara and spouse John Robinson had three children. Connie Robinson Bruhn and John, Jr. live in Anchorage; Bonnie Robinson Spier lives in Tacoma, Washington. John Robinson, Sr. died in 1998. Son Herbert McKinney and spouse had two sons, Lee and David, both living in Anchorage. Daughter Shirley McKinney Briggs Clark had no children.

LOUIS STRUTZ was born in Oaks, North Dakota on January 7, 1897. When he was two, his family moved to Montesano, Washington, where he spent his youth. He played the tuba in the Montesano Band. On March 28, 1917 he joined the United States Army, giving his occupation as a musician. After the end of WWI he was assigned to Anchorage, Alaska, arriving here on November 5, 1919 with Company B, 21st Infantry.

After his discharge, Louis felt that Anchorage would be a good place to live and asked the love of his life, ALINE SAWHILL, to join him. Aline was born on the Tyler Ranch in Nimrod, Montana, July 16, 1899. She attended elementary and high schools in Nimrod and Blakely, Montana and business college at Missoula and Thompson Falls, Montana. She was employed by the division storekeeper of the Northern Pacific Railroad in Parkwater, Washington, and it was there that she met Louis Strutz. Aline and Louis were married in the Presbyterian Church in Anchorage on April 12, 1920.

Louis started a dairy farm with fourteen cows and five hundred chickens. He purchased a home and property at 516 P Street and, with the family increasing in size, he sold off the farm animals and went to work for the Alaska Railroad from 1926 to 1941. He then went to work for the Northern Commercial Company until his retirement in 1962. Louis was not only kept busy at work and at home, but still found time to play the tuba and drums in the local Anchorage Band.

Louis Strutz

Aline Strutz

Aline kept busy raising six children, caring for the large vegetable garden, and living a true subsistence life, canning salmon, vegetables and fruits. The children all had their chores to help out. Aline had many hobbies; however, her favorite was collecting and photographing Alaska wild flowers. She visited many areas seeking wild plants and transplanted them in her yard. She eventually collected over two thousand specimens. She wrote articles for gardening journals and contributed to rock and garden bulletins in the United States as well as in Britain. Many of her photos were published in the *Alaska-Yukon Wild Flower Guide*. As a member of the Anchorage Garden Club, she participated in all of the flower shows, winning many honors. A plant variety named after her is the "Artemisia Campestris borealis, H & G var. strutzea Welsh." After her death Aline was honored by the Legislature, citing her many accomplishments and contributions to the State, with her strong pioneer spirit and dedication in helping to make Alaska the great land that it is.

Original Home

Aline in Garden

The 1964 earthquake severely damaged their home and grounds, but they faced the challenge of restoration and turned the rubble into an attractive home and garden, which was on the local home and garden tour for many years. The home is still standing, however is no longer owned by the family.

Home After Earthquake, 1964

The union of Aline and Louis Strutz produced six children, twenty-six grandchildren, sixty-two great-grandchildren and seven great-great-grandchildren. Louis Strutz died February 22, 1977 at the age of eighty, and Aline died on November 12, 1995 at the age of ninety-six. They are both buried in the Pioneer Tract of Anchorage Memorial Park Cemetery.

Clella, Jo Ann and Gayle Strutz

Daughter Clella Lou Strutz Fowler had two children. Janis Aline Fowler Bradbury lives in Chandler, Arizona; Richard William lives in Arlington, Texas. Daughter Jo Ann Strutz Nattress bore three children. Michael lives in Edgewater, Florida; Gregory lives in Fremont, Nebraska; and Penny Nattress Brandt lives in Bellevue, Washington. Daughter Gayle Strutz Ryan had four children. Timothy and Joseph live in Oroville, California; Mary Ann Ryan Edwards lives in Sacramento, California; and Abigail Ryan Hensley lives in Fairfax Station, Virginia. Daughter Ermalee Strutz Hickel had six children. Theodore J. lives in Portland, Oregon; Robert J., Walter, Jr., Jack E., Joseph W. and Karl all live in Anchorage, Alaska. Son Lloyd Louis Strutz had four children. Sharon Lou lives in Anchorage; Debora Jean Strutz Studnek lives in Girdwood; William Louis and Margaret Ann Strutz Hanrath live in Anchorage. Son Richard Kenneth Strutz had seven children. Richard, James Paul, Colleen Halsey and Cindy Ann Lamson all live in Anchorage; Marie Ray Scouler lives in Salt Lake City, Utah; and Ronda Lee Strutz Martens lives in Sitka, Alaska.

Ermalee, Lloyd and Richard Strutz

DAN, SR. and CATHERINE KENNEDY were early arrivals in Alaska during the 1850's. They spent most of their lives in southeast Alaska, primarily in the Juneau and Sitka areas. Dan, Sr. passed away early in life, and Catherine spent her last years in Anchorage, living with her son Dan, Jr. until her death in 1935.

Dan and Catherine had four sons: James, Dan, George and John. James was born in Juneau in 1881, and Dan was born in Sitka in 1884. Both of these brothers lived in various parts of southeast Alaska including Skagway, Cordova and Ketchikan. In 1919 both Dan and James arrived in Anchorage and opened a haberdashery store on 4th Avenue and E Street adjacent to Hewitts Photo.

James died in 1934 in Seattle after a short illness. He and his spouse had two daughters: Frances Kennedy Truitt of Juneau, and Catherine Kennedy Poland Silides, who presently resides in the Pioneer Home in Anchorage.

After the death of James, brother Dan moved across 4th Avenue and opened the clothing store known as the Hub Clothing. Dan passed away in 1944 while visiting Circle Hot Springs. He was married to Gertrude Watson, the daughter of Charles and Grace Watson, also original Anchorage and Alaska Pioneers. Charles Watson was a former United States Deputy Marshal in Anchorage. Gertrude was a schoolteacher and taught in various places on the railbelt. Gertrude passed away in 1953 in Anchorage. She was born in Whitehorse in 1903. Dan and Gertrude had no children. They are both buried in the Catholic Tract, Anchorage Memorial Park.

George Kennedy arrived in Anchorage in the early 1920's, along with his brother John. George opened a hardware store on 4th Avenue and D Street and was highly successful. He was a tall, gangly, cigar-chewing glad-hander and was most popular on 4th Avenue as a practical joker. George had a favorite term he used on all of his friends. If he called you "asmodius," you were accepted. If he didn't call you "asmodius," it meant you were not accepted in his group as yet.

When WWII arrived George sold out of the hardware business and moved to Seattle. A few years later he and Jack Waterworth opened a hardware store in the Seattle area. George was killed in an auto accident sometime in the 50's in Seattle and is presumably buried in Seattle. He was married but had no children. John Kennedy worked for George and Dan during their years in Anchorage. It is unknown where John died and where he is buried. John never married. There is much more history somewhere on the Kennedys, however finding any family survivors is difficult if not impossible.

THE FIRST HIGH SCHOOL GRADUATES

Three boys and three girls graduated in the first Anchorage High School class of 1919.

HELEN NIEMI, who became Helen Carlquist, with her husband had several businesses in Anchorage. They eventually bought out the Eckman Furniture store and operated successfully for many years. Helen was a member of the Pioneer Niemi family. LOIS PRICE was the daughter of Mr. and Mrs. Tom Price. Mr. Price was the United States Commissioner and also magistrate of Anchorage. Lois married Doctor Arthur D. Haverstock and lived in Seward and Anchorage. MARGARET SIMONSON was a member of the Pioneer Simonson family and was married to Al Monsen, well-known Alaska bush pilot and later Pan American Captain. ARTHUR FRODENBERG and his wife opened Sally's Sweet Shop on 4th Avenue

Anchorage High School, 1919, on 5th Avenue Between F and G Streets

between G and H Streets. They remained in Anchorage until the early 1940's. Little or nothing is known of KEITH DENTON and his family. Presumably they left Anchorage in the late twenties, however it is unknown where they settled. CLARENCE THATCHER

Keith Denton

Art Frodenburg

worked for the Alaska Railroad as a locomotive engineer. He lived in Anchorage and Seward. Clarence was a well-known baseball player in Anchorage and played on various teams here. He passed away suddenly in Seward in February 1951 at the age of fifty. He presumably is buried in Seward.

Margaret Simonson

Helen Niemi

Lois Price

Clarence Thatcher

Anchorage School, 1922

CHAPTER III

1920

The year 1920 was a memorable one in the history of Anchorage. It was the year that the city became legally incorporated, elected a Mayor and a City Council, and took on the daily functions of municipal government. The first City Council meeting was held on November 26, 1920, and the minutes of this meeting were as follows:

> The first regular meeting of the councilmen of the City of Anchorage, Anchorage, Alaska, was held at seven-o-clock P.M. November 26th, 1920, at a place known as the townsite office.
>
> Those present were: Leopold David, Frank I. Reed, John J. Longacre, Isadore Bayles, D. H. Williams, A. C. Craig and Ralph N. Moyer, all of whom were properly sworn in before Judge Lindley Green, Notary Public in and for the Territory of Alaska.
>
> By unanimous vote, Leopold David was elected president of the Council and Ex-Officio Mayor of Anchorage. R. N. Moyer was designated as temporary Clerk.

Leopold David, Mayor 1920

> By unanimous vote of the council, the regular meeting time of the council was set for Wednesday of each week at the hour of 7:30 P.M. [Taken from City Council archives Loussac Library.] The council thereupon adjourned, signed by R. N. Moyer, Temporary Clerk.

LEOPOLD DAVID was therefore elected first Mayor of Anchorage, and Judge Fred M. Brown signed the necessary papers declaring Anchorage an incorporated city on November 20, 1920. The population of the new city of Anchorage was eighteen hundred fifty-six people. The incorporation election vote was three hundred twenty-eight for and one hundred thirty against. From November 26 all new arrivals into the city of Anchorage and all who were residents prior to November 26 would be subject to the laws, rules and regulations of the new city.

The year 1920 also welcomed the second graduating class of Anchorage High School. The class consisted of three boys and three girls. To the best of my knowledge, all of the graduates of this class are deceased.

Gerald Arbuckle

Loretta Coberly

Esther Denton

Edna Purvis

Rasmus Simonson

William Stolt

CHARLES ALBERT BERG was born in Dalarna Province, Sweden in 1871. He came to the United States in 1882 with his parents, who settled in Lake Park, Minnesota. He first entered Alaska in 1906 at Valdez, where he went over the Valdez trail to Fairbanks. He left Fairbanks for Nome in 1908, and in 1910 he landed in Iditarod after pretty well covering most of the major gold camps at the time.

In 1915 he moved down to Susitna Station, where he bought a small sawmill from Oscar Gill. At Susitna Station he met PHOEBE JANE NAGLEY, and after a short courtship they traveled to Knik via dogteam and were married there by the Rev. T. P. Howard. Phoebe was born in Anacortes, Washington in 1884 and grew up in Marysville and Cashmere, Washington. She attended normal school in Ellensburg and Bellingham and became a teacher. She came to Susitna Station in 1915 to help her brother H. W. Nagley in the operation of his store.

Ora Dee Clark had a contract with the B.I.A. to teach school at Susitna Station; however, she was offered the job to teach in Anchorage, and prevailed upon Phoebe to take over the Susitna School. Ora Dee held a master's degree and was qualified to organize the school system in Anchorage, which she preferred to do.

Charles and Phoebe Berg

Home on L Street

In 1916 Charles moved his sawmill to Talkeetna where he took on a contract to cut ties for the Railroad. In 1920 the family moved to Anchorage and built their home at 647 L Street. Charles operated sawmills at Caswell, Indian and Portage during the railroad construction days.

The marriage of Charles and Phoebe produced three children. Daughter Virginia and spouse Earl Lagergren had four children, all living in Washington.

Earl and Virginia Lagergren

Virginia as Miss Alaska

Berg Family

Eric lives in Port Orchard; Edward lives in Olympia; and Arne and Jane M. live in Seattle. Son Carl Albert Berg and spouse Elsena had one daughter, Kimberly Chris Berg, who lives in Anchorage. Daughter Frances Mary Berg Snow had four children. Sandra Louise is now deceased; Geoffrey Eugene lives in Seattle, Washington; John Palmer lives in Anchorage, Alaska; and Judith Eileen lives in Enumclaw, Washington. Charles Albert Berg died in 1959 in Seattle, Washington, and Phoebe Jane Berg died in 1993 in Renton, Washington at the age of one hundred nine.

Francis Snow

Mary and Carl Berg

In the same month that the Charles Berg family arrived, BARTLEY HOWARD moved to Anchorage from Cordova. Bartley was born in Fordsville, Kentucky in 1878. He first arrived in Alaska in 1903, settling in Eagle for a period of time. He then returned to Kentucky and in 1907 came back to Alaska and settled in Cordova, where he started and operated a construction business. He later was employed by the Copper River and Northwestern Railway until 1920, when he moved to Anchorage.

Bartley first came to Anchorage for the specific purpose of building the Elks home on 3rd Avenue and G Street. After he completed the Elks building, he remained in Anchorage and was employed by the ARR as superintendent of buildings and bridges. After he supervised the construction of the Curry Hotel for the ARR, he was employed as manager of the Alaska Matanuska Coal Corporation at Moose Creek until the mine was flooded out in 1933. In 1925 Bartley won a seat in the Territorial Senate and served until 1929 when he became associated with the Juneau Lumber Company for a short time. His final employment was with the Ketchikan Lumber Mills in Anchorage.

Bartley married EMMA MILLER in Fordsville, Kentucky in 1931 and brought her to

Bartley and Emma Howard

Henry and Elsie Sogn

Anchorage that same year. The Howards had one daughter, Ophelia, who married Dr. Harold Sogn, the son of another Pioneer Anchorage family. HENRY SOGN, Harold's father, was born in Iowa in 1874. The family moved to South Dakota in his early years, and there he spent his early youth. In 1898 Henry made his first venture to the north country and joined the gold rush to the Valdez mining district.

With three partners, he arrived in Valdez in 1898 and proceeded to pack over the Valdez Glacier and up the Copper River. The partners built four boats from the native trees, whipsawing trees to make lumber for the boats. They reached the head of the Klutina River in the fall, which was too late to do any prospecting. They then returned to the village of Copper Center, where it was decided that Sogn and another man would return to Valdez to resupply their camp so they could prepare for the spring mining. Sogn and his partner each took one boat and headed down river for Valdez. His partner never made it, so Sogn sent word to the other partners in Copper Center to come to Valdez. They never showed up, and he therefore left for South Dakota and joined the Railway Mail Service.

In 1920 Henry convinced his wife that there was still gold in Alaska, and they set out for the west coast and Alaska. While in Seattle he injured his foot in a fall from a dock, and the injury turned out to be permanent. This then prevented his going to the gold fields, so they decided to settle in the new city of Anchorage. Upon their arrival in Anchorage, he went to work for the ARR for one year and then was appointed assistant postmaster. He served as postmaster for eight years thereafter and in 1932 went into private business as a real estate and insurance agent.

ELSIE DAVIS was born in Beresford, South Dakota in 1883. She came north with her husband Henry in 1920 and was active in the community affairs of the day as well as being an officer of the Pioneer Auxiliary and a supporter of the Womans Club.

Henry and Elsie had one son, Harold E. Sogn. Harold studied medicine and received his degree from Columbia University in New York City in 1937. He returned to Anchorage and opened his practice here in 1940. He, along with Z. J. Loussac, built one of the first permanent office buildings in Anchorage and aptly named it the Loussac Sogn Building, which still remains on the corner of 5th Avenue and D Street.

Harold and Ophelia had three children. Son Harold H. lives in Anacortes, Washington and is a retired dentist; daughter Kristin passed away in 2001; daughter Karen Feek lives in Bellevue, Washington.

Harold E. Sogn

Ophelia Sogn and Son Harold

Daughters, Kristin Sogn and Karen Feek

Bartley Howard died in 1941, and Emma Howard died in 1950. Elsie Sogn died in 1951, and Henry S. Sogn died in 1952. They are all buried in the Masonic Tract, Anchorage Memorial Park Cemetery. Harold E. Sogn died in 1954, and Ophelia died in 1982. They are both buried in Angelus Memorial Park in Anchorage.

MARTIN and MATTIE LECKWOLD were two of the first homesteaders in the Matanuska Valley in 1913. Martin was born in Oxdal Selbu, Norway in 1972 and came to America with his parents at the age of four. The family settled in Minnesota, and Martin lived there until he got the urge to travel. Mattie Culbertson was born in Clarissa, Minnesota in 1892, and it was there that she met Martin and was destined to be his wife.

When Martin achieved manhood he traveled west to Washington where he was employed in the Bremerton Navy Yard. He served in the Spanish American War in 1898, and when the war ended he went to Alaska in 1909. In 1910 he returned to Minnesota where he and Mattie were married that same year. In 1913 he returned to Alaska alone and homesteaded in the Matanuska Valley. In 1914 Mattie joined him on the homestead and kept herself busy as the first postmistress in the Matanuska area. Martin was employed as a black-smith with the ARR until they moved to Anchorage in 1920.

Martin continued to work for the ARR until his sudden death in 1935. He passed away in the Marine Veterans Hospital in Seattle and is buried in the Veterans Cemetery near Bremerton, Washington. His sudden passing left Mattie as sole support of the family. She was employed in various capacities with the Railroad until her retirement to the Pioneers Home in Palmer in 1969, where she passed away in 1978.

Mattie and Martin Leckwold

Marcella Leckwold

Harry Leckwold

Weldon Leckwold

Martin and Mattie had three children, Marcella, Harry and Weldon. The Leckwold grandchildren, sons and daughters of Harry and Barbara, live in various parts of the country. Brian lives in Middleburg, Florida; David lives in Brighton, Colorado; Sandra Handley lives in Vancouver, Washington; and Laurie Wilson lives in Wasilla, Alaska.

Last Home, Now Marx
Brothers Restaurant

Home on 3rd Avenue

A former miner from Nevada arrived in Anchorage in 1920 to work in the construction of the tunnels on the Alaska Railroad. He was ARTHUR M. LeCOUMP, and he was employed with the ARR from 1921 to 1943. After the completion of the Railroad he became the heating plant fireman until his retirement.

In his spare time Art dabbled in real estate and built several homes and apartments in Anchorage. He had liquidated all of his properties at the time of retirement in preparation for moving to Seattle.

While driving his car to Valdez to ship it via Alaska Steam to Seattle, he had a head on collision with a truck in Thompson Pass and was killed instantly. His wife, Agnes, had preceded him to Seattle and was in Wisconsin caring for a sick parent when the accident occurred. He was killed in September 1944, and Agnes Sedy LeCoump passed away in California in 1987. Both Agnes and Art are buried in the Masonic Tract, Anchorage Memorial Park.

Frank Martin

FRANK H. MARTIN, ROSE MARTIN and son FRANK R. MARTIN arrived in Anchorage in 1915. The senior Martin worked for the Alaska Engineering Commission as a private cook for Colonel Mears, who was the chief engineer of the AEC. The family resided in Anchorage for three years when Frank R. enlisted in the Army at the advent of WWI.

Frank R. Martin married JEANNE MARIE CAMBRET in France in 1919 and came directly to Anchorage in 1920 after his discharge. Frank was eventually employed as a brakeman on the ARR. A daughter Francine was born in Anchorage in 1920, and the family made their home at 910 I Street. Some years were spent in Curry on the ARR where Jeanne was employed as a cook for the Curry section crew.

5th Avenue Looking west

House at 910 I Street

Francine and Wesley
Skogsbergh

Frank R. Martin was born in Stampede, Washington in 1888 and
died in Rochester, Minnesota in 1934. Jean Marie Cambret Martin
was born in Anncey, France in 1901 and passed away in 1998 in
Renton, Washington. Francine married Wesley Skogsbergh, and
they had four children, all living in Washington. Lee Martin lives in
Seattle; Garry lives in Tukwila; Karen Washington and Craig Skogsbergh
live in Snohomish.

More professional people--educators, doctors, lawyers and politicians--were arriving in the frontier city to start or expand a career. One such person was Doctor
CLAYTON A. POLLARD, a dentist from Colorado. Clayton Pollard was born in
Mexico, Missouri in 1887. The family of seven boys moved to Cordele, Texas where
he was raised. Part of the family moved to New Mexico and Clayton went to Colorado, wherᵒe he
entered dental college in 1910. He resided in Colorado after completing his dental training, and in 1919
he was married in Cedar Edge, Colorado. His wife passed away of pneumonia less than one month after
they were married.

Jean Marie Martin

In 1920 Dr. Pollard came to Anchorage and opened a
dental office. Using Anchorage as his base of operations,
he traveled all around the Territory on a government contract with the B.I.A., tending to the dental needs of the
Alaska Natives and Eskimos. He later went into partnership with Lawlor W. Seeley and opened a dental practice
in the McKinley Building on 4th Avenue and D Street.

In 1928 Clayton, Alfred Benson, Tom Price, Bob
Romig, Tom Bevers, Emil Pfeil, Bill Murray, E. R.
Tarwater, Ray Mathison, Art LaRue, Matt Raich
and Scotty Allen formed a company called
Anchorage Fur Farm Association. It was a mink

Pollard Ranch in Kasilof

Lucy and Clayton
Pollard

Clayton Pollard and Son,
George

Clay Pollard and His
Mother, Lucy

ranch located on eight acres owned by Clayton on what is now 10th Avenue and M Street.

Clayton served on the Anchorage City Council for three years during the 1920's. He purchased a ranch in Kasilof where the family spent the summers, and in 1946 he closed his dental office and moved permanently to Kasilof and lived on the ranch. He served as a representative for the 3rd Judicial District in the Territorial Legislature in the regular session in 1945 and the special session in 1946 and was re-elected on the democratic ticket in 1946.

LUCY MAY MATTSON was born in Lake Crystal, Minnesota in 1889. Lucy entered Bible College in Iowa and upon completion of her studies was sent to the Baptist Orphanage on Woody Island near Kodiak. There she met Clayton Pollard, and they were married in Anchorage in 1923. Two sons were born of this union, and the family resided in Anchorage until 1946 when they all moved to Kasilof.

Clayton Pollard passed away in 1960 and is buried in the Kasilof Cemetery. Lucy moved to Redondo Beach, California in 1965, and in 1972 she moved to San Pedro, California where she died in 1978. Son Clayton J. became a teacher and librarian and lives in San Pedro, California. Son George became a Licensed Alaska Guide and still lives on the ranch in Kasilof.

An early athlete who captured the hearts of the local baseball fans, JOHN VICTOR NELSON was born in Ridgeway, Pennsylvania in 1896. He arrived in Anchorage to be a mine inspector for the United States Bureau of Mines at the Eska Mine on Moose Creek. He met his spouse, HULDA CAMPBELL, in Anchorage in 1921, and they were married in Seward in 1922. Hulda was born in East St. Louis, Illinois in 1897. She came to Anchorage to visit a friend, and the visit turned into many years after she met "Vic" Nelson.

Vic Nelson

Hulda Nelson

Vic and Hulda Nelson

Ball Team

After the Eska Mine closed down, they moved to Anchorage, and Vic was employed by the Alaska Railroad as chief timekeeper until his retirement in 1951. During the years in Anchorage Vic was well known as a baseball player. His specialty was pitching, and many in Anchorage considered him one of Alaska's greats of baseball. He was honored at the Centennial All Sports Banquet in 1967 and received an award for his past activities on behalf of baseball.

John Victor Nelson

Joan Wahto

James Nelson

Vic and Hulda moved to Homer after his retirement and remained there until Vic passed away in 1968. Hulda died in 1994. Vic is buried in the Pioneer Tract of Anchorage Memorial Park Cemetery. Hulda had her ashes scattered over Kachemak Bay.

Home on Government Hill

Vic and Hulda had three children. John Victor never married and lives in Anchorage. James R. never married and passed away in 1981. Joan Nelson Wahto and spouse Gordon Wahto had three children. David lives in Anchorage, Cody Sontag lives in Shoreline, Washington, and Susan T. Rivers lives in Salem, Oregon.

———

ARNE SIMON KRISTOFER ERICKSON was a Norwegian import who spent his life in the mining game in Iditarod and on Crow Creek. He was born in Bergen, Norway in 1887. He immigrated to the United States in 1909 and almost directly proceeded to Fairbanks in search of the elusive gold. He prospected around Fairbanks for approximately one year until the strike in Iditarod caught his fancy. In 1910 he proceeded to Iditarod and was prospecting near the Dave Strandberg property near discovery on Otter Creek. There he met **JOSEPHINE JOHANNSON**, who had come to Iditarod and Flat in 1913 to visit her sister, Jennie Strandberg. Arne and Josephine were married in Flat in 1913 and remained there until 1920. Josephine was born in Malmo, Sweden in 1888 and immigrated to the United States in 1910, spending a year in Tacoma, Washington prior to her visit to her sister in Flat.

Arne and Josephine had two sons, and in 1920 Arne sent them "outside," as the mining camps of Flat and Iditarod were losing population due to the decrease in

John Erickson

Arne at Strand-berg Mine

Hans Erickson

Erickson Family

Josephine and Arne Erickson

mining. In late October 1920 Arne and a friend, referred to only as Oscar, proceeded to "mush" over the Iditarod trail from Flat to Anchorage. What follows is the Arne's actual diary from the day he started out on October 28, 1920 until he finished in Anchorage on November 18, 1920. This diary testifies to the hardiness of these pioneers who thought nothing of walking three hundred fifty miles from Flat to Anchorage. The settlements of Flat, Flat City, Iditarod and Discovery all are within four miles of each other, and the four names refer to nearly the same location.

Diary of Arne Erickson from Flat Creek to Anchorage, Alaska by way of the Iditarod Trail. Nothing is changed, including punctuation and spelling. Permission to relate this was given by Arne's granddaughter, Marjorie A. McConnell.

Oct. 28, 1920
Oscar and I brought down the rest of our stuff from the Up Grade and left that claim for good. Was up to Dave Strandberg's for supper. Left his house at about 9 A. M. and went to bed at Abe Weiss.

First day out. Oct. 29
Started for the outside. Fine weather. Left Flat at twelve noon. Stopped in at Mrs. Harms and Jim Farrells. Had a cup of coffe and left Jims at l0 minutes to 1 P.M. Got to Ruby roadhouse at 6:30 P.M. Good road but pack pretty heavy and my shoulder is awful sore. 16 miles from Otter. [Note Otter Creek and Flat are synonymous.]

Second day out. Oct 30
Started from Ruby roadhouse 7:30 A.M. Stopped for lunch 8 miles out. Got to Moore Creek 9 P.M. Pretty tough going. Had to snowshoe about half way. 22 miles from Ruby roadhouse.

Third day out. Oct. 31, 1920
Left Moore at 6:30 A.M. Lots of snow. Had to snowshoe all the way. Tough going. Started to make camp at 5 P.M. 11 miles from Moore Creek. Put pot of beans on camp fire and had supper when beans was cooked and they was burnt all to hell. Got pretty sick after eating burnt beans and went to bed under a tree. Snowing all day and night.

Fourth day out. Nov. I
Left camp at 5:30 A.M. Had some of the burnt beans. Was sick as a dog all day. Had to take a dose of salts. On the snowshoes all day. Made ten miles to Halfway House. Cooked up the last of our grub. Pretty tough house to stay in-old smoky heater. Had to sleep on table. 58 1/2 miles from Flat.

Fifth day out. Nov. 2, 1920
Left Halfway House at 7 A.M. Was on snowshoes all day. Got to Big River Roadhouse at 3 P.M. Nobody home so we had to go up river to an Indian Village. Nobody home there either. We broke into a cache and found a little flour and sugar. On our way up I shot one grouse and one ptarmigan so we will have supper tonight. Oscar is cook. 72 3/4 miles from Flat.

Sixth day out. Nov. 3, 1920
Left Indian village at 8 A.M. Got to big River at 9:30 A.M. Put on our packs and started off. Oscar and I left 2 dollars in flour sack and 1 dollar on the table for the lodging and grub. Had to snowshoe down the river about 8 miles. Nothing to eat all day. Hard going. Arrived at Takotna about 6:30 P.M. All well.

Seventh day out. Nov. 4
Layed over today. Heard it was too crowded at McGrath. Went to call on Mrs. Lowery All's well. Paid $5.00 for a two and half months subscription to Kusko Times.

Eighth day out, Nov. 5
Left Takotna at 8 A.M. Good mushing to McGrath. Got in at 2 P.M. 16 miles.

Ninth day out. Nov. 6 1920
Left McGrath at 7 A., M. Made twelve miles by noon. Had lunch and went twelve miles farther, 24 miles today. Good walking. Got in at 6 P.M. Had to sleep on floor.
[Evidently overnight at Berry.]

Tenth day out. Nov. 7
Left Berry on Big River at 7 A. M. Walked 17 miles today. Arrived Salmon Roadhouse at 1 P.M. 149 miles from Flat. Good mushing today. Had big supper and feeling fine 30 above.

Eleventh day out. Nov. 8
Left Salmon at 6:30 A. M. Mushed 12 miles. Had lunch and mushed another nine miles. Got in at Piluck at 3 P.M. in good order. Trail good, mushing fine today. No Snow.

Twelfth day out. Nov. 9 1920
Left Piluck at 6:45 A. M. Raining a little in the morning then turning into snow. Mushing fine, no snow on ground. All creeks frozen. 190 miles from Flat. Got to French Joes at 2 P.M. Twenty miles mushing today. Alls well.

Thirteenth day out. Nov. 10
Left French Joes at 6;30 A.M. Blowing to beat the band. Mushed about 19 1/2 miles. Got in at 2:30 in good shape. Mushing fine from French Joes to Davis on Rohn River. All's well.

Fourteenth day out. November 11, 1920
Left Davis at 6:40 A.M. Good walking for about nine miles up Dills Canyon She was a bad one on Rainy Pass snowing and blowing. Got to Andersons 6:20 P.M. 12 hours out, had to snowshoe from summit on down. Mushed 24 miles today. Feeling fine.

Fifteenth day out. Nov. 12 1920
Left Andersons at 6:30 A.M. Mushed 29 miles. Got in at 9 P.M. not too bad. Got in to Happy feeling fine. Paid for Oscar $6 and $4 for lunch.

Sixteenth day out. Nov. 13
Left Happy Roadhouse at 6:40 A.M. Caught up with and passed a dog team that was hauling a big shipment of gold ($150,000) from dredge at Candle Creek to Anchorage for shipment to Seattle. Had to snowshoe all the way to Mountian Climbers 21 1/2 miles. Got in at 8 P.M. Pretty tired and nobody at roadhouse and nothing to eat. Hungry as a bear. When dog team drove in I talked driver out of a small piece of reindeer meat (his dog feed). Cooked this and devided it up between six of us. Saved a bit of the broth for morning. Collected $l.00 from the boys except Oscar. Feeling fine.

Seventeenth day out. Nov. 14
Left Mountian Climbers at 6:30 A.M. Had about half a cup of reindeer soup for breakfast. Good mushing to Skwentha. Made twenty miles. Was in at Skwentha Crossing about 3 P.M. and had a big supper. Feeling fine. 295 miles from Iditarod.

Eighteenth day out. Nov. 15
Left Skwentha Crossing at 7 A.M. Got into Lake View at 3:45 P.M. Pretty wet mushing. Raining more or less all day. Been thinking about wife and kiddies. Getting closer every day. Feeling fine.

Nineteenth day out Nov. 16 1920
Left Lake View at 6 A. M. Got in to Susitna at 2:40 P.M. Was nine mushers together along the trail--not too bad. Cost $1.00 to get across the river. River broke a couple of day ago. Had a good feed when we got in. Everything in good order. Feeling fine. 335 miles from Iditarod.

Twentieth day out. Nov. 17
Left Susitna at 7 A. M. got into Little Susitna at 2:30 P.M. Wet snow half the way then turn to rain. Got pretty wet before we got in. Ate lunch we had along as roadhouse was not open. Paid $7.00 at Susitna. 353 1/2 miles from Iditarod. Feeling fine.

Twenty first day out. Nov. 18, 1920
Left Little Susitna at 7 A. M. Got to Knik at l P. M. Stopped for lunch and boat was ready to leave for Anchorage at 5:30 P.M. Every place filled up. Finally got a room at the Northern Hotel. [The Northern Hotel was located at 5th Avenue and K Street.] Bought a full suit of clothes and a grip. Paid $ l5l. 75. Also bought some fruit for $I.50. Was pretty hungry for fruit. Too late to send telegram to wife. Feeling fine. [Evidently Josephine and boys were in Seattle.]

This diary attests to the rugged individualism of these true Alaska Pioneers who let nothing stop them from their quest for gold and would hike three hundred fifty miles as if it were a common event. In 1922 Arne was hired as superintendent of the Girdwood Gold Mine. In 1930 he filed his own claim and worked the Crow Creek Mine until 1940. He was a skilled furniture maker and, during his retirement, specialized in making grandfather clocks.

One of Arne and Josephine's sons, Hans G., passed away in 1957. Hans had one daughter, Kathryn Erickson Navaille, who lives in Colton, California. Son, John A., passed away in 1971 and had three children. Arne Gerald lives in Naknek; Marjorie Anne Erickson McConnell lives in Nevada City, California; and Joan Kristine Erickson lives in Bellaire, Texas. Josephine passed away in 1955 and is buried in the Pioneer Tract, Anchorage Memorial Park. Arne remarried in 1961 and passed away in 1978 at the Fairbanks Pioneer Home. He is buried in the Fairbanks Cemetery.

After WWI many veterans found their way to Alaska and to Anchorage. They were looking for a new start in life or looking for employment at a decent wage. One of these young veterans was STEVE WILLIAM OSTRANDER. He was born in North Port, Long Island, New York. When he was one year old the family moved cross-country to Portland, Oregon where Steve grew up. He lived in foster homes during part of his youth and was raised by a Mrs. Frank Brown, whom he considered family.

House on L Street

Hazel and Steve
Ostrander

In 1914 Steve went to work in the woods out of Longview, Washington as one of the first high climbers on the Columbia River. He lived in logging camps for a number of years until he enlisted in the Navy in 1917 during WWI. When he was mustered out in Bremerton, Washington in 1919, he decided to head for Alaska. He arrived in Anchorage in 1920 and immediately went to work on the railroad dock being constructed by the AEC. He later moved into the butcher shop when the railroad commissary opened up and finally to the stores department until he retired as general storekeeper in 1955.

HAZEL ROSE TEELAND was born in Nome, Alaska in 1908, a daughter of the Pioneer John Teeland family, whose history you will find in another chapter. She and Steve were married in 1936 and lived in their home on L Street until they moved to Salem, Oregon after Steve's retirement.

Loreen Wells

Steve Ostrander, Jr.

Hazel and Steve reared two children. Steve, Jr. lives in Medford, Oregon, and Loreen Wells lives in Salem. Steve died in 1970, and Hazel died in 1993. They are both buried in Salem, Oregon.

One of many immigrants who entered the United States looking for a new life and a decent living, BALDO "BOB" KUVARA was born in Slovenia in 1878 and entered the United States about 1900 at the age of fourteen. It is unknown where he spent his young life, but when he arrived in Anchorage he was already an experienced chef and, upon his arrival in Anchorage, immediately set about to acquire a restaurant. He acquired the Union Café in 1920, and in 1921 it burned down. He purchased a lot across 4th Avenue from the Union and rebuilt immediately with a new name, the Frisco Café. Bob operated the Frisco and also owned the Panhandle building across the street. In 1929 he returned to Slovenia for his first visit in over thirty years.

In 1938 Bob married VIOLET DESPET, who also was from Slovenia. In 1942 he suffered another loss when the Frisco Café burned down. He rebuilt the building, and then in 1952 he moved his family to the Seattle area. Bob and Violet had four children, two boys and two girls, all presumably living in Washington. He passed away in 1953, and Violet passed away in 1993.

Early Anchorage resident JOHN JAMES McISAAC was born at Fair View, Prince Edward Island. He left his home at about twenty years of age and spent time in and around Massachusetts, Maine and other eastern states and ports before setting out for Alaska in 1897. He joined the stampede to the Klondike that year and lived in Dawson, Yukon Territory until 1906 when he returned to Seattle, Washington. In 1920 he returned to Alaska, but this time to the new city of Anchorage. Here he established himself by building a small hotel at 215 4th Avenue. He also built the 5th Avenue Hotel, located between C and D Streets on the south side of 5th Avenue where the J. C. Penney building now stands. He disposed of the 5th Avenue Hotel in 1936, and he and his wife made their home in the McIsaac Rooms building.

John McIsaac was born in 1865 and passed away in Anchorage in 1942. He is buried in the Catholic Tract, Anchorage Memorial Park. At the time of his death he had two daughters living in Seattle, Washington: Mrs. W. R. Colvin and Mrs. C. H. Lindbergh. His son George lived in Anchorage, however it is unknown where he now resides.

The Alaska Railroad attracted another immigrant to Anchorage in May 1920. CARL RIVERS arrived in Anchorage from Brainerd, Minnesota to work on the Alaska Railroad as an air brake repairman. He had been hired away from the Northern Pacific Railroad in

Carl and Hilma Rivers

Hilma Rivers and Children

Lily Rivers Stolt

Rivers Home

Minnesota to come to Anchorage. He was born in Oulu, Finland in 1882 and immigrated to the United States in 1900. He spent most of his younger life in Minnesota, and in 1915 he married HILMA LAUREN, who was also a Finnish immigrant born in 1882.

In July 1920 Hilma and their two daughters arrived in Anchorage to join Carl and moved into their four-room log home located at 8th Avenue and F Street, which Carl had purchased for three hundred seventy-five dollars.

Hilma operated a small restaurant in Anchorage for a short period of time; however, most of their interest was in their membership in the Suomi Finn Club. They also were active members of the Pioneers of Alaska. Carl retired from the ARR in 1946, and he and Hilma moved to warmer climes in Auburn, Washington.

Carl passed away in 1957, and Hilma died in 1970. They are both buried in the Pioneer section of Anchorage Memorial Park. Daughter Rose married Ralph Holdiman, a member of another Pioneer family, whose history is taken up in another section. Ralph passed away in 1958, and Rose passed away in 1966. Lillian married William Stolt, also a descendant of a Pioneer family. Her further history is taken up in the Stolt family story.

Anchorage was almost completely out of the tent city classification when HARRY GEORGE SELLER arrived with his family. Harry was born in London, England in 1876, the son of an English army officer. He fought in the Boer War and was awarded the Queen Victoria Cross by Queen Victoria. He immigrated to the United States in early 1900 and spent some time on the east coast working as a newspaper reporter and photographer. He met KATHRYN DYAKANOFF in Atlantic City.

Katherine Seller, Daughters Marj Dorbandt and Betty Blalock and Granddaughter Pat Dorbandt

Kathryn was selected by the first Commissioner of Education, Sheldon Jackson, to go to the Carlisle Indian Institute in Pennsylvania to receive a formal education. Upon her graduation from Carlisle, Kathryn entered Westchester State Normal School where she received her teaching degree in 1907. Her first teaching assignment by the B.I.A. was Sitka, Alaska in 1908. In the spring of 1908 Kathryn returned to Seattle where Harry was waiting for her, and they were married in Seattle in 1909.

They took their honeymoon trip to Atka, Alaska on a sailing schooner with one hundred seventy dollars worth of construction materials and three special items the government had conceded to Kathryn: an organ, a cow and a bull. They were commissioned

Harry Seller

Katherine Seller

Betty Blalock and Spouse

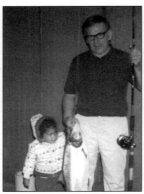
John Seller

Harry Seller

Renee Showell

by the B.I.A. to build the first government schoolhouse in the Aleutian Islands. It is interesting to note that they refunded fifty dollars of the original one hundred seventy dollars to the government. The schoolhouse, which was also their home, was completed and ready for use in 1909.

Their early teaching in the Aleutians took them to many villages besides Atka--Alitak, Uyak, Akiak, Unalaska and finally Tyonek where they taught for one year. From Tyonek they moved their family to Anchorage in 1920 so their children could attend high school. Harry was the first game warden in Anchorage and covered the Seward area as well. He also contributed a great deal of his time and effort to establishing the first Anchorage library, along with Mrs. Wever, and was instrumental in getting KFQD, the first radio station, established. He was employed by the Alaska Railroad until his untimely death.

Kathryn Dyakanoff was always a strong pro-native activist. She was very involved with the native peoples' problems during all of her years of teaching. In 1936, after the death of Harry, she began teaching again, and her assignments included Beaver, Tyonek, Alitak, Eklutna, Lake Illiamna and parts of southeast Alaska. Due to her native heritage, she did not receive her teaching certificate from the Territory for twenty years. Her perseverance and dedication to the native people of Alaska was recognized by the Department of Interior in 1950 when she received a special award for commendable service. That same year Congress awarded her a medal for "outstanding service to her people."

Author Will Hudson wrote a narrative of his trip to Atka in a book called *Icy Hell*. After meeting Kathryn he wrote: "The little native school was under the direction of an Aleut girl who received her education in the States. If ever there was a saint living on earth, I am sure it was this faithful cultured Aleut maiden, who was slaving herself half to death in an effort to help her charges in faraway, lonely Atka."

The union of Harry and Kathryn produced six children. Renee Lois Seller Showell had no children, and she passed away in 1945. Alfred drowned when he stepped off an ice float in Alitak when he was seven years old. Marjorie had one daughter, Patricia Dorbandt, who lives in California. Marjorie passed away in 1983. Harry George was killed in Unalaska during the Japanese invasion of the Aleutians in WWII. John had three daughters and one son all living in California. Betty Seller Blalock had one son, Blaine John Brown, now living in California.

Harry Seller passed away in 1936 and is buried in Tract 3, Anchorage Memorial Park Cemetery. Kathryn passed away in San Francisco in 1980 and is buried there. Renee Seller McCullough is buried next to her father in Tract 3, Anchorage Memorial Park.

———

In 1920 a young man of seventeen arrived in Anchorage for a visit and instead stayed for sixty-eight years. BERTEL A. WENNERSTROM met VIOLET MAE ELLIOT, and they were married in 1927.

Violet Mae, her mother VIOLET BALL, and her sister Jeanne "Happy" arrived in Anchorage in 1916. They joined their father, WILLIAM SHERMAN ELLIOT who had arrived earlier that same year to work for the ARR as a crane engineer. William was born in May Creek, Washington in 1881. He was killed in a bridge accident in 1922 shortly after he built a home on 8th Avenue between C and D Streets.

Bert was born in Southbridge, Massachusetts in 1903, found his way to Anchorage, landing here on April 15, 1920, and went to work for the ARR on the eighteenth of April as a laborer in the materials yard. He worked as janitor and mail clerk before advancing to manager of the employment office, the position he had when he and Mae were married.

Mae worked for the Railroad as a bookkeeper from 1922 until 1929 and in later years was a stenographer for the Superior Court and the United States Department of Justice. She was later employed as medical secretary to Dr. Harold S. Sogn and in 1956 was legal secretary to attorney Paul F. Robinson.

For the next fifty years the couple lived at the 415 West 8th Avenue address. Bert was active with the Elks lodge and the Pioneers of Alaska and was a staunch supporter of the Fur Rendezvous. He played the part of Dr. Knutsen on a KFQD radio show and sang a song

Mae Elliot

Burt Wennerstrom

Vi Elliot

William Elliot

Mae and Son, Justin
Wennerstrom

Home on 8th Avenue

Bruce
Wennerstrom

Burt and Mae
Wennerstrom

entitled "When the Ice Worms Nest Again." He was a history buff and was a member of the boards of Cook Inlet Historical Society, the Museum of History and Art, and the Fine Arts Commission. He and Mae were King and Queen Regent for the 1969 Fur Rendezvous. Bert passed away in 1988, and Mae died in 1996. They are both buried in the Elks Tract, Anchorage Memorial Park Cemetery.

The union of Bert and Mae produced three sons. Justin lives in Oakland, California; Harold was born in 1932 and died in 1937; Bruce lives in Santa Barbara, California and has six children. Lisa Gaye Murray, Julie Anne Dashek Craig Ivor, Chad Elliott and Todd Sherman live in Santa Barbara, California. Robert Bruce lives in Aubrey, Texas.

Charles and Bessie
Quinton

John Bagoy, Charles Quinton and
Wally Burnett

Another prospector and miner who came north to Nome in 1901 and finally settled in Anchorage, CHARLES F. QUINTON was born in Dexter, Maine in 1883. As a young man he made his way across the United States to the west coast and headed for the gold fields of Nome, Alaska in 1901. After two

Harry Quinton

Howard Quinton

Griffin Quinton

Bessie Quinton and
Sister Edith

Charley Quinton
and Boys

unsuccessful years he headed back south and attended a barber college with the idea of having a back-up trade if he did not make it rich in the gold mining business. He returned to Alaska in 1905 and prospected the Copper River Country and the Kantishna during the summer months. In 1920 he finally settled in Anchorage and opened a barbershop.

BESSIE GRIFFIN came to Anchorage from Montana to visit her sister Edith Knapp, and she married Charley in 1922 in Anchorage. Bessie worked as a bookkeeper for various stores and also was employed as a court reporter. She was born in Louisville, Colorado in 1894.

Charley continued to have the "gold fever" and at every opportunity was off prospecting with his partners in the Kantishna area.

The union of Bessie and Charley produced three sons. Son Griffin lives in Anchorage and had three children. Jodie Tupuola lives in Anchorage; Dianne passed away in 2001; and Greg lives in Irvine, California. Son Harry lives in Spokane, Washington and has no children. Son Howard lives in Grants Pass, Oregon and has three children. One daughter lives in Portland, Oregon, and one daughter and son live in Grants Pass, Oregon.

Charley passed away in 1952, and Bessie died in 1975. Both are buried in Angelus Memorial Park, Anchorage.

Another 1920 boomer who arrived in Anchorage to seek his fortune, JOEL KLOUDA was born in Racine, Wisconsin and came to Anchorage to work as a machinist for the ARR. He married ANNA SIMMONS, who was born in Kodiak in 1897. The family lived in a log home at 8th Avenue and F Street, which is now the location of the All Saints Episcopal Church.

The Klouda Boys   James Klouda

MARY and FRED SIMMONS, the parents of Anna, lived in the Hope and Sunrise area about 1910. They moved to Knik and lived there for a number of years prior to moving to Anchorage in 1920. Fred Simmons and his son Adam worked for the Alaska Railroad as cranemen. In 1941 Anna Simmons Klouda, Mary Simmons and Fred Simmons passed away, leaving four Klouda children.

With both the parents and grandparents gone, the four Klouda children were left to

Fred and Pat Klouda   Pat and Joe Klouda

manage on their own. The eldest son, Joseph C., married Patricia Rieten, and they had three children. Bernard lives in Anchorage and is the owner of Bernie's Pharmacy; James passed away in 1951; Terrance lives in Anchorage. Joseph passed away in 1988 after a successful career with Berts Drug Stores. Son Fred married Patricia Stafford and they had four children. Mary Ann, Fred, Jr. and Joseph all live in Anchorage; Colleen lives in Kodiak. Fred retired from the FAA as an air carrier inspector and now lives in Sterling, Alaska. Son James Klouda lives in Ontario, Oregon. He worked as a cowboy for many years and never married. Daughter Colleen Klouda Neese lived in Seattle, Washington and passed away in 1999.

A young boy of twelve arrived in Anchorage in 1920 to live with his aunt, Delly Weber, a sled dog trainer. HALFORD P. NOGGLE was born in Los Angeles, California in 1908. He grew up in Anchorage and was in the high school graduating class of 1925. Upon graduating from high school he entered the University of Washington; however, he was unable to continue due to lack of funds. He returned to Anchorage and began working for the ARR in a number of locations. While working in Curry he met FLORENCE EMILY HAYES who was working at the Curry Hotel. Florence was born in St. Paul, Minnesota, and came to Anchorage in 1924. Her mother, Teresa Seavy, was living in Anchorage and ran a boarding house on 5th Avenue. Florence came to Anchorage to join her mother after graduating from high school in 1924.

Halford Noggle

Hal and Flo Noggle in Curry

Florence and Hal married in 1929 and moved to Anchorage shortly after their marriage. He left the employ of the Alaska Railroad and did various odd jobs around Anchorage including reading the news on KFQD radio at six and ten in the evening, as well as singing solos until midnight. These jobs were all done while he studied the law in the office of Warren Cuddy. He passed the bar in 1938 and was admitted to the practice of law in Alaska.

Florence and Halford Noggle

Flo and Daughter, Ann

Noggle Home on M Street

His first assignment was as assistant district attorney in Cordova, and then he worked a year at the same job in Seward. In 1939 Hal enlisted in the Naval Reserve and spent the next five years in the Navy in the Aleutians and in the South Pacific. He was discharged with a commission as Captain in the Naval Reserve.

After WWII Hal and family homesteaded in the Fire Lake area and built a home. He was appointed regional attorney for the CAA, now the FAA. In 1949, the family left the homestead and moved to Seattle, Washington and then to Washington, D.C. where Hal was assistant administrator for the FAA. He retired from the FAA, and in 1997, some time after the death of Florence, he moved to Denver, Colorado to be near his daughter. He passed away in March 1999 at the age of ninety.

The union of Hal and Florence produced one daughter, Anne Noggle Uhlman. She had two children, Nancy Anne Young and James Halford Krall, both of whom live in Friday Harbor, Washington.

The homesteaders were beginning to move into various areas around the townsite in 1920. North of town on what is called the Loop Road was the most popular area, and one of the early families to move there was the EMIL SAVOLA family.

Emil was born in Finland in 1886 and immigrated to Canada about 1910. He arrived in Anchorage about 1920 and worked for the ARR on the section crew. ERIKA PEKKALO was also born in Finland and arrived in Anchorage about the same time as Emil. She was living with friends in Anchorage when she and Emil met and were married in 1920. Emil had been previously married, however his first wife passed away in 1915, leaving Emil with a daughter Anna.

Emil homesteaded on Green Lake on the Loop Road north of Anchorage. He did not, however, file patent to the land until 1924. He was an excellent builder and was well-known for his abilities as a carpenter. His log home on Green Lake was a model of workmanship with two stories, a kitchen and living area downstairs and bedrooms upstairs.

A daughter, Helen, was born in 1922 and another daughter, Frances, in 1924. In 1931 disaster struck the family when Erika mistakenly used gasoline to start her kitchen stove, thinking it was kerosene. The explosion set her and daughter Anna aflame and caused both of their deaths. Emil sold his homestead after the disastrous fire and continued to work for the ARR until his death in 1941. Emil, Erika and Anna are buried in the Moose Tract, Anchorage Memorial Park Cemetery.

Erika Savola

Emil Savola

Anna Savola

Helen Savola Kelly

Frances Savola Lahti

Savola Home on Green Lake

Daughter Helen Savola Kelly and spouse had four children. Beverly Weston, Russell Cooper, Jerri Cooper and Dean Kelly all live in Oregon. Daughter Frances Savola married Andy Lahti and they had four sons. Andrew Arnold and Wayne live in Anchorage; Vennard lives in Lacy, Washington; and David lives in Shelton, Washington.

In 1973 Andrew Lahti, the spouse of Frances Savola Lahti, became the first employee of the city of Anchorage to have worked for the City for thirty years. Upon his retirement in 1976 he had completed thirty-three years with the City water department. He was presented a plaque on a June day in 1973 to celebrate his thirty years, and the day was named Andy Lahti Day by the Mayor.

Frances and Andy Lahti died in 1986, and Helen Kelly died in 1996. Frances and Andy are buried in the Pioneer Tract, Anchorage Memorial Park Cemetery. Helen is buried in Florence, Oregon.

———

The growing community was attracting more and more professionals who were opening offices in the new town. WILLIAM H. RAGER opened his law practice soon after his arrival in Anchorage in 1920. He was born in Frederick, Maryland in 1882 and came to Anchorage from Montana where he had been practicing law for some time. He first formed a law partnership with Jerry Murphy and later with M. J. Conroy, former Mayor of Anchorage. In the latter part of 1921 he was appointed United States Commissioner by District Judge E. E. Ritchie. He held that office until 1926 when he retired from public service to devote full time to his private law practice. Judge Ritchie was quoted as saying that William was the only commissioner ever appointed by him who had no complaints registered against him.

William Rager, Sr.

Katherine Rager

Last Home

Rager First Home

William Rager, Jr.

In late 1920 KATHERINE G. DeWALD left her teaching career to come to Anchorage from Montana for the express purpose of marrying William. After William's death in 1927 Katherine again began teaching school, and in 1932 she moved to Seward where she taught high school English and Latin. She later worked for the Corps of Engineers in Seward until she retired and moved back to Anchorage to be with her son William, who still lives here. Katherine was born in Salem, Virginia in 1891. She died in 1960 and is buried in the Pioneer Tract, Anchorage Memorial Park.

The year 1920 brought the KEIST, HILE, WILLIAMS and PEYSER clans to Anchorage. The patriarch of the clan, Louis Henry Keist, and his spouse, Anne House Keist, arrived in Alaska during the 1898 gold rush to the Klondike. Louis was born in 1857 in Iowa, and Anne House was born in Ohio. They spent several years in the Juneau-Douglas area where Anne passed away and is buried. The union of Louis and Anne produced a son and a daughter. Son Samuel O. was born in Jessup, Iowa in 1881. He came to Alaska in 1907 with his spouse Nora, first arriving in Juneau where they operated a candy shop. Daughter SARAH MAUDE KEIST was born in 1878 in Charleston, Illinois and lived in Iowa for some years prior to coming to Alaska. She lived in Cordova in 1916 and was in business there until she moved to Anchorage in 1921.

Sam Keist and his spouse Nora had no children. Sarah Maude Keist first married Fred Hile, and had six children. This marriage ended in Juneau, and Sarah married Max Peyser, who was a professional tailor. This marriage produced one son Edward.

All of the Hile children remained in Alaska and Anchorage with the exception of daughter Veneta, who married

Sarah Maude Keist

Sam Keist

Carl Williams, Sr. with Esther and Carl, Jr.

Venetta and Fred Hile

George Grenlee and moved to the Chicago area. Daughter Esther, born in 1902, married Carl G. Williams. He was a conductor on the Alaska Railroad, and in later years he and brother-in-law Woody Hile operated the Anchorage Laundry on 5th Avenue between C and D Streets for many years. Carl died in 1962 and is buried in Angelus Memorial Park. Esther passed away in Anchorage in 1995 and is buried in the Pioneer Tract, Anchorage Memorial Park. They had one son, Carl, Jr., who passed away in Anchorage in 1999. His cremated remains are buried with his mother and with his father.

Louis Hile, Sam Keist and Woodrow Hile

Son Louis Hile married Ivy Lothrop, and they had three children. Louis was an ardent baseball player in Anchorage, playing the position of catcher on local teams. He was born in Cordova in 1910 and was employed by the Alaska Railroad. Their two daughters moved to California. Son Edward died in 1965. Louis Hile is buried in the Catholic Tract, and son Edward is buried in Tract 18, Anchorage Memorial Park.

Sarah's and Fred's daughters Gertrude and Ruby died at the age of six and seven respectively. Son Woodrow, Carl Williams' partner in the laundry, was born in Douglas in 1913 and came to Anchorage in 1920. He married Valerie M. Coxey and they had two children, who still live in Anchorage. Woodrow is buried in Angelus Memorial Park.

Patriarch Louis Henry Keist and his two children, Samuel O. Keist and Sarah Maude Keist Hile Peyser, are buried in the Elks Tract, Anchorage Memorial Park.

LOGAN STIPP arrived in Knik in 1917 and moved to Anchorage in 1920 where he was employed by the Alaska Railroad, first as a locomotive fireman and later as a locomotive engineer. Prior to moving to Alaska, Logan was employed as a prison

Logan Stipp at Age 32

Bertha and Logan Stipp

Logan Stipp on North Star
Express

Wanda Stipp

Bertha Stipp
with Wanda

Logan and Wanda Stipp,
1926

guard at San Quentin prison in California. He was born in Downing, Missouri in 1885 and came west as a young man. He met BERTHA HUBBARD in Anchorage, and they were married in Yreka, California. Bertha was born in San Francisco and was raised near Yreka on the Klamath River. She first came to Anchorage with her brother, John Hubbard, who was employed by the city of Anchorage.

During their time in Anchorage, Logan and Bertha purchased the Winn Hotel located on the corner of 4th Avenue and B Street. It was recently destroyed by fire. Logan and Bertha had one daughter, Wanda Stipp, born in Anchorage in 1920.

Logan Stipp, Sheep Hunting

After thirty years of service with the ARR, Bertha and Logan retired to Yreka, California, where they both are buried. Wanda Stipp remains in Anchorage and is retired from the Anchorage Telephone Department.

JACOB C. "JAKE" KNAPP was born in Mystic, Iowa in 1886 and left his native state as a young man to seek his future in the west. He worked in the coal mines in Montana for a number of years. There he met and married EDITH GRIFFIN. Jake soon tired of the coal mining business, and he and Edith moved to Prince Rupert, British Columbia, where he obtained work in the shipyards.

John "Jack" Knapp

Edith Knapp

Jake and Edith
Knapp

Jake Knapp

Jacob C. Knapp, Jr.

Edith Knapp with
Jacob C., Jr.
and Jack

Family Home on 8th Avenue
and I Street

Jake finally decided to head for Alaska, which he had been hearing so much about, and sent Edith back to Montana, with the promise that he would send for her as soon as he got established. He first stopped in Juneau, but found nothing of interest there. He proceeded to Anchorage in the latter part of 1920 and landed a job with the Alaska Railroad.

He was able to establish permanent employment with the ARR in 1921 as an electrician, and sent for Edith to join him. They first lived at 109 4th Avenue and later bought a log cabin at 8th Avenue and L Street. After twenty years with the ARR, Jake transferred to the Post Engineers in 1941 and remained there until he retired in 1949.

Edith kept busy as a housewife and mother of two boys. She was active with the Pioneers of Alaska and the Eastern Star. Eldest son, Jack, was born in 1924 and second son, Jacob C., was born in 1926. Both sons followed in their father's footsteps and worked for the Alaska Railroad. John F. "Jack" and spouse had no children and live in Washington. Jacob C., Jr. and spouse Mildred Snyder Knapp live in Anchorage, and they had three children. Eric R., Amy C. and Edith Ann all live in Anchorage. Edith died in 1957, and Jacob, Sr. died in 1961. Jacob is buried in Grants Pass, Oregon, and Edith is buried in Angelus Memorial Park, Anchorage.

CHAPTER IV

1921

In 1921 the first great bank robbery occurred in Anchorage. Miss Wanda Nolan, later named Gelles, was the clerk on duty when the robbery occurred. She and the one customer in the bank were locked in the vault until help arrived.

The High School graduating class that year consisted of five students, all of whom are deceased.

Albert Heckey

Vera Kimball

William Niemi

Herbert Schell

Selma Simonson

The Mayor remained the same.

The first train ran from Seward to Fairbanks.

Another one of those grizzled prospectors who settled in Anchorage in the twenties, PETER FREDERICK CLAVEAU was born in San Francisco in 1979 and made his way to Alaska in 1902, first landing in Valdez. He was another boomer looking for gold and was heading for the gold fields of Fairbanks. After his sojourn in Fairbanks and other places, he settled in Anchorage in 1921.

In his own words:

> *I left Valdez in April of 1903 and necked a sled through Keystone Canyon to Tonsina, then packed over the U. S. Government Telegraph Line trail through Mentasta Pass. Lived on 'dog' ribs, which we got from some soldiers stationed in cabins along the telegraph line. We built a raft at Tanana crossing, shot all the rapids on the Tanana river to Chena. Arrived in Fairbanks, June 10, 1903. Went prospecting with Bob Martin, George Mutchler, and Scotty Brown of Rampart. Wanted to stake 10, 11 and 12 below on Cleary. Bob Martin and George Mutchler said lets get the hell out of here, there is nothing on this creek.*
>
> *Formed the town of CARO on the Chandalar River, prospected the Koyukuk, Chandalar, Poorman, Ruby and every other damn creek in the country.*

Pete died in 1970. It is unknown where he is buried. This, however, is a typical situation of these oldtimers who prospected this country.

———

HARRY JOHNSON was another oldtimer who came to Anchorage in 1921, and his story upon entering Alaska is as follows, in his own words.

On or about April 6, 1921, I and a number of other workers took passage on the Steamer Northwestern out of Seattle to come to Alaska to work on the Alaska Railroad. Or as it was then known as the AEC. After about six days on the boat, we landed in Seward, where we were held for five to six days on account of a snowstorm. Then we took a freight one morning out to Hunter where we unloaded to shovel snow. We worked at that stuff until we were snow blind. Most of us then walked over the summit and came into Anchorage.

Harry was born in Tromso, Norway in 1886. He immigrated to the United States in 1902 and came to Alaska almost immediately. He was employed as a carpenter with the ARR for many years. He left Anchorage for a stint in Ketchikan from 1933 to 1939 and then in Kodiak from 1939 to 1940. Harry died in 1954 and is buried in Tract 18, Anchorage Memorial Park in an unmarked grave.

———

A well-known Finnish carpenter by the name of OLLI KOHORNEN arrived in Anchorage in 1921 to work for the ARR. He first came to Anchorage in 1916, but returned to Seattle, Washington for four years prior to returning to Alaska. Olli was born in Vesanto, Finland in 1887 and met his wife Hilja in Anchorage. HILJA VANAJA was widowed, and she had one son, Reino. The couple lived in Anchorage until 1950 when Olli retired, and they moved up to Blodgett Lake in the Matanuska Valley. Olli died in 1960 in Palmer and is presumably buried there. Stepson Reino moved to Greenbank, Washington. No positive record is available as to the burial place of Olli or Hilja.

———

The year 1921 brought another young hopeful to Anchorage. AZRO WILLARD was born in Sedro Wooley, Washington in 1895. He served in WWI, and soon after discharge he headed for Alaska and, in particular, Anchorage, where he had heard of the great opportunities in the new city. Upon his arrival he immediately gained employment with the Alaska Railroad in the commissary department.

Polly and Azro Willard

Azro was a farmer at heart and was soon pursuing the idea of a homestead in the Anchorage area. He located one hundred sixty acres on Spenard Road, which encompassed the SE 1/4 of Section 26, Township 13, North of Range 4 and West of the Seward Meridian. He received the patent on the land in July 1924. He built his cabin and later home on a

Lake Spenard, 1936

Haying on Homestead

Sunflowers on Homestead

rise adjacent to Fish Creek and almost exactly where Gwennies Restaurant is today.

In 1929 Azro and POLLY DEMIDOFF were married and moved onto the homestead. Polly was born in Kenai in 1897, and homesteading was nothing new to her. While Azro kept his employment with the ARR, Polly kept the home fires burning and saw to the raising of the two children. The homestead was a good three miles from town by road, and Azro had an automobile which got him to and from work. However, on days when it snowed heavily and the road was not plowed, he put on his skis and skied to work and back, taking short-cuts cross-country.

Azro and Polly moved off the homestead in 1946 and moved to Sedro Wooley, Washington. He returned a few short years later and finished out his employment with the Alaska Railroad and then retired in the early fifties.

Mabel and Elmer Martin

Son, Frank Willard

Azro and Polly had two children. Son Frank lives in Mt. Vernon, Washington and has one son, Andrew. Daughter Mabel lives in Mesa, Arizona and has one son, Willard Martin. Polly died in 1980, and Azro died in 1981. Both are buried in Sedro Wooley, Washington.

PETE WOLDEN was a Norwegian immigrant who arrived in Anchorage in 1921 and engaged in commercial fishing and mining. He had been a superintendent for local and Cordova canneries and at one time was stores supervisor for the Independence Mine. From 1937 until the war closed down the mines, Pete was trucking for the Pacific Alaska Mines between Anchorage and Hatcher Pass and also from Knik-Goose Bay to the Mines. For five years he was employed by the city of Anchorage. He was born in Norway in 1884, and passed away in Anchorage in 1951. He is buried in Tract 14, Anchorage Memorial Park.

ROLAND HEALY was a Pioneer trader on the Susitna River. He arrived on the Anchorage scene in 1916 and in 1917 moved up the Susitna River to Susitna Station where he was employed by H. W. Nagley in his trading post. After a few years with the Nagley Company, Roland started his own trading business and for fifteen years operated on the Susitna dealing primarily with the trappers and the fur trade.

He was born in Arklow, Ireland in 1884, came to the United States around 1899, arrived in Alaska first in 1908 for a short period, and then returned to the Anchorage area in 1916-17. He was well-known among the trappers of the area and had many friends in Anchorage, where he visited constantly. He enjoyed chartering an airplane and inviting his Anchorage friends to take trips touring the area. Roland died in 1936 and is buried in Tract 3, Anchorage Memorial Park, in an unmarked grave.

A man from "down under" arrived in Anchorage in 1921 after working the major gold strikes in Alaska and the Yukon. JOHN FRANCIS MONKMAN was born in Brisbane, Australia in 1866. He spent his youth in New Zealand and came to the United States at the age of twenty-one in 1887. He lived in Humboldt County California until 1897 when he made the trip to Dawson over the Atlin trail. He and a partner used up three horses on this journey. In 1903 he moved to Fairbanks, where he mined on Dome Creek, Cleary Creek and Goldstream until he headed for the new strike at Iditarod in 1910. In 1912 he moved over to Flat and Discovery, and there he met and married MARGARET O'MEARA, a school teacher who came to Flat from Victoria, British Columbia, where she was born in 1878.

She and John lived in Flat until 1921, when, like so many others, they left the area due to the decrease in mining and came to Anchorage. After two years they moved to Chatanika, where John took another try at mining, and then returned to Anchorage again in 1925.

John and Margaret had one daughter, Moana. Moana married Harry Lundell, and they had one daughter, Bonnie. John and Margaret moved to Fairbanks in later years to live with their daughter. John died in 1947, and Margaret died in 1968. They are presumably buried in Fairbanks

A well-known Alaska politician and businessman, CARL FREDERICK LOTTSFELDT was born in San Francisco in 1898 and first arrived in Alaska at Cordova in 1919, where he was employed with a local salmon cannery. He moved on to Anchorage in 1921 and joined the Alaska Road Commission and served for fourteen years. He worked in Takotna, Ophir and McGrath developing bush airfields.

His career in Alaska included a stint with the Park Service in McKinley Park, where he was chief clerk. He also served as civil works administrator at Lynn Canal, and as the postmaster and store owner in Ophir.

Carl and Sophia Lottsfeldt

Carl Lottsfeldt with Senator
Ernest Gruening

Son, Buzz
Lottsfeldt

Carl with Lead Dog

Sophie and Carl
Lottsfeldt, 1959

Carl met SOPHIA ANDERSON in Juneau in 1928, and they were married in Juneau that same year. Sophia was born in Douglas, Alaska in 1907 and spent her young life in southeast Alaska until she married Carl. She was a graduate registered nurse and worked in the Juneau hospital as well as in Anchorage. She also operated a health store in Anchorage for a number of years.

When Carl retired from government service he went into private business selling heavy equipment and mining machinery. He was a well-known legislator and served as a member of the State House from 1962 to 1966. He was running for the State Senate when he suddenly passed away in 1976. Carl was also known for his efforts on behalf of the Pioneers' Homes in Alaska and lobbied long and hard for their establishment.

The union of Carl and Sophia produced two children. Daughter Frances Marie Lottsfeldt Leon was born in 1929, and son Carl F. "Buzz" was born in 1931. Carl, Jr. had three children, Jim, John and Joellen, all living in Anchorage. Frances had no children. Sophia passed away in 1975; Carl, Sr. passed away in 1976. Carl, Jr. passed away in 1997, and Frances passed away in 2000. All are buried in the Pioneer Section of Anchorage Memorial Park.

One of the early families to homestead in Anchorage was the WILLIAM GILLIES MARSH family. William was born in Lawton, Michigan in 1886. He first arrived in Alaska in 1915 at Cordova. In 1919 he came to Anchorage with the intention of homesteading. He filed for a homestead on Loop Road in October 1919. In 1921 his family joined him. Several sons and daughters all filed for homestead rights and eventually accumulated over six hundred acres of land on the combined farms.

In 1887 William married MARIOLA ELVIRA HIGH, who was born in Brockway, Michigan in 1869. They lived in northern Michigan for some years and then moved to Oregon and finally to Aberdeen, Washington. William and Mariola developed the Aberdeen Ranch on Loop Road. It proved to be a great success, producing vegetables, potatoes, chickens, pigs, chinchillas and goats.

William and Mariola Marsh

Marsh Extended Family

William and Mariola had nine children, four boys and five girls. All of them, including the in-laws, were involved in Aberdeen Ranch at one time or another. We will not go into the entire Marsh family as, needless to say, the tree is huge. We have already discussed the Bayer side of the family, and will deal here with the Richard Sessions family, the Jess Storm family, and, briefly, with the other children. William died in 1937, and Mariola passed away in 1942. They are both buried in the Masonic Tract, Anchorage Memorial Park.

Daughter IRMA WINIFRED MARSH was born in Aberdeen, Washington and married ARTHUR RICHARD SESSIONS in 1924. " Dick" Sessions was born in Dubuque, Iowa in 1902. He came to Anchorage in 1919-20 and was employed with the Alaska Railroad. He worked his way up to chief clerk and in 1947 was moved to Seattle as assistant to the general manager in charge of the Seattle office. Upon his retirement, he was commended by Secretary of the Interior Stewart Udall for his work in helping to plan and organize overseas transportation facilities. He was also honored by Udall for his work in speeding emergency supplies to Alaska after the 1964 earthquake.

Sessions Family

Irma died in 1956, and Dick passed away in Seattle in 1973. They had two children, William Richard, who passed away in 1979, and Barbara Ann Nelson, who lives in Aberdeen, Washington.

Daughter EDNA LULU MARSH married JESSE HERBERT STORM in 1913. Edna was born in Michigan in 1893 and came to Anchorage with her family. Jesse Storm was born in Kansas and came to Anchorage in 1920. He was active with the Anchorage Volunteer Fire Department and worked for the Alaska Railroad in the freight department. After WWII he was fire chief at Fort Richardson. In 1952 he retired and the family moved to Stevens Lake, Washington.

Edna passed away in 1968, and Jesse died in 1976. They had two sons, Jack Harold, who died in 1977, and Charles Clark, who lives in Snohomish, Washington.

MARIOLA ENID MARSH married BENJAMIN HENRY KENNETH BAYER. Mariola was born in West Branch, Michigan, and Kenneth Bayer was born in Nelson, British Columbia. The rest of the story of Enid and Kenneth is found with the Frank Bayer family history in another section.

WILLIAM GILLIES MARSH, JR. was born in Dearborn, Michigan. He married ELLEN MARIE GYLLAND in 1916. Ellen died in 1928, and William died in 1956. They had three children. Harvey Golden married Ethel Adams. Harvey was born in 1888 and died in 1957. Ethel was born in 1889 and died in 1945. Ellen Laura "Nellie" was born in Flint, Michigan in 1898 and passed away in 1961. She married Mason Charles S. Skinner who was born in Iowa in 1878 and died in 1944. Donald Howard was born in The Dalles, Oregon in 1912. He lived most of his life in Anchorage and died in 1962.

Edna and Jess Storm

HENRY FRANKLIN BOWMAN was born in Illinois in 1857 of Scottish parents who were among the earliest settlers in Virginia. His parents moved to Illinois and later to Texas shortly after the Civil War. At the age of nineteen Henry became a cowboy and rode the range in Texas until the family moved to Idaho. In Meadows, Idaho he started the famous "Bar B" Ranch. In 1899 he married DOLLY KINGBAN. They had four children, one of whom was FRED BOWMAN.

In 1907 Henry came to Alaska and became involved in businesses with his son Fred. In 1912 Fred married ANNA ALHOLM, who was born in Oulu, Finland in 1885. They operated the Golden Gate Hotel in Fairbanks prior to moving to Anchorage in 1921.

Fred and Anna Bowman

In 1930 Fred and his sons located a homestead at what is now Bragaw and DeBarr Roads. Fred later became secretary treasurer of the Anchorage Commercial Company, predecessor to the

Harry Bowman, 1925

Edward, Fred and Harry Bowman

Homestead Near Bragaw and DeBarr

Harry Bowman

Edward
Bowman

Howard
Bowman

Northern Commercial Company. From 1933 to 1936 he operated Bowman Airways, which is believed to be the first company to schedule charter flights to Seattle. After 1938 Fred lived at Lake Clark, Port Alsworth, where he operated a placer mine.

Anna passed away in 1953, and Fred passed away in 1959. Son Harry lives in California. Edward was a pilot for Alaska Airlines and was killed in a plane crash in 1961. Howard lives at Lake Clark. Fred and Henry are buried in the Elks Tract, Anchorage Memorial Park.

Railroader EARL BARNETT landed in Anchorage in 1921 after jobs in numerous places throughout the United States. He was born in Youngstown, Ohio in 1890 and spent his youth there. His family moved to Meadville, Pennsylvania where he and his father both worked in engine service for the Erie Railroad. When work became slow and temporary, the family moved to Jerome, Arizona, where they found work in the copper mines. Earl later moved to Ely, Nevada, where he operated an overhead crane in a mine smelter.

HETTY CLASSEN was born in Essen, Germany in 1887 and immigrated to the United States in 1892 with her parents and three sisters. They proceeded to Corning, Ohio and lived on a farm with her grandparents while her father worked in the coal mines. The family moved to West Virginia where her father again found work in the coal mines. A strike in the mines occurred, so the family moved to O'Fallon, Illinois and settled on a farm. Hetty grew up there and worked as a housekeeper and cook.

Earl Barnett

Hetty started doing some traveling and in Ely, Nevada found employment in the diet section of a hospital and later as a nurse.

Home on 8th Avenue

Earl in Front of First Home

Hetty Barnett

There she met Earl Barnett, and they were married in 1915. The smelter shut down, and Earl was out of work, so they moved to Oregon, where Earl's uncle was logging. Their first son, Robert, was born there in 1915. They next moved to Miami, Arizona, and number two son, Glen, was born in 1916. The

Virginia Barnett

Robert Barnett

Donald Barnett

Glen Barnett

mine in Miami shut down so the family moved back to Meadville, Pennsylvania. There Donald and Virginia were born in 1918 and 1920 respectively. Earl, constantly looking for permanent work, then left for Tampico, Mexico to work in the oil fields.

After a year in Mexico, Earl decided to go to Alaska as the Railroad was now operating in Anchorage. He landed in Anchorage in 1921 and went to work in engine service for the ARR. In 1922 he brought the family up, and they settled permanently in Anchorage. Earl retired from the Railroad as road foreman of engines in 1952.

Dog Driver

Earl passed away in 1964; Hetty passed away in 1981 at the Pioneer Home in Anchorage. Their daughter, Virginia, died in 1944 and is buried in Meadville, Pennsylvania. Son Donald, who still lives in Anchorage, had two children, Thomas and Elizabeth. Son Robert, who lives in Homer, had three children. David Earl lives in Anchorage, Allen S. lives in Sitka, and Sally Slusser lives in Ellensburg, Washington. Son C. Glen died in 1998 and had one son, Gary, who is also deceased. Earl, Hetty, Glen and Gary are all buried in Angelus Memorial Park in Anchorage.

A German immigrant who found his destiny in Alaska, EMIL H. PFEIL was born in Seisen, Germany in 1886 and as a young man sailed before the mast to many ports of the world prior to coming to Alaska in 1919. In 1920 Emil arrived in Anchorage and went to work for the AEC as a tie cutter in Sutton. When the headquarters buildings were built in Anchorage for the Railroad, he became the first blacksmith and eventually headed up that department. He put in a

Muriel Anderson Pfeil

Emil Pfeil

Pfeil Family   Caroline Pfeil

Muriel Adele Pfeil   Robert Pfeil

few years prospecting and in 1924 returned to work for the Railroad until he retired in 1941.

He became interested in real estate after his retirement and constructed a number of homes in Anchorage. With partner Tom Bevers, he built the Bevers and Pfeil apartment and store building on the corner of 4th Avenue and E Street. Being long interested in civic affairs, he served on the Public Utility Board, the City Council and a term on the Anchorage Chamber of Commerce board.

In 1929 he met MURIEL CAROLINE ANDERSON, a schoolteacher who arrived in Anchorage in 1925 to take on a teaching job with the Anchorage School District. She eventually became school principal and taught commercial subjects. Muriel was born in Spokane, Washington in 1899 and was raised and educated in Washington. Emil and Muriel were married in 1929, and she gave up her teaching career to be a mother and a housewife.

The union of Emil and Muriel produced three children, Muriel, Caroline and Robert. Muriel operated a travel agency, Caroline became a registered nurse, and Robert was a Captain for Alaska Airlines. Emil was killed in a plane crash in 1954 and is buried in the Elks Tract, Anchorage Memorial Park. Muriel is living in Providence Horizon House and is one hundred one years of age at this writing.

An American born in Vienna, Austria, GUSTAV GELLES' parents were visiting Austria at the time of his birth. He was brought back to New York when he was only a few months old. As a young man, "Gus," as he was known to all, came to Alaska to represent the National Grocery Company for the entire Territory. He headquartered in Juneau but made frequent trips to the north prior to Anchorage becoming a tent city. In 1920 he moved permanently to Anchorage and made it his headquarters.

WANDA NOLAN came to Anchorage in 1918 to be a cashier for the Bank of Alaska. In 1921 she was locked in the bank vault with the only customer during the first

Wanda Nolan Gelles   Gustav Gelles

bank robbery in Anchorage. Gus and Wanda were married in 1921, and she left her position in the bank to become a mother and housewife. She served on the school board for nine years and ran Gus's office as well.

Knik Arm Towers

Gus Gelles with Friend

First Home on L Street

Wanda Griffin

Gus was known throughout the Territory as the "Optimo Kid" because of his prowess as a sales agent for Optimo Cigars. Gus made the first commercial flight from Anchorage to Kodiak with Russel Merrill. He was instrumental in organizing radio station KFQD, Anchorage's first station, the Evan Jones Coal Company and the Alaska Guides. In 1926, along with A. A. Shonbeck and Alonzo Cope, Gus organized the Anchorage Airways with Russel Merrill as chief pilot. The first aircraft was bought from Travel Air Manufacturing Company in Wichita, Kansas. Other local residents who were stockholders in the new venture were Oscar Anderson, Jack Collins, A. D. Balderston, Robert S. Bragaw, Jr., Pete Olson and Fred Parsons. Gus was constantly promoting Anchorage and was one of its best boosters. In 1935 Gus, Grant Reed, Herb Reed, and Frank Dorbandt as pilot left for Seattle in a Bowman Airways Travel Air. Gus returned with Dorbandt to Anchorage and became the first round trip passenger on an airplane between Anchorage and the States.

Robert Gelles

Wanda Nolan Gelles was born in Almota, Washington in 1892 and passed away in Anchorage in 1940. Gus Gelles died in 1943. The union of Gus and Wanda produced three children. Daughter Wanda Gelles Griffin had four children. Charles Robert lives in Palmer, Katherine Jorene and Sue Granderry live in San Francisco, and Marie Trueblood lives in Anchorage. Son Robert Gelles had three children. Laura and Leslie Eldine live in Los Angeles, and Amalie lives in New York City. Daughter Katherine Urie had two children. Anthony lives in Seattle, and Judith Theresa Fulp lives in Kodiak. Wanda and Gus are buried in the Elks Tract, Anchorage Memorial Park. Katherine Gelles Urie passed away in 1989 and Robert passed away in 1992 in California. Wanda Gelles Griffin still lives in Anchorage.

CHARLEY and MILJA WAHL came to Anchorage in 1921 from North Dakota. Charley worked independently as a carpenter in Anchorage for many years. He also spent time as a Cook Inlet fisherman and was a hardrock miner in the Willow Creek district.

Katherine Urie

Charlie Wahl

Milja Wahl

Home and Rental

Irma Wahl Crocker

They had one daughter, Irma, who married Eugene Crocker, a member of another Pioneer family. They had three children. Linda Gene White, Arlene M. Bennett and Eugene Charles Crocker all live in Anchorage.

After his retirement, Charley and Milja operated several rental units on 3rd Avenue between Cordova and Barrow Streets. Charley maintained a hobby making jewelry.

Charley was born in Wassa, Finland in 1888, and Milja Korpi was born in Finland in 1892. Charley died in 1962, and Milja died in 1972. Daughter Irma Wahl Crocker died in 1968. All three are buried in Tract 18, Anchorage Memorial Park. Eugene Crocker died in 1990 and is buried in Tract 3 next to his father in Anchorage Memorial Park.

ADOLF WILLIAM YOUNG was another prospector-miner turned railroader. He was born in Fredricksburg, Texas in 1883 and grew up there. He arrived in Alaska after the Spanish American War in search of gold. He landed in the Hope and Sunrise district during their goldrush heyday; however, he was not too successful in mining. In 1920 he moved to Anchorage and went to work for the Alaska Railroad. He retired as a conductor after thirty-five years of service.

Doris and Adolf Young

Adolf as Conductor on ARR

House on 8th Avenue

Adolph was of German extraction and his true name was Jung. However, when he signed up for the Spanish American War and was asked his name, they wrote it down as "Young," and he never corrected it.

Red Brennan and
Adolph, Sr.

Adolf Young, Jr.

Shortly after his arrival in Anchorage he met DORIS OSKOLKOFF, who was born in Ninilchik, and they were married in 1921. This union bore two children, Adolph W., Jr. and John Charles, both living in Seattle, Washington. Adolph, Jr. and spouse Elizabeth had two daughters, Christy Anne Rowe and Stephanie Jo Cooper. Christy lives in Seattle, and Stephanie lives in Issaquah, Washington. After Adolph retired, the family left Anchorage and settled in Seattle, Washington.

One of the early building contractors in Anchorage was HAROLD L. BLISS. He was the owner and operator of the Bliss Construction Company, which has operated in Anchorage since 1924. Harold was born in Ellsworth County, Kansas in 1884 and came to Anchorage in 1920. He was first employed by the ARR as a master carpenter and later left the Railroad to enter private business as a general contractor. He first was partnered with Earl Lewis and later with Ray C. Larson until he bought out his partners' interests and became sole owner of the business. He built many homes and buildings during his thirty-five years in Anchorage. Prior to his arrival in Anchorage he was general foreman of the AKU silver mines in the Aleutian Chain.

Elizabeth Bliss

ELIZABETH HOLMES was born February 4, 1887 in Niles, Ohio. She and Harold Bliss were married in Cleveland, Ohio in 1917. They came to Anchorage in 1921 and moved into their home at 321 L Street. Elizabeth was a life member of the Anchorage Garden Club, and their home was considered the Eden of Anchorage because of her flower gardens. Harold died 1957, and Elizabeth died in 1979. They are both buried in Angelus Memorial Park in Anchorage.

WILLIAM THOMAS LINKS arrived in Anchorage in 1921 from points north. He was born in Vancouver, Washington in 1871 and was adopted by an aunt after his mother passed away when he was ten years old. At the age of fourteen he worked for the Hudson Bay Company in Canada where he learned the fur trade. When the gold rush started in Dawson, he headed north and followed the gold rushes to Fairbanks, Nome, Ruby and Iditarod. He operated a restaurant in Nenana prior to coming to Anchorage in 1921 and started a mink ranch near what is now the Travelers Inn on 7th Avenue and Gambell Street.

William was married to LILA L. BARNES, who died during childbirth of their daughter, Lila Louise. William then married HILDA B., who was born in Backaryd Blekinge, Sweden in 1886. Sometime after their arrival in Anchorage, William and Hilda separated, and Hilda and daughter Lila remained on the Anchorage property at 634 Gambell Street.

William passed away in 1952 at his moose camp near Hunter Station on the ARR. Hilda died in April 1963, and Lila died in 1982. William is buried in Tract 14, Anchorage Memorial Park, and Hilda and Lila are buried in Tract 18, Anchorage Memorial Park.

———

Another hard-luck prospector and miner from the Iditarod country moved into Anchorage in 1921. ROBERT "BOB" DUNN was born in Scotland in 1857. He made the Klondike gold rush and was in Nome in 1900 and in Fairbanks in 1908. He came to Iditarod in 1910 when the great gold rush started there. He spent the next ten years of his life in Flat and Iditarod and then moved to Anchorage in 1921.

Sometime during the years between 1898 and 1921, Bob spent some time in prison for an unknown crime. While he was incarcerated he supposedly wrote the poem that follows. This poem was given to fifteen-year-old Peter Bagoy in Flat, Alaska. It has never been publicly read, and very few, if any, have heard it other than members of the Peter Bagoy family.

THE UNGRATEFUL MAN
by Robert "Bob" Dunn
as told to Peter J. Bagoy in 1915 in Flat, Alaska

He hit my camp on a rainy day, coming from God knows where.
With a busted place in his overalls, and burrs in his tangled hair.
He wasn't a fop nor he wasn't a dude, but surely he was kind to me,
for he said my method of cooking beans was the best he ever did see.
Well I bedded him down the best I could, and showed him the whiskey jug,
I didn't sleep good on the ground that night, but the stranger was warm and snug.

He was the most grateful man I think, that ever came up that pass,
he praised my grub and he praised my claim and he bragged on my old jackass.
He praised the coffee I brought to him, before he was out of bed,
till my worn out hat got far to small for the size of my swelling head.
Well he stayed and stayed till the spring sun came, and the hill slopes all turned
brown, and the drab flood riffled in the old sluice box, with the snow thaw
coming down.

Then he went away, and I was needing help, for the bacon was low you see,
and the sluicing water it didn't last long, but he had been so kind to me,
I couldn't bear to mention, you understand, that I needed help. So he shed some tears,
and gratefully shook my hand, then borrowed my shovel and frying pan, tobacco
and grub, and went singing away up the Trinity Pass, and never came back again.

He never came back, but he struck a lead at the forks of the little Bear,
a six-foot lead of the Peacock Blue, and now he's a millionaire.
For the hills are high and the days are long, and lone times in between, when
a man forgets that he has a tongue and his starving soul grows lean.
For God put in the first man's heart, the longing for human praise,
and down through the change of many years, that hankering stays and stays.

Well, I met him once plumb face to face on the Red Bluff road last fall,
he looked my way as his car went by, but he never saw me at all.
He never saw me and my feelings ached, as I stood in that dusty trail,
a cheery grin was all I asked, and maybe a friendly hail,
For the hills are high land the days are long, and the lone times in between,
I wanted a grin, and all I got was the stink from his gasoline.
Well I suppose there's lots of things when a fella's a millionaire,
that fill his mind so his poor old friends are crowded clean out of there,
but once he was terribly kind to me, he's rich and I'm sure I'm glad,
but I wish he'd bring that old shovel back for I'm needing it mighty bad.

Bob Dunn died in 1952 and is buried in the Pioneer Tract, Anchorage Memorial Park Cemetery.

Among the many immigrants arriving in Alaska from other countries looking for a new life
was the JOSEPH MERENDA family. Father JOSEPH, spouse NICOLINA, daughter ROSA,
and son SAMUEL arrived in the Juneau-Douglas area in 1914. Joseph found employment
with the Treadwell Mine in Douglas and after two years, in 1916, moved the family to
Anchorage. He found employment with the AEC at the Eska Coal Mine as did his son Sam.

The family lived at the Jonesville, Eska and Premier coal mines where
Joseph was employed. World War I came along, and son Sam was
called to serve. Upon his discharge in 1921 he returned to Eska,
bringing with him an old Army buddy, named JAKE ANGELI.

Sam and Rosa Merenda

Joseph, Rosa, Samuel and Nicoline Merenda

Rosa with Daughters

Jacopo "Jake" Angeli

Joe Merenda, Jake Angeli and Buddies

Louise, Anita and Gloria
at Eska Mine

Gloria, Louise, Anita, Rosa, Sam Merenda and
Jake Angeli in Anchorage

Jake met Rosa Merenda, and the courtship began. They were married in 1922 and set up housekeeping at the mine. The union of Jake and Rosa bore four children, three daughters and one son. Son Giovanni died at the age of two. The children grew up in the coal mining camps until Jake sent the family to Anchorage in 1936 to continue their schooling.

Jake worked at the Premier Mine until it flooded in 1935. He then went to work for the Evan Jones Coal Mine until the disastrous explosion in 1937. This was the worst mine disaster in Alaska history. Fourteen men were killed in the explosion. Jake Angeli was one of four men who survived. The fourteen men who were killed, all friends of Jake, were Abel Asikainen, Joe Cernick, Pete Ferreni, Asel Huttila, Lester Lamson, Joe Lucas, John Mattson, Frank Melznek, Otto Mikkola, Robert Nakki, Peter Olson, Jack Saarela, Paul Williams, and Augustine Yerbich.

Jake moved into Anchorage to be with the family and was employed by the city of Anchorage at the pump station. Rosa stayed home, raising the children and tending her garden. She started working at the Federal Building after Jake passed away and was retired just prior to her death in 1967.

Jake was born in Italy in 1892 and died in Anchorage in 1945. Rosa was born in Catabria, Italy in 1896 and died in Anchorage in 1967. Patriarch Joseph Merenda died in 1940, and matriarch Nicolina Merenda died in Anchorage in 1938.

Jake's and Rosa's daughter Gloria Angeli married Joseph Breyer, and they had two children, John J. and Barbara J. Breyer O'Leary, who both live in Anchorage. Daughter Anita never married. Daughter Louise and James Nichols had one daughter, Sandra Lee, who lives in Anchorage. Son Giovanni is buried in the Moose Tract, Anchorage Memorial Park Cemetery. Joseph and Nicolina Merenda and Jake and Rosa Angeli are buried in the Catholic Tract, Anchorage Memorial Park Cemetery.

Another family that emigrated from Italy and arrived in Alaska in 1917 was SILVIO and MARIA RAUTH and daughter MARY RAUTH. They first settled in Arizona soon after their arrival in the United States in 1916. They were attracted to the new land of Alaska and moved to Juneau in 1917. Silvio and Maria operated the Savoy Restaurant in Juneau doing the cooking and managing, while Mary worked as the waitress.

Maria and Silvio, Rauth and Sam Figurelli

Tony and Mary Pastro

In 1918 Mary Rauth met a hardrock miner named SAM FIGURELLI, and they were married in 1919. Mary was born in Tyrol, Switzerland in 1900. Their first child was born in Juneau in 1920. After hearing about the new town of Anchorage and the completion of the Alaska Railroad, the Rauth family and the new family of Figurelli all moved to Anchorage in 1921. Soon after their arrival in Anchorage, Sam and Mary had a set of twins, one of whom died at birth. In 1924 another son was born to them. One month after the birth of the second son, Sam was killed in a cave-in while working for the city of Anchorage in the installation of water lines.

Mary at Age 80

In 1925 Mary married TONY PASTRO, a coal miner who was working at the Premier Mine in the Matanuska Valley. Tony was born in Treviso, Italy in 1885 and came to Alaska in 1915. He did contract work for the AEC during the construction days of the Alaska Railroad. In 1930 Tony and his father-in-law, Silvio Rauth, purchased the Nevada Hotel and Café located one lot in from the corner of 4th Avenue and B Street. In 1933 Silvio sold his interest in the Hotel to Tony's brother George Pastro and retired to Elsinore, California. In 1937 Tony and Mary built the Lido Hotel and Café on the corner lot next to the Nevada Hotel, which was torn down and replaced with a bowling alley.

The Lido Café and Hotel building was two stories with the café on the main floor and twenty rooms upstairs. In the basement were a cocktail lounge and the Aleutian Gardens nightclub. During WWII Keith Capper, a newly arrived entrepreneur, leased the bowling alleys and the Aleutian Gardens cocktail lounge. During the war years the entire building was destroyed by fire and was rebuilt. In 1953 Mary and Tony retired and sold the Lido complex to an investor. It was again destroyed by the 1964 earthquake. At the time of the quake, Bagoy's Flowers had opened their new

Lido Café

Lido Hotel and Cafe

Pastro Home

Eugene Pastro

Richard Pastro

shop in the space occupied by the Lido Café, and it was also destroyed by the quake.

Mary Pastro and Sam Figurelli had three children who took the last name of their stepfather,

Tony Pastro. Son Rudy, whose twin died at birth, never married and lives in Oregon. Son Richard and spouse, Lois, had two children. James R. lives at Anchor Point, Alaska, and Anthony J. lives in Fairbanks. Son Eugene and spouse, Emily, had seven children. Rosemarie Pastro de Farias, Mary Anne Pastro Gee, Patricia Louise Pastro Sullivan, Theresa Catherine Pastro Mar and David Anthony Pastro all live in Seattle, Washington. Sister Margaret Mary Pastro, a Catholic nun, lives in Portland, Oregon, and Father Vincent Jerome Pastro, a Catholic priest, lives in Tacoma, Washington. Tony Pastro died in 1961 in California. Mary Pastro died in 1994. Both are buried in Seattle, Washington.

The JOHN B. BAGOY family arrived in Anchorage in 1921 from Flat, Alaska. John Bagoy was born in the village of Dunave' in the state of Dalmatia and the country of Croatia in 1869. His family were poor farmers and lived a peasant's life on the land. At the age of seventeen he was conscripted into the Austro-Hungarian army and served two hitches. He was subject to further conscription as a reservist.

In 1893 he left for the United States in search of a better life. He did not find it in New York, and with a new-found friend and countryman set out for California. They first landed in Angels Camp, California and worked in the silver and gold mines.

John B. Bagoy

Marie Bagoy

The cry of gold in the Klondike lured him to Skagway and the Chilkoot in 1896. He worked his way over the pass by packing loads for other stampeders. He earned enough to get his twelve hundred pound grubstake by 1897-98 and was on his way. Upon arriving at Dawson he found that most of the ground was well staked and there wasn't much left to choose from. He joined a concession with a man named Johnson who held three claims on

Hunker Creek. Johnson held the claims, and miners worked for him on shares. This arrangement was called a concession.

He earned a pretty good stake and left for Nome in 1900, but there he found nothing. He returned to Bakersfield, California and, with a partner, opened a general store. He decided to take out his citizenship in 1906 and then take a trip to visit the "old country."

In the village of Trebinje, just north of Dubrovnik, he met MARIE ANTOINETTE VLAHUSIC', a twenty year old beauty who was born in Linz, Austria in 1886. Her father was a civilian concessionaire with the Austrian Army and moved to various military posts operating commissaries. A whirlwind courtship ensued, and they were married in 1907. In 1908 they departed for the United States, first settling in Tonopah, Nevada, where John found work in the silver mines and where first child, Peter, was born that same year.

The cry of "gold" was again heard, and this time in Fairbanks, Alaska. John packed up two-month old Peter and Marie, and off they went by stage to San Francisco and then by train to Seattle and steamer to Skagway. The White Pass and Yukon Railway was built by then, so the trip to Whitehorse was easy. They boarded a steamer and headed for Ft. Gibbon and up the Tanana to Nenana and then up the Chena to Fairbanks.

Roadhouse on Discovery

That fall John staked a claim on Fox Gulch and spent the first winter in a tent, mucking out a drift. Marie cranked the windlass hauling up the bucket of muck at thirty below zero with young Peter on her back. In the spring John gave up on Fox Gulch and moved over to Goldstream, where his luck did not improve. The winter of 1909 found them moving into town into a log cabin on Garden Island, where Marie took in washing and John found work as a waiter and bartender in town.

Again John heard the call of "gold," this time in Iditarod. Down river they went in 1910, landing in Iditarod that summer. Marie was with child again, and in November 1910 a daughter, Doris, was born. She was the first child born in the Iditarod mining camp and was the talk of the town.

Flat, 1916

John's mining luck was all bad, and he went from job to job to keep the family afloat, doing some prospecting and "sniping old claims" in between times. He had three roadhouses that befell the water from floods and the Riley Investment Company dredges. He finally found some bottomland on Flat Creek--a house, a barn and a large root cellar--and decided to be a farmer again. By this time, 1919, their sixth child was born. By 1921 the mining was falling off and eldest daughter and son Peter needed a high school education, so John formed a lottery and sold tickets on his farm and raised enough money to move to Anchorage. Another long and arduous trip ensued from

Anchorage First Home and Greenhouse

Flower Shop Home, 1941

Flower Shop in Lido Building
After the Earthquake

Peter J. Bagoy

Doris Bagoy Faroe

Iditarod to Anchorage on which the family lost most of their worldly goods and mementos in the Nenana River.

Arriving in Anchorage in 1921, the family of eight found temporary lodging in the Gitchell Hotel, and then John located two cabins on 4th Avenue and A Street. He pulled the two of them together and made a livable place. He landed a job with the ARR in the foundry and worked the greenhouse and garden in the evenings along with Marie. They were able to make a decent living, raising hothouse tomatoes, cucumbers, and other vegetables and selling them to the local stores. Marie was talented with her flowers, and in the summer she did well arranging flowers for weddings and funerals. In the winter she made her own flowers and dipped them in wax to make wreaths and other items. They were becoming successful in this venture and in 1935 were able to build a new home and also open the first florist shop in Anchorage and also in Alaska.

John passed away in 1940, and Marie carried on until she had to retire before her time in 1953. Daughter Mary Lakshas and her husband took over the shop and operated it until the death of Otto Lakshas. Mary sold the shop in 1972, but the name still remains the same in Anchorage, as the first and oldest flower shop in Anchorage and in Alaska.

The union of John Bagoy and Marie Vlahusic' produced eight children. Eldest child Peter married Helen Wilson and had two step-daughters who live in Anchorage, Donna Hobson and Delores Weiler. Peter J. Bagoy, Jr. lives in Anchorage. The second child, a boy, was stillborn in Fairbanks, and the third child was stillborn in Iditarod. Eldest daughter, Doris, married H. A. Cappy Faroe, and they had one daughter, Alexandra Marie, who passed away in 1987. Daughter Mary married Otto Lakshas and they had one son, Jeffrey, who lives in Florida. Daughter Eileen married Richard Bell, and they had one son John, who lives in Las Vegas, Nevada. Daughter Gabrielle married Roy Holm, and they had two daughters. Julie Holm Kavanaugh lives in Livermore, California, and Eileen Holm Quakenbush lives in Seattle, Washington. The youngest son, John, married Thelma Osbo, and they had three children. John, Jr. lives in Coos Bay, Oregon, Rayna Bagoy Larson lives in Klamath Falls, Oregon, and Candice Bagoy lives in Anchorage.

Mary Bagoy
Lakshas

Gabrielle
Bagoy Holm

Eileen Bagoy
Bell

John P. Bagoy

John B. Bagoy, Sr. died in 1940; Marie A. Bagoy died in 1982. Peter J. Bagoy died in 1997; his spouse Helen Bagoy died in 1992. H. A. "Cappy" Faroe died in 1982, and Doris Bagoy Faroe died in 2000. All are buried in the Catholic Tract, Anchorage Memorial Park Cemetery.

In January 1906 LEE VINCENT RAY arrived in Seward at the age of twenty-eight. He was born in Brookline, Massachusetts in 1878. He studied for the bar under several attorneys, spent a year in Ketchikan prior to going to Seward, and opened his law office in the Harriman bank building in Seward in 1906. In April 1907 he was appointed Assistant U. S. Attorney in the third judicial division and was initially stationed in Seward but subsequently was transferred to Valdez, where he met and married HAZEL SHELDON.

Lee Vincent Ray   Hazel Sheldon Ray

Hazel first arrived in Alaska in 1900 at the age of eleven in the company of her parents and brother Charles. Hazel was born in Seattle. Washington in 1888 and grew up in Seattle. Prior to coming to Alaska, the family lived in Cape Arago, Oregon, where her father operated the lighthouse. Then he became employed by a company that proposed to construct a railroad from the west side of Cook Inlet to Nome. The first year in Alaska they operated a road-house on the shore of Lake Illiamna. When the venture failed, the family returned to Seattle. Hazel returned to Valdez in 1904 and was working as a telephone operator when she met L. V.

1913, First Territorial Legislative Meeting

The famous Keystone Canyon War trial was going on, and shortly after their marriage the trial was moved to Juneau. The newlyweds accompanied the court until the trial ended, and then they moved back to Valdez. Then in l910 they moved back to Seward.

In 1912 Alaska became a United States Territory, and the first Territorial Legislature met in March 1913. L. V. Ray participated in this historic event as President of the newly formed Senate. A landmark decision was made by this group seven years prior to the passing of the nineteenth amendment to the United States

L. V. with President Harding

Lee V. Ray, Jr.

Patricia Ray

Constitution. The first act of this first Alaska Legislature was to grant women the right to vote.

In 1919 when the Railroad was completed to Anchorage, L. V. could then travel easily to Anchorage and represent his clients here. He spent a good share of his time in Anchorage representing his clients and traveled constantly between the two cities. In 1921, just after Anchorage was incorporated and Leopold David began his first years as Mayor of Anchorage, David and L. V. formed a partnership with David operating the Anchorage portion of their firm.

L. V. served as Mayor of Seward for three terms and officiated at the Seward portion of the visit to Alaska by President Harding in 1923. He served as President of the Board of Law Examiners and was city attorney for many years.

In 1946 L. V. Ray died at the age of sixty-eight. A permanent commemoration of him is the mountain near Mile 32 on the Seward Highway named in his honor, the L. V. Ray Peak.

The union of L. V. and Hazel produced two children. L. V. Ray, Jr. died accidentally in 1941 and had never married. Patricia Ray Williams still lives in Seward. She had two children, Derick Williams who lives in Texas and Patricia Erickson who lives in Anchorage. L. V. died in 1946, and Hazel died in 1982. They are both buried in the Seward Municipal Cemetery.

CHAPTER V

1922

The year 1922 found Mayor LEOPOLD DAVID still in office and three new members added to the City Council:

DR. J. B. BEESON
HARRY CRIBB
W. S. HORNING

It was a quiet year, as the only startling news was that fire chief Dolan resigned and Carl Martin was appointed temporary chief.

Anchorage High School graduated nine students, five boys and four girls, all of whom are deceased.

IRMA MARSH (No photo)
RICHARD SESSIONS (No photo)
MARGARET STEWART (No photo)

Violet Elliot

Edward McMahill

Ulah Murphy

Layton Schell

Selby Seeley

Harold Sogn

An oldtimer who came to Nome in 1902, JOHN RODGERS was Anchorage's oldest resident at the time of his death. He was born in Scotland in 1841 and roamed the United States in his youth until he went to Nome. He opened a restaurant in Nome in 1903 and operated it until he moved to Anchorage in 1922. He was unable to work for many years and lived on a small pension and income from several lots he owned in town. John died in 1942 at the ripe old age of one hundred one years. He is buried in the Pioneer Tract, Anchorage Memorial Park Cemetery.

A well-known Anchorage businessman, GRANT REED came to Alaska in 1900, landing in Skagway where he was agent for the White Pass and Yukon Railway. Eight years later he was appointed agent for the Alaska Steamship Company in Skagway and still later was agent for the Copper River and Northwestern Railway in Cordova. In 1915 he established a mercantile business in Chisana, which he operated until 1917 when he again became agent for the Copper River road. He was later transferred to McCarthy as the lines agent and again opened a mercantile store there until it was destroyed by fire two years later.

Grant Reed

Grant joined the Alaska Railroad in 1920, starting at Tunnel, then Matanuska, and finally Anchorage in 1921. Soon after his arrival in Anchorage he opened a women's shop and named it Reed's Store. It was jointly operated by him and his wife, Sadie.

Grant served one term as Mayor of Anchorage in 1928, however still held his job with the Alaska Railroad. He retired from the Railroad in 1936 and sold his interest in the store several years after Sadie passed away. He became a semi-invalid and needed daily care, so he hired a nurse, Agnes Sayers of Ketchikan, whom he married in 1939. Grant disposed of his business interests, and he and Agnes retired to Long Beach, California in 1940. Grant passed away in 1942 in Long Beach.

GEORGE LEONARD JOHNSON arrived in Anchorage in January 1922. He first came to Cordova in 1908 and lived there for three years working on the Copper River Railroad. He moved to Katalla in 1911, was a forest ranger on Fox Island, and then started a mink ranch on Little Kayak Island. The same year of 1911 he married MAY S. KIRKHOM, and they then moved south to Douglas where George worked in the Treadwell Mine until he moved to Anchorage in 1922. He engaged in raising mink and was a part-time special agent for the Alaska Railroad. He and his wife also engaged in tinting photographs and later sold this business to Denny Hewitt. May stayed with Hewitts and ran the tinting department, and George worked full-time as special agent for the ARR.

George and May had one son, Leonard, who had a career with the Alaska Railroad as a conductor. After Leonard's retirement to California he continued the hobby of painting and tinting portraits, following his parents' tradition. It is unknown where George and May went when they retired and what year they passed away. Son Leonard died in California in 1999.

ISAAC COLE MCFARLAND arrived in Anchorage in 1922. He first landed in Alaska in Cordova in 1919 where he was employed by the Carlisle Packing Company until he moved to Anchorage. He spent the next ten years in Anchorage while working in the bakery business. He spent the next thirteen years chasing gold in Ophir and Fairbanks. Cole, as he was known, was born in Prosser, Washington in 1902. He and MARGARET were married in 1924. She was born in Spokane, Washington in 1904.

Cole died in Spokane, Washington in 1976. It is unknown where Margaret died. Their marriage bore two children. It is unknown where son, Cole E., and daughter, Patricia McFarland Melendrey, presently reside.

BURT A. DOOL was another arrival in Anchorage in 1922 and was immediately involved in business. He was born in Cassopolis, Michigan in 1880 and was the oldest child of a family of ten brothers and sisters. He made his way to the west coast in search of opportunity and became involved in the laundry business, working for the Metropolitan Laundry in Seattle, Washington. He eventually became superintendent of the plant until 1922 when he moved his family to Anchorage.

In 1915 Eli DeHon, brother of Mrs. Dool, started the Pioneer Laundry in Anchorage and was joined by Burt in 1922. Some years later Burt became sole owner of the plant and operated it until his passing in 1934. He is buried in the I.O.O.F. Tract, Anchorage Memorial Park Cemetery.

A well-known and prominent attorney in Alaska, GEORGE B. GRIGSBY was born in Sioux Falls, South Dakota in 1874. He received his education at the University of South Dakota and was admitted to the bar in 1896. He opened his first law office in his native state of South Dakota in 1898.

When the Spanish American War broke out, George received a commission as First Lieutenant in his father's command, which was part of Teddy Roosevelt's Rough Riders.

George first set up practice in Alaska in Ketchikan in 1900 and in 1902 went to Nome to join his father, Colonel Melville Grigsby, Retired, who had been appointed United States district attorney for the second judicial district. Young George took a position on his father's staff as an assistant district attorney and remained in that position for six years. He was then elevated to the position of United States district attorney serving until 1910.

George left the government service in 1912 and set up private practice in Nome. In 1914 he was elected Mayor of Nome and in 1916 was elected attorney general for the Territory of Alaska. After assuming this office he moved to Juneau. In 1919 he was elected delegate to Congress from Alaska to fill the unexpired term of the late Delegate Sulzer. After completing his term as delegate he moved to Anchorage in 1922 and practiced here for many years. He was President of the Anchorage Bar Association at the time of his death in 1962 in Santa Rosa, California, where he was spending the winter. [Reprinted from *The Alaska Weekly*, August 28, 1928, and *The Nome and Seward Peninsula*, 1905.]

One of Alaska's most admired and honored publishers, editors and newsmen, ROYAL GRATTON SOUTHWORTH came north to Dawson during the 1898 stampede and worked his way south as a newspaper publisher in Fairbanks, Nenana and other towns until he became editor of the *Anchorage Daily Times* in 1922. He was born in Stockton, California in 1876, and came over the Chilkoot in 1898 enroute to the Klondike.

The story of his career in Alaska sounds like the history of the progress of the Territory. As a newspaper reporter and publisher he met and knew almost every oldtimer in Alaska, and he interviewed almost every important visitor for half a century. He witnessed the change of transportation from the days of the Dyea and Chilkoot to the modern railroads and the development of the airline business.

When Nenana became the temporary northern terminus of the Railroad in 1916, Roy sold his interest in the Fairbanks paper and moved down to Nenana. He was there when President Harding drove the golden spike linking the northern and southern ends of the railroad. He printed the first ice pool tickets when there were only a few hundred local people around.

When the division point of the Railroad became Anchorage, Roy and family moved here, and he became editor of the *Anchorage Daily Times* until he retired. After his retirement he became Secretary of the local Elks lodge and stayed in that position for nine years. He and his wife retired to Grass Valley, California in 1952, and he died one year later in 1953. He is buried in Grass Valley. Roy married CAMILLE HUTTON in Fairbanks in 1915, and the marriage bore one daughter, Margaret Southworth Dyer, whose last known residence was Juneau.

———

RALPH GROVER'S job with the military brought him and his wife ILONA to Anchorage in 1922. Ralph was a reserve Lieutenant in the Signal Corp. He was a part-time bookkeeper and temporary postmaster and owned a paint store for several years. His wife Ilona worked as secretary to attorney Warren Cuddy for ten years. Ralph was an active leader in the American Legion and held various offices in the Legion. Ralph was born in 1887 and died in 1955. Ilona was born in 1888 and died in 1956. Both are buried in the Elks Tract, Anchorage Memorial Park.

———

A man who had a hand in the construction of many pioneer roads in southcentral Alaska, FRED SPACH was born in Somonauk, Illinois in 1883. He was trained as a civil engineer and started his career in Idaho where he worked for the highway department. In Idaho he met and married his wife, HENRIETTA, who was born in Mora, Minnesota in 1892.

Fred first came to Anchorage in 1922 and worked for the Alaska Railroad. In 1924 he was appointed city clerk of Anchorage until 1926, when he started with the Alaska Road Commission as assistant engineer. In 1934 Fred was in charge of the vast Kuskokwim area for the construction of roads, trails and landing fields for the United States Government under the direction of the Alaska Road Commission. The Kuskokwim Road District covers all of the area between the Alaska Range and the Yukon River from a line extending from Lake Minchumina through Poorman and thence to the coast.

Fred was reassigned in later years to the Anchorage District, working under Superintendent Christopher Edmonds. He was assistant engineer on the

Fred Spach

Henrietta Spach

Glenn Highway project from Palmer to Glenallen in 1941, as well as on many other local roads and highways.

Fred died in Portland, Oregon in 1953, and Henrietta died in Spokane, Washington in 1981. They had one son, Roger Spach, who lives in Anchorage.

Roger Spach

PAUL and ELEANOR MARSCH arrived in Anchorage in 1922, like so many others, to help build the Alaska Railroad. Paul worked for the ARR for a number of years and then worked for W. J. Boudreau Company, a wholesale grocer. In 1936 and 1937 Paul served on the City Council. In 1941 Paul went to work for the government at what is now Elmendorf Air Force Base and was there until his retirement in 1957.

Paul was born in Portland, Oregon in 1889, and Eleanor was born in Minnesota in 1894. Eleanor helped found the Ladies Auxiliary of Jack Henry Post #1, American Legion, and served as its President. During WWII she headed up the Selective Service Commission in Anchorage. An ardent housewife and mother and a superb poker player, she still found time for community service.

Eleanor Marsch

Paul Marsch

The marriage of Paul and Eleanor in 1918 produced two children. Peggy Marsch married Herb Enberg and they had two children. Karen Enberg Foster lives in Chattaroy, Washington, and Richard C. lives in Anchorage. Son Burton and spouse Lou had two children, Kurt P., who lives in Anchorage, and Vonn M., who lives in San Francisco, California.

Paul and Peggy Marsch

Paul and Burt Marsch

Marsch Family

Paul died in 1976 in St. Petersburg, Florida. Eleanor died in 1978, and daughter Peggy Enberg died in 1999. Eleanor is buried at Angelus Memorial Park in the Pioneer section, and Peggy and Paul had their ashes scattered.

Burt Marsch

Peggy Enberg

George and Jeannette Mumford

Charlotte and Her Mother
Jeannette

Mumford Home

Charlotte Mumford Simpson Family

Another professional who came to Anchorage in 1922, GEORGE F. MUMFORD was born in Maryland in 1895 and was raised in Maryland and Delaware. He was working for the Pennsylvania Railroad in Wilmington, Delaware when he got the urge to travel to Alaska. It was a land he read about in travel books and publications of the day. He had a penchant for travel and often said that his hotel bills from traveling kept him broke.

George arrived in Anchorage in the spring of 1922 and immediately went to work for the Alaska Railroad, earning money for his next planned trip. His travel plans changed, however, when he met a young lady named JEANNETTE NIEMENEN.

Jeannette was born in Eveleth, Minnesota in 1901 and came to Anchorage to visit her brother, Matt Nieminen, a local bush pilot making a name for himself in Alaska flying. She was employed in the National Bank of Alaska, and, after their marriage in 1923, George also went to work for the same bank. They were the entire bank staff for many years and were well known throughout Alaska's financial circles. George remained with the bank for thirty-seven years and was one of the officers who helped guide it from a small territorial bank to the State's largest financial institution. After 1935 George served as a director and officer of the Anchorage Daily Times Publishing Company. His fraternal and civic activities included Exalted Ruler of the Elks, member of the City Public Utilities Board, and President of the Alaska Rural Rehabilitation Corporation, which was responsible for the Matanuska Valley colonization project.

After Jeannette left the bank, she managed the Mumford Apartments at 135 Christenson Drive. George retired as vice-president and director of the bank in 1961 and became involved in the ownership of the Parsons Hotel, the Lane Hotel and the 5th Avenue Hotel, along with son George, Jr., who managed two of the properties.

George and Jeannette had been planning a world cruise and in 1964 left for a sixty-three day trip around the world. While in Montevideo, Uruguay George suffered a heart attack and passed away. Jeannette died in 1978.

George and Jeannette had two children. Son George, Jr. lived in Pleasanton, California and passed away in

2000. He had two daughters, Stephanie Anne Mumford, who lives in Rockville, Maryland, and Jeannette Mumford Perrera, who lives in Pleasanton, California. Daughter Charlotte Mumford Simpson married Lewis Simpson and they had four children. Lewis, Jr. lives in Wasilla, Alaska; John Scott lives in Puyallup, Washington; Steve lives in Big Lake, Alaska; and Stacy Moe lives in Eagle River. Charlotte died in 1983.

First-class salesman CLARK ANDRESEN was born in Minneapolis, Minnesota in 1904 and was two years old when his family moved to Seattle, Washington. At the age of eighteen Clark left for Anchorage to join his brother, Moritz, who had already settled here. Clark finished high school in Anchorage and graduated with the class of 1925. While in high school, he obtained a part-time job with Brown and Hawkins mercantile company, and, when the Anchorage store closed in 1927, he was transferred to Seward. He managed the hardware department in the Seward store until he was offered a job with the Hunt and Mottet Hardware wholesaler in Tacoma, Washington.

Clark and Midge Andresen

The Hunt and Mottet people recognized Clark's sales ability and wanted him on their team as the Alaska representative. They were not wrong in their judgment, as Clark proved to be a real go-getter and literally put Hunt and Mottet on the map in Alaska. He traveled throughout Alaska for the next forty-two years and took on other lines, including Zellerbach Paper Company and Brown and Bigelow.

First Home

In 1939 Clark married a young beauty named MARJORIE "MIDGE" REEVE. Midge was born in Roseburg, Oregon and came to Alaska with her parents in 1933. Midge and Clark married in Fairbanks, however they settled in Anchorage, where they raised their family. Clark was an avid baseball fan and was known throughout Alaska as "Mr. Baseball" due to his prowess as a player in his younger days.

Last Home

Clark and Midge retired to the Seattle area in 1976 where he spent all of his spare time watching the baseball games.

The union of Clark and Midge produced three daughters. Daughter Scarlett Kay DuBois lives in Anchorage, and she had one son and one daughter. Kash Shawn Brouillet lives in Los Angeles; Tara Desiree Rosenbaum lives in Seattle, Washington. Daughter Judy LaVerne Rosenberg lives in Anchorage, and she had one

Whole Andresen Family

Clark with Brothers

Scarlett Kay Bubois

Judy Rosenberg

Candace Jennings

son and one daughter. Robert Clark Martin lives in Yokosuka, Japan; Machele Kristen Ruthemeyer lives in San Luis Obispo, California. Daughter Candice Reeve Jennings had one son and one daughter. Lewis Paul and Greta Maria both live on Vashon Island, Washington. Clark passed away in 1992 in Seattle. Midge returned to Anchorage and presently lives here.

RUFUS HORTON NICHOLS and spouse, MARTHA, arrived in Anchorage in 1922 with their family. Rufus worked for the Alaska Railroad as a telegrapher in Anchorage and at McKinley Park. He later was hired as a police officer for the city of Anchorage.

Martha and Rufus Nichols

Rufus Nichols and Family

They had five children, three sons and two daughters. Daughter Frances worked as a telephone operator for the city of Anchorage. She married John Andresen and they had one son David, who lives in Seattle, Washington. Son Marion and spouse, Madge, moved to Ashland, Oregon, and they had one daughter, Phyllis Nichols Garrison, who lives in Ashland, Oregon. Son Orrin was a conductor on the ARR. He married Louise Palmer, and they had two children. Luella Nichols McKinley lives in Melberta, Nebraska; Lorrin lives in El Cajon, California.

Son Ralph owned a drug store and also a Dairy Queen ice cream parlor. He and his spouse, Margo, had three daughters. Barbara Nichols Kau lives in Bend, Oregon; Beverly lives in Dusseldorf, Germany; Linda lives in Junction City, Oregon. Daughter Bessie married Deward Benton, and they had three children. David lives in Merit Island, Florida; Martha lives in Coco, Florida; and Deward lives in Rockledge, Florida. All of the original Nichols family first and second generation are deceased.

One of the early legal minds who came to Anchorage in 1922, LAWRENCE D. ROACH was born in County Cork, Ireland in 1885 and immigrated to Canada in 1901 with his family. He entered Alaska in 1908 as a representative of the Northern Navigation Company, which operated sternwheeler steamers from St. Michael to the Dawson gold fields on the Yukon River. He later became agent in Cordova for the North Pacific Line, which was operated by the Guggenheim copper interests and which later became the Alaska Steamship Company.

Edna Roach

Hillard Roach

While laid up for the winter in Fairbanks when the river froze over, Lawrence took up studying law under a Fairbanks attorney. He and his wife, EDNA BURNHAM ROACH, were living in Juneau when he received his license to practice law. Edna was with child that year, and, having complications, she was sent to Seattle for medical attention and died in childbirth.

Lawrence served several posts in Alaska including being commissioner in Kodiak in 1921 and later practicing law in Juneau and Seward. He came to Anchorage in 1922 and lived here until 1962. He was elected to the City Council in 1936, and in 1938 he became the first city judge for Anchorage. Judge Roach died in 1962, and at that time he was the oldest practicing attorney in Anchorage in time of service. His son Hillard became a Captain in the Merchant Marine and now resides in the Matanuska Valley.

L. D. with Pipe

WILLIAM FRANCIS MULCAHY was born in New Haven, Connecticut in 1896. He spent his young life in New Haven and married GERTRUDE EMMA GUTHRIE in 1916. In 1922 Bill and family moved to Anchorage where he had accepted employment with the newly completed Alaska Railroad. During his tenure with the ARR, he held many positions--claim agent, auditor of station accounts, auditor, acting chief accountant and general auditor.

In his spare time William served the youth of Anchorage promoting recreational activities and sports facilities. He promoted facilities for basketball, hockey and baseball by interesting civic leaders and clubs in providing these facilities. Baseball, however, was his favorite, and in 1947 he was named Alaska's first National Baseball Congress Commissioner of baseball, a post he filled for three years. In 1950 he introduced Little League baseball to Anchorage. He was active in the YMCA, serving on its first board of directors, and worked with the USO and Red Cross.

While Bill was promoting baseball, Gertrude was busy bringing entertainment to Anchorage through the formation of the Anchorage Little Theater group. She opened the first "dancing and dramatic art school," which was called "The Gertrude Mulcahy Studio."

Gertrude Mulcahy

William Mulcahy

Alys Mulcahy in
Snow White

Gertrude Mulcahy as
an Actress

First Home on
Government Hill

Mark and Alys LaFollette

She produced many plays and built her own props and costumes. Gertrude was an accomplished actress, and, prior to coming to Alaska, she and her sister, at a young age, were billed as the "Haven Sisters" and were on the "Bill" along with Mae West in New York City.

Gertrude and Bill received numerous awards and recognition as devoted volunteers for the USO and as promoters of baseball, the YMCA and other organizations in Anchorage.

Dave Mulcahy

The following poem was supposedly written by Gertrude Mulcahy and is re-printed here with the permission of her daughter, Alys LaFollette.

> If once you have lived in Alaska
> You'll never be quite the same
> Even though you look as you've always looked
> And your name is the same old name.
>
> You may travel the world for the rest of your days
> Or simply stay home and sew
> But Alaska days and Alaska ways
> Will follow where'er you go.
>
> You may hobnob with the finest bunch
> Or with an ordinary group just keep
> But you'll always remember Alaskans and Alaskan ways
> And dream of them in your sleep.
>
> And you don't know why or can't say how
> And you'll never even know
> Why Alaska is buried right in your soul
> Be you cheechako or sourdough.
>
> For there's something about this very land
> Which leaves its mark forever
> And it could be the touch of the master's hand
> Bringing you closer to his endeavor.

Joe Mulcahy

Bill and family moved to Milford, Connecticut in 1953 following his retirement from the Railroad. He and Gertrude had three children. Son Joseph had three children: Robert J. of East Haven, Connecticut, Geralyn Rakich of Pembroke, New Hampshire, and Mary Anne who lives in Naugatuck. Daughter, Alys Mulcahy LaFollette, lives in Albuquerque, New Mexico, and she had two children. Suzanne LaFollette Cameron and Barbara N. Senne live in Pinehurst, North Carolina. Son David had one daughter, Bonnie Irene, who resides in West Haven, Connecticut. Bill Mulcahy died in 1965, and Gertrude died in 1974. David died in 1955, and Joseph died in 1995. All are buried in New Haven, Connecticut.

BESSIE HARRISON was running a boarding house in Cripple Creek, Colorado in 1905. She was a widow with two children, Jack and Wilma. Jack was born in Cripple Creek in 1907, and Wilma was born in 1911. Bessie married for the second time to Daily Sullivan, and they had two children, Doris and Charles.

Bessie and Family

In 1921 the family packed up and headed for Alaska, first moving to Chickaloon, Seward, and finally to Anchorage in 1922. In 1922 the family returned to Seward, with the exception of Jack who stayed in Anchorage to finish high school. After completing high school, Jack was employed as the youngest big game guide in Alaska at the time. Jack met and married LORENE CUTHBERSON in 1930 in Estes Park, Colorado. Lorene was born in Sterling, Kansas in 1905. She arrived in Anchorage as a home economics and music teacher in 1928. Jack was employed with the Alaska Railroad as a locomotive engineer. In 1945 he established a cinder block plant in Anchorage, which was the forerunner of Anchorage Sand and Gravel Company. In 1946 he joined the Anchorage Sand and Gravel Company as vice-president and served for the next twenty years until his health forced him to retire.

Doris Sullivan

Charles Sullivan

Lorene was kept busy raising their two daughters and was extremely active in various music and theater organizations. After Jack's death in 1968, Lorene opened the Hat Box, a ladies' ready-to-wear specializing in hats. Her activities and interest in music made her a popular figure in Anchorage. She organized the United Choir of all Faiths, which was the forerunner of the Anchorage Community Chorus. In 1992 she was named Alaskan of the Year, and, when the Anchorage Performing Arts Center was built, a lobby of the center was named in her honor.

Jack Harrison

Wilma Harrison

Lorene Harrison

Jack Harrison

Jack and Lorene with Family

Jack died in 1968 and is buried in the Pioneer Tract, Anchorage Memorial Park Cemetery. Lorene presently resides in the Anchorage Pioneer Home. The couple had two daughters. Daughter Carol Ann Dodd had four children. Kelly Dodd Watt lives in Michigan; Diane Harrison lives in Crested Butte, Colorado; Romney Dodd Ortland and Edward Harrison Dodd live in Anchorage. Daughter Peggy Harrison Vielbig had two sons. Earl is deceased; Eric lives in Boulder, Colorado.

IRA S. BAILEY was born in Mt. Vernon, Texas in 1890. As a young man he learned the trade of interior decorating and was plying his trade when WWI broke out. He enlisted in the United States Army at Corsicana, Texas and served from July 1917 to April 1919.

Mattie Bailey

Ira Bailey

Two weeks before he left for overseas duty, he married MATTIE MATHISON, who was teaching school in Texas. Mattie was born in Texas in 1894. Her parents, Claude and Ida Mathison, went from Texas to Hope, Alaska in 1901 in search of gold. Not having any luck in Hope, the family moved to Seward in 1904, and then back to Texas in late 1904. After about one year they moved back to Alaska, landing in Unga on the Aleutian chain, where Claude worked in a coal mine. They moved back to Seward again and stayed until 1911 when Ida took the family back to Texas and lived there for the next seven years. Ira and Mattie were married in Corsicana, Texas.

When Ira sailed for France, Ida, Mattie's mother, took all of the family back to Seward, Alaska. Mattie was pregnant at the time and the firstborn son, Ira S., Jr., was born in Seward in 1918. When WWI ended and Ira was discharged, he immediately sailed for Seward where he rejoined the family.

Bailey Kids

Ira took up his trade as a painter again while in Seward and soon was employed by the AEC as a painter and then timekeeper. From 1920 until 1921 he worked for the ARR in Seward and then moved to Anchorage in

1922. In 1931 he was appointed assistant fire chief and held that position until his untimely death. Ira was active as a baseball player and also manager of the team. He organized the first Boy Scout troop in Anchorage under the auspices of the American Legion.

Ira passed away in 1937, and Mattie was left with six children. She worked for the ARR during the summers of 1938 and 1939 and also taught school in Hope, Ellamar and Eagle.

The marriage of Ira and Mattie produced six children, five boys and one girl. Eldest son, Ira S., Jr., best known as "Stan," had two daughters, Barbara Jean and Monica. Son, Robert, had one daughter, Michelle, and a son, Ira. Son, Albert, had two daughters and one son, Susan, Allison and Scott. Son, William, had two children, William and Carolyn. Warren had four children; Jeff, Robert, James and Lorri. Daughter, Lucille Bailey Gardiner, had no children.

Ira S. Bailey, Sr. died in Anchorage in 1937 and is buried in the American Legion Tract, Anchorage Memorial Park Cemetery. Mattie Bailey died in 1977, Ira S., Jr. died in 1993, and Warren died in 1989.

Mattie, Winner of the Pilsbury Bake-off

Al, Bob and Bill Bailey

Lucille Gardiner and Spouse

CHAPTER VI

1923

1923 was a big year.

The President of the United States, Warren Harding, visited Alaska to commemorate the completion of the Alaska Railroad. He arrived in Anchorage on July 13 enroute to Nenana to drive the golden spike. On the same day, the Alaska Engineering Commission was abolished, and the Alaska Railroad was substituted thereafter.

The City had a new Mayor in that JOE CONROY was appointed to fill out the term of Leopold David, who unexpectedly died in office.

Five new members were elected to the City Council:

CHARLES W. BUSH
WILLIAM H. HOWARD
GRANT REED
A. A. SHONBECK
R. S. TEMME

Anchorage Airfield is Now the Park Strip

Mayor Joseph Conroy

President Harding Driving the Golden Spike

Anchorage had its first Municipal Airfield on what is now the Park Strip, with landings and takeoffs beginning that year.

The high school graduating class of 1923 consisted of six boys and eight girls:

Bernice Allen

Eric Anderson

Maurice Anderson

John Dunn

Myrtle Elliot

Alta Herzer

Decema Kimball

Amy MacFarland

Allen Morrisson

Hilma Niemi

Paul Prather

Lawlor Seeley

Gertrude Watson

Myrtle Wendler

JOHN TOMPKINS was born in Skagway in 1900. He worked in the Treadwell Mine in Douglas and at the A. J. Mine in Juneau. He moved to Haines for a year and then to Anchorage. He went to work for the ARR in the mechanical department in 1923. "Tommy," as he was known, was an excellent baseball player and was very popular among the fans. His untimely death in 1930 left a gap in the ARR baseball team. He is buried in Tract 3 in an unmarked grave in Anchorage Memorial Park.

FRANCIS LARUE was born in Minot, South Dakota in 1902. He spent his young life there and moved to Anchorage in 1923 to work for the Alaska Railroad in the erection department where he eventually became foreman. He was Exalted Ruler of the Elks Lodge in 1935-36. At the outbreak of WWII he enlisted and after three years service was discharged as a Captain. He retired from the Railroad in 1948 and moved to Montana. He passed away in 1961 in Missoula, Montana and is presumably buried there.

CHARLES STANFORD, a well-known dog musher in his day in Flat and Iditarod, came to Alaska in 1900, landing in Nome in search of gold. Charley gave up on finding gold and took a job as a baker, which was what he was trained to do. It is unknown where he came from; however, he lived in Idaho for a number of years, and he was married in Chilliwack, British Columbia prior to coming to Alaska.

Charley finally came to Iditarod in 1912 and took up dog mushing for a living. He developed a good team of dogs and started freighting and carrying the United States mail from Seward to Nome. He headquartered in Flat and worked both directions, carrying mail, gold bullion, freight and passengers when space permitted. Charley and his wife were separated for many years. She taught school in Ft. Yukon and also in Tanana and Nenana.

In 1923 things slowed down in Flat and Iditarod, and Charley headed for Anchorage. He worked a short time for the Alaska Railroad and then for the Alaska Road Commission as a baker. In 1935 he retired fully and lived in a small cabin on 4th Avenue between A and B Streets. He was a frequent visitor to the home of his old friend John Bagoy. Almost every evening after dinner Charley would arrive to read the evening paper. When John answered the door, he would say, "How are you tonight, Charley," and Charley's regular reply would be, "John, I think my every breath is going to be my next one."

Charley met his maker in 1939 at the age of seventy. He is buried in the Pioneer Tract in Anchorage Memorial Park.

GEORGE CONKLIN came to Anchorage in 1923 from Nome, where he prospected and located several claims. He kept these claims for many years, hoping to go back some day and take out the gold that he knew was there. He went into the paperhanging and painting business in Anchorage. He had a shop on 4th Avenue between H and I Streets.

George was a tall man, six foot four, and a "string bean." He built a small boat, twenty-one feet long, and traveled the Inlet to Hope, Sunrise, Knik and other points, just to cruise around and take friends for rides. He had a small pilot house on the boat with a hatch in the roof so he could stand up with his head sticking out and pilot his boat. He was a comical figure to see as he cruised down Ship Creek with the tide heading out into the Inlet. George was an ardent duck hunter and fisherman. He netted dozens of salmon and shot hundreds of ducks and kept his wife busy cleaning and canning ducks and fish.

He retired from his business in 1938, although he did not want to. He felt his customers no longer thought that he could handle the work any longer and that he was growing too old. George became very despondent and left Anchorage for Nome, where he was going to work the claims that he had held for so many years. About one year after he left Anchorage, George took his own life in Nome. He felt that he was of no use to anyone any longer. He is buried in the Nome City Cemetery.

One of the better-known traveling salesmen in Alaska, JOE FREEMAN was born in Pawling, New York in 1885 and spent the better part of his life in the western states and in Alaska. He was employed by the Seattle Hardware Company as their Alaska representative. Joe made his headquarters in Anchorage and in particular at Kennedy's Hardware.

He was well-known throughout the Territory not only for his prowess as a salesman but also for his interest in the American Legion and the VFW. Joe was past Commander of the Legion and was a dedicated member of both organizations. He was a veteran of WWI and fought in four major battles in France including the Marne, St. Mihiel, and the Meuse-Argonne. Joe died in 1944 in Anchorage and is buried in the Legion Tract, Anchorage Memorial Park.

NORA BLACK came to Alaska in 1904, first locating in Fairbanks and then in Tanana, where she operated a roadhouse. In 1923 she moved into Anchorage and remained here until her death. She was married to CHARLEY BLACK, who was employed at the Alaska Railroad.

Nora was known far and wide in Alaska as an outstanding cook and chef. During her years in Anchorage she was in constant demand to furnish food at various receptions and to plan and provide food for many dinner parties, including those of Mayor Loussac, who would not use anyone but Nora for his planned parties.

In her later years Nora was employed by the Elks Lodge as receptionist in the ladies' lounge. She was held in high esteem in every community where she resided and had the respect of all who knew her. She died in 1940 and is buried in the Veterans Tract of Anchorage Memorial Park Cemetery. She was not a veteran nor was her husband; however, she had brothers who were veterans and also relatives in the Northern Army during the Civil War. This indicates the high esteem in which she was held by the citizens of Anchorage. Nora was one of the very few colored ladies who resided in Anchorage during the early years.

Entrepreneur and jack-of-all-trades, ALGERNON "AL" SIDNEY JONES was born in Knoxville, Tennessee on August 20, 1900. In 1904, along with his mother, father, sister and two older brothers, he moved to Seattle, Washington. Al grew up in Seattle and at the age of seventeen, in 1917, joined the United States Army, serving twenty-two months at Ft. Lewis, Washington.

Al Jones

After the war Al worked as a farm hand in Washington until 1923, when he came to Anchorage, Alaska to seek his fortune. He was employed as a janitor for the Alaska Railroad Hospital in Anchorage, where he met R. LEE BARTHOLF, a nurse, whose family was engaged in the mining business in the Willow Creek district. They were married on January 19, 1924.

Al opened a small grocery store at 442 4th Avenue in 1924. He soon closed this store and started to pursue an early interest which he had in aviation. He purchased a Boeing C-11S biplane from C. O. Hammontree. Ray Troxell, a friend of Al's, test hopped the plane for him, but, unfortunately, the plane stalled on takeoff and crashed in the Inlet. No one was hurt other than Al's pocketbook.

His next venture was moving to Hope, where he had a tie cutting contract for the ARR, in 1925. In 1926 he became an Alaska registered guide, and he and Lee opened up a hunting lodge on Tustemena Lake. In 1927 he decided to venture into a salmon packing cannery. He started the Kustatan Packing Company on lower Cook Inlet across the Inlet from Kenai. He operated the cannery during the summer months each year and spent the winters in Anchorage. In 1933 Al moved his Kustatan Packing Company to Anchorage and continued to operate it until 1937.

In 1934 he took up flying again and received his student permit. The same year Al and Lee separated, and she took their two children and moved to Park City, Montana. In 1936 he married Anne Tinker in Seattle, and they continued to operate the packing company until he sold out to Al Soeneke in 1937. In 1937-38 he received his private pilot's license and opened Anchorage Airways with pilots John Amundsen and Gordon McKenzie flying a Fairchild 71 and a Fairchild 42. This venture lasted one year, and in late 1938 he and his wife moved to Bethel to be near their mining operations. He closed down his mining operations in 1943 and received his commercial pilot's license the same year. He opened up Al Jones Airways in 1943 and operated out of Bethel.

In 1947, while returning from a flight to Nunivak Island, Al lost the engine on approach to the Bethel airport and crashed and was killed. The marriage between Al and R. Lee Bartholf produced two children, Evelyn Ann and Al Ray. Al Ray lives in Golden, Colorado. It is unknown where daughter Evelyn resides. Al is buried in the Elks Tract of Anchorage Memorial Park Cemetery. All information on Al Jones was contributed by his family and the *Anchorage Times*.

———

One of the most tragic stories of 1923 was the beginning of a series of accidents relating to the Frank Smith family. FRANK SMITH was born in Palma, Idaho in 1890. He enlisted in the United States Army during WWI, spent several years in the service after the war, and arrived in Anchorage in 1923. He homesteaded a fishing site at the mouth of the Chuitt River close to Tyonek. He spent his summers at his fish camp and the winters in Anchorage.

In 1924 he met MARY GERTRUDE RIFF, who was a registered nurse and had come to the Kenai-Tyonek area as a public health nurse employed by the Bureau of Indian Affairs. Mary was born in Columbus, Ohio in 1890 and was trained as a nurse. She enlisted in the Army Reserve Nurse Corps in WWI and served in France under combat conditions.

Mary Smith

The union of Frank and Mary produced three sons, and the children grew up as fishermen following their father's trade. They spent the summer season at the fish camp and then moved into Anchorage for the winter months to attend school.

In the summer of 1934 Frank Smith was drowned in an accident at his fish site. He got his leg caught in an anchor rope tied to a fish net and, before help could reach him, he drowned. His body was never found.

In 1950 son Rowland was pinned under his dory during a storm at their fishing site and was drowned, almost sixteen years to the day after his father met his death at approximately the same location. He was twenty years old and was born in Anchorage.

In 1953 son Byrne was drowned during a hunting expedition on the Olympic Peninsula in northwestern Washington. After the drowning of his brother in 1950, Byrne had taken a job as engineer on a cannery tender for H. J. Emard Company. He was wintering in Seattle when the boat was in the shipyard for overhaul. He and friends were elk hunting and were coming down a wild river when they hit a rock and capsized. Byrne never made it out, and his body was found several days later.

Mary Smith was still grief-stricken from the loss of her two sons when, in 1954, her son Gerard became the fourth member of the family to die by drowning. He also met his death at almost the same location as his father and brother. His body was found, however, and was brought to Anchorage to be buried with his siblings.

All of these tragedies were bearing down on this woman who had lost her husband and entire family to the elements. At the time of Rowland's death in 1950, Mary took a bad fall on the ice and fell with her head hitting the ground, causing the loss of her sight in her left eye. After the death of son Gerard she again fell and this time injured her right eye to the point where she was almost blind. In the spring of 1957 her many friends assisted her in funding a trip to the Retinal Associates at Massachusetts General Hospital in Boston. The doctors were, fortunately, able to restore some sight in her right eye.

This woman suffered more tragedy in her lifetime than is seemingly possible. With all of the heartbreak and suffering, she still maintained an attitude of cheerfulness, and her compassion for people she felt were less fortunate than she was remarkable. Her faith in her God and in her church kept her going as she suffered one tragedy after another.

Mary entered the Palmer Pioneers Home in 1972 where she remained until her death in 1977. Up until she died, her friends in the home told of her visiting other residents and cheering them up even though by then she was completely blind. She was a true Pioneer woman of the north, who, in spite of her own troubles, had the time to help her fellow human beings.

Mary and sons Rowland, Gerard and Byrne are all buried side-by-side in the Catholic Tract of Anchorage Memorial Park. Frank Smith has a headstone with the family although his body was never found.

WALTER GEORGE CULVER was hired by the Bureau of Indian Affairs, Bureau of Education, Alaska Division, to teach Eskimo and Aleut children at Port Moller, Harendeen Bay, Alaska in July 1915. Walter was born in Reading Township, Hillsdale County, Michigan in 1890. He met MILDRED AILEEN ROWE in Seattle, Washington, and they were married in May 1915. Mildred was born in San Francisco, California in 1890. They spent their honeymoon in Port Moller, building the schoolhouse and living quarters prior to their starting to teach the students. They spent three years at Port Moller, and during his teaching appointment Walter was asked to herd reindeer to another area to provide food for the natives. While Walter served as reindeer superintendent appointee, Mildred was left to teach school alone. In 1917 Walter delivered stillborn boy and girl twins. In the spring of 1918 Walter and Mildred left Port Moller, and he enlisted in the Army during WWI.

During Walter's time in the service, Mildred, who was pregnant at the time, moved in with Walter's parents in McMinnville, Oregon. In the winter of 1919 Walter was discharged from the Army, and in the spring of the same year the Bureau of Education asked him to return to the Aleutians, where he and Mildred continued teaching for another three years.

Walter Culver

Mildred Culver

Culver Family, (left to right) Walter, Franklin, Harold, Margaret and Mildred

First Home

In 1922 Walter was employed by the Department of Agriculture, Biological Survey, with headquarters in Juneau, and left this service in 1923. After leaving Juneau, Walter and family moved to Fox Island, started a fox farm, and from there moved to Anchorage in 1923. From 1923 until 1926 he was employed as fur warden, United States deputy game warden, United States deputy marshall, and chief of police of Anchorage in 1925 and 1926. In July 1926 he was employed by the Alaska Railroad as claim investigator and then as assistant chief special agent until 1933. Taking some time off from his job in 1930, he took the census in Anchorage and enumerated two thousand three hundred eighty-three people in and around Anchorage.

He resigned from the Alaska Railroad in 1933 and went to prospecting in the Goodnews Bay district until 1943, when he and Mildred sold their home and moved to Warrenton, Oregon, and later to Edmonds, Washington. They made a final move to Hemet, California and remained there for the rest of their lives.

Margaret and George Nappe with
Walter and Mildred Culver

Judy and Harold Culver

Franklin and Iola
Culver

The union of Walter Culver and Mildred Rowe produced three children. Son, Harold, the eldest, married Judy Holberg in 1947, and they had three children. Lawrence Walter lives in Columbus, Ohio; Barbara Louise Culver Regas lives in San Diego, California; and Nancy Irene Culver Laing lives in Oceanside, California. Daughter Margaret Culver Nappe and her spouse had three children. Gary Wayne lives in Florida; Leslie Nappe Sinclair lives in Seattle, Washington; and Brian Eugene lives in Stevenson, Washington. Son Franklin married Iola Clymer, who had two sons who were legally adopted by Franklin.

Walter died in Hemet, California in 1968, and Mildred died in Hemet in 1972. Franklin died in 1975, and Harold died in 1997. Margaret lives in Bellingham, Washington.

———

A man who was to become a veteran of the Alaska Road Commission, JOHN ARTHUR BORGES was born in Chicago, Illinois in 1876 and grew up there. As a young man he worked for the Cook County treasurer's office after completing high school. In 1904 he moved to Pasadena, California where he was employed by the Pacific Electric Railway Company. In late 1904 he decided to move north to Seattle, Washington, where he was employed by the McMillan Company.

Eliizabeth Pierce
Borges

John Arthur Borges

While living in Seattle and doing some business travel to Bellingham, Washington, Arthur met ELIZABETH ISABEL PIERCE. They were married in Bellingham in 1909. Elizabeth was born in Bellingham in 1880 as one of nine children. She attended elementary and high school in Whatcom County and later became a teacher. She taught school at the Laurel School for a time and then was employed by Montague and McHugh in Bellingham as a bookkeeper and cashier.

Two years after their marriage they left Washington for Alaska. In 1911 they landed in Valdez, where Arthur was employed by the Alaska Road Commission on the Richardson Highway Project which was being built by the United States War Department. He began his career with the ARC as disbursing agent in Valdez until 1917 when he transferred to Juneau. Two children were born to the couple while in Valdez in l913 and 1916.

John Borges with Jack and Janet

Family Home, 10th and E Street, 1938

In 1923 the family was transferred to the Anchorage District of the ARC. The family first lived on 6th Avenue, where Arthur purchased the east and west one-half of Lot 9, Block 54. He moved two separate structures onto acre tracts #5 and #4, Block 20, South Addition to the Anchorage Townsite, and combined them into the family home on 10th Avenue and E Street. The home stands in the same place today. Arthur served on the Anchorage School Board for a time; Elizabeth was active with the Rainbow Girls and taught Sunday school.

Arthur and Elizabeth moved to Santa Barbara, California in 1943 due to Arthur's health. He passed away in 1948 in Santa Barbara, and Elizabeth moved back to

Janet and Ed Barber with Sons Hugh, Guy and Dick

Anchorage after his death. She lived with her daughter and son-in-law, Janet and Ed Barber, until she passed away in 1949. Elizabeth is buried in the Pioneer Tract, Anchorage Memorial Park, and Arthur is buried in Santa Barbara, California.

Arthur and Isabel had one daughter and one son. Son John Arthur, Jr. married Pauline Lillard, and they had one son, John Arthur III, who lives in California. Daughter Janet married Edward Barber, a member of another Anchorage Pioneer family, and they had three children. Guy, Hugh and Dick all live in Anchorage.

———

Alaska had several true entrepreneurial types who eventually settled in Anchorage. They all brought development to Alaska and to Anchorage in one form or another. In their own way they pioneered businesses that ranged from theaters, to food distribution, to fox farming, to shipping, to water transportation, to mining--all establishments that not only benefited themselves but benefited the Territory and the people in it. One of these men was HEINIE BERGER. Heinie

Heinie Berger

Alice Berger

was born in Hamburg, Germany in 1888. He immigrated to the United States in 1903 at the age of fifteen. Little is known of his life from the time he came to the United States until he showed up on the Alaska scene in about 1914 at Seward, where he and a partner supposedly established a tailor shop.

He must have had experience as a seaman, as he held masters papers as early as 1923; however, it is unknown when or where he received them. He acquired a boat named the *Discovery* and operated out of Seward, Seldovia and ports in the lower Inlet. In 1926 he started his freight and passenger service between Seldovia, Homer, Tyonek, Kenai and Anchorage.

He changed the name of the boat to the *Discoverer*. It was a thirty ton gas schooner, fifty-three feet long, with a fourteen foot beam. It had a one hundred horsepower engine and was built at the Seabeck Yard in Seattle, Washington. The boat was first owned by a man named Walton who had converted the engine to a sixty horsepower Fairbanks Morse Diesel, and Heinie acquired the boat sometime in 1922.

Heinie operated between Seward and Seldovia in 1932, making two trips per month carrying mail, passengers and freight. In November 1932 he was making his last trip from Anchorage and ran into heavy ice when the boat suddenly started taking on water, and almost immediately the engine room was flooded. Heinie and his crew of three barely had time to get a skiff off the deck and into the water before the boat went down. All they were able to grab before abandoning ship were a few blankets, a handful of grub, some matches and a five-gallon can of kerosene. They were about eight miles offshore from Tyonek; however, they headed for the east shore as it was closer. They fought their way through some weather and strong surf and finally swamped the dory on the beach between Kenai and Kasilof. They were soaking wet and the temperature was twenty-three degrees. They kept themselves alive by building fires with the kerosene.

Heinie, engineer Jack Wilkinson, cook and deck hand Oscar Wick, and deck hand Fred Bergman walked twenty-three miles to the Kasilof Fox Ranch that Heinie and his wife Alice owned. Within three days they were all flown to Anchorage by pilot Matt Niemenen who had spotted them on the beach but could not land immediately due to weather.

Heinie had developed a long friendship with Allen Hardy, who with his wife, Alice, owned a fox farm on the Kasilof River. Allen lost his life in an accidental drowning on the river in 1930. Alice was widowed for one year, and then she and Heinie were married in 1931. Heinie made the fox farm his headquarters while running the Inlet, stopping off to see Alice on every trip.

In 1929 Heinie won part of the Ice Pool and still had about fifteen thousand dollars left. He immediately headed to Seattle, bent on getting another boat. He found one under construction at the Berg Shipyard and bought it immediately. It was seventy-six feet long, with a 17.6 foot beam and a two hundred horsepower Washington diesel engine, and could handle fourteen passengers on a cabin deck and fifty tons of cargo in the hold and on the deck. He named it the *Discoverer* and started a run from Seattle to Anchorage, making six trips per year carrying passengers and automobiles on the deck and forty to fifty tons of groceries in the hold for local grocery stores in Anchorage.

Business was booming for Heinie. He decided to buy another boat to take care of the local runs on the Inlet. He had a sixty-one foot, thirty-ton wooden hull boat built at the Berg Shipyard in Seattle. It had a sixty horsepower Fairbanks Morse diesel, a fifteen-foot beam, and carried ten passengers. Heinie needed a name for the boat, so he put out a notice in the *Anchorage Times*, with a fifty-dollar prize for any school kid to come up with a name. Local boy Ted Bystedt won the prize with the name *Kasilof*. The *Kasilof* started the local run on the inlet in 1937.

MV Kasilof

Heinie decided to expand into the entertainment business in 1937. He bought a partially completed building on the corner of 6th Avenue and C Street and named it the Ambassador Club. It was the finest club in town in those days, with a huge dance floor, three sides of booths and tables, a bandstand, and a private entrance. You did not have to go through the adjacent bar to get in. He had a partner, Chris Terry, who managed the club. Heinie established the Berger Distributing Company in 1937 and hired Chris Terry to run the business. Chris was a crackerjack salesman and did well in selling

MV Discoverer

Golden Glow Ale, Hamms Beer and other products up and down the railbelt and on the Inlet. Chris was able to handle both the Ambassador Club and the distributing business, while Heinie took care of the transportation business.

In 1938 Heinie brought in three Wurlitzer juke boxes and put one in Richmonds Soda Fountain, one in the D and D café, and one in the Anchorage Grill. The Grill had a good dance floor and was frequented by the teen crowd, as was Richmonds. His entertainment business was flourishing and so was his transportation business. In 1938 he bought a scow, which he loaded up with groceries and freight amounting to about two hundred tons. He carried lumber, automobiles, groceries and miscellaneous freight for Anchorage merchants at a freight rate with which the Alaska Steamship Company and the Railroad could not compete. Colonel Otto F. Ohlson considered the small fifty-ton operator as no competition, but it was a different story when Berger started hauling two-hundred-ton loads.

Colonel Otto F. Ohlson, general manager of the ARR, was not about to stand for this competition. Heinie was offloading at the old City dock, which was on Railroad property but was leased to the City. To reach the dock on the second bend of Ship Creek, you had to cross the main line of the Railroad. Ohlson placed a string of railcars across the road, blocking entrance to the dock. This created a lawsuit, which Heinie lost, and he appealed to the San Francisco Court of Appeals. The suit finally died a natural death when WWII started, however it forced Heinie to pay the ARR one dollar twenty-five cents per ton wharfage. You could ship an automobile from Seattle to Anchorage for an average cost of twenty dollars, and cargo at twenty dollars per ton.

Heinie operated power barges and the *MV Garland* after the war. Jim Arness of Kenai, Elmer Dow, and Jack Wilkinson all had turns as skipper on one or the other of Heinie's power scows and had many stories to tell of the days with the Heinie Berger Transportation Company. The life of Heinie would fill a book in itself. Jim Arness of Kenai was an important contributor to the history of Heinie Berger, as was Chris Terry. Both of these men worked for Berger, and both said he was the finest man that they ever worked for.

Heinie died in Seattle in 1954 after a long illness. His wife Alice was left with the estate; however, Heinie left no will, and the settlement of the estate cost her dearly. She tried to hold on and run the business but finally had to sell out. She retired to eastern Washington and passed away there in 1960.

Jim Arness recalls the fate of the *Discoverer* and the *Kasilof*. The Navy chartered the Discoverer in WWII, and she was used as a submarine net-tender at Adak. She was sold as surplus property after the war and was used as a mailboat from Ketchikan to various villages in southeast Alaska. She was wrecked on that run in the early 70's. The *Kasilof* stayed on the freight run from Seattle to Anchorage during WWII with Jack Wilkinson and Elmer Dow as rotating captains. Rumor has it that she burned to the waterline in the 1980's somewhere in southeast Alaska.

Heinie's good friend and partner CHRISTOPHER TERRY must be mentioned here, as he was part and parcel of the Heinie Berger history. Chris was born in Vancouver, British Columbia in 1907. His father was a Canadian mountie, and his mother passed away when he was two years old. He was sent to England with his siblings to live with relatives after his mother passed away. When Chris was eleven he was enrolled in the Royal Navy Cadet School, which was a cross between an orphanage and a reform school. After a few years of harsh discipline and minimal education, he was automatically enlisted in the Royal Navy.

He vividly recalls the years he spent shoveling coal in the ships' boilers during his years in the Navy. When his hitch was up he took his discharge in Vancouver, British Columbia and sought out his father, but the reunion was not pleasant. He went to Seattle, where he met a recruiter for the Alaska Railroad, and came to Anchorage in 1930. He was severely injured in a crane accident on the Railroad and spent two years in the hospital before he was completely healed from a broken back.

After he was able to walk again, he found a job with Heinie Berger in 1933 that developed into his being the agent for Berger Distributing and manager of the Ambassador Club. In 1934 he met Alice Berger's visiting niece Dorothy, and they were married in Anchorage.

When WWII started and changes in business were taking place, Chris left Berger and opened a bar in Seward. He sold then his bar in Seward, went to work for Milt Odom as a liquor salesman, and retired from that to a homestead in Willow. Dorothy died in 1961 and is buried in Anchorage Memorial Park. Chris moved to a rest home in Peoria, Arizona, and the last contact the writer was able to make with him was in 1999.

Following are more people involved in the Heinie Berger and the Chris Terry Saga, and I would be remiss if I left them out of the picture, as they also were early day Anchorage Pioneers.

ALICE BERGER and MARY PETERSON, the OTTO sisters

Hester Johnson Otto and Julius William Otto had nine daughters, all born in Wisconsin. Mary Otto and her identical twin, Clara, were numbers six and seven; Alice was two years younger. Julius came from a solid middle class family, although he had weaknesses such as alcohol and gambling. In 1904 he moved his family by wagon to Washington to get a new start in life. He soon disappeared from the family and never showed up again until he was in his eighties and needed care.

Hester was from solid Norwegian farmer stock. She worked hard, had high standards of deportment for her daughters, and insisted that the girls stay in school until at least the eighth grade. Mary was the first married. She married Harry Myers who died less than a year later. Three years later she married Glen Smith, but once again tragedy struck, and he died eleven months later. Alice married John Stratton, a Seattle dentist. Their three and one-half year old son died of a fever, and at the same time her husband asked for a divorce. Alice and Mary then decided to build a new life, and, instead of giving in to despair, they left for Alaska with nothing more than a hand carried bag apiece.

Bright, pretty and energetic, they landed in Anchorage in 1924, and it was not long before they were in business, opening a sweet shop and soda fountain. In 1926 Alice met Allen Hardy, and they were married and moved to Kasilof to start a fox farm. Fur farming was a popular venture at the time in Alaska, and their location on the Kasilof River was a lonely one, as the only means of contact was by water. Heinie Berger operated boats up and down the Inlet, and they became great friends. When Allen drowned, Alice and Heinie were married a year later. You know the rest of her story.

Mary had settled in Fairbanks and remained in the interior the rest of her life. She owned and operated several roadhouses and cooked at many locations including the Healy River Coal Company mine at Suntrana. She had a lodge on the 40-Mile, and, when the Alaska Highway was built, she opened the Triangle Lodge. At the time of her death she operated the Tortella Lodge in Nenana. Mary married twice. Her last husband, John Peterson, and she were married in 1929. She remembered the years with him as being the happiest in her life. He died of a ruptured appendix in 1946. This story is told by Barbara Henrichs, whose husband, Glen, was the nephew of Alice Berger.

One of the early-day homesteader families in south Anchorage was the family of ENGELHARD K. SPERSTAD. He was born in Norway in 1884 and immigrated to the United States sometime around

Engelhard Sperstad

Anna Sperstad

the turn of the century. He first arrived in Valdez in 1906, hoping to find employment in the Valdez district gold claims. He spent his prospecting time in and out of Valdez, and while in Valdez he met and married ANNA SERINA ABRAHAMSON. Anna was born in Valsoy Fjorn, Norway in 1885 and came to Valdez as a domestic, like so many other women who immigrated to the United States at the time. Anna was employed by Judge Thomas Donohoe in Valdez as cook and housekeeper.

Two sons were born to the couple while in Valdez, and in 1923 they decided to head for Anchorage, which was a booming city where opportunity existed. The couple filed for a one hundred sixty acre homestead in what is now **the Spenard area adjacent to Arctic**

Homestead Cabin

Evelyn Ann Watsjold

Hope Lucille Lowe

John Sperstad

Thomas W. Sperstad

Boulevard and International Airport Road. The only access to the homestead at the time was the Railroad, which intersected their property near Campbell station. Access by road was a branch off Spenard Road at Deadmans Curve. It was a pioneer unmaintained road with two ruts suitable for wagons in the summer and bobsleds and horses in the winter.

The family lived a subsistence lifestyle, raising vegetables on the homestead, fishing for salmon in the Inlet during the summer, picking berries, and hunting moose, rabbits, grouse and ptarmigan. Anna's expertise at preserving and canning kept the family larder full. It was a long way to school for the children. From the homestead to downtown Anchorage was about four miles, and there were many times that they had to walk all the way to town and back to attend school.

The union between Anna and Englehard produced four children, two boys and two girls. Son John had no children and lives in Fairbanks. Son Thomas had no children and died at his hunting camp in the Wrangell Mountains in 1990. Daughter Evelyn Ann Watsjold had three children, John Eric, Kim Allen and Dan, all living in Anchorage. Evelyn Ann passed away in 1983, and she and Thomas had their ashes scattered. Daughter Hope Lucille Lowe had four children. Karen Ann Brian, Inez, Nelson and Carl all live in Anchorage. Englehard and Anna are both buried in Angelus Memorial Park.

Jenny Strandberg in her Garden in Anchorage

Dave Strandberg at Mine Office in Flat

The patriarch of one of the most prominent mining families in Alaska, DAVID STRANDBERG was born in Halmstad, Sweden in 1875. Obtaining his early education in Sweden, he came to the United States and resided in Seattle, Washington where he attended the Wilson Business College. He was employed in the timber country of Washington and in various mines prior to coming to Alaska in 1898 during the great rush to the Klondike. Little did he know that his venture in gold mining would lead to his being the father of one of the most prominent mining families in Alaska.

After trudging over the Dyea, he prospected and mined around Dawson until 1905 when he decided to move on to Fairbanks. He went down the Yukon and located on Ester Creek just out of Fairbanks. Dave met JENNY SOPHIA JOHANSON, who was born

Harold Strandberg

Olga Strandberg Doheny

in Smoland, Sweden in 1884. She came to the United States in 1904 and arrived in Dawson in 1905. She moved to Fairbanks to live with an aunt, and there she met Dave Strandberg. They were married in 1908 and lived and prospected on Ester Creek for two years before departing for the Iditarod. Dave staked some claims on Flat Creek and proceeded to develop them for the next ten or twelve years.

Ted Strandberg

Bill Strandberg

Genevieve Strandberg
Crawford

Odin Strandberg

In 1923 he moved the family to Anchorage, and from that period on he made Anchorage his headquarters for the operation of mining properties in Candle Creek, Cripple Creek, Utopia Creek, property on the Koyukuk River, and platinum ground in the Goodnews Bay country. Dave's sons became his mining partners as they grew older, and in 1932 they formed the Standberg and Sons Mining Company and first operated in Folger.

Jenny and Dave had four sons and two daughters. Eldest son, Harold, married Barbara Carlquist, daughter of a Pioneer Anchorage family, and they had three children. David Harold lives in Prescott, Arizona; Steven Frederick lives in San Francisco; and Douglas Frank lives in Friday Harbor, Washington. Harold died in Green Valley, Arizona in 1995. Daughter Olga married Larry Doheny and they had three children. Kathleen Hennessy lives in Lubbock, Texas; Michael died in 1980; and Jenny lives in Anchorage. Olga died in Anchorage in 1991. Son Theodore and wife, Gail, had one daughter who lives on Mercer Island, Washington. Ted died of a heart attack at the Folger mine in 1955. Son William never married and was killed by a black bear at the mining camp in Eureka Creek in 1961. Son Odin married Marie Nordstrom, and they had four children. Odin, Jr. passed away in Fairbanks in March 2000; Sigvold John lives in Fairbanks; James lives in Anchorage; Barrent lives in Wasilla. Daughter Genevieve Strandberg Crawford had six children and lives in California.

Dave Strandberg died in Anchorage in 1951, and Jenny died in 1954. Dave, Jenny, Ted, Bill, and Olga are all buried in the Pioneer Tract, Anchorage Memorial Park.

Joe and Lauretta Reno

Family in Girdwood

One of many who came to Alaska looking for a better life, GAETANO "JOE" IANNONE RENO was born in Compobasso, Italy in 1866. He arrived in the United States in 1890 after giving up his studies for the priesthood. He met LAURETTA PESCO in Salt Lake City, Utah, and after a long courtship they were married in 1904. Lauretta was born in Palermo, Sicily in 1884 and was living with family in Salt Lake City.

Store and Hotel

Joe kept hearing of the construction of a railroad in the north. He saw this as an opportunity to establish himself in business and as a great place to raise a family. After their second child was born, they left Salt Lake and landed in Seward, Alaska in 1906. Joe obtained work on the railroad construction and decided Girdwood would be a good location to establish a store and roadhouse, as it was a construction camp for the south district of the line.

Joe built a good-sized log cabin roadhouse and store, and business was good during the construction years. When 1923 rolled around and the Railroad was completed, Joe and family, now grown to nine, moved into Anchorage, the headquarters of the ARR.

He opened a general store on the corner of 4th Avenue and C Street in 1924. He sold general merchandise and miscellaneous clothing, but mostly groceries, with Italian specialties. With the large family he now had, he was never wanting for help in the store. They operated on this corner until 1937, when he moved one block down the hill to 3rd Avenue and C Street, where he had purchased an existing building and small store from Mr. Bauman. He also built a small hotel next door to the store and operated in this location until his death.

Joe was often asked about his nickname, and his explanation was that when he worked for the Railroad the paymaster could never get his name straight the way he pronounced Iannone, so the paymaster simply called him "Reno," and the name stuck.

Joe and Loretta had ten children, two born in Salt Lake and the others born in Alaska. Son Floyd Iannone had two children. Floyd, Jr. is deceased, and Violet Jean lives in Seattle, Washington. Daughter Mary Iannone Reno Agbaba had four children. Milan, Steven, Dan and Jean are all deceased. Daughter Mary Eberhardt

Reno Family

lives in Fairbanks. Daughter Jessie Iannone Reno Corliss had three girls. Betty Corliss Haynes lives in Fairbanks; Janet Corliss Shaw is deceased; and Nancy Peifer lives in Glendale, Arizona. Daughter Lela Iannone Reno Johnson had no children. Daughter Margie Iannone Reno Weseman had two children. George lives in Kent, Washington, and Loretta Sims lives in Umpqua, Oregon. Daughter Addie Iannone Reno Hausman had three children. Lester E. is deceased; Chester lives in Sedro Wooley, Washington; Donna Sicks lives in Duluth, Minnesota. Son James Iannone Reno had no children nor did daughter Elvera Iannone Reno Sidars. James is now deceased, and Elvera lives in Mt. Vernon, Washington. Daughter Virginia Iannone Reno Johnston had one son, Leroy James, Jr., and he lives in Kansas City, Missouri.

Elvera Reno Sidars

Lauretta died in 1936, and Joe died in 1942. Both are buried in Anchorage Memorial Park in the Catholic Section.

CHAPTER VII

1924

KFQD

The year 1924 was not a startling year. The big news was the establishment of the first radio station in Anchorage, KFQD. It was located on the corner of 5th Avenue and E Street in a wood frame building. See photo showing two antenna poles with antenna extending across 5th Avenue. (Photo courtesy AMHA B-91.9. 12.)

The high school graduating class of 1924 was low key as well and published no high school annual as there were only three graduates:

ARTHUR PRICKETT (No photo)
ETHEL REEDER (No photo)
LILY RIVERS

Lillian Rivers Stolt

A new Mayor was appointed when Joe Conroy resigned on October 2, 1924. Councilman CHARLES BUSH was appointed Mayor to fill out Conroy's term.

The new members on the City Council were:

CARL W. BOLTE
CHRIS ECKMAN
T. SCOTT OLIVER
CHARLES PEDERSON
W. A. SHERMAN

Joseph Conroy

Mayor Charles Bush

ART and BLANCHE O'NEIL arrived in Anchorage in 1924 from Missoula, Montana. Art obtained work with the Alaska Railroad in the roundhouse. The couple had three children. Dennis, the eldest son, worked for the Alaska Railroad until he retired as a locomotive engineer. With his spouse, Joy, he moved to Roseburg, Oregon where he passed away in 1989. Denny

Dennis and Joy O'Neil

Dennis O'Neil

had no children. Son Barney passed away in Fairbanks in the 1960's, and daughter Peggy Hannah had two daughters who live in Roseburg, Oregon.

Kathleen Schuetz Jones

GEORGE H. SCHUETZ was born in St. Louis, Missouri in 1872 and arrived in Anchorage in 1924. KATHRYN TAMKE was born in Deer Lodge, Montana in 1878 and arrived in Anchorage in 1926. While in Anchorage, George owned and operated the Club Bar in downtown Anchorage. The couple had one daughter, Kathleen, and one stepson, Claire "Beef" Spensley, who was a locomotive engineer on the Railroad.

The family left Alaska in 1935 and settled in Montana. George died in 1935, and Kathryn died in 1954. Kathleen Schuetz Jones and her spouse had three children. Claire E. passed away in 1998; Daryl F. lives in San Jose, California; and Dennis W. lives in Juneau, Alaska.

One of the legal minds that came to Alaska via the Klondike, J. LINDLEY GREEN was born in Missouri of Quaker parents in 1858. He moved to Utah as a young man and engaged in politics in Salt Lake City for some time before moving to Seattle, Washington.

Judge Lindley Green

Lindley Green in Garden

He left Seattle in 1898, joining the thousands of men and women in the great stampede to the Klondike. He left Dawson poorer but wiser and moved down river to Rampart where he was appointed the first United States commissioner in the town. From Rampart he moved to Fairbanks, where he practiced law for a few years, and then moved down to Seward, where he became assistant district attorney of the third judicial district.

In 1924 he moved to Anchorage and became registrar of the Anchorage Land Office and held that post for ten years. He and his wife IDA built a home at 9th Avenue and M Street, where they took up light farming with their own large garden and a small greenhouse. J. Lindley also settled on a homestead just east of what is now Mountain View, about six miles east of downtown Anchorage. J. Lindley passed away on July 17, 1941. He is buried in the Pioneer Tract, Anchorage Memorial Park.

Another Klondike stampeder who found his way to Anchorage in 1924, DELBERT G. HOSLER was a man who made and lost several gold mining fortunes over the years. Del was born in 1876 in Flint, Michigan, and as a young man made his way to Alaska via the Chilkoot in 1898 on his way to the Klondike and Dawson.

In 1899 he went back to Michigan to marry his spouse to be, OLIVE ELIZABETH SHUTT, who was born in 1877, also in Flint, Michigan. Del returned to Dawson the same year, and Olive followed in 1900. They spent some time in Dawson and then moved on to Ester near Fairbanks in 1908 and on to the discovery in Tofty in 1914. In 1914 they again moved on to Woodchopper and remained there until 1923.

Their final move was made to Anchorage in 1924 so the children could attend high school. They built a two-story log home at the corner of 8th Avenue and M Street overlooking the Inlet, and their yard and landscaping were the envy of many homeowners at the time. Del was one of the first residents to plant trees in the divider strips between the street and the sidewalk. Both he and Olive were interested in the growth of Anchorage and its beautification. Del did construction work and also worked as an engine hostler for the Alaska Railroad.

His claim to fame was that he was present when "Soapy Smith" was shot in Skagway. Hosler mined on his own and did underground and placer mining, employing up to seventy men at times. He said his best venture was a mine on Ready Bullion Creek near Fairbanks, which he worked for seven months and where he made a good-sized stake. When that ground was worked, he took a lease on another piece and lost all he had made on Bullion Creek. This was the story of his life, make it and lose it.

Five children were born of this union. Jack McDonald was born in 1902 and passed away in 1939. Amy Julie was born in 1904 and passed away in 1927. Elmer D. passed away in 1985 in Escondido, California. Delbert passed away in Anchorage in 1982. Frances Elizabeth Hosler Kohler had three children. Adele Vergin, Bill Kohler and Sally Duber all live in Fairbanks, as does Frances. Olive died in 1964, and Delbert G. died in 1968. They, and all of their children except Elmer and Frances, are buried in Anchorage Memorial Park in the Pioneer section.

An old-timer railroader and his spouse arrived in Anchorage from Cordova in 1924. WILLIAM H. and ANNA CANNON were both born in Portsmouth, England. Anne was born in 1887, and Bill was born in 1889. Bill sailed halfway around the world before he settled in New York and wrote for Anna to come to New York so they could marry. They had known each other in England when both were apprentices, he learning to sail and she learning to be a tailor.

Bill and Anna Cannon

Janice Cannon Hickel

Gwen Cannon

For the next ten years they made their way across America and lived in Montana, and then in Bremerton, Washington. By 1923 they decided to go to Alaska and finally to Anchorage. Bill worked for the Alaska Railroad as a boilermaker, and Anna worked as a tailor and seamstress. Their first home, which was little more than a cabin, was on L Street, and a year later they were able to move to Government Hill where theirs was one of the first twelve homes built by the Railroad. Bill retired from the Railroad in 1951, and they moved to Kent, Washington. However, they returned to Anchorage seven years later.

Bill and Anna had three children. A son Vernon died at the age of ten, and youngest daughter, Janice Cannon Hickel, died in 1941, two years after she and Walter Hickel were married. Eldest daughter, Gwendolyn Cannon Risch, passed away in 1987. Gwen had five children. Ronald, Vern, William Fred, and Jennifer live in Anchorage. Marianne Risch Corey lives in Homer, Alaska. Janice and husband had one son, Ted Hickel, who resides in Oregon. William Cannon died in 1977, and Anna died in 1986. They and son Vernon are buried in the Masonic Tract, Anchorage Memorial Park.

Another oldtimer who came to Alaska via the United States Army, JERRY T. ALLEN was born in Oblong, Illinois in 1876. He enlisted in the Army in 1899 and became a baseball and track star in his division while in the Army. He served in Madrid, Cuba and the Philippines during the Spanish American War and was also a veteran of WWI. While stationed in San Francisco in 1906, he assisted in rendering aid to the victims of the earthquake and fire. While stationed as a military guard at Alcatraz Prison, Jerry met and married Miss ALBINA KODYM, who was born in San Francisco in 1888. She accompanied Jerry on his last assignment to Ft. Liscum, and there a first child was born.

Jerry and Albina Allen

Jerry in U.S. Army

First Home on 4th Avenue and A Street

Jerry was sent to Nome in the military contingent before being assigned to Ft. Liscum, which is now the location of the Alyeska Pipeline terminus in Valdez. While in Liscum he was appointed postmaster in 1917 and held that post until the base closed in 1924.

In 1924 Jerry took his retirement as First Sergeant and moved the family to Anchorage. He was employed by the Alaska Road Commission and also worked part-time for the city of Anchorage. Jerry kept up his interest in baseball and spent time with the youth of Anchorage coaching base-ball. He acquired rental property on 4th Avenue and A Street adjacent to his home and spent most of his time maintaining the properties.

Jerry, Jerry and Jerry Allen

Last Home on 5th Avenue and H Street

Jerry and Albina had one son, Jerry A., who married Mary E. Unger, and they had two children, Mary Lou Allen Story, who lives in Arkansas, and Jerry Lee, who lives in Anchorage. Albina died in Anchorage in 1953 and is buried in Anchorage Memorial Park in the Masonic Tract. Jerry T. died in 1965 in Oblong, Illinois, and Jerry A. died in 1977.

Jerry Allen as a Conductor

A railroader who came to Anchorage via Cordova, FRED ROZELLE HOLDIMAN was born in Tacoma, Washington in 1883 and grew up there. While living in Livingston, Montana in 1906 he met and married LAURA MAUDE AKAM, who was born in Clinton, Ontario, Canada in 1885. After a few years in Livingston, they moved to Othello, Washington, and in 1917 they moved to Auburn, Washington. Fred was a trained machinist and his trade was in demand by railroads during this time. The couple then had five children, and Fred heard of the opportunities in Alaska.

In 1922 he packed up the family and left for Cordova, Alaska, where he had a job lined up with the Copper River Railroad. Two years later they moved on to Anchorage when the Alaska Railroad was completed, and Fred got a job as a machinist. When they first arrived they lived on Government Hill and then moved to Cottage #18 on 2nd Avenue and remained there after purchasing the home, which was renumbered to 518 2nd Avenue.

Fred and Maude Holdiman

Fred retired from the Railroad in 1945, and in 1949 he and Maude moved back to Auburn, Washington. Fred had been active in the Federation of Government Employees for several years and was instrumental in obtaining the government homes, when they came up for sale, at appraised value so that the current occupants and employees could purchase them. Maude had her garden, and while the children were in school she served as President of the P.T.A. for several years.

Second Home

Ruth Holdiman

Ralph Holdiman

Roy Holdiman

Reetha Holdiman

Roberta Holdiman

Reona Holdiman

Maude died in Auburn, Washington in 1951, and Fred died in Auburn in 1976. The union of Fred and Maude produced six children. Daughter Ruth Holdiman Smith had three children. Keith passed away in 1995; Clyde passed away in 1999; and Karen Larsen lives in Seattle, Washington. Ruth's husband, Jim Smith, died in 1974, and Ruth died in 1996. Son Ralph married Rose Rivers, a member of another Anchorage Pioneer family, and they had three children. Joy Holdiman Hurlbert lives in Shelton, Washington, and Sally Larimore and David live in Anchorage. Ralph died in 1958, and Rose died in 1966. Both are buried in Anchorage Memorial Park. Son Roy Holdiman and Marcella Eyer Holdiman had two daughters, Sandra and Kay, who live in Anchorage. Daughter Reetha Holdiman Martin lives in Kalispell, Montana. Daughter Roberta Holdiman Simmons had four children, all living in Washington. Carolyn Hatley lives in Bellevue; Lenard lives in Spokane; Sue Fleming lives in Renton; and Dale lives in Buckley. Roberta divorced in 1963, married Bill Dodte in 1967, and lives in Renton, Washington. Daughter Reona Holdiman Baker lives in Auburn, Washington and has two sons, Michael and Andrew. The family lives in Auburn, Washington.

H. A. "CAPPY" FAROE was a Norwegian immigrant who arrived in the United States at San Francisco in 1921. He was born in Bergen, Norway in 1898 and spent his youth in Bergen close to the sea, which he loved. When he was twenty years old and in the Norwegian Army, he was selected for the King's Guard, a position of honor in the military. The King's Guard was used primarily in official presentations and guarding the government buildings and their gates. In 1975 King Olav of Norway visited Anchorage, and Cappy had the opportunity to visit with him and remembered him as the Crown Prince at the time he was in the Guard.

Cappy landed in San Francisco aboard the *M.D. George Washington* and later served as quartermaster aboard ships of the Admiral Line which plied the west coast. In 1923 he arrived in Alaska as the skipper aboard the cannery tender *North Cape*, owned by the Emard Packing Company and the Gorman Company. He barely made the trip across the Gulf of Alaska, as they were towing a barge full of fish trap equipment when a storm engulfed them. Faroe refused to cut the barge loose and made it into Cook Inlet safe and sound.

Cappy in the Kings Guard

Cappy at Independence Mine

Doris Ann Bagoy Faroe

H. A. Cappy Faroe

In 1928 he met and married DORIS ANN BAGOY in Anchorage. Doris was the eldest daughter of Marie and John Bagoy, early Alaska Pioneers. She was born in Iditarod, Alaska in 1910 and was the first child born in the mining camp. The newspaper of the day proclaimed her as the "first real Iditaroder," and she was the darling of the camp.

Faroe ran cannery tenders for Libby, McNeil and Libby for several years and then moved permanently to Anchorage in 1924. He was a skilled carpenter, did various detail work for local establishments, and also built several houses in Anchorage, including a new home for John Bagoy. He became seriously interested in mining and was gradually supplying specialized mining equipment to the Willow Creek Mines, sometimes delivering parts carried on his packboard and skiing up Hatcher Pass to the mines.

He and Doris eventually established a retail electrical-industrial store in Anchorage, located on 4th Avenue between C and D Streets. In 1953 they launched into the wholesale business,

Cappy's Business, Northern Supply

Sandra Marie Faroe Noonan

and the Northern Supply became the first electrical wholesale house in Alaska. In 1971 he sold his business to a national concern and went into retirement. While in business, he served on the Chamber of Commerce board for many years and the Anchorage Power Commission. In 1962 he was awarded the Chamber Gold Pan award and in 1973 was named outstanding Alaskan of the Year by the State Chamber of Commerce.

The marriage of Doris and Cappy produced one daughter, Alexandra "Sandra" Marie Faroe. She married Richard Noonan and they had three children. Daughter Stephanie Drachkovitch lives in Los Angeles, and sons Burke and Richard live in Wilsonville, Oregon. Cappy died in 1982, and Doris passed away in 2000. They are both buried in Anchorage Memorial Park Cemetery, Catholic Section. Daughter Sandra Noonan passed away in 1985 in Portland, Oregon and is buried in the military cemetery there.

Another immigrant who came to Alaska and found his future in the cannery and fish business in Anchorage, EMIL HARLACHER was born in Urdorf, Switzerland in 1894. Emil immigrated to the United States in his late teens and became naturalized in 1918. He first came to Alaska in 1922 to work seasonally in the fish canneries of southeast Alaska.

Margaret Elliot Harlacher

Emil Harlacher

Harlacher Home

Chapter VII • 1927

Emil met MARGARET ELLIOT in Portland and corresponded with her for two years prior to their marriage. Margaret was born in Detroit, Michigan in 1903 and came west with her family in later years. Emil brought his family up to southeast Alaska in 1922-23, first living off Edeleen Island between Wrangell and Ketchikan. Living on the island was lonely, as supply ships called only twice annually, and there was no medical assistance. Emil packed up the family in 1924 and moved to Anchorage where he was employed by Henry J. Emard Packing Company as machinist and manager of the cannery. During the winter months when the packing season was over, Emil remained as caretaker of the plant and overhauled equipment for the coming season.

In 1941 Emil retired from the cannery business and was employed by the government at Elmendorf Air Force Base, where he was foreman of the machine shop until he retired.

Cannery Bus

Betty Ann Kampfer   Dorothy Jean Larsen

Margaret and Emil had two daughters. Eldest daughter, Betty Ann Harlacher Kampfer, passed away in 1983. Margaret passed away in 1985, and Emil passed away in 1987. Daughter Dorothy Jean Harlacher Larsen and spouse live in Sun City, Arizona. Emil and Margaret are buried in Anchorage Memorial Park in the Masonic Tract.

A German immigrant who came to Alaska in 1922, ERNEST GEORGE MATTSCHEI was born in Dortmund, Germany in 1890. He immigrated to the United States aboard a sailing ship named the Oratava, sailing out of Hamburg. He manned sailing ships sailing out of Hamburg to Santa Rosalia,

Government Hill Home   Mattschei Family   Ella and Ernest Mattschei

Anchorage Legends & Legacies ————————————————————————— **261**

Mary and Ernie Mattschei

Helen and Andrew
Wisnewski

Robert Mattschei

Baja, California. Ernest was a machinist by trade and left the sailing life when he met ELLA ADELAIDE ZELLMAN, who was born in Ferus Falls, Minnesota in 1900.

Two children were born prior to their moving to Seward, Alaska where Ernest was employed as a mechanic for Ogles Garage. The following year they moved to Kenai where he was employed by the Libby Cannery as a machinist. In 1924 they moved to Anchorage, and he worked for the Alaska Railroad in the machine shops until he retired. He also operated the Brill Car on the railroad when required. His mechanical ability made him in demand, and he did part time work for the downtown stores, repairing radios and small appliances. In early 1942 the family moved to Seattle for their retirement.

The marriage of Ernest and Ella produced three children. The eldest was son Ernest, Jr., who had two children, Robert who passed away and Barbara who resides in Fresno, California. Daughter Helen Mattschei Wisnewski had five children. Timothy is deceased; Cheryl O'Neill, Candace Barbieri, Pamela Carson, and Melinda Holing all live in Seattle, Washington. Son Robert had one son, Mark, who lives in Wenatchee, Washington.

Ella died in 1966, Ernest, Sr. died in 1974, Ernest, Jr. died in 1990, and Robert died in 1991. Helen lives in Seattle, Washington.

"A man before his time," CECIL MOORE WELLS was born in Litchfield, Pennsylvania in 1902. He attended grade school and high school in Spencer, New York and followed that with his true calling in automobile school. Cecil married ELMIRA BATTY in 1920 at the age of eighteen when he was a resident of Spencer, New York. He was working for his father in his garage when, in 1924, he decided to spread his wings and seek his fortune in Alaska. He packed up his wife and, with two children, headed north to the great land of Alaska, which was getting national publicity due to the completion of the Alaska Railroad.

Cecil, Elmira and Phyllis Wells

He arrived in Anchorage in 1924, and immediately found employment with the ARR, working in the foundry. In 1929 he partnered up with Bob Loudermilch, the local undertaker, who had opened up a winter storage garage for automobiles and a machine shop, which enabled him to keep his own equipment running as well as that of other local folks.

Wells Family

In 1930 Cecil opened up his own establishment and named it Wells Garage. It was located on 5th Avenue between E and F Streets. He obtained the dealership for General Motors cars and was the first to put a car on the lot so people could feel and touch a car they wanted to buy. Up until that time, you could only order a car by catalog, sight unseen. He shipped in his cars with Heinie Berger Transportation Company on the *MV Discoverer* as deck load. The first year of business he sold seven cars, which boded well for his garage business. He brought in the first mobile home to Anchorage and put it on display, and people were again stunned at being able to view what they wanted to buy. He started the first bus line that ran to the Willow Creek mines over the newly built Palmer Highway. When the Alcan Highway was completed during the war years, he brought in the first cars again by hauling them over the highway. He, however, did not consider the low overhead bridge structures on the highway, and, when his first car came up on the top load of a truck, a Cadillac Limo had its top torn off. This, of course, ended the highway method of bringing in cars. Cecil Wells gave the people of Anchorage what they needed before they knew they needed it, and as a result he played a large role in the development of Anchorage and of Alaska.

In 1939 Cecil married for the third time and left Anchorage, moving to Fairbanks to start again by opening Wells Alaska Motors in that city. He was vitally interested in Alaskan progress and worked diligently with the Chamber of Commerce. In 1953 he was named President of the State Chamber of Commerce. His many business interests included partnership in Amy Creek Mining Company and an apartment house development with Lloyd Martin Company in Hawaii.

In 1944 his former wife Nanele Wells sold the Wells Garage Company to local investors Max Kirkpatrick, Denny Hewitt and Jack Clawson, who changed the name to Alaska Sales and Service, which still operates today.

Graduation of Auto School

Wells Garage on 5th Avenue Between E and F Streets

Wells Family on the Road

In 1934 Cecil made a trip back to New York on business and spent some time with his parents. His brother MAX H. WELLS talked him into letting him return to Alaska with him. In 1934 they left New York by bus heading for Pontiac, Michigan where they picked up a GMC truck for Pete Wolden and Lee Hartley, and then to Lansing, Michigan where they picked up a new Oldsmobile for Nels Kleven. They delivered the vehicles in Anchorage after coming on the Alaska Steamship vessel *Northwestern*. Max finished high school in Anchorage and worked for his brother at Wells Motors in Anchorage and also in Fairbanks.

Cecil Wells

Betty and Max Wells

Max met BETTY BUZBY in Fairbanks, and they were married in 1940. In 1952 they moved to Valdez where they opened Wells Commercial Company and operated until the '64 earthquake put them out of business. Max then went to work for the State of Alaska as a supply officer and retired in 1982. He served as President of the Chamber of Commerce, Mayor of Valdez, on the school board and in many other organizations.

Cecil was killed in October 1953 and is buried in Fairbanks. He had six children by five different wives. Phyllis Evelyn Wells Rafferty lives in Edmonds, Washington; Clayton Edwin passed away in 1983; Joyce Elmina lives in Klamath Falls, Oregon; Cecil Warren George lives in Raleigh, North Carolina; Wendel Reuben lives in Las Vegas, Nevada; and it is unknown where Marquam Lathrop Wells lives.

Max and Betty Wells had eight children: Lynn Mae Bellezza, Mary Katherine Wegner, Jean Leslie Sutton, Jason Carl, Grace Ann Brayton, David Rush, Laura Louise Phillips, and Theodore Max.

CHAPTER VIII

1925

The year 1925 was no more exciting than 1924 was!

CHARLES BUSH was elected Mayor.

New members of the City Council were:

WILL CLAYSON
U. G. CROCKER
W. B. DEAN
HENRY POPE

Anchorage High School graduated eleven seniors pictured here.

"The official opening of the Anchorage Golf Links occurred in 1925 and in June the sand greens were completed and Mr. Wilson, the instructor, will soon have a driving range and putting green ready for beginners."

Another big news item was that L. A. Powless was reappointed as chief of police, and Z. J. Loussac and D. H. Williams were the new officers of the Western Alaska Fair Association.

Another railroader who was hired outside, EDGAR R. TARWATER was born in Knoxville, Tennessee in 1880. He was hired as a special disbursing agent for the Department of the Interior in 1916 and was stationed in Seward. He had previously worked

Mayor Charles Bush

Clark Andresen

Paul Beeson

Elaine Cameron

Vic Gill

William Gill

Ruth Holdiman

Ophelia Howard

Sam Moyer

Waino Niemi

Hal Noggle

Dorothy Stiles

for the Department of Interior in the Philippine Islands where he went immediately following the Spanish-American War. He held the post of Commissioner of Education on the Island of Luzon until 1915 and then spent a year on a world tour before reporting to his new post in Alaska.

In 1916 he left the service of the Interior Department and went into the banking business with the Brown and Hawkins Company in Seward, an association that lasted for many years. Edgar then came to Anchorage in 1925 when he joined the Bank of Anchorage, which was taken over by the Bank of Alaska, and became its vice president. He held the post of vice president until his retirement in 1938.

He took an active part in civic affairs of the day and was an ardent baseball fan as well as being one of the better golfers at the time. He was an organizer of the Anchorage Golf Club and assisted in laying out the course. He died in the Swedish Hospital in Seattle, Washington in 1944 and was buried in his home state of Tennessee in the town of Neubert.

Paul and Odile Meier

Meier Family

PAUL and ODILE MEIER were married in Butte, Montana in 1900. They came to Alaska in 1923, first landing at LaTouche where Paul found temporary employment. They moved to Anchorage in 1925 when LaTouche started to go the way of a ghost town, and it was difficult to earn a living there. Paul found work with the ARR in Anchorage almost immediately as a steamfitter and sheetmetal man.

Although Paul and Odile moved to Washington in 1931, five of their sons stayed on in Anchorage and made their homes here. Odile was born in Manchester, New Hampshire and died in Seattle in 1952. Paul was born in Saxony, Germany in 1876 and died in Seattle in 1957. Son Art died in 1965; Paul H. died in 1919. Both are buried in Anchorage Memorial Park. William J. died in 1914; Herman L. died in 1926; Alvin "Lovey" died in 1972; Edwin H. died in 1995; and Sylvan lives in California.

Art Meier

Alvin Lovey Meier

Edwin Meier

Sylvan Meier

MYRON EDWIN "JOHN" AMES was another one of the Klondike stampeders who entered Alaska and the Yukon in 1898 and met with nothing more than disappointment rather than gold. John was born in Loveland, Colorado in 1875 and, after his stint to the Klondike, returned to Loveland where he married EDITH BELLE GREENOUGH, who was born in Loveland in 1885.

After his return to Colorado, and some years after his marriage, John returned to Alaska with two of his eldest sons. They settled in Kukak Bay on Shelikof Strait in 1923. Edith and the rest of the family arrived in 1924, and then all

Ames Home

John and Edith Ames

of them moved into Anchorage in 1925. John spent each winter trapping the Kahiltna River until 1932 when he decided to stay in town year round. He purchased the Anchorage Public Scales, which was used to weigh truckloads of coal, the fuel used in Anchorage at the time. John also had a mink ranch at Bird Creek, and the family would spend summers down there. Between 1932 and 1935 John ran a weekly mailboat named the *Alert* from Anchorage to the Susitna River serving Susitna Station, McDougal, and Skwentna.

In 1935 John passed away suddenly, and Edith was left with the scale house to run, which she did, with son Phillip's help. When WWII started, Edith sold the house on F Street and the scale house and moved to Seattle where she spent the rest of her years.

John and Edith had five children, four boys and one daughter. Mildred Ames Fernald was born in 1912 and died in 1976; Ollie "Jinx" was born in 1908 and died in 1981; Bob was born in 1907 and died in 1993; Dick was born in 1927 and died in 1998. Phil was born in 1921 and lives in Kenai with his wife Betty Anne. Phil and Betty Anne had five children. Bradley Gordon lives in Port Lions, Alaska; Martha Ellen Ames Ellis lives in Kenai, Alaska; Warren Rodell was born in 1950 and passed away in 1973; Kathy Anne Ames Stewart lives in Bellingham, Washington; and Brannon Scott lives in Sterling, Alaska. John died in Anchorage in 1935 and is buried in Anchorage Memorial Park. Edith died in Seattle in 1969.

Mildred Ames Fernald

Ollie Jinx Ames

Robert, Phil and Dick Ames

John Ames and Boys

J. R. and Agnes Sherwood   Sherwood Home

JAY R. SHERWOOD was born in New York City in 1885 and ran away from home and went to sea as a young man. He later apprenticed as a trainman and also worked on fishing boats in southeast Alaska.

AGNES BANNER was born in Victoria, British Columbia in 1894 and married Jay in Victoria, British Columbia in 1913. After he served in WWI in France, Jay worked on several railroads in California. In 1925 he moved his family to Anchorage where he did construction work prior to hiring on with the Alaska Railroad. He did some commercial fishing and also some mining to fill in between jobs. In 1932 he was hired on permanently with the ARR and stayed on with them until he retired in 1947 as a conductor.

Jay R. died in 1964, and Agnes died in 1969. They are both buried in Escondido, California. Son Jay R., Jr. had three children, Jay R. III, Kenneth H., and David. Jay R., Jr. lives in Washington.

Daughter Elsie Sherwod Mazur had five children: Mary A., Stanley F., John R., Michael A., and Elizabeth. Elsie died in 1999. Daughter Ruth Sherwood Holman had two children, Paul and Lee Carol Holman Patterson. Ruth is buried in Ephrata,

Elsie Sherwood   Jay R.   Ruth Sherwood   Morgan and Warren
Mazur   Sherwood, Jr.   Holman   Sherwood

Washington. Son Morgan had no children and died in 2000. He is buried in Davis, California. Son Warren lives in Halibut Cove, Alaska.

One of the most colorful characters to come to Anchorage in 1925, WILLIAM A. C. "LUCKY" BALDWIN arrived here with his wife MAME S. BALDWIN from Juneau where they had lived since 1922. When they arrived in Anchorage, they went their separate ways. Lucky opened a grocery store on 4th Avenue between D and E Streets, and Mame opened a grocery store on 4th Avenue between E and F Streets.

Lucky had spent many years with the Royal Canadian Mounted Police prior to coming to Juneau. He suffered from paralysis and was relegated to an electric three-wheel cart, which he operated up and down the streets. Lucky was full of wisecracks and, in many cases, bawled out his customers at will. His motto was "In God we trust, all others pay cash." This he had painted on his store windows on huge silver dollars.

Lucky's Self Service Grocery was the first self-service grocery in Anchorage and was always on the competitive edge. He shipped by boat with Heinie Berger Transportation and chided the Alaska Railroad employees to come into his store and buy more cheaply than the stores that shipped by rail from Seward. His customers seemed to love his chiding attitude. He would sit in his cart by the stove and growl at them as they shopped. As an example, a lady came in to buy bird seed, and, when the clerk went to get it for her, Lucky said, "What in the hell are you doing trying to raise a canary when you can't even take care of your family."

He often bragged that he was the only man in Alaska who could prove he was sane. He held discharge papers from Morningside Hospital in Portland, Oregon stating he was sane.

Lucky died in 1942 and is buried in the Pioneer Tract, Anchorage Memorial Park Cemetery. His tombstone was cast from concrete by John Oden and was inscribed, "Here Lies Lucky And Always Will Lie." This same tombstone was stored in the living quarters in the rear of the store, and, when Louis Odsather worked for Lucky, he and his wife had to move the stone from under the bed every night prior to retiring. Mame Baldwin died in Seattle in 1944 and is buried there.

A professional man who arrived on the Anchorage scene in 1925, DR. LAFAYETTE LAMB HUFMAN was a dentist who was born in Bremerton, Washington in 1895. After serving in the Balloon Corps during WWI, he attended dental school at the University of Minnesota. Following his graduation he associated with Dr. Pollard, a practicing dentist in Anchorage. Hufman took the dental exam in Juneau in 1925 and then proceeded to Anchorage to start his practice.

He moved his family to Fairbanks in 1929 and became active in civic affairs. He was an early promoter of hockey and baseball in Fairbanks and was an avid hunter and fisherman. In 1941 he gave up his dental practice and moved to his summer cabin on Paxson Lake, where he pursued his interests in hunting and trapping.

Hufman Home, 1926

Dr. L. L. and Kay Hufman

Robert and Betty Huffman and
Brother Donald

Hufman Family

MARY CATHERINE LEE
was born in Franklin, Ohio in
1897. She attended the
Cincinnati Conservatory of
Music before coming to
Anchorage and was an accomplished musician in both voice
and piano. She was one of the
driving forces behind the
development of the Fairbanks
Winter Carnival in 1934.

Mary and Doc Hufman had two children. Son Donald Lee and spouse Jenny Doheny had one son,
Stefan, who lives in Wasilla. Son Robert Lee and Betty Jean Clark had four sons. David Lee lives in
Medford, Oregon; Joseph Dean lives in Anchorage; and John Clark and Paul Galen live in
Fairbanks. Mary died in Ashland, Oregon in 1966, and Doc Hufman died at Paxson Lake in 1984.

Another long time ARR employee arrived in Alaska in 1925, coming directly to Cordova from
Kellinghausen, Germany where he was born in 1898. RUDOLF KRUEGER came to Cordova to
work for the Copper River and Northwestern Railway and was stationed in McCarthy. With his
spouse, MARIA AHRENS KRUEGER, who was born in Wittorf-Holstein, Germany in 1897, he
moved to Anchorage in late 1925, where went to work for the ARR as section foreman at
Hurricane Gulch. Marie accompanied him and was hired on as cook for the section crews wherever they were stationed.

The Kruegers worked for the Railroad at various sections including Hurricane, Willow,
Montana, Birchwood, Honolulu and Portage, which was their last station, and they remained
there until their retirement
in 1956.

Marie and Rudolph Krueger

Patricia and Rudy Krueger

The Kruegers had one son,
Rudolf who married Patricia
Chisholm, a member of
another Pioneer Anchorage
family. They had three sons.
Kurt Rudolf lives in Mt.
Pleasant, South Carolina; Paul
Quinn lives in Beaverton,
Oregon; and John Chisholm
lives in Las Vegas, Nevada.
Rudolf Krueger, Sr. and Maria
both passed away in 1960 in

Bellevue, Washington. Rudolf, Jr. died in 1974. Rudolph, Sr., Maria, Rudolph, Jr. and Patricia Chisholm Krueger are all interred in Acacia Memorial Park, Seattle, Washington.

GLENN EDGAR BURRELL was born in 1893 in Stockton, Nebraska. He moved west and attended the Colorado School of Mines for two years. He arrived in Anchorage in 1925 and worked for the ARR on the bridge crew at Curry and later moved to Fairbanks where he was employed by the F. E. Company. From 1927 to 1929 he owned and operated a freight line between Fairbanks and Valdez on the Richardson Highway. He moved to Cordova in 1929 and worked for the Kennecott Copper Company in both Cordova and Chitina and moved permanently to Anchorage in 1939. He died at the Pioneer Home in 1979 and is buried in the Pioneer Tract of Anchorage Memorial Park.

CHAPTER IX

1926

Chris Eckman

The year 1926 was uneventful.

CHRIS ECKMAN was elected Mayor.

New Councilmen were:

C. A. POLLARD
GRANT REED
C. A. MATHESON
J. W. TINKLER

There were five high school graduates:

EDNA ALLENBAUGH
EDNA BROOKS (No photo)
VANNY JONES
HULDA LOTHROP (No photo)
TANIA SHADURA (No photo)

Edna Allenbaugh

Vanny Jones

The big local news was that the first commercial airline in Alaska was being headquartered here, Anchorage Air Transport, organized by GUS GELLES and ART SHONBECK. RUSSEL MERRILL was hired as their first pilot.

The other big news in 1926 was the solving of the Great Dog Team Mail Robbery that took place near Flat in November 1923. Postal inspectors arrested William C. Shermeyer, a roadhouse operator, and Nellie Beattie, known throughout the territory as the "Black Bear." Shermeyer had confessed and implicated the woman in the robbery of a dog team mail carrier in the amount of thirty-three thousand, one hundred seventy-three dollars. The money was taken from mail bags while the team was enroute from the Railroad to Flat. When the team reached Shermeyer's roadhouse, just twenty-four miles from Flat, it stopped for the night, and no money could be found after the team left that point.

The money was in two consignments, including twenty-seven thousand five hundred dollars which was being sent by the Dexter Horton Bank of Seattle to Thomas P. Aitken, a mine operator, and two thousand two hundred fifty dollars sent by Decker Brothers, fur buyers of New York, to Ed C. Jolme.

Shermeyer took a trip to Los Angeles after the robbery and openly bragged about the "heist." The postal inspectors followed him back to Flat, and the mystery was solved. (This information taken from the *Anchorage Times,* June 15, 1926.)

JOHN JOSEPH O'SHEA was born in Fairbanks in March 1910. He was reared in Fairbanks and graduated from the University of Alaska with a B.S. in chemistry. He was the President of the University of Alaska Alumni Association in 1942-43. He was a member of the Territorial Legislature in 1943, was employed as clean-up foreman for the U.S. Smelting Refining and Mining Company for several years, and was a part-time assayer. He later became coal inspector for the Alaska Railroad. John went into business for himself as an independent insurance agent and real estate broker.

He had a long history of public service beyond his legislative years in that he was chairman of the southcentral chapter of the National Foundation for Infantile Paralysis. He was awarded the distinguished service award and was the Alaska chairman of the March of Dimes from 1955 to 1957. In 1971 he was appointed deputy director of the State Division of Insurance in Anchorage, and in 1973 he became the director of the Division of Insurance in Juneau. In 1973 he received the Distinguished Alumnus Award from the University of Alaska.

John's wife, Florence, was living in the Pioneers Home in Anchorage when she passed away in 1990. John passed away in 1992 in Anchorage. John and Florence had two children, Mary Jane who lives in Maryland and William who lives in Seward.

LELAND and FRANCES STRICKLAND arrived in Anchorage in 1924. Strickland became an employee of the Alaska Railroad and Frances operated a dressmaking and pattern shop. Their original home in Anchorage was located between 7th and 8th Avenues on L Street and is still standing, now known as the J. Vic Brown home.

Frances had twin sons by a former marriage, ALLEN and EDWARD TURNER, who were born in Chicago, Illinois. They came to Anchorage to join their mother and step-father in 1926 and entered the third grade here. Both boys grew up in Anchorage and attended Anchorage schools.

Ed and Allen Turner

Allen moved to Fairbanks in 1935 where he lived with his aunt and uncle. After he finished high school in Fairbanks, he worked in various mining camps during the summers, and in 1941 he went into the Army prior to WWII. He was in the Army Air Corps as a radio operator in both the European and the China-Burma theaters. In 1941 he and DOROTHY DAVENPORT were married in Iowa. This union produced two children. Son Terry Turner is a practicing attorney and lives in Anchorage; daughter Mary Kaye is employed in the Anchorage School District and also lives in Anchorage. Allen and Dorothy now reside in the Anchorage Pioneer Home.

Edward's career began with his entry into the Episcopal ministry. He was ordained a priest in 1944 in Washota, Wisconsin, and his first assignment was in Seward, Alaska in St. Peter's Parish. Edward moved up in the church hierarchy, being assigned to New York City in the overseas department. He traveled the world performing his duties for the church in many foreign countries. After Edward and Anne Pfeiler were married, he again asked for parish work, and his next assignment was in the Caribbean where he became Canon of the Cathedral in San Juan, Puerto Rico. He then went back to parish work in the Virgin Islands and eventually became Bishop of the Diocese of the Virgin Islands.

He retired in 1973, and he and his wife moved to Arizona. Diabetes and its problems caused his death in Nevada in 1996, and he is buried in the St. Paul churchyard, Fredericksted, Virgin Islands. Edward and Anne had two children. Daughter Susan lives in Missouri, and son Edward lives in Wisconsin.

Frances Turner Strickland was born in Edgemont, South Dakota in 1902. She passed away in Seward, Alaska in 1977. Her ashes are buried in the Seward Cemetery.

Simeon Oliver

One of Alaska's and Anchorage's early teachers, ETHEL ROSS came to the Anchorage area in 1926 with her husband ERNEST ROSS. They worked a trapline on the upper reaches of the Skwentna River from 1926 until 1935, spending each winter on the trapline and the summers in Anchorage, where Ernest fished commercially.

In 1935 Ernest passed away, and Ethel left for Washington. She furthered her education and returned to Anchorage in 1937 with a teacher's certificate. She immediately started teaching in Palmer, the same year that the colonists arrived. In 1938 she started teaching in Anchorage and continued teaching here until the early 80's.

In 1940 she married SIMEON OLIVER, an Aleut who was a well-known pianist and author. Together they spent a year in the Aleutian Islands, assisting the natives in resettling after WWII. She authored the book *Journal of an Aleutian Year*, detailing the time they spent on this venture. She also authored two other books, *Aleutian Boy* and *Eskimo Tales Retold*. She was awarded an honorary doctorate from the University of Alaska for her written works and her life of teaching.

Ethel Oliver

Ethel was born in Valley, Washington in 1902 and was educated in Washington prior to coming to Alaska. She and Ernest Ross had one son, Ernest, Jr., who passed away in Ferndale, Washington in 1997. Ethel died in Ferndale, Washington in 1995, and she is buried there.

John Reekie and Family

William and Ina Reekie

Elizabeth Reekie

A railroader who came to Anchorage in 1926, JOHN REEKIE was born in Scotland in 1893 and, accompanied by his wife, ELIZABETH HENDERSON REEKIE, came to the United States looking for a better life. Elizabeth was born in Dysart, Scotland in 1898. When they arrived in Anchorage, John obtained a job with the Alaska Railroad as a machinist and stayed with the ARR until his retirement when Elizabeth and John moved to Seattle. He passed away there in 1971.

Elizabeth returned to Anchorage and entered the Pioneer Home where she lived until she passed away in 1992.

John and Elizabeth had three children. William, the eldest son, married widow Ina Findlay, who had three children, and they had one daughter together. Iain lives in Muirfield, Texas; Drew lives in Grand Junction, Colorado; Margo Findlay lives in Fairbanks; and Elizabeth lives in Pt. Barrow. William, Sr. passed away in 1979 and is buried in Angelus Memorial Park. Son James had four children. Raymond lives in Eagle River, Robert and Bruce live in Anchorage, and daughter Linda lives in Juneau. John "Jack," Jr. had three children. Kathy Reekie Morino and Patty Steadman live in Seattle, Washington, and Becky Morino lives in Wasilla. Jack died in 1985, and his ashes are buried at their lake cabin along with the ashes of his mother Elizabeth.

A true veteran of the north, JAMES CLIMIE arrived in Anchorage in 1926. He was born in 1877 in Kilmarnock, Scotland where he grew up. He was barely twenty years old when he immigrated to the United States and went directly to Alaska, joining the stampede to the Klondike. In 1900 he went to Nome where he spent a short period of time prospecting. From Nome he moved to Manley Hot Springs and then to Rampart. He had previously mined on American Creek in Hot Springs, and in Rampart he worked Little Minnook Creek.

In August 1908 AGNES arrived in Rampart from Johannesburg, South Africa to marry James whom she had known in Scotland. For the next fourteen years they lived in Rampart while James was mining for gold. They moved to Anchorage where James was employed by the Alaska Railroad, starting as a laborer and then a blacksmith helper and finally a carpenter on the B and B #3 gang, a job which he held until he retired.

Climie was vitally interested in the labor union movement. He was past president of the American Federation of Government Employees, and during his early years in Rampart he was president of the Miners Union.

Agnes and James had two sons, James and Charles. James won an appointment to Annapolis and after graduation went into the Marine Corps. He was stationed in Peiping, China as a Captain in the Embassy Guard when WWII broke out. He was taken prisoner by the Japanese and held in Northern China until the war ended. Son Charles passed away in the east in 1950. James Climie, Sr. passed away in Anchorage in 1940 and is buried in the Pioneer Tract, Anchorage Memorial Park. Agnes entered the Pioneer Home in Sitka in 1951 and passed away there in 1957. She is buried in the Sitka Cemetery Pioneer Section.

One of Alaska's greats in the flying business, RUSSEL HYDE MERRILL was born in Des Moines, Iowa in 1894 and was educated and grew to manhood in Des Moines. He attended Grinnell College and Cornell University in Ithaca, New York. In 1915 he enlisted in the United States Navy Reserve as a Seaman Second Class. He reported for duty in 1917 at Newport, Rhode Island, and from 1917 until 1921 he was in the Naval Flying Corps, appointed a Naval Aviator, and promoted to Lieutenant Junior Grade. He was discharged in 1921, then was re-appointed in the Naval Reserve Flying Corps in 1922 and discharged in 1925. He had received a B.S. in chemistry from Cornell in 1919, and, in serving in the reserve over the years, he spent only the required time each year serving on active duty.

Russel Hyde Merrill

In 1920 he joined the Crown Willamette Paper Company at Camas, Washington. There he met a secretary named Thyra Allen and a long friendship started. He was transferred to Floristan. California in 1921 as plant manager; however, he and Thyra kept in touch. He left the company to move to Palo Alto, California to be with his mother who had only twelve months to live. After she died he returned to Portland, and he and Thyra continued the relationship where it left off and were married. He had helped to organize the Ken Clay Products Company in Portland and became its general manager.

In 1925 he saw an advertisement offering a flying boat for sale in Portland. The plane's owner was Roy J. Davis, an aviation pioneer who now lived in Portland and had been flying commercially for five years. He told Merrill that he would not sell his airplane if he could find someone who would be interested in starting an aviation business in Alaska. Merrill was interested.

Merrill with Anchorage Airways Plane

On May 19, 1925, Merrill, Davis and Cyril Rugner flew into Seattle from Portland and the following day headed north. Just out of Cape Scott oil began streaming out of the engine, and they had to put down. An Indian in a small boat towed them to Alert Bay. They made their repairs and left for Bella Bella after two days. On May 25, 1925 they arrived at Ketchikan and flew from one town to the other on the Alaska coast, heading for Seward. On August 1,

1925 Davis and Merrill set out for Seward across the Gulf of Alaska. Their mechanic, Rugner, went back to Portland, as they no longer needed him. After many trials and tribulations the two pioneer pilots arrived in Seward on August 3, 1925. They crossed the Gulf of Alaska on the first commercial flight ever attempted in ten hours and twenty minutes of flying time.

The Curtis Flying Boat of the Roy J. Davis Airplane Company was the first airplane ever to fly into Anchorage. Roy Davis and Russel Merrill landed unannounced at 8:30 PM on August 20, l925. They carried a passenger, one Frank Murphy, from Seward to Anchorage.

Gus Gelles of Anchorage chartered Merrill to fly him to Kodiak on a sales trip. On their return they were forced down on Chugach Island, and the plane was demolished by the high winds and tides. All they could save was the boat and the engine. Gelles said after the trip: "It was a wonderful experience."

Merrill and Davis renamed their company and operated out of Portland for a time, and then the company disbanded and Merrill looked for a flying job. He was contacted by Gus Gelles and Art Shonbeck, who organized the Anchorage Air Transport Company. They hired Alonzo Cope as a mechanic and sent him to Wichita, Kansas to purchase two Travel Air planes. The pair of Travel Air airplanes arrived in Anchorage on March l, 1927. They were packed in eleven crates and shipped via Alaska Steamship Company to Seward and then by ARR from Seward to Anchorage. There had been a heavy snow in Anchorage, and the owners felt they should wait for spring to construct a hangar. The crates were stored in Oscar Gills' garage, just five blocks from the airfield, which is now the Delaney Park Strip.

Ed Young was hired as another pilot for the company, and in the early spring the planes were assembled and test hopped. The planes were named *Anchorage #l* and *Anchorage #2*. When they test hopped *Anchorage #2*, it broke through snow crust and damaged one ski and the wing.

Merrill and Young and Cope were all flying for Anchorage Air Transport when it was sold to Alaska Airways, Inc. in 1929. The new company retained all of the pilots, and many hazardous trips and adventures ensued during the years. On September 16, 1929, after making a flight to a camp where James Stillman and J. H. Durrell of New York City were hunting, Merrill departed from Anchorage alone bound for Akiak village and was never heard from again. In October 1929 a piece of fabric, which was identified as being part of his plane, was found on Cook Inlet near Tyonek.

The Anchorage airport of Merrill Field was named in his honor, and the Anchorage Womans Club contributed a bronze plaque on the beacon tower, which was erected there by popular subscription as a memorial to him. Merrill Pass was also named in his honor as the man who founded the route.

(All of the information given here, including photos, is from the book by Robert Merrill MacLean, *Flying Cold*.)

Alonzo Cope and Matt Nieminen

Another member of the Flying North Pioneers, ALONZO COPE was born in Oklahoma in 1897 where he grew up near Oklahoma City. "Lon," as he was known among Anchorage friends, came to Anchorage in 1926 after hearing of the opportunities with the Alaska Railroad. He was trained as a mechanic and worked in the mechanical department of the Railroad until 1926. Then he got involved in flying through his acquaintance with A. A. Shonbeck, who approached him in joining him and Gus Gelles in the development of an airline. Cope was well known for his mechanical ability and was therefore an immediate asset to the proposed company.

In 1927 the company, Anchorage Air Transport, was organized with Russel Merrill as chief pilot and Lon Cope as mechanic. Ed Young was hired later when the company got its second plane in operation. Many of Cope's challenges were repairing planes that cracked up in the bush and making them flyable. In one instance he mushed in by snowshoe with parts and pieces on his back to a crash site to repair a plane. He salvaged all of the fabric and even the nails to rebuild the plane and made it flyable again.

In 1929 Ben Eilson purchased Anchorage Air Transport, and the company name was changed to Alaska Airways. Lon remained with the new team as mechanic. In late 1929 he married MARGARET A. BALF in Anchorage. Margaret was born in Wisconsin in 1901 and was educated as a business education teacher. She taught in Montana and Washington before she came to Anchorage to join the staff of Anchorage High School.

In 1930 Frank Dorbandt, another famous air pioneer, and Lon organized their own firm, calling it Dorbandt-Cope, and proceeded to bid against dog teams for mail carrying contracts on the Kuskokwim and Yukon Rivers. In 1931 Lon and Dorbandt sold out to Pacific International Airways. Lon joined their firm, and Frank Dorbandt went elsewhere. During the time that Lon was with P.I.A., he learned to fly. A short time later, P.I.A. was bought out by Pacific Alaska Airways, and Lon again joined this group. In 1932 he was transferred in service to Pan American World Airways in Brownsville, Texas, making scheduled flights out of that base.

In 1938 Lon left P.A.A. and returned to Alaska and started flying independently out of Juneau. While on a flight from Ketchikan to Juneau in March 1939, he crashed near Grand Island while in a snowstorm. Lon and his four passengers were all killed instantly.

After Lon's death Margaret moved to Palmer where she taught school for the next twenty-nine years before she retired to Redlands, California. She died in Redlands in 1983 and is buried there. Lon is buried in the Elks Tract of Anchorage Memorial Park. A stillborn daughter, Josephine Cope, who died in 1931, is buried in the same grave with her father.

M. C. Edmunds

Betty Edmunds and Children

The man responsible for the construction of the early roads and trails in the Anchorage-Fairbanks area, MORGAN CHRISTOPHER EDMUNDS, known as "Chris," was born in Liandough, Wales in 1883, the youngest of six children. He obtained an engineering degree in Cardiff where he lived most of his young life. He traveled around the world several times aboard sailing ships and was at one time a professional pugilist and was also a runner for the Army during the South African Boer War.

Chris Edmunds with Son

His mother and father had immigrated to Johannesburg in 1896, and, soon after his mother passed away, his itchy feet sent him again to sea, as he wanted to see America. He got off his boat in Seattle, Washington and headed for the Iditarod country where he did some unsuccessful prospecting.

Chris returned to Wales for a visit with relatives and then returned to Alaska in 1916 to work for the Alaska Railroad. During the flu epidemic of that year he was sent with a group of Railroad employees to Ft. Yukon as a burial detail to assist the missionaries. This is where he met LULU BEATRICE NUNEVILLE, a deaconess missionary nurse who was on the staff at Ft. Yukon. Betty, as she was called, was born

Sarah Edmunds

Morgan Edmunds and Family

in Germantown, Pennsylvania in 1886. She attended deaconess school in Philadelphia, and after graduation she was accepted at the Episcopal School of Nursing in Philadelphia. Upon her graduation she was sent by the church to Ft. Yukon to work with Archdeacon Hudson Stuck during the rampaging flu epidemic.

Chris and Betty were married in 1920 in Tanana and then moved to Healy where Chris was employed by the ARR. In 1923 the family moved to Fairbanks where Chris was appointed to the post of superintendent of the Alaska Road Commission, Fairbanks District. In 1926 he was moved to Anchorage where he held the same position in the third judicial district.

Elizabeth and Tom Donohoe

The family had increased to five when they settled in Anchorage, and Chris and Betty took up their activities in the church as well as participating in public causes. Chris retired from the ARC in 1949, and he and Betty moved to Seattle, Washington. By 1942 Chris had a laundry list of accomplishments with the ARC. Under his command, the portion of the Glenn Highway from Palmer to Glenallen was built, the road in McKinley Park from the hotel to Wonder Lake was built, the old Seward Highway from Anchorage to Potter was completed, the Anchorage-Palmer highway was completed, the Homer spit road and sea wall were built, the connecting road from Pile Bay to Lake Illiamna was done as well as the interconnecting roads in the Matanuska Valley and Hatcher Pass. These were all a part of his district. In 1939-40 he was instructed by the government to dig a canal connecting Lake Spenard with Lake Hood, as the aircraft industry was expanding and more and larger planes were being used.

One of his foremen from McKinley Park was in for the winter after the Park had shut down, so he assigned Pete Bagoy and Noble McCrea to dig the canal. They had an old Bucyrus dragline, which was an open frame with no cab and no heat. Bagoy was the operator, and McCrea was the oiler. They spent two cold winters digging this canal, which was eighteen hundred feet long, two hundred feet wide and four feet deep. They moved seventy-five thousand cubic yards of dirt and finished the job in the spring of 1940.

The union of Chris and Betty produced three children, two girls and one boy. Eldest daughter, Sarah, married Willard Nagley II, and they had one son, Willard III, who lives in Kirkland, Washington. Daughter Elizabeth married Tom Donohoe and they had two sons, Thomas Christopher and Patrick Keeler. Son Morgan Christopher, Jr. married Mary Elizabeth Call, and they had four children: Megan Elizabeth, Lucinda Ann and Mary Mathilda all live in Virginia, and son David Christopher lives in Anchorage. Chris Edmunds died in Seattle in 1958, and Betty died in Seattle in 1980. Daughter Sarah Edmunds Nagley died in 1979 in Anchorage.

CHAPTER X

1927

New Mayor WILL CLAYSON was sworn in as were three new Councilmen:

IKE BAYLES
M. J. CONROY
R. C. LOUDERMILCH

The big news in Alaska in 1927 was the cave-in and flooding of the huge Treadwell Mine in Douglas, along with the lesser mines of the Mexican and the Seven Hundred and with the loss of two lives. "It is doubtful if the mine will ever open again. The financial loss exceeds 10 million dollars and the economic loss of 1000 jobs is devastating to the community." (*Anchorage Times*, April 16, 1927)

William Clayson

Municipal Airfield

Arthur Adams

The big news in the year 1927 in Anchorage was the arrival of two Travel Air aircraft for the newly formed Anchorage Air Transport and the beginning of commercial air travel out of Anchorage.

Anchorage High School graduated six students that year, all boys!

Anchorage Air Transport Travel Air

Joe Bell

Sidney Black

Phillip Gill

Harold Strandberg

Harlan Youel

A well-known mining engineer and one of the early graduates of the University of Alaska School of Mines, LAWRENCE CHRISTOFER "LARRY" DOHENY was born in Merrill, Wisconsin in 1902. He first came to Alaska in 1927 to attend the University of Alaska and graduated in 1930. After graduation he was employed by the U.S. Smelting, Mining and Refining Company. He was well known as a mining engineer throughout the Territory. He was supervisory engineer for the Reconstruction Finance Corporation for a time and later with the soils testing division of the Corps of Engineers.

In 1931 he married Olga Strandberg, a daughter of the well-known Strandberg mining family, and they had three children. Son Michael passed away in 1984; daughter Kathleen Doheny Hennessy lives in Texas; and daughter Jenny lives in Anchorage. Larry passed away in 1952, and Olga passed away in 1993.

An old-timer newspaperman and mining authority in both Alaska and the Yukon, CHARLES R. SETTLEMEIR was born in Albany, Oregon in 1873 and received his early schooling there. He obtained his newspaper training in Tacoma, Washington and in 1898, like so many other stampeders, he headed for Dawson and the Klondike gold fields.

In 1899-1901 Charley acquired a part interest in the *Dawson News*, however, his gold fever was still active, and in a few years he sold his newspaper interest and took part in a silver prospect in the Mayo district of Yukon Territory. He had the reputation of being one of the most well-informed men in the mining business and mining law, and his opinions during his newspaper days were often written with authority.

Charley departed the Yukon and was heading back to Seattle; however, he decided to take a detour to visit his old friend Roy Southworth in Anchorage, who at the time was editor of the *Anchorage Daily Times*. Roy Southworth prevailed upon him to take over the editorial job, which he did, and remained editor of the *Times* until 1936.

Charles Settlemeir

Charley left the *Anchorage Times* in the fall of 1936 and moved to Fairbanks to become editor of the *Fairbanks News Mine*r. In 1942 he accepted the position of editor of the *Alaska Weekly* in Seattle. He passed away in Seattle in 1947.

Charley and his wife had two children. A daughter and a son were born in Los Angeles and lived in Dawson with their parents for several years. Charles and his wife went their separate ways in 1910, and the children lived with Mrs. Settlemeir. The daughter, Marion, died under mysterious circumstances in Los Angeles in 1934, and son, Weston, died in San Francisco just three months before Charley passed away in Seattle.

A well-known Anchorage grocer, with his partner, established the first grocery store in Anchorage that priced "to the penny." Up until that time all prices were rounded off to the nickel. Pennies were almost unheard of in Anchorage and in some places were not even accepted as legal tender. This gentleman was WILLIAM "BILL" MELLISH. He was born in Kenmore, Alberta in 1892 and attended grade and high school in Dawson, Yukon Territory. His father came to Dawson during the gold rush, and shortly thereafter he and his mother followed. The school he attended was located at the Forks, which was the junction of the Bonanza and Eldorado Creeks, the greatest gold bearing streams in the area. In 1909 Bill left Dawson, headed for Alaska, and followed the gold trails looking for the yellow dust, but, like so many other stampeders of the day, he came up empty-handed.

He enlisted in the United States Army during WWI, and as a result of his enlistment he received his citizenship papers. After his discharge he became a storekeeper in Fairbanks, and in 1926 he married MONICA HUGG. Monica was the daughter of Mr. and Mrs. H. L. Hugg who came to Anchorage in 1916 where H. L. was a dispatcher and agent of the ARR stationed in Matanuska.

In 1927 the family moved down to Anchorage, and Bill went to work for the Northern Commercial Company and the Alaska Railroad. In 1935, when the settlers moved into the valley, he was employed by the co-op in Palmer. The family moved back to Anchorage in 1940, and Bill became a partner in the Pay n' Takit Grocery on 4th Avenue between C and D Streets.

Monica was an avid golfer, and she helped organize the Anchorage Golf Club. In 1930 she won the Rasmuson Women's Open Championship and later won the Z. J. Loussac AGC Women's Trophy in 1934, 1935 and 1936. When WWII broke out, Monica was the adjutant of the Anchorage Women's Motor Corps.

Bill and Monica had one son, Donald Mellish, who became president and executive officer of the Bank of Alaska. He and his wife, the former Susan Schmelzer, had three children: Gabriele lives in Anchorage; John lives in Kenai; and Robert lives in New York City. Bill Mellish died in Spokane, Washington in 1971, and Monica died in California.

A well-known grocer who came to Anchorage in 1927, HERBERT LESLIE REED was born in Columbus, Ohio in 1895 and grew up there. In 1924 Herb acquired the franchise for the establishment of Piggly Wiggly stores in Alaska. The Piggly Wiggly stores were a retail grocery chain operating in the south forty-eight states.

Herb packed up his wife GERTRUDE GEBHART REED and, with their daughter, left for Alaska in 1924. Gertrude was born in Columbus, Ohio in 1898, and had come west with her husband and daughter, joining Herb in his business ventures. They first arrived in Ketchikan and surveyed the area to see if it warranted a store. They

Herbert Leslie Reed

Verna and Son Anthony

Verna Reed Lazarnik

kept moving north to Cordova and then to Anchorage, where they settled on opening a store in 1927.

Herb opened the first Piggly Wiggly store in Anchorage and later a second one in Fairbanks. Both stores were highly successful and operated profitably well into 1938 when Herb's health began to deteriorate. Herb passed away in 1938, and Gertrude operated the stores until she sold out to local interests a short time later.

Herb and Gertrude had one daughter, Verna Reed Hall. She had two children with Hall, who was in the Air Force during the Korean War and was declared missing in action in 1951. She married N. Peter Canlis some years later, and he passed away in 1978. She now lives in San Diego and is married to George A. Lazarnik. Of her two sons, Anthony Reed Hall Canlis lives in Sammamish, Washington, and Christopher Burns Hall Canlis lives in Seattle. Gertrude passed away in Seattle in 1990. Both she and Herb are buried in Evergreen-Washelli Cemetery in Seattle, Washington.

A veteran who spent time in Uncle Sam's Army in Alaska in 1924, ISAAC H. H. "IKE" HEFFENTRAGER was born in Skippack, Pennsylvania in 1899 and, as a young man, joined the Army in 1924 and was stationed in Alaska. He served his three-year hitch and was discharged at Vancouver Barracks, Washington in 1927. He had Alaska in his blood and returned to Anchorage the same year. He worked as a night policeman for the City for a time and then went to work for the Alaska Railroad in 1930, retiring after thirty years of service in 1960.

In Anchorage Ike met ANNA WAGNER, who was born in Plauen, Germany in 1912. She had come to the United States with her mother Gertrude in 1915. Her father had passed away

Isaac and Anna Heffentrager

Heffentrager Home

Family on Rabbit Hunt

and her father's brother, C. W. Wagner, had sent for them to come to the United States. Anna and her mother traveled across the United States via train to California. They had some difficulty in making their way as neither of them could speak or understand English, which was nothing unusual for that time.

Gertrude and Wagner were married in California and then moved to Alaska. They lived in the towns of Seldovia, Fairbanks and on a homestead near Eska. They finally settled in Anchorage and lived on L Street near where Ike and a friend lived as close neighbors. Ike and Anna were married in 1929 and soon bought their house at 136 7th Avenue. The house was built in 1919 and is in the history books as the Bieri-Heffentrager House.

The union of Anna and Ike produced three children, one son and two daughters. Their son Frank lives in Anchorage, and he and his spouse, Bonnie Maxwell, had three children. Carl and Leslie Heffertrager Fontaine live in Anchorage; Laurie Heffentreger Earl lives in Bothell, Washington. Daughter Mary Margaret and spouse Edson Anderson were presumed dead when they were lost on Cook Inlet on a fishing and hunting trip in 1951. Daughter Gertrude Katherine Heffentrager Hinds lives in Marston Mills, Maine. She had six children. Linda Hinds Halstead lives in Hyattsville, Maryland; Danny lives in Pocasset, Maine; Mike lives in Falmouth, Maine; Susan Hinds Eldridge lives in Waterloo, Maine; Elizabeth lives in Marston Hills, Maine; and Thomas lives in Valdosta, Georgia. Anna died on January 10, 1999, and Ike passed away in June 1999. Both are buried in Evergreen-Washelli Cemetery in Seattle, Washington.

Heffentrager Family

MARGUERITTE EPPERSON-WILKENSON arrived in Anchorage in 1927 with her seven-year-old daughter, Eleanor. Margueritte was born in Illinois in 1904 and raised in Colorado. Daughter Eleanor was born in Richmond, Virginia in 1921. Shortly after their arrival they moved up the Susitna River to Susitna Station, where they leased the Roadhouse from Bill Dennison. Margueritte made a living serving family style meals and renting rooms to travelers on the river.

Eleanor, Bill and Margueritte

Willis Epperson

Margueritte, Mike Trepte, Eleanor

Shortly after they began operating the roadhouse, Margueritte's brother, WILLIS EPPER-SON, arrived at Susitna Station to help his sister in the roadhouse. Willis, his sister, and Bill Dennison were taking a trip up-river in a scow that belonged to Dennison, when, by some freak occurrence, the scow swamped, and everyone was thrown into the water. Willis saw Dennison in trouble and tried to rescue him, but he slipped out of his grip and was lost. He then noticed his sister drifting downstream, holding on to an empty gas can. He swam to her and pulled her ashore on an island sand bar. He left her there and proceeded to build a four-log raft on the river bank. He used his shoelaces to tie the logs together, put Margueritte aboard, and headed down-river to safety. It was getting late, and they spotted a cabin on shore and made for it. Willis was suffering from hypothermia and collapsed when they reached the cabin. Margueritte left him there and started out for another cabin for help. She found blankets and headed back to where she left her brother and found him dead.

Willis Epperson was hailed as a hero in his attempt to rescue Bill Dennison and for rescuing his sister from the icy waters of the Susitna. Willis was born in 1908 in Colorado and was just twenty-one years old when he met his death on the Susitna River. He is buried in Anchorage Memorial Park Cemetery.

Following the accident, Margueritte and Eleanor returned to Seattle where they lived until 1931. There Margueritte met MIKE TREPTE, and they were married in Seattle in 1931. Mike was born in Dresden, Germany in 1892, and made his way to Valdez in 1917. He

Dutch Creek Mine

Hiking Through Talkeetna

Trapping Cabin on
the Yentna

prospected around Cache Creek and established a trap line on the forks of the Yentna about seventy-five miles from Talkeetna.

After their marriage in Seattle, Margueritte and Mike left for Talkeetna where they operated a gold claim on Dutch Creek forty-five miles from Talkeetna in the summer and trapped on the Yentna in the winter.

Eleanor Trepte married Robert Seitz and they had two children. Son Robert lives in Chugiak, and daughter Margaret Ann Seitz Jenks lives in Marysville, Washington. Eleanor and Robert were divorced in 1957, and she later married Hubert Martin. This marriage produced one son, Troy Martin, who lives in Tucson, Arizona. Eleanor and Hubert live in Green Valley, Arizona. Her mother Margueritte died in 1983.

Eleanor and Hubert Martin

One of the Pioneer women who mushed the Chilkoot with the gold seekers, ELIZABETH FLOWER was known from Fairbanks to Juneau and from Dawson to the Koyokuk after spending more than forty years in the north.

She and a woman companion were initiated into the rigors of the trail when no facilities for passengers could be found on a steamer from Whitehorse to Dawson. The two ladies finally persuaded a barge operator to let them ride the top of the load to Dawson. Upon their arrival at Dawson they found work immediately in a clothing store.

In Dawson she met J. H. Flower, whom she married in 1914. The couple left Dawson for the new strike at Wiseman on the Chandalar River. They opened a bakery there and operated it until 1917. They moved to Nenana on the Alaska Railroad, which was the division point of construction. There they opened a bakery again, and in 1921 they moved to Seward where they opened another bakery. In 1927 Elizabeth and her husband parted company. She went to Anchorage, and he moved south to Juneau. She lived out her years in Anchorage and died in 1940. She is buried in the Pioneer section of Anchorage Memorial Park.

A railroader who came to Anchorage from Norway in 1927, IVER NOTTVIET was born in Norway in 1892 and came to the United States in 1906. During WWI he joined the Army and served in France, thereby receiving his citizenship. After the War he worked for the Alaska Railroad as a conductor until his retirement in 1942.

MARIE "BILLIE" NOTTVIET was born in St. Elexis, Quebec, Canada in 1896. Her first stop in Alaska was in Livengood in 1923. She moved to Anchorage in 1925 and worked for Reeds, a women's clothing store. She and Iver were married in Anchorage in 1924, and in 1935 they bought the store from Grant Reed. In 1941 they sold the store and moved to Santa Barbara, California, where they lived out their lives. Billie died in 1982, and Iver died in 1989.

Charles and Gertrude Davis

A cowboy, rancher, hunting guide, ranger and miner came to Alaska from Wyoming in 1927. He was CHARLES A. DAVIS, SR., who was born in Clarinda, Iowa, and in 1881 his family moved to Sheridan, Wyoming, where they operated a cattle ranch. He became a United States deputy marshal and a forest ranger before he became a hunting guide. He first entered Alaska when he was a marshall and had followed a fugitive to Alaska and ended the search in Anchorage. He was so impressed with Alaska that it always stayed in the back of his mind.

He and GERTRUDE BELLE HUNT were married in 1905 in Sheridan. She was born in Buffalo, Wyoming in 1887 and was no novice to the rigors of ranch life and rural living. After his mission to Alaska, Charles returned to Wyoming and had a very successful life and career as a dude rancher in partnership with his family. They had a herd of cattle and many horses and a guiding service that took clients into the Big Horn Mountains and into the Rockies.

Davis Home in Hope

In 1927 the desire to return to Alaska overcame all doubts, and the family packed up the five children and seventy-five horses and moved to Anchorage. When they arrived in Anchorage they put on the first rodeo ever held in the town. They organized the Alaska Guide Association, and the business prospered for the first years. When the depression hit, the clientele, mostly from the south 48, shrunk to the point where the family could not afford to feed the horses. It therefore became necessary to sell the horses and quit the guide service.

Davis Family

The family chose to remain in Alaska, and Charles took up trapping and worked for the Alaska Railroad as well. He moved the family to Indian while searching for a homestead location and finally settled on Hope, across Turnagain Arm. Charles, with the aid of two of the boys, built a beautiful log home, and Charles proceeded with mining on Resurrection and Palmer Creeks. The children all grew up in Hope and mostly went to high school in Anchorage. The family lived a subsistence life in Hope, raising their own vegetables and hunting wild game. Small boats owned by the

Charles Davis, Jr. with Wife Fay

Mathison brothers, Billy Austin and John Ames, provided mail service and transportation in the summer months.

Charles and Gertrude had five children, one daughter and four sons. Son Lawrence and spouse, Margaret Mahlum, had two daughters. Susan lives on the San Juan Islands, Washington, and Larilee lives in Kelso, Washington. Daughter Dorothea Davis Cotter and spouse, John Cotter, had two children. J. Lawrence lives in Dallas, Texas, and G. Joan lives in Hillsboro, Oregon. Son Arthur never married. Son Robert and spouse, Faye Havenhill, had two children. Sharon lives in Vancouver, Washington, and Jeannette lives in Florida. Son Charles and spouse, Faye Dahl, had three children. Charles III lives in Midland, Texas; Nancy lives in Seattle, Washington; and son Gerald lives in Wrangell, Alaska.

Gertrude and Charles moved to Seattle, Washington in 1952. Charles died in 1964, and Gertrude passed away in 1970. Son Robert died in 1970, and son Larry died in 1973.

Gertrude penned a poem to CARL "BEN" EIELSON, one of Alaska's hero pilots, which was printed in the *Anchorage Times*, March 14, 1930.

TO "BEN" EIELSON

Long will Alaska mourn the one who, undaunted,
Flew across the Arctic wastes, shunning pomp and splendor,
To be lovingly known as "Ben" who knew not fear nor selfish gain;
Whose deeds of bravery in history shall remain.

Those who hold him dear shall look upon his cold, still face
And know he gave his life not in vain,
But striving to reach the icebound ship
To rescue those whom the cruel Arctic blasts had forced to remain.

No braver deed can a man perform
Than going to the rescue of others in the face of an Arctic storm.
His spirit shall linger with us,
And when we see the northern lights more bright
We shall know it's "Ben" who's calling, bidding farewell to this Arctic land,
Where he took his last brave flight.

Forever will the name of "Ben"
Remind us of the one who laughed at death to fly across the "poles;"
Who today could fly where throngs would wait to welcome him,
Yet came back to this Arctic place to leave us with his "soul."

Mrs. Gertrude Davis

Henry Pope

Henry Wolfe

Sheet Metal Shop

Another old-timer who stampeded into the Klondike in 1898, HENRY POPE left Vancouver, British Columbia in the spring of 1898 headed for Dawson. He arrived in Dawson that same year and spent seven fruitless years chasing the gold dust. In 1906 he mushed downriver to Fairbanks, again looking to strike it rich. He finally gave it up in Fairbanks and left to go back to Vancouver, British Columbia. Seven years later in 1915, like so many others, he returned to Alaska, except this time he came to Anchorage.

In 1915 Henry and partner Henry Wolfe opened up the Pioneer Sheet Metal Works on the corner of 5th Avenue and C Street. In 1930 he bought out Henry Wolfe and became the sole owner of the shop. Henry served one term on the City Council in 1935, and the following year he sold the shop to Ray G. Wolfe. Henry moved south to Sacramento, California in 1942 and passed away there the same year.

RAY G. WOLFE was born in West Liberty, Iowa, September 23, 1905. He came to Anchorage in 1927 to work for his uncle Henry Wolfe, who was part owner of the Pioneer Sheet Metal Works. When Henry Pope bought out Henry Wolfe in 1930, Ray continued to work for Pope and eventually bought him out in 1936.

Ray met ESTHER HEV-ERLING in Anchorage in March 1932, and they were married in March 1937. Esther was born in Vernonia, Oregon in 1903 and became a registered nurse, practicing in the Swedish Hospital in Seattle, Washington prior to coming to Anchorage in

Ray and Esther Wolfe

Wolfe's Department Store

1931. She had worked for both Dr. J. H. Romig and Dr. A. S. Walkowski from 1931 to 1933 in the Railroad Hospital.

Ray purchased the Sheet Metal shop in 1936 and in a few short years the shop was torn down, and a two-story combination apartment and store building replaced it. Ray's twin brother, Robert Wolfe, joined in the ownership along with other partners. The business developed into Wolfe's Hardware, then to Wolfe's Furniture, then to Wolfe's Department Store, and in later years to Wolfe's Furnishings. In 1970 Jerry Wolfe, Ray's nephew, purchased the store and still operates it today under the name of Wolfe's Maytag Home Appliance Center. They now specialize in appliances only.

Home on 10th Avenue

Ray retired in 1970 and got involved in the mining game. He was president of Alaska Mines and Mineral Company, which evolved from the DeCoursey Mountain Mining Company, which operated a mine in Red Devil, Alaska in the mining of cinnabar, the raw form of mercury. Ray became interested in civic affairs and for two years served on the City Council in 1942 and 1943. He served one term as Anchorage Mayor in 1944. He served on the Anchorage Planning Commission, the Off-Street Parking Commission, and was on the national board of advisors for the SBA.

The union of Ray and Esther produced two daughters. Patricia Ann Wolfe married Craig Kaufman and they had three children. Debra Ann Kaufman Wilson lives in Eagle River; Rebecca Lynn Kauffman Duda lives in Issaquah, Washington; Michelle Renee Kauffman Holler lives in Wasilla, Alaska. Roberta Ray Wolfe Mabey had two children. Kristine Elaine lives in Eagle River, and Raymond Gregory lives in Newburg, Oregon. Ray died of a heart attack on October 5, 1977. Esther still lives in her home and is presently going on ninety-eight years of age. Another hardy Alaska woman!

Patricia and Craig Kaufman

Roberta Mabey

TOM MCCROSKEY was the Anchorage Mayor in 1933, serving for one term. He arrived in Anchorage from Fairbanks in 1927 when he was transferred to the Anchorage district of the Alaska Road Commission. He first came to Fairbanks in 1904 during the gold rush. He

Tom McCroskey

was born in Santa Barbara, California in 1874 of a pioneer family that had settled in the Santa Maria Valley. His first wife, Minnie, passed away in Anchorage in 1927 shortly after arriving here. She was a pioneer in her own right, as she braved the elements and the times in Dawson and the Klondike, and it was in Fairbanks that she met and married Tom in 1917.

Tom married again in 1938 and retired to Santa Barbara, California. He passed away in 1948 and is buried in Santa Barbara. His first wife, Minnie, is buried in the Anchorage Memorial Park Cemetery.

CHAPTER XI

1928

The big news locally was the appointment of Colonel Otto F. Ohlson as the new general manager of the Alaska Railroad.

The new Mayor was GRANT REED, and the new council members were:

CHARLES CARLSON
FRANK MORRISON

The other news was that KFQD, Anchorage's one and only radio station, was on the brink of disaster. It was dying financially as it had to live on advertising, and there simply was not enough income to support the station. The godfather of KFQD was Bert Wennerstrom, who, with some friends, bought time on Friday nights putting on a program organized by the Ice Worms' Club. He put on a live radio show, with local talent, such as Evelyn Landstrom, Eileen Bagoy and Mae Wennerstrom as vocalists.

Mayor Grant Reed

His monolog of Dr. Knudsen in the humorous accent and the theme song of "When the Ice Worms Nest Again" brought in donations for the support of the station. Frank O. Berry read the news every night, and he and all the other volunteers saved the station. In 1935 under J. P. Hannon, the station finally was able to stand on its own with the advent of the Matanuska Valley farmers entry into the Valley. The local businessman now had an audience and potential customers to advertise to.

4th Avenue Between D and E Streets, Snow Removal

The High School graduating class consisted of seventeen students:

Doris Bagoy

Ed Barber

Sue Bell Clayton

James Climie

Ann Diamond

Thomas Ek   Donald Gordon   Janice Koslosky   Enid Marsh   Margaret Porter

Paul Reed   Lyda Shaw   Roland Snodgrass   Olga Strandberg   Albert Suomela

Reino Vanaja   Helen Welch

Another '98 stampeder to Dawson, ANDREW EDGAR was a son of the old sod, born in Straband, Ireland in 1876. He immigrated to the United States via Ontario, Canada in 1897 and joined the rush to Dawson the following year. Like so many others, he had a long hard chase looking for the elusive gold and never found it in any quantity.

He gave up on Dawson and the Yukon in 1907 and started prospecting in the Marshall district on the lower Yukon. He and his spouse ANNA EDGAR endured the hardships of remote Alaska mining camps until 1928 when they moved to Anchorage and Andrew found work with the Alaska Railroad.

Anna passed away in 1934, and Andrew died in 1942. They are both buried in the Pioneer Tract of Anchorage Memorial Park. Anna and Edgar had an adopted daughter, Ramoka Kamkoff Miller, whose present whereabouts is unknown.

An Anchorage oldtimer who was truly the father of organized ski-jumping in Anchorage, EDVART KJOSEN arrived in Anchorage in 1928 from points unknown and was engaged as a commercial fisherman in the summer months. Like so many bachelors of the day, he fished in the summer months and spent the winters in his cabin waiting for the coming spring to start fishing again. Ed was born in

Norway and was naturalized in Anchorage in 1936. He was a former ski-jumper in Norway and an expert in cross country skiing.

He was not satisfied to sit in his winter cabin and smoke his pipe, but carried on with his love of skiing. He could be seen skiing downtown from his cabin on East 2nd Avenue on almost a daily basis. With a pack-sack on his back, he would do his meager shopping for groceries and ski back home. The local kids were attracted to him, and soon he was teaching them the art of jumping and cross-country skiing.

Edvart Kjosen

The first ski jump in Anchorage was built by Ed on the south side of Chester Creek about in line with I Street and at the brow of the hill on approximately 17th Avenue, aptly named Kjosen Hill. In 1936 the locals took more interest, and, in anticipation of the 1937 Fur Rendezvous, the group decided to build another jump on the opposite side of Chester Creek

A group of local enthusiasts met in 1937 to form the Anchorage Ski Club. Some of the members were, of course, Edvart Kjosen, and also Al Corey, George Rengard, Ralph Soberg, Fred Soberg, John Hylen and Axel Hanson. This was the beginning of organized skiing in Anchorage. None of these gentlemen is alive today, but they were the nucleus that started it all, led by Ed Kjosen. George Rengard was also an activist in skiing. He was the driving force behind getting the new jump built on the hill adjacent to where the Native Hospital was. Downhill and slalom courses were laid out in the same location. The next skiing location to be developed was Arctic Valley.

George Rengard

Ed Kjosen passed away in 1944 after a long illness and is buried in Anchorage Memorial Park in an unmarked grave.

A man who became one of Alaska's best-known gold miners, WALTER WILLIAM STOLL was born in St. Paul, Minnesota in 1887 and moved to Seattle, Washington in 1900, where he later graduated from the University of Washington School of Engineering in 1911. He first entered Alaska in 1922 and later came to Anchorage in 1928. He was president of the Alaska Pacific Consolidated Gold Mining Company, a firm in which many Alaskans held stock. Its prime property was the Independence Mine, the second highest producer of gold in Alaska, in the Willow Creek district.

When WWII started, the gold operations all had to shut down, and Stoll, with a group of local investors, took over the Buffalo Coal Mine and produced coal for the military in Alaska as well as for civilian use. Stoll was elected president of the Buffalo Coal Mining Company; Frank Colabuffalo was vice-president, Emil Pfeil was named treasurer, John Manders was named secretary-treasurer, and other directors were Ed McElligott, Joe Brunie and Tom Bevers.

When WWII ended Stoll went back to the Independence and started the process of reopening the mine. The Independence Mine was known as one of the most efficient mines in Alaska under Stoll's management. The camp and facilities were unsurpassed as being one of the finest camps in Alaska.

Before he entered the mining business, Stoll operated the Farwest Packing Company, a fish cannery located on what is now the city of Anchorage port. When the dock was built it was called the Ocean Dock, and the first company to open cannery operations was the Gorman family out of Seattle. Stoll was hired as manager, and the company used both names of Far West and Gorman. Walter Stoll died in Seattle at the age of sixty-one.

Two brothers who stampeded to the Klondike gold fields together in 1898, JACK and SAM TANSY were both born in Worthington, Indiana, Jack in 1867 and Sam in 1870. After leaving the Dawson country Sam moved to Fairbanks, where he lived for a number of years. When the railroad construction started he moved down to the Nenana division and remained there until about 1923. In 1924 he moved down to Girdwood and operated a roadhouse until he moved back to Anchorage in 1928.

Jack had been employed with the National Park Service in Yellowstone National Park prior to his coming to Alaska. At one time he had been a guide for President Teddy Roosevelt when he toured the Park. When Jack left the Dawson country he moved to Circle and then to Eagle and then to Valdez. In 1912 he moved to Seldovia and lived there and in Anchorage until he died. He was employed by the Bureau of Fisheries as a stream warden and also as a camp cook. He worked on and off for the Bureau and owned his own boat, which he used in his line of work. Jack died in 1939, and Sam died in 1941. They are both buried in the Elks Tract, Anchorage Memorial Park, in unmarked graves.

One of Anchorage's and Alaska's greatest and most colorful early-day bush pilots, FRANK G. DORBANDT was born in Detroit, Michigan in 1893. Little is known of his early life and where or when he learned to fly. He appeared on the Anchorage scene in 1929, when he was hired by Anchorage Air Transport as a second pilot. He joined Alaska Airways later and also flew for PIA.

Frank was credited with more mercy flights in all kinds of weather than any other pilot of his day. He had an aggressive, argumentative and cantankerous personality, but he knew how to fly. In 1930 he made a mercy flight to the north coast of Siberia to bring the captain of an icebound Russian trading vessel, the *Karise*, to Nome for hospitalization. The next year he made another rescue mission to Siberia to rescue the Jochinson party.

He was instrumental in making Anchorage the center of commercial aviation, both passenger and freight. In 1934 Frank brought in the largest aircraft ever seen in Anchorage. It was the

Tri-motor Ford owned by the newly formed Ptarmigan Airways. Frank flew the "tin goose" up from Los Angeles, with Don Glass as co-pilot and Jack Carr as mechanic. Frank died in Fairbanks in 1935 and is buried in Anchorage Memorial Park.

Frank G. Dorbandt

A logger from Arlington, Washington and a schoolteacher from Seattle, Washington arrived in Skagway four months apart in 1924, although they didn't meet each other there. The logger, FOSTER HEAVEN, was born in Florence, Washington in 1890, and the teacher, DAISY SPIESIKE, was born in Seattle, Washington in 1897.

After a short period of time, Foster moved to Juneau where he worked in the Treadwell Mine. In 1926 he moved to Houston on the Alaska Railroad, where his brother was mink farming. In 1928 they sold the mink farm, and both brothers moved to Anchorage and worked for the ARR. Foster was a crane operator and machinist for some years, then worked in the round house. Foster bought a two-room log cabin at 716 K Street and made it his Anchorage home.

Foster Heaven   Daisy Heaven

Daisy, LeRoi and Wythle Heaven

Daisy Spiesike stayed in Skagway and worked at the Pullen House as a desk clerk. She taught school in Skagway, Seldovia and Kodiak for the next six years. While visiting her friend Polly Willard, in Anchorage in 1930, she met Foster Heaven who was a dinner guest at the Willards, and a long friendship ensued. Daisy and Foster were married in Anchorage in June 1931. The Heavens made their home at 716 K Street. Foster continued to work at the Railroad, and Daisy was a substitute teacher.

The Heaven Home

In 1952 Foster retired from the Railroad, and the family moved to the Matanuska Valley. Foster was caretaker of

LeRoi and Margaret Heaven

Wythle and Allen Gershmel

King's Lake Camp for two years prior to moving to a forty-acre farm on Fairview Loop Road. They lived on the farm until their deaths in July and August of 1970.

Foster and Daisy had two children. Son Foster LeRoi married Margaret Ann Johnson, and they had a son, Troy Bradley, who lives in Denver, Colorado. Daughter Wythle Jourine Heaven married Allan Gershmel, and they had five children. Brian Earl, Charlene Gershmel Kunnuk, Marietta Jourine Gershmel Bragg and Patty Jo Gershmel all live in Wasilla, and Bruce Charles lives in Colorado Springs, Colorado.

A Spenard Road homesteader who arrived in Anchorage in 1928, HOWARD A. McRAE was born in Sedro-Wooley, Washington in 1898, and his parents took him to Skagway on their way to the Klondike when he was three months old. They arrived in time to live through the experience of being in Skagway when the infamous Soapy Smith was shot. They did not go to Dawson, but went to Atlin, British Columbia instead. The gold eluded them, so they returned to Skagway and then to Haines, where the senior McRae filed for a homestead.

JANET MILLER was born in New York City in 1895. She grew up in New York and was trained as a nurse. When WWI broke out she went to France and served there with the Army until the end of the war. After a period of illness she wanted to change her vocation. Through her church she found that there was a Presbyterian Mission School in Haines, Alaska, and off she went, headed for a new adventure.

Janet, Mother and Howard

In Haines she met Howard McRae, and they were married in Skagway in about 1927. In 1928 they moved to Anchorage in search of steady employment. Howard worked for a short time for a transfer company and then took a correspondence course in electricity and worked for the Alaska Railroad until he took a medical retirement in 1945.

They lived in a small home on 4th Avenue and L Street for a short time and then filed on a homestead just west of the railroad crossing on Spenard Road. They built a road back to the homesite where they built a home. Howard's brother had arrived in the meantime, and he helped build the road to the home. The road exists today and is, naturally, listed on the city maps as the McRae Road.

Howard and Janet had five children. Jean McRae Clayton lives in Juneau; Howard, Jr., Evelyn, Charles and Bethea are deceased.

In 1946 the family moved back to Haines where Howard built a home on his father's old homestead, eight miles south of Haines. Howard took up oil painting as a hobby and was good at it. He also kept busy part time working in a cannery operating the steam retorts. Janet died in Haines in 1958, and Howard died in 1979. They are both buried in the McRae family plot in Haines.

———

A well-known Russian Orthodox priest came to the United States in 1898, first landing in New York City where he was supposedly assigned. He suddenly found that this was not the case and found himself in Kodiak, Alaska instead. His name was ALEXANDER PAUL SHADURA. He was born in Russia in 1875 and at the age of twenty-three was sent to America as a seminarian.

In 1901 Paul Alexandrov Shadura and KATHERINE L. HUBLEY were married. Kate, as she was called, was born in Unga, Alaska in 1882. Her father, Isaac Hubley, came to Alaska from Halifax, Nova Scotia, Canada, where he was born in 1838. He was a veteran of the Civil War and remained in the military after the war. He was assigned to the west coast of the United States and was at Kodiak when Alaska was purchased from Russia.

Katherine and Rev. Alexander Shadura

Fr. Shadura and Kate moved to Kenai in 1907 where he headquartered and lived for over forty-five years, serving his flock full time and being a commercial fisherman part time.

His post in Kenai required him to travel at least once a year to the various villages in the district, first to Tyonek, then to Susitna Station, McDougal and Knik. All of his travel was by small boat, some with motors and some without. He made his first trip to Anchorage in 1922 and held services at the Episcopal Church. At the same time he made arrangements for housing his children who were becoming of high school age. Tania lived with the Ward family. Two years later daughter Madge moved to Anchorage. Pete followed in 1826, then Alex came in 1928, and Isaac followed in 1932.

The couple had six children. Son Paul, the eldest, was born in 1902 and married Fiokla Backoff in 1933. Fiokla and child died during childbirth. Daughter Tatiana "Tania" married Jonus A. Ellison in 1932, and they had one daughter, Laura Joy Ellison. Daughter Parascovia "Madge" married Marion Nichols in 1933, and they had one daughter, Phyllis Garrison. Son Peter married Ruby Peyton in 1939. They were divorced in 1946. Pete then married Margaret Stelzner in 1949, and they had no children. Son Alexander Paul married Leda Tardonov, and they had four children: Natasha Shadura Potebrnya, Tamura Shadura O'Neal, Leda Shadura Barnes and Paul Alexander. Son Isaac Paul married Donna Borego, and

Son, Paul and Alex Shadura

The Shadura Family

they had one daughter, Artha Lois "Bonnie" Shadura Piccolo. Paul died in 1956, and Kate died in 1957. They are both buried in the Russian Orthodox Section of Washelli Cemetery in Seattle, Washington.

CHARLES E. SMITH was another Klondike stampeder who found his way to Anchorage in 1928. He and MABEL REEDER CHANDLER were married in 1928 and, with Mabel's son, William Chandler, moved to Anchorage in that same year. Mabel was born in Lake City, Minnesota in 1882 and was married to William Blaine Chandler, who was born in San Francisco in 1879 and died in 1915. Mabel and her two-year-old son William continued to live in Butte, Montana until 1928 when she married Charles Smith.

The Chandler Family

Charles was a miner-prospector and, after his Klondike days, was occupied as a fisherman and a big game guide. He ran dog teams from Fairbanks to Nome carrying the United States mail and did freighting by boat on the Yukon River.

The family arrived in Anchorage in 1928 and settled in a small home located at 3rd Avenue and I Street. The day after their arrival, fifteen-year-old William went to work in the local fish cannery and the following summer worked for the Alaska Railroad as a section hand. Bill graduated from Anchorage High School in 1930 and worked for the Alaska Road Commission,

Mabel Reeder Chandler Smith

William Chandler

Clair and Bill Chandler

alternately going to college at the University of Washington. He graduated from the University of Washington in 1938 with a degree in civil engineering. Immediately after graduation he worked for Standard Oil Company of California in San Francisco and then was assigned to Saudi Arabia. He had a long career with Standard Oil Company in pipeline construction and was assigned in various places from Alaska to Arabia. He became the president and CEO of Tapline in 1963 and held this post until his retirement in 1972.

In 1940 he and his spouse Clair were married in Honolulu and this union produced three children: Barbara Chandler Harris, Gail Chandler Hawkins and William Blaine II.

———

The man who was appointed general manager of the Alaska Railroad in 1928 by President Calvin Coolidge, COLONEL OTTO F. OHLSON was born in Halmstadt, Sweden in 1870, and, after completing his basic education, he attended the Electric Technique in Stockholm, graduating at the age of twenty.

He said that he was a victim of "wanderlust" and wanted to travel and see the world. In 1890 he left Sweden and first went to South Africa, then to India and then to America, traveling as an able-bodied seaman from India to the United States.

After his arrival in the United States, he went to work for the Northern Pacific Railway in 1901 and stayed with them for twenty-seven years. He was chosen for the job as general manager of the Alaska Railroad when he accompanied President Coolidge on a fishing trip when he was division superintendent of the Northern Pacific. President Coolidge was so impressed with him that he asked him if he would be interested in the job in Alaska, and Ohlson accepted.

The job as general manager of the ARR was, during the early years, the most prestigious, the most powerful, and the highest paid position in Alaska. The man who ran the Alaska Railroad was next to God in Anchorage. Ohlson had a long career as a tough-minded, hard-nosed individual who was intent on having the Railroad make a profit, even though it was not built for that purpose. After the completion of the road, Ohlson decided it was time for the Railroad to operate in the black. He accomplished this by increasing freight rates, and this brought the wrath of every merchant from Seward to Fairbanks down on him.

Ohlson said the "subsidy" was over; the Railroad must stand on its own. He drove home his ideas of operating for profit by not allowing competition, such as Heinie Berger and his gas boats bringing in merchandise at far lower freight rates. Ohlson blocked Berger from crossing the railroad tracks so he could deliver his cargo

Otto Ohlson

The Colonel's House

The Railroad Staff

uptown. When the Anchorage Times shipped a load of paper with Berger, Ohlson discontinued all advertising. He opened and closed the Railroad commissary to federal employees depending on how he felt toward the local merchants who were prone to ship with Heinie Berger. Lucky Baldwin, a local grocer, constantly kept Ohlson off-balance by advertising groceries at cheaper prices because he didn't pay the high freight rates of the Alaska Raiload.

It was a well-known fact that the Railroad never paid a freight claim until after Ohlson left the service. The Railroad contracted with the Evan Jones Coal Company for its annual purchase of coal. If the price was not right, the Colonel would threaten to open his own coal mine, and he did so on more than one occasion.

All in all, Colonel Ohlson was a controversial character; however, he did have his good sides. He gave summer employment to many high school kids to work on the extra gangs and on the sections. During the 1946 longshoremen strike, the Colonel opened the commissary to the public to relieve the shortage of food. He instructed his engineers and trainmen to stop and pick up anyone on the track with a flag hitching a ride.

Ohlson had a tough job. He had to satisfy his customers and the Congress of the United States who were poles apart in their thinking. He did a great job and kept the Railroad running, eventually at a profit. He will long be remembered by many oldtimers as a fair man to work for and by others as a tyrant running his own fiefdom.

Ohlson married MARIE E. RICKETTS in Chicago in 1897. She and the Colonel lived in the manager's home on 2nd Avenue and Christensen Road. She was a generous hostess and entertained many of the local women in her home. She never let the Railroad enter any conversations and maintained a friendly relationship with the local ladies, who thought very highly of her.

Marie Ohlson passed away in 1939, and Ohlson resigned from the ARR in 1945. He traveled extensively throughout the world and settled in Seattle, Washington for a few years. He then moved to the east coast where, in 1956, he entered a Veterans Hospital in Hampton, Virginia, and died there in 1956. Marie was buried in Chicago, and, as far as can be determined, Ohlson is buried in a veterans cemetery in Virginia. (All information supplied here was taken from the *Anchorage Times*, Alaska Railroad, the *Fairbanks Daily News Miner* and the *Seward Gateway.* All photos are courtesy of the Anchorage Museum of History and Art.)

CHAPTER XII

1929

The big news this year was the stock market crash.

On the local scene, the news was the dedication by the Anchorage Womans Club of the plaque and beacon tower at Merrill Field in memory of Russel Merrill.

Anchorage had a new mayor in JAMES J. DELANEY.

New Council members elected were:

OSCAR GILL
NICK GAIKEMA
H. H. MCCUTCHEON
CARL MARTIN

The High School graduating class held fifteen students, six girls and nine boys:

Mayor James Delaney

Ralph Holdiman

Del Hosler

Ivy Lothrop

Dorothy Miller

Jack Morton

Frances Nichols

Walter Niemi

Hubert Oliver

Renee Seller

Madge Shadura

William Snodgrass

Jean Staser

William Strandberg

George Valear

Jess Ward

An emigrant from Czechoslovakia landed in New York City in 1913. He had just completed his hitch in the Austro-Hungarian Army and had been practicing as a pharmacist in his homeland. Like so many other men of European descent, he left to come to America, as he was not sure from one day to the next if he would be conscripted into the Army again. Such was ALEX LISKA, an educated man who could speak seven languages fluently. He was employed by a large eastern bank in New York City as an interpreter and later moved on to Chicago where he practiced the same profession.

He got the gold fever after hearing of all of the incredible amounts of gold arriving from the Yukon. He never got to Dawson, but prospected along the Yukon, the 40-Mile, Circle, Fairbanks and other points. He was known throughout his travels as a wrestler and an exceptional athlete. Soon after his arrival in Anchorage he became interested in osteopathy and took a correspondence course reading and learning and still going out on prospecting trips, taking his books with him. He later completed his education at a Chicago chiropractic school and set up his practice in Anchorage.

He was well known in Anchorage in his trade. The local oldtimers remember Alex as a brute of a man. He was barrel-chested, with shoulders and arms like a typical wrestler. He stood about five foot seven and weighed about two hundred pounds. His patients soon found out about his strength of manipulation. Many of the local residents who were young children at the time would stand on the sidewalk and listen to the moans and groans and screams emanating from his upstairs office at the corner of 4th Avenue and G Street.

Alex left Anchorage in 1953 and moved to California for reasons of health. He passed away the next year in 1954.

Another professional man who made his way to Anchorage in 1929, DR. KENDRICK PIERCE was a dentist who had practiced in Fairbanks and other mining regions of the north prior to his coming to Anchorage. He set up his office in the Masonic Building at the corner of 4th Avenue and F Street. He practiced there until 1947 when he moved to Salem, Oregon with his wife, Pedita. Dr. Pierce passed away in Salem in 1949.

Many remembered ED NIGHTENGALE as an accordion player who played with the local orchestras at the various Saturday night dances. He was born in Philadelphia, Pennsylvania in 1897 and came north to Cordova in 1924 to work for the Copper River and Northern Railway as a machinist and boiler fireman. He worked for the A. J. Mine in Juneau and for the North American Dredging Company in Flat before coming to Anchorage in 1929 to work for the Alaska Railroad.

Ed married BEULAH DRYDEN in 1932 in Seward. They had two children, Donald A. of Pacific Grove, California and Helen Nightengale Jarrie of Woonsocket, Rhode Island. Ed passed away in 1972, and Beulah passed away in 1979. They are both buried in the Pioneer Tract, Anchorage Memorial Park.

ISABELLE PRESTON arrived in Anchorage in 1929. She was born in Swansea, South Wales in 1865. Before coming to Alaska she lived in Houston, Texas and St. Louis, Missouri. She arrived in Seward in 1925 and then moved to Anchorage in 1929. She was active in the Womans Club and was a permanent fixture in the third district court, never missing a session and always seated in the same seat. She made her own costumes for the annual Fur Rendezvous and was recognized by most residents as always carrying a cane while strolling on 4th Avenue.

Her husband, JOHN O. PRESTON, was a retired gold miner, and they resided at 121 6th Avenue. Isabelle died in 1952, and John died in 1956. They are both buried in the Pioneer Tract, Anchorage Memorial Park.

A well-known Anchorage jeweler, JAMES VICTOR "VIC" BROWN was born in Port Arthur, Canada in 1893. He and his spouse, JEAN SIMPSON, who was born in London, England in 1890, took their two children and immigrated to the United States. They entered through Sweet Grass, Montana in 1916 and traveled to Juneau, where Vic was engaged as a jeweler and watchmaker.

In 1917 a Fairbanks jeweler, Harry Avakoff, had heard of Vic's talents and offered him a job in his firm in Fairbanks for the attractive amount of one hundred twenty-five dollars per month. Vic had been earning one hundred dollars per month, and this raise was attractive enough for him to pack up the family and move to Fairbanks. They took a boat to Skagway where they caught the White Pass and Yukon Railway to Whitehorse and then down the river to Nenana and up the Tanana and the Chena to Fairbanks.

Vic went into business with Harry, and they formed the partnership of Avakoff and Brown Jewelers. They operated the

Jean and Vic Brown

Raymond "Deac" Brown

J. Vic, Jr. and Marie Brown

business for a number of years until 1929 when they decided to part company. Vic decided they should move to the relatively new and bustling city of Anchorage, and in the fall of 1929 they made their move. The family had now grown to four children, and they found a home at 8th Avenue and E Street. Vic opened his shop at the corner of 4th Avenue and E Street under the name of J. Vic Brown and Sons, Jewelers.

Ernie and Bertha Brown Holm

As business progressed and Anchorage grew, the business became successful, and the family bought their first home in 1935 at 727 L Street. They added a second story on the home to accommodate the family, and they lived there until Vic retired in 1941.

Vic had been a semi-pro hockey player in Canada and took an interest in the youth of Anchorage in coaching a hockey team. They would have to go all the way out to Lake Spenard to practice, as there was no local rink. He was also an avid golfer, and in 1937 the Anchorage Golf Club had its first tournament. This, of course, was on what is now the Delaney Park Strip. Gold mine operator W. E. Dunkle was the first tournament winner, and the rest of the players were Dr. Howard G. Romig, Vic Brown, George Vaara, Bob Albritton and Warren Cuddy. There were about five holes, so to get eighteen you had to go around more than three times.

Vic's and Jean's son Albert Edward "Ted" was born in Medicine Hat, Alberta, Canada. He and his spouse, Frances Sheldon, had three children: Maxine, who resides in Hawaii, and Shirley Jean and Albert Edward, who reside in Oregon. Son Raymer Simpson "Deac" was also born in Medicine Hat, Alberta, Canada. He and his wife, Charlotte Manning, had four children. Michael resides in Anchorage, and Ida Lou, Patrick and Raymer, Jr. are all deceased. Daughter Bertha Elizabeth "Bert" was born in Fairbanks, married Ernest Holm, and had two children. Jeanne Holm Patrick resides in Seattle, and Christopher lives in Anchorage. J. Vic "Bud," Jr. was born in Fairbanks and married Marie Laurie. They had three children. J. Vic "J.V." III lives in Idaho, and Deborah Brown Sedwick and Dawn Brown Wilcox live in Anchorage.

ALBERT H. "HANK" DYER first came to Alaska in 1923, landing at Scow Bay (Doyhof) as a crew member on a fishing boat. He was born in Duwata, Washington in 1896, and the lure of Alaska brought him north. Hank had already been married prior to his sailing north, and in 1928 he sent for his wife and son to join him in Scow Bay. MARY MOLSEE was born in Goldendale, Washington in 1895, and, after joining her husband, she worked as a cook for the United States Forest Service in Petersburg,

After spending two years in Scow Bay, Hank and the family moved to Seward. He took a job with the ARR, working on the section at Hunter and Indian. He later worked at the Jonesville Mine, and Mary and son were with him all the way. She cooked for the section crews on the Railroad until 1929 when they moved to Anchorage so their son could attend school.

After they arrived in Anchorage, Hank worked for the City as a truck driver and also as a part time city jailer. They lived in a home on the west end of 4th Avenue near where the Oscar Anderson house now sits. Hank filed on a one hundred sixty acre homestead during the years that he and Mary both worked in Anchorage. She worked every summer for the Emard Packing Company until 1935 when they moved to the homestead.

After the start of WWII Hank worked for contractors on the Aleutian chain until the war ended. After the war and until his death in 1973, he worked his placer mine on Friday Creek in the Kantishna. Mary died in 1983 in the Pioneers Home in Anchorage. They are both buried in the Pioneer Tract, Anchorage Memorial Park.

Hank and Mary had one son, Robert, who married Violet Dodge in 1941, and they had two girls. Bonnie Dyer Frey lives in Washington, and Patricia Dyer Smith lives in Fairbanks, Alaska.

Another railroader who arrived in Anchorage in 1929, ARTHUR M. REEKIE was born in Kirkcaldy, Scotland in 1897. He and his wife, JEAN REEKIE, arrived in Anchorage in 1929 with their two children. Jean was born in Boness, Scotland in 1902. Art was employed with the Alaska Railroad until his retirement. He was a section stock-

Vi and Bob Dyer   Hank and Mary Dyer

Dyer Family

Art Reekie   Jean Reekie

Reekie Family

Jean Elizabeth Reekie

man for many years. Jean was employed as a clerk in several Anchorage retail stores over the years, besides being active in various fraternal organizations.

Jean and Art had three children. William, the eldest, passed away in 1967. Second son, Arthur, Jr. and his spouse had four children. Michael lives in Anchorage; Judy is deceased; Janice Czako lives in Detroit, Michigan; and Joan Amruz lives in Anchorage. Daughter Jean Elizabeth Lee had one daughter, Jackie Cappers, who lives in Anchorage. Jean, Arthur and son William are all buried in the Elks Tract of Anchorage Memorial Park.

A pioneer of the northland who came to the Yukon before the gold rush to the Klondike, JOHN EMMETT "JACK" KINNALEY was born in Ireland in 1865. Little is known of his early life prior to coming to Alaska. He was prospecting around Dawson in 1895 and for many years after the big strikes. Jack never married. He traveled from one mining camp to another, eking out a living, sometimes finding some pay dirt, however, finding just dirt most of the time.

He was known to have gone to Wiseman during that rush and later spent one winter by himself with his dog up the Chandalar River and into the Brooks Range. In 1918 Jack decided he had enough of chasing gold and heard about the new town of Anchorage and the construction of the Railroad. He moved to Anchorage that same year and worked, in the summers only, for the Railroad as a part-time cook on Paddy Cohen's bridge crew for several years.

In 1929 Jack hooked up with another oldtimer, JULIUS FRITZEN, and the two of them rented a cabin owned by John Bagoy and spent the rest of their days in retirement, Jack smoking his pipe and telling stories about his travels in Alaska, and Julius smoking his cigar and telling stories about WWI when he was in the German Army. As a boy, this writer spent many hours on Saturdays listening to these to oldtimers spin their tales. Jack gave me a first edition booklet of Robert Service poems that was printed in Dawson.

Jack died in 1935 and is buried in the Pioneer Tract, Anchorage Memorial Park. Julius went to the Pioneer Home in Sitka in 1939 and is buried in the Pioneer section of the Sitka Cemetery.

The saga of CLIFFORD H. PHILLIPS. This is the story of the life of a stampeder to the Klondike. It is taken partially from the *Anchorage Times*, December 7, 1949.

Phillips was born in Quakerstown, Pennsylvania, June 3, 1872 and spent his childhood on a farm. At the age of sixteen he went to work for a brokerage firm in Philadelphia. He became imbued with the "call of the west" when his employers sent him to Kansas, miles from the civilization of those days, to make land appraisals. From there in 1893 he went to Colorado and Wyoming.

His first interest in mining camps was fostered by a visit to Cripple Creek, Colorado in 1894. He heeded the "call of the north" and left for Juneau, Alaska on January 7, 1897 aboard the *City of Topeka*. In March of the same year he traveled, in company with Ed Currier, Gus Johnson and Bill Kerr, along the Dyea trail, arriving at the head of Lake Bennett. On April 20 Phillips celebrated his twenty-fifth birthday by rowing a scow through Miles Canyon, covering the distance of two miles in one and three quarters minutes. After many harrowing experiences they arrived in Dawson on June 9, 1897. Gold fever was in the air, and young Phillips took part in the strikes at Eldorado, Bonanza, and Fraction No. 5 below Discovery on Hunker Creek.

The excitement and hardship proved to be too much for his health, and he was forced to return to Seattle for the winter. The lure of Alaska was in his blood, however, and in 1900 he again headed north on a three-masted schooner bound for Nome, arriving there on June 5. Hearing of a strike on Tigidik Island south of Kodiak, he continued on to what was called the Island of Gold. He then carried on in the traditional manner of most early pioneers by traveling to Valdez, Homer and into the Cook Inlet country.

The winter of 1901 again saw him in Seattle; however, he could not resist the call to Alaska, and he returned to Valdez in 1902 with the Robert Blei party, with horses to be taken to the Nizina and Copper River areas.

In 1906 he returned to his home in Philadelphia, and there he met and married Fannie, a widow with two small children. In February 1907, accompanied by his wife and family, he returned to Valdez, then Cordova and finally Chitina, where he was employed by the Copper River and Northwestern Railroad as relay agent and oil station manager.

After his adopted children left the nest, he and Fannie spent a year in Seattle and then returned to Anchorage in 1929. In Anchorage he worked for the Railroad for a time and was later appointed court librarian and bailiff by Judge Anthony J. Dimond, a post he held until shortly before his death. He was the Secretary of Igloo #15, Pioneers of Alaska, for fifteen years, and also, at the time of his death, he was Secretary to the Grand Igloo. Fannie held the position of President of the Womens Auxiliary of the Pioneers in both Anchorage and Cordova.

The dedication which he wrote for his unfinished book aptly sums up his life as a Pioneer.

> In acknowledgement and gratitude to my heavenly father for having watched over me and protected me from death, during my many treacherous journeys I made while working and exploring in the virgin and wild sections of the West, Northwest and Alaska.

For permitting me to see beauty and indescribable grandeur of his work in the mountains, valleys, rivers, bays and oceans.

For the fortitude, courage and faith he gave me when so many times about to despair.

For having given unto me Christian parents, and a mother who taught me at her knee how to pray.

For having led me to marry a widow with two children—a lovable and devoted wife an helpmate, who has been such a real comfort during the many years of struggle, whose children have loved and honored me as though I were their own father.

Clifford H. Phillips died in Anchorage in 1949 and is buried in the Pioneer Tract of Anchorage Memorial Park Cemetery. Fannie is buried in Acacia Memorial Park in Seattle, Washington.

Mary Bagoy and Otto Lakshas, 1939

A young man from Snoqualmie, Washington arrived in Anchorage in 1929 to take on a summer job at the Jonesville Coal Mine. He was hired by Oscar Anderson to fulfill a commitment to hire athletic scholarship recipients from the University of Washington. OTTO LAKSHAS was one of these athletes. He was born in Snoqualmie, Washington in 1907 and after high school was offered an athletic scholarship at the University of Washington.

He worked the summer of '29 driving a blind mule, pulling coal cars out of the mine and dumping them in the stockpile. In September of the same year he won a Ford automobile at the Anchorage Fair, and this ended his scholarship. He stayed on in Anchorage and never went back to school. He took a job with the Alaska Railroad in the commissary department. In 1930 he met and married Gertrude Nelson, a marriage that ended in divorce two years later.

He stepped up from the commissary at the ARR to crane operator and tie inspector and finally to yard foreman. In 1938 he married MARY BAGOY, a member of the Pioneer Bagoy family, and together they took over the operation of the Bagoy Flower Shop in 1952 when Marie

Mary and Otto Lakshas, 1967

Son, Jeffery Lakshas

Bagoy retired. They survived the earthquake of '64 and rebuilt the shop on the corner of 6th Avenue and A Street. In 1968 Otto's health was failing and the shop was sold in 1969.

Mary and Otto had one son, Jeffrey, who lives in Florida. Otto died in 1970 and is buried in Angelus Memorial Park. Mary resides in Seattle, Washington.

Another early day stampeder entered the country in 1898 on his way to the Klondike. He prospected around Dawson for years, and later he had hit almost every camp in the country including Fairbanks, Circle, 40-Mile, Ruby, Iditarod and Nome. The man was WILLIAM SARGENT, one of the best-known miners and prospectors in the country. No one knows where he came from, as he spoke little of his past. He was one of the real types of early prospectors who helped develop the gold fields but never lucked out in hitting it rich. Bill never married and lived a bachelor's life.

In 1929 he arrived on the Anchorage scene, went to work for the Alaska Road Commission, and stayed with them until his death in 1934. Bill is buried in the Pioneer section of Anchorage Memorial Park.

A young man from Brooklyn, New York joined the Merchant Marine in 1926, and, after three years at sea, he wound up in Anchorage, Alaska in 1929. EDWARD R. McELLIGOTT was born in Brooklyn, New York in 1907 and was reared there until he reached the age of nineteen when he went to sea.

Esther Olund McElligott

Edward McElligott

He came to Alaska, like so many others of the day, looking for work. He found it in the Alaska Railroad, working in the freight depot. He soon left the ARR and joined W. J. Boudreau Company, a wholesale grocer, and received a good background of the grocery business. It was not long before he opened his own grocery store, the Anchorage Grocery, located on the corner of 4th Avenue and H Street.

ESTHER OLUND, a young graduate nurse who was hired by the Department of Interior on a one year contract to work as a registered nurse at the Railroad Hospital, came to Anchorage in 1930. She was born in Manchester, Washington in 1907 and, after her schooling, went into training at Swedish Hospital in Seattle to become a registered nurse.

First Home on 8th Avenue and H Street

McElligott Family

Ed sold out of the grocery business and invested in an insurance firm in Anchorage and then in Automotive Parts and Equipment Company. It was the largest distributor of auto parts in Alaska at one time. He served two terms on the Anchorage City Council and was a member of other civic groups. Esther was one of the founders of the Bishop's Attic, and still serves on the Board of Directors. She was also a member of the Board of Directors that planned, started and built the Anchorage Senior Center.

Ed and Esther reared five children. Eldest son, James Morgan, died at the age of sixteen. Daughter Marymae married James Duncan, and they had five children. Mark lives in Port Orchard, Washington; Robert lives in Peach City, Georgia; Greg lives in Crescent City, California; Jeff lives in Morrisville, North Carolina; and Elizabeth lives on Mercer Island, Washington. Daughter Margaret Ann married Howard Gass, and they had three children: David, Stephan and Margaret Esther. Son Edward Michael married Marianne Hartlieb, and they had three children: E. Michael II, Kirstin Michelle and James Morgan. Daughter Esther Lynn married Walter Hickel, Jr. and lives in Anchorage. They had three children, Walter J. III and twin girls, Morgan Brittany and Kolby Alexandria. Ed died in 1991 and is buried in the Catholic Tract of Anchorage Memorial Park. Esther still resides in Anchorage.

A man who came to Anchorage in 1929 to play the organ and piano in the Empress Theater, KENNETH LAUGHLIN was born in Portland, Oregon in 1900 and was raised in Portland and nearby Yamhill, Oregon. He played professional piano and organ for fifteen years in Oregon, Washington and Alberta, Canada, prior to answering Cap Lathrop's call for a pre-movie organist for his theater. After one year, with the advent of "talking pictures," Ken taught music in the public schools and also gave private lessons in piano and organ. In 1934 he homesteaded on Upper Fire Lake and built a small restaurant, called the "Shack," adjacent to the lake.

From 1935 to 1940 he worked as an announcer and then program manager at radio station KFQD. He was later promoted to station manager at KFQD and then to state manager for the Alaska Broadcasting Company. In 1946 he and ESTHER NELSON were married. Esther was born in Karisham, Sweden in 1903 and went to Juneau with her parents, prior to coming to Anchorage in 1924.

In 1950 Ken left the broadcasting business rather than accepting the job of national sales manager for the firm and being stationed in Seattle. In the same year he accepted the position of advertising manager of the Anchorage Daily Times. Ken was the first president of the Anchorage Chapter of the Advertising Club of Alaska.

Ken and Esther had no children between them, however Esther had a son by a previous marriage. Charles Parker and wife Katherine live in Soldotna, and they had one child, Patricia, who also lives in Soldotna. Ken died in 1979, and Esther died in 1987. They are both buried in the Pioneer Tract of Anchorage Memorial Park Cemetery.

CHAPTER XIII

1930

MAYOR DELANEY served his second term.

The new City Council member was E. R. TARWATER.

The Anchorage population was 2736.

Anchorage High School graduated fifteen students, ten girls and five boys:

Janet Borges

Emmett Cavanaugh

William Chandler

Louise Gill

Jean Horning

Lillie Johanson

Gladys Koslosky

Ed Meier

Evelyn Meyer

Mary Mikami

Ruby Olson

Rose Rivers

Pete Shadura

Ted Strandberg

Vivian Jones not pictured.

The depression years were taking hold in the United States, and hundreds of men looking for work were coming to Alaska and, in particular, to Anchorage. One of these was CHESTER LAMPERT. Chet was born in Cincinnati, Ohio in 1907 and, as a young man, trained as an electrician. He landed a job with Pacific Alaska Fisheries at Squaw Harbor and later with Wood Bay Packing on Admiralty Island in southeast Alaska. He moved north to Latouche in 1928 and worked for the Kennecott Corporation.

He arrived in Anchorage in 1930 and landed a job with Anchorage Light and Power as an electrician in the power plant. He then moved on to the Alaska Road Commission and worked in McKinley Park for two years. In 1933 he homesteaded at what is now Gambell and Fireweed Lane, where Sears Mall and Fred Meyer now stand.

Chet worked for various contractors from 1933 to 1940, and then he was employed on Elmendorf Air Force Base. He subdivided and sold off some of his homestead property in 1946, and after that he worked with the tools off and on. Chet passed away in 1989.

Another young man looking for a future came to Alaska, first landing in Ketchikan in 1925. LESTER JOHN "SPEED" SWIFT was born in Merton, Wisconsin in 1900. The family moved west to Hoquiam, Washington in 1904, and Speed went through school there and graduated from the University of Washington in 1922. He held a degree in pharmacy and worked in a drug store in Ketchikan prior to moving on to Anchorage in 1930, where he was employed by the Anchorage Drug Store until 1939.

In 1938 Speed married Ann Diamond, the daughter of Anchorage Pioneer Joseph Diamond. After their marriage Speed went to work for the Alaska Railroad until he retired. He and Ann had one daughter, Carrol Ann Swift. The family left Anchorage and moved to California after his retirement, and no more is known of them.

CHARLEY HARVARD was another railroader who landed in Anchorage in 1930. It is unknown from whence Charley came, and very little is known of this bachelor engineer who worked for the Alaska Railroad as resident engineer. Harvard Avenue on Government Hill is named after Charley, as he was the man who laid out the streets and drew the first plat that laid out the dimensions of the lots and streets. In 1935 Charley and Anton Anderson went to the Matanuska Valley and laid out the forty-acre tracts that were turned over to the settlers brought in by the Federal Emergency Relief Administration. Charley died in 1979 at the age of eighty-seven.

A pioneer aircraft mechanic or "mechanician" as they were called in those days, CECIL LEROY "CECE" HIGGINS was born in Edora, Iowa in 1903, and his family moved to Chadron, Nebraska where he grew up across the street from a future Alaska aviation pioneer, Harold Gillam. In 1923 Cece and Gillam came to Alaska, first landing in Cordova and then Chitina. They both worked for the Alaska Road Commission in the construction of the Richardson Highway.

In 1928 both Cece and Gillam got jobs with the Bennet-Rodebaugh Airplane Transportation Company in Fairbanks. In 1929 the company was purchased by Carl Ben Eielson. Cece moved down to Anchorage in 1930 and became the first certified aircraft mechanic at the newly opened Merrill Field. In August 1930 Cece and pilot Matt Neimenen took the first flight without oxygen over Mt. McKinley in a Fairchild 71 monoplane belonging to Alaska Airways. They broke all Alaska altitude records for flying without oxygen at that altitude of over twenty thousand three hundred feet.

Cecil Higgins

They stripped the plane down, leaving no seats, and lightened up as much as possible, including only enough gasoline to get there and back. On the return they ran out of gas at Susitna Station and glided in about twenty miles, making a safe landing at Merrill Field. Higgins said it was "dead stick all the way."

Cece met CLARA PETERSON, an Anchorage schoolteacher, in 1930, and they were married in Seward in 1934, making a special trip by air to Seward with Jack Waterworth. The ceremony was performed by Dr. Joseph H. Romig, of Alaska medical fame. It was the first wedding ceremony he performed in twenty-five years. Clara came to Anchorage from Burke, Idaho where she was born. She graduated from Teachers

Cecil Higgins and Plane

Matt Neimenen and Plane

Matt Neimenen

College in Cheney, Washington, and taught school in various towns in Washington and Idaho prior to coming to Anchorage in 1930.

Higgins worked for Alaska Star Airlines for five years as chief of maintenance, and during WWII he was drafted by Colonel E. Davis, commander of Ft. Richardson Elmendorf Field, and became foreman of the Alaska General Air Depot, supervising the maintenance of the Army's combat aircraft during the Aleutian Campaign.

After WWII he left the aircraft industry and worked for many years as a salesman in the clothing business and at Hoyt Motors, Anchorage Hardware, Northern Supply and Steel Fabricators. In 1980, after the death of Clara, he moved into the Anchorage Pioneer Home, and in 1989 he moved to Tacoma, Washington to live with his son. Cece prided himself as being one of the founders of the Alaska Aviation Heritage Museum, and the restoration facility was named in his honor, Cecil Higgins Restoration Facility.

Cecil died in 1990 in Tacoma, Washington. His ashes were scattered over the Chugach Mountains. He and Clara had a son and daughter. Their daughter, Sally Higgins, lives in Fairbanks, and son Dan lives in Tacoma, Washington. Dan had two daughters, Debora M. and Dianne, both living in Kent, Washington.

A well-known miner and mining engineer who came to Anchorage in 1930 from elsewhere in Alaska, WESLEY EARL DUNKLE was born in Warren, Pennsylvania in 1887. He was educated in Pennsylvania in grade and high school and in Sheffield Scientific School and then graduated from Yale University in 1908.

Wesley joined the Oliver Iron Mining Company in Minnesota in 1908 to 1909 just after his graduation from Yale. He joined the Consolidated Copper Mining Company in Nevada in 1910 and then came to Alaska for the Kennecott Mining interests in Cordova. He stayed with Kennecott

Wesley Earl Dunkle

until 1930 when he first arrived in Anchorage. He took over active management of the Lucky Shot Mine and operated as manager until his backers pulled out in 1938. He started development on the Golden Horn Mine in Flat until it flooded out.

Dunkle was active in other interests as well and became seriously interested in flying. He bought his own plane, which he flew for many years in the area. In 1934 he flew his new "ambulance" plane up from Seattle in thirteen and one half hours, setting a record. His four-place plane had folding seats to make up a stretcher bed and room for a nurse. It was Alaska's first. Dunkle's interest in aircraft brought him and other investors to the development of the Star Airways, which was the forerunner of Alaska Airlines. He was president of the line from 1932 to 1938.

His primary interest, however, was always mining, and in 1938 he developed the Golden Zone Mine out of Broad Pass, with stockholders, Alex McDonald, E. R. Tarwater, A. A. Shonbeck, and Warren Cuddy. Gold mining was shut down during the war years, and then he easily shifted his own operations to the coal prospects in the area of Colorado Station on the Alaska Railroad. He spent his remaining years working on the development of the Golden Zone Mine.

Wesley died in the hills near his Golden Zone camp in 1957. He and Florence Hull were married in the early years of his life, and they had two children, John H. and William E. She passed away during the boys' childhood, and Dunkle married again in 1934 to Gladys E. Borthwick, and they had one son, Bruce.

Mrs. Dunkle was also a pilot. She and her spouse were probably the best-known mining family in Alaska during their time. Mrs. Dunkle moved to the east after closing the Golden Zone Mine and passed away in 1962 in Washington, D.C. They are both buried in Angelus Memorial Park in Anchorage.

One of the early physicians to arrive in Anchorage in 1930, Dr. AUGUST STANLEY WALKOWSKI was born in Bessemer, Michigan in 1898 and was educated at the University of Michigan Medical School, graduating in 1927. He first arrived in Alaska in 1928 when he was hired by the Kennicott Copper Corporation as a resident physician at their Latouche operation.

In 1928 he and GRACE MCKEOWN were married in Chicago, Illinois. Grace was a registered nurse, and when they moved to Latouche she was his aide and assistant. Grace was born in Lawrenceville, Illinois in 1904 and met "Wally" at the Ann Arbor Hospital in Ann Arbor, Michigan. When Providence Hospital was built in Anchorage, she was prominent in the women's auxiliary.

In 1930 Wally and Grace moved to Anchorage where he took the job of resident physician for the Alaska Railroad Hospital, and later in 1939-40 he joined the staff of Providence Hospital, as well as holding his private practice.

Wally had a reputation of being available for any emergency that arose. He made dozens of mercy flights with local bush pilots, providing emergency medical care to people living in the bush. In one mission alone, he spent thirty-six hours flying and riding horseback to save the life of a patient who could not reach medical facilities. He made national headlines in 1932 [see photo] when he and Grace went into a village which had an outbreak of measles and gave medical aid to the sick.

Wally and Grace Walkowski

Dr. Walkowski never sent out a bill, believe it or not. I personally can attest to that. You would have to go to his office or call

Dr. A. S. Walkowski

him to find out what his fee was. Wally always had the best interests of his patients at heart, and with a dry sense of humor he had a great rapport with his patients. It was said by many that you never knew if you had a fifty dollar illness or a three hundred dollar illness until you called him to give you a bill. Wally was an ardent duck hunter and made many trips with Nick Gaikema to the duck flats each hunting season.

Wally and Grace were divorced for a number of years, and in 1963 he married Doris Ervin, the widow of Wells Ervin who was killed in a plane crash.

The union of Grace and Wally produced three children. Eldest daughter, Frances Ann Walkowski Waters, lives in Kent, Ohio and had three children. George A. lives in

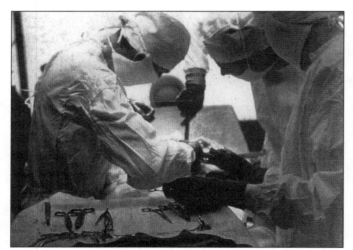

Dr. A. S. Walkowski in Surgery

Chapel Hill, North Carolina; Helen Marie lives in Agoura Hills, California; and Robert Lipscombe lives in San Francisco. Daughter Mary Jane Walkowski Emard had three children. Madeleine Ann died in 1996; Sarah Elizabeth lives in Kirkland, Washington; and Michael E. lives in Mesa, Arizona. Son Philip McKeown Walkowski lives in North Hollywood, California.

Grace died in Seattle in 1976; Wally died in the Anchorage Pioneers Home in 1979; Doris Ervin Walkowski died in Anchorage in 1983; and daughter Mary Jane Emard died in Ft. Worth, Texas in 1990.

Anne Walkowski

Mary Jane Walkowski

Phillip Walkowski

CHAPTER XIV

1931

MAYOR JAMES DELANEY served his third term.

New City councilmen were:

ROBERT H. ROMIG
IRA BAILEY

Anchorage High School graduated fourteen students, six girls and eight boys:

Rex Anderson

Mary Bagoy

Bill Barber

Lawrence Bayer

Charles Climie

Leroy Crawford

William Harriman

Romaka Kamkoff

John Meyer

Alice Mikami

Frank Reed

Addie Reno

May Teeland

Dora Werner

There was nothing startling happening in 1931, other than it being the second year of the great depression. However, Alaskans were mostly affected in that many people were coming north seeking employment, which was unavailable down south. By 1931 the Federal Government had invested seventy million dollars in the Alaska Railroad and had not shown a profit, nor had the Railroad fulfilled its role in developing Alaska's economy. A special committee was sent that year to investigate the problem and recommended drastic increases in the freight and passenger rates. Alaskans protested the increases and started taking their business elsewhere. This led to further decreases in Railroad revenue. (*Anchorage Times* and Chamber of Commerce reports 1931.)

———

Among the many young men coming north to Alaska in 1931, DAVID A. DREW was born in Baraboo, Wisconsin in 1901. His family moved to Bloomington, Indiana when he was eight years old and then moved again to western Washington. He attended college for two years and then worked in sawmills and various lumber camps until 1924. He then worked as a projectionist and stagehand for a theater in Butte, Montana, and when the depression hit he cast his eyes north to Alaska and landed in Anchorage in 1931.

Like so many others, he took any job he could find. He started out as a section hand, a helper on a mink ranch, and spent one winter as a novice trapper. He finally secured steady work with the Railroad on the section and spent ten years with the ARR, leaving this job as section foreman in 1942. In 1948 he returned to government service as a jail guard in Anchorage and was appointed United States deputy marshal in 1949, under James Patterson. Dave passed away in Anchorage in 1981.

———

The era of the bush pilots and organized airlines had arrived in Anchorage in the early 1930's. One of the "air entrepreneurs," LINIOUS "MAC" MCGEE was born in Francesville, Indiana in 1897, and during his early years he worked for his grandfather, who was a banker in a small Montana town. Although Mac had learned to fly, he shined at management and organization, which were things taught to him by his grandfather.

In 1931 he stood on the dock in Seattle, Washington, looking north to Alaska. With little or no cash in his pocket, he decided to head north. He

Mac McGee

Mac and Helen McGee and Nephew

stowed away on the Alaska Steamer *Aleutian* and six days later arrived in Seward. He made his way to Anchorage where he landed a job with A. A. Shonbeck, who was the Standard Oil dealer in Anchorage at the time. His duties were driving truck, delivering, and every other odd job that came along. He soon got himself involved in the fur business, buying, selling and trading, and it was not long before he owned a Stinson airplane and was doing some local flying on a charter basis.

Mac partnered with A. H. Barnhill, who was a pilot. He later bought out Barnhill and hired Oscar Winchell and later his half brother, Estol Call, and other pilots followed: Roy Dickson, Ken Neese and others. McGee Airways was successful and doing great business. Mac did the business end, and his pilots did the rest. He worked out a commission pay basis for them and started installing radios in his three Stinsons. He also set up trappers who had cabins in the passes and the routes to the interior with radios so his pilots could communicate and gauge the weather.

In 1936 he merged with Star Airways and managed the outfit for a year. One of his ex-pilots, Kenny Neese, then took over management for a time. Mac went back to mining, which was

his first love. He operated on Utopia Creek, Manley and various other locations throughout the interior. In the fifties he worked the old Oscar Dahl property on the Seward Highway just north of Summit Lake.

McGee Airways with Furs Covering the Stinson

In 1935 Mac and HELEN SEABURG were married. Helen was the eldest daughter of the Pioneer August Seaburg family. She was born in Seattle in 1915 and was brought to Anchorage in 1916 when her father obtained work with the ARR and sent for her mother and her.

She and Mac started wintering in Reno, Nevada and spending summers on the gold claims. In 1973 they were involved in an auto accident, and Helen was severely injured. She died of her injuries in 1975. Several years later Mac remarried and continued his mining until he passed

Fleet of McGee Air's Stinsons

away in Reno in 1988. Helen is buried in Denver, Colorado with her mother and sister. Mac is buried in Reno, Nevada.

Oscar Winchell

Another of Alaska's greatest bush pilots was OSCAR WINCHELL, "The Flying Cowboy." He was born in Verdigre, Nebraska in 1903. In 1921 Oscar began his flying career in Redfield, South Dakota when he saw an airplane land in a hay-field. He spent his last fifteen dollars to get a ride in that plane, and from then on he was hooked. He followed airplanes from then on until he eventually learned to fly, and in those days it did not take long to learn. He soloed after four hours!

Oscar's daughter quotes her father as saying: "I've always want-ed to fly since I can remember. I wanted to fly around like a bird. Walking ain't no damn good." Flying was more than just for transportation for this old barnstormer. He said to me, "I didn't have a job. I felt like I was going to heaven."

In 1927 he bought his first plane, a six hundred dollar Jenny, with money he earned by stacking oats in South Dakota. Later he and partner George Ice founded Pioneer Airways, which later became Rapid City Airlines. Oscar taught flying and developed the idea of a fly-ing club where people pooled their money to buy and fly one plane.

The 1929 crash meant ruin for many pilots, and Oscar looked for greener pastures. To him, Alaska seemed like the best bet, and in 1931 he arrived in Anchorage, and the flying cowboy started a new adventure in the far north. His first job was with McGee Airways flying Mac's Stinson. Oscar spent time ferrying passengers and freight that Mac had lined up.

In 1936 two young nurses arrived in Anchorage and were immediately put to work by Dr. Walkowski. Florence Gue and Pauline Cain came to Alaska for adventure and found it in Anchorage, especially Florence, who married Oscar Winchell in 1937. In 1940 Oscar left Star Airways and started flying his own ship out of McGrath under the name of Oscar Winchell Flying Service. He flew food, equipment and passengers throughout the area, from McGrath up and down the Yukon and Kuskokwim Rivers, Flat, Takotna, Ophir, Ruby, Anchorage and Fairbanks or to anywhere there was a payload.

In 1953 Oscar and Florence moved to California and remained there until Oscar died in 1987. He is buried in San Dimas, California. Oscar and Florence had one daughter, Patricia Marie Winchell Wachel. She passed away in 1999 in Covina, California. Patricia had one daughter Nancy Winchell Wachel Smith, who lives in LaVerne, California. (Information given here came from Partricia Wachel's book, *The Flying Cowboy*.)

Home on 15th and Karluk

Paul and Lee Rees on 50th
Anniversary

Another young couple arrived in Anchorage in 1931 from California. PAUL DAVID REES and LaNEVA "LEE" PLATT REES both left good jobs in California to come to the land of adventure. Paul was born in Wymore, Nebraska in 1903, and in 1927 he moved to Long Beach, California where he met and married LaNeva Platt. Lee was born in Pine Island, Minnesota in 1903. After their marriage they decided to move to Alaska, and, upon their arrival in Anchorage, Paul immediately acquired work with the Alaska Railroad. He held the position of freight agent for many years and also worked in the accounting department.

Lee was a true animal lover and began a career of raising husky dogs and driving a dog team for her own enjoyment. Most of her dogs were of a matched quality and attracted attention wherever they went. She and her team were often photographed and were on the cover of various magazines during the period.

Daughter, June Barker, with Paul Rees on
His 95th Birthday

In 1933 Paul and Lee built their first home at 9th Avenue and K Street and lived there until they required more space for the dogs. In 1938 they moved out in the "woods," approximately where 16th Avenue and Karluk would be. This was about two miles from downtown and a mile from

Lee and Dog Team

their closest neighbor. They acquired seven acres from Paddy Welch and built a log home, which still stands today.

Paul was active in the Lions and Masonic Lodge and was awarded the Melvin Jones Award for outstanding dedication to the Lions in 1996. He is now at the young age of ninety-six and is "snowbirding" in Mesa, Arizona for the winters. Lee passed away after a short illness in 1991; however, she will long be remembered by oldtimers as the first lady of dog mushing in Anchorage.

Florence Hoffman

Paul and Lee had one daughter, June Rees Barker. She and her spouse had three children. Donald, Tyra Lee and Reesa all live in California.

One of the best-known and best-loved lawmen who came to Alaska in the early days was A. FRANK HOFFMAN. He was born in St. Louis, Missouri in 1871, and as a boy of thirteen he left home and traveled to the Dakotas and other parts of the west looking for adventure.

He found his way to Alaska during the great gold rush of 1898. He did not, however, head for Dawson, but instead opted for Valdez and the Copper River and Chisana country. He was an early friend of Anthony J. Dimond, and together they prospected the Chisana district in 1913. Soon after his coming into Valdez and Chisana he joined the Valdez police department and became chief for several years. He then received an appointment as United States deputy marshall in Chisana at the same time as his old friend Tony Dimond was appointed United States commissioner.

Frank Hoffman

Frank had a varied career prior to becoming a peace officer. He started out as a cowpuncher in the Dakotas, and then worked as a prospector, miner, teamster and freighter. He was so well known in the area that his appointment as a marshall was well received. Frank was a "moose" of a man, according to one of his admirers, and a man who had a disposition that could never be ruffled. He had the ability to handle dangerous men, and another who knew him at Chisana during the wild days said, "Frank was never compelled to make any real spectacular arrests, because his presence inspired obedience to the law. Wherever he was, little trouble resulted."

An article appeared in the Valdez newspaper after his death telling of some of his arrests. It got so that it was considered an honor for a tough guy to be arrested by Frank, and many a bar room tale was told by men whom he had taken to the hoosegow. One time a would-be tough hombre came all the way from the interior to "lick" Frank, but when he tackled the job, Frank put him away with one punch.

Frank and FLORENCE HAUGHLAN were married in Anchorage in 1916 when he was marshall in Matanuska Landing. They made their home alternately in Matanuska and in Anchorage. Florence often said that the high point in Frank's life was his appointment to guard President Harding when he visited Alaska in 1923. In 1933 Frank was appointed United States marshall for the Anchorage district of the third Alaska division. He replaced Harry Staser who resigned in 1932. Frank passed away in 1937, and Florence died in 1970. They are both buried in the Elks Tract, Anchorage Memorial Park.

A true Alaska medical missionary arrived in Bethel, Alaska in 1896. JOSEPH HERMAN ROMIG was born in 1873 into a family of missionaries and was raised with his nine brothers and sisters on Chippewa Mission Farm near Independence, Kansas. He attended Hahnemann Medical School in Philadelphia, Pennsylvania under the auspices of the Moravian church, his church having provided for his medical training in exchange for his promise to serve for seven years without salary as a doctor at a mission.

Dr. J. H. and Ella Romig

Ella Ervin Romig

Soon after receiving his medical degree, he married the girl of his choice, a trained nurse whom he had met in medical school. ELLA MAE ERVIN was born in Kingston, Pennsylvania in 1871. She moved to Forty Fort, Pennsylvania with her parents and then to Philadelphia where she attended nursing school and met Joseph Romig. Ella had become interested in Joe's plans of going to Alaska to serve his term in the mission at Bethel. The reason he chose Bethel was because his sister and brother-in-law, John Henry Kilbuck, had been working as missionaries at Bethel for a number of years. Kilbuck was a full-blooded Delaware Indian who had gone to teach the Eskimos of the Kuskokwim River area. He was a linguist and had a good rapport with the natives. Thus Joseph Romig felt that he would have a better chance using the experience of his sister and brother-in-law in completing his mission.

Dr. J. H. Romig

The newlyweds set sail from San Francisco, stopping over

Bethel Mission, 1896

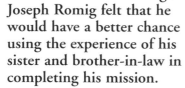

J. H. Romig and Emily Craig

J. H. and Robert Romig
and Friend

at Unalaska and then going on to Bethel upriver from the mouth of the Kuskokwim. They were met offshore by the Kilbucks, accompanied by a host of Eskimos. Bethel was not much of a village, as it consisted only of four houses occupied by white families, a chapel, an old Russian bath house and a small store. The Romig home was a simple two-room structure, which served as both residence and hospital. The newlyweds immediately took hold of the situation and in short order had a reasonable looking clinic and home.

Romig Family and Friends

The villages were rife with tuberculosis in those days, and epidemics of influenza and whooping cough were common. Broken bones, cuts bruises and other maladies were rapidly treated by Dr. Romig. With his magic potions and healing powers, the periods of recuperation were shortened considerably from the primitive methods previously used. Romig was soon named "Yung-Chawista," person working for others, or "Remaker of People."

Romig soon became expert at dog mushing, as his practice stretched for hundreds of miles, and all of his missions were related to saving lives. There were no planes, no highways, no snow machines, nothing but dogs or snowshoes in the winter, and rowboats, kayaks and the like in the summer.

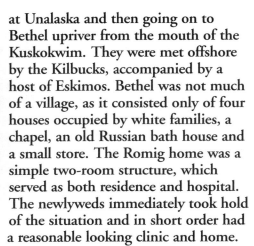

Margaret and Elizabeth, 1918

In the fall of 1899 the re-supply ship never made it into the river, and this created a food problem for the village with winter coming on. Romig rounded up about twenty men and a half dozen rowboats and headed up-river to portage and slog across to the Yukon and down to Russian Mission for supplies. Upon arriving there they found little or nothing, and they headed down the Yukon to St. Michael where they were able to get supplies. The return trip was just as miserable, fighting man-eating mosquitoes and weather. When they finally got back to Bethel, they had covered over one thousand miles on this relief mission.

While Romig was gone, Ella held down the fort, performing minor surgery, setting bones and doing everything that Romig could do except major surgery. Their life was one hardship after another; however, they were totally dedicated people and were undaunted by the elements.

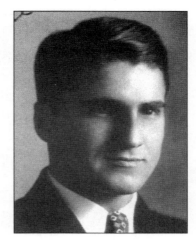

Howard Romig, 1929

In 1903, after completing their mission, they returned to San Francisco where Romig ran an emergency hospital during the aftermath of the 1906 earthquake. Before long he was again called back to the north by the Nusgagak Packing Company, which offered him a job as company physician at Nushagak. He accepted, and again the family moved north. He was appointed United States commissioner while there and held court on the ships that traveled from port to port.

After leaving Nushagak, Romig and family moved to Seward where he opened a small hospital in 1921, but he had to close it in 1922. From Seward he was hired by the St. Joseph Hospital in Fairbanks as chief surgeon, and from there he went to Nenana, where he opened a hospital for the Alaska Railroad. In 1930 he was called to Anchorage by the Railroad to take over the Railroad Hospital as chief of staff to replace Dr. Haverstock, who was moving to Seward.

Robert's Wife Louise with J. H. Romig

His son Howard G. Romig had graduated from Stanford and had done his internship and returned to Anchorage. He and his father went into private practice together for a short time. In 1937 Ella Romig passed away, and two years later Romig married Emily Craig, who had been chief of nursing at the Railroad hospital and was an old friend of both Ella and Dr. Romig. In 1937 he agreed to serve one term as Mayor of Anchorage and did a commendable job, but politics was not in his nature. Romig Junior High School was named in his honor, and the name of Romig Hill stuck from the days that he occupied the log house at the top of the hill where a group of condominiums now stands.

St. Joseph's Hospital in Fairbanks

Moosehorn Ranch on Romig Hill

Alaska Railroad Hospital, 1930

In 1939-40 he became chief surgeon at the new Providence Hospital, and shortly there after he retired from practice. Dr. Romig purchased several acres of land on what is now Romig Hill and where West High School now stands. Henry Easterly had a cabin on his homestead at the top of the hill and called it "Moosehorn Ranch." Romig added on to the log home and started his "Board of Directors" organization. He and friends put on an annual wild game dinner. The guests each brought a wild game entrée they had cooked. This turned out to be an annual affair, and eventually the same group became the beginning of the Anchorage Rotary Club. Dr. Romig and Emily retired to Colorado Springs, Colorado, and he passed away there in 1951.

Dr. Joseph H. Romig and Ella Ervin Romig had four children. Three of them were born in Bethel. Robert H. was born in 1897 and died in Anchorage in 1962. Margaret Romig Hannon was born in 1898 and died in Anchorage in 1968.

Nenana Hospital, 1916

Providence Hospital, 1939

Jean Elizabeth Romig Daily was born in 1900 and died in 1965. Howard G. was born in Seward in 1911 and died in Anchorage in 1987. Margaret had two daughters, Molly and Patricia. Robert and spouse, Louise, had no children nor did Elizabeth Daily. Howard married three times and had fifteen children.

All of the first and second generation Romigs are buried in the Masonic Tract of Anchorage Memorial Park Cemetery. One grandchild and the spouse of Robert are also buried with the family. Dr. J. H. Romig died in Colorado Springs, however he was disinterred and brought to Anchorage and buried in the family plot. Emily Craig Romig is buried in Colorado Springs.

CHAPTER XV

1932

OSCAR GILL was elected Mayor of Anchorage.

The new Councilmen were:

ART SHONBECK
U. G. CROCKER
JACK B. WADMAN

Anchorage High School graduated fourteen students, seven girls and seven boys:

Mayor, Oscar Gill

Bob Abernathy

Gwen Cannon

Robert Carlson

Clarence Ekland

Myrtle Fleckenstein

Frances Hosler

Charles Jasper

Moana Monkman

Antoinette Schodde

Helen Seaburg

Marjorie Seller

Alex Shadura

Odin Strandberg

Henry Swanson

The biggest event for this year was the beginning of construction of the highway from Anchorage to Palmer by the Alaska Road Commission.

A Greek immigrant came to the United States in 1912 at the age of seventeen looking for work. SOTER D. "SAM" CHIAMIS was born in Thebes, Greece in 1895. He left Greece for the United States heading for Seattle, Washington, where his brother was living. As he said, "there were no jobs back home, so I left for America looking for work."

His first job was with the Chicago-Milwaukee Railroad on the Oregon and Washington segments. Work was scarce on the railroads and unsteady, so Sam opened a newspaper stand in downtown Seattle. Hearing of the railroad being built in Alaska he sold his newstands and bought an eighteen-dollar steerage ticket to Seward on the Alaska Steamship *Northwestern*.

He arrived in Seward on March 17, 1917 and got work on the ARR. He was in Nenana when President Harding drove the golden spike in 1923. After the completion of the road, Sam continued to work for the ARR as section foreman at various locations from one end of the road to the other. His last job was foreman at the Potter section.

After twenty-five years with the ARR, Sam, with partner Harold Koslosky, opened "Sams" liquor store on 4th Avenue. He later bought out Harold and bought the Panhandle Bar, opened two more liquor stores, and operated the Chiamis apartment building. Sam became a real estate developer, dealing in buildings and land. He suffered extreme damage in the 1964 earthquake; however, this did not deter him from rebuilding.

In 1937 Sam took a trip back to the old country, and there he met and married his wife MERSINA, and they spent the next fifty years together in Anchorage, raising four children.

Mersina died in 1981, and Sam died in 1988. His son John died in 1943, and son James died in 1976. Sam and Mersina are buried in the Pioneer Tract of Anchorage Memorial Park and sons John and James are buried in Tract 13. Daughters Des Chiamis Lester and Zoe Kennedy presumably live in Anchorage.

Another stampeder who navigated the Chilkoot to Dawson, HEMAN A. LA ZELLE was born in Lorain County, Ohio in 1857 and lived there until he joined the great stampede to the Klondike in 1898. He mined for years in both the Dawson and Fairbanks camps and later gave up the quest for gold and settled down to doing mechanical and blacksmith work.

He and his spouse, ANNETTE, moved from Fairbanks to Anchorage in 1932 to join two daughters who were employed by the Alaska Railroad. Annette died in 1932; Heman passed away in 1934. They are both buried in the Masonic Tract of Anchorage Memorial Park. They had four children, daughters Harriet LaZelle and Hazel Campbell and sons, Mason, who was killed in a plane crash, and Harvey. The whereabouts of the remaining family members is unknown.

Clyde Ellis

A well known attorney and a man prominent in veterans affairs in Anchorage, CLYDE R. ELLIS came to Anchorage in 1932. He was born in Peru, Iowa in 1896 and received his law degree from Willamette University in Portland, Oregon. He served as assistant U.S. attorney for the third district and later went into private practice with John Manders. He was a past Territorial Commander of the American Legion and the VFW. He served in two world wars and was the driving force in organizing the Reserve Officers Association in Anchorage.

Clyde was secretary of Mt. McKinley Airways, a past President of the Chamber of Commerce and the manager of the 1938 Anchorage Fur Rendezvous. Wherever he went he was a promoter of Anchorage. During WWII while in the service he promoted the naming of a Liberty ship after the City of Anchorage.

Ellis, at the time that he was Chairman of the Chamber of Commerce, was influential in convincing United States Postmaster General Farley to build a federal building in Anchorage. Farley came to Anchorage in 1938 to determine the need. Ellis was in charge of the committee to see to the needs of Farley and to make sure he got the true picture of what Anchorage had to offer. Farley, on his return to D.C., got the money, and the Anchorage Federal Building at the corner of 4th Avenue and F Street became a reality. It was under construction within one year of Farley's visit.

Clyde and his spouse Nancy had two children, a daughter Mabel and a son Clyde, Jr. Clyde died in Seattle in 1947 while on a business trip.

The depression was taking its toll on many young men in the United States in 1932, and Alaska was purported to be the place to head for as far as work was concerned. It was not necessarily so; however, they still kept coming. Another of these young men who came and stayed and was successful in his endeavors, THOMAS CULHANE was born in Ferguslea, Ontario, Canada in 1903. He immigrated to the United States at the age of seventeen and became a citizen shortly thereafter.

He found work in Detroit, Michigan with the U. S. Rubber Company in their tire manufacturing division. There was much

Rena and Tom Culhane

Tom and Rena in 1993

The Culhane Children

unrest in the industries with the depression in full swing, and, with labor unions striving for work and better conditions, it was almost impossible to get steady work. Tom had three good friends with whom he worked, George and Bill Justin and Herb Schroeder. George Justin had just read a book on Alaska and told the others about it. Tom read the book and said, "when do we leave?"

The four friends bought a two hundred fifty dollar car and drove to Seattle, camping out all of the way. They bought steerage tickets to Seward on the Alaska Steamship *Yukon* and six days later landed in Seward. They found little work with the exception of the extra gangs on the Railroad and those were only during the summer months, with wages at sixty-two cents per hour. There was work in Fairbanks with the F. E. Company driving points, so the partners split up. Tom stayed in Anchorage, and the other three headed to Fairbanks.

Tom After a Successful Sheep Hunt

Tom found reasonable work with the Railroad, and in 1933 he sent for his fiancée, RENA LAJAMBE. Rena was born in Oklee, Minnesota in 1907 and met Tom in Detroit. Tom met Rena at the boat in Seward, and they were married that same day. They went on up to Anchorage and settled in a two-room cabin rented from Marie Bagoy. Rena found work in John Meyer's North Pole Bakery, and Tom worked whatever jobs he could.

The Crew at Anchorage Refuse

A friend Art Meier told Tom that Walt Teeland wanted to sell his transfer business. Tom got a loan from E. R. Tarwater, an officer of the National Bank of Alaska, and bought the trucking business for two thousand five hundred dollars with terms of twenty-five dollars per month at eight percent interest. Walt's Transfer had a 1932 GMC flat bed combination dump truck and a 1932 Ford one-and-one-half ton flatbed. His business was selling and delivering coal and wood and hauling anything he could move.

Walt's Transfer evolved into Arctic Fuel and Appliance Company, and Culhane was in the propane gas business as well as diesel fuel and stove and furnace oil. He sold the propane business and bought a private refuse company operating outside the city limits of Anchorage. This business evolved into Anchorage Refuse Company, and at the time Tom sold this company he had one hundred thirty employees and was operating a business doing several million dollars per year. It was not bad for a young man who came to Alaska to find a better life, and, like so many others, who stayed and found success through just plain hard work. Tom learned to fly in the late thirties and was an accomplished private pilot. He was a great hunter and fisherman, and his boys followed in the love of flying both fixed wing aircraft and helicopters.

Tom and Rena had four children. Daughter Marguerite had one son, Brian, who lives in Anchorage. Eldest son, Jack, was killed in a tragic airplane accident in March 1991. He and his spouse, Anne, had two children, Heather Culhane Field, who lives in Charles City, Iowa, and Patrick Scott, who died with his father in the same accident. Son Thomas and Sharon Oskolkoff Culhane had five children. Tanya Lynn Culhane Henrikson, Timothy R., and Sarah L. Culhane Johnson all live in Anchorage. Tricia M. lives in Baltimore, Maryland; and Katherine died in 1993. Son Gerald and spouse, Beth, had three children. Sabrina Culhane Herrick and Corena L. both live in Anchorage, and Jerrica E. lives in Washington.

Tom passed away in 1997 and is buried in the Catholic Tract, Anchorage Memorial Park with son Jack and the Culhane grandchildren Patrick and Katherine. Rena is now ninety-four years young and lives at home.

Ken Neese

The early thirties were the years of the bush pilots arriving in Anchorage. Star Airways, McGee Airways, Bowman Airways, Woodley Airways, Jim Dodson Air Service, Ptarmigan Airways, Peterson Airways, Bethel Airways, Al Jones Airways, Hakon Christensen Air Service, Pacific International Airways, Pacific Alaska Airways, Dorbandt and Cope, Cope Air Service and many others long forgotten all demanded pilots, and Anchorage was rapidly becoming the air capital of Alaska.

Another of these early-day pilots who came up in 1932, KENNETH "KENNY" WAYNE NEESE was

Kenny and Mary Neese

Mary Neese

Mary and Betty Neese

Kenny Neese and the Ox-5

Kenny Neese, Johnny Moore and
Oscar Winchell

born in Waterloo, Iowa in 1903. He learned to fly in Fresno, California and entered into commercial flying in Oakland, California. He gave flying lessons in Oakland in 1928 and 1929 and entered cross-country air races from Mines Field in Los Angeles to Cleveland, Ohio. In 1929 he was offered a job with Varney Air Service in Portland, Oregon to fly the mail from Seattle to Portland, and he had to do night flying. In November 1929 he had a bad accident and crash landed in a farmer's field. His plane caught fire, and the farmer pulled him out of the plane, but he was left with scars on this face, arms and legs. After being hospitalized for several weeks, he gave up flying with the Varney people. In 1930 the family moved back to Oakland, and he started teaching students for the Dolores Gunther Monarch Air Service. He did stunt flying on the side as well as putting on air shows in small towns.

In 1930 an old friend and pilot, Al Monsen, told Kenny that Anchorage needed pilots, so Al sent him the fare for a ticket, and Kenny arrived in Anchorage in 1932. He left his wife and daughter in Fresno in care of his mother and family. He arrived in Anchorage in January and immediately went out to Merrill Field and met Mac McGee, who owned McGee Airways, and Mac put him to work immediately. By this time Mac had three Stinsons, and now three pilots, Estol Call, Oscar Winchell and Kenny Neese.

When McGee sold out to Star Airways, Kenny stayed on with them and flew mostly the Bristol Bay run on floats during the summer. He soon became one of the best-known pilots in the area and the most well respected for his flying ability and efficiency. He drew many requests from Star customers. "I won't fly unless Neese is the pilot."

When Star Airways bought the first stagger wing Beechcraft, they sent Kenny out to the states to get it. He became famous in the interior for the high speed of this new aircraft and established new speed records between towns. He was popularly called "Buck Rogers" after his appearance in the speedy Beechcraft. Neese had his close calls and forced landings and performed many mercy flights. There were no radios in the planes in those days, and these pilots all flew by the seats of their pants. Kenny and family left Alaska for good in 1941, and he went to Florida to ferry bombers for Pan American Air Ferries to Africa and Persia. He flew Martin B-25's from Palm Beach, Florida to Africa via Brazil. It was not known in 1942 whether he was shot down while crossing the Atlantic or crashed in Africa, South America or the United States, however death came on the last flight before he was to retire.

The McGee Stinsons on the Mud Flats

Kenny married Mary Elizabeth Morford, who was born in Gallatin, Missouri in 1910, and, like most pilots' wives in those days, she followed her man to wherever he had to go to fly. Kenny and Mary had one daughter, Betty Neese Guyer. She and her spouse, Bob, had four children. Jay Melissa lives in the Matanuska Valley; Kenneth Arthur lives in Denver, Colorado; Kim Allison lives in Phoenix, Arizona; and Dawn Elyse Craig lives in Tempe, Arizona. Kenny died in 1942, and Mary passed away in Hawaii in 1999.

More pilots were coming to Anchorage everyday. Some of them starting their own bush airlines. Competition was getting strong, and every devious method the pilots could think of was used to get customers. One of the early Anchorage air entrepreneurs, ARTHUR GORDON WOODLEY was born in New York in 1906 and was educated at Boston College. He learned to fly in 1928 in the Army Air Corps and was an active pilot ever after that. He established Woodley Airways in 1932 with a four place Travel Air and a four place Waco A. Art did most of the flying himself, but also hired pilot A. H. Barnhill, and, in later years, Don Glass, Roy Holm, and Roy Dickson were added to the pilot staff.

In 1928 Art and his brother, Rev. Fr. George Woodley, a Catholic priest, came to Anchorage where Fr. Woodley was to be stationed to relieve Father Dane, the local priest. Fr. Woodley was to be sta-

tioned at Nulato Mission, and he owned a Bellanca airplane in New York, donated by friends, to be used in his missionary work.

Art and his brother, with their father, flew the plane to Anchorage. Both brothers were ardent hunters and decided on a sheep hunt in the Talkeetna

Roy Holm

Don Glass

Art Woodley

Mountains before Father Woodley departed for his mission in Nulato. With their friend Dan Kennedy, they started their hunt, and Fr. Woodley was killed when he fell into a gorge after shooting his sheep.

Art stayed in Anchorage and started his own airline, calling it Woodley Airways. He painted a huge flying "W" on the fuselage. Art did most of his own flying and was a highly successful operator. With Mary Diamond running the office and handling the customers, Art's Woodley Airways was a profitable operation.

In 1934 a young pilot arrived in Anchorage and for a short time flew as co-pilot for Frank Dorbandt. His name was DON GLASS. He was born in San Ramon, California in 1904 and was raised around Oakland and Berkeley. He worked for both Boeing and Douglas in the assembly plants and as a pilot. In 1938 Don went to work for Art Woodley, flying a Waco and Travel Air and, in 1942-43, a new Stinson Tri-motor Airliner. In 1943 on a scheduled return trip from Juneau, he had problems with one of the engines not starting. He unloaded his passengers and some freight and took off with two engines. His plan was to start the third engine in the air. He crashed in Gastineau Channel and lost his life.

In 1937 Art had three pilots, in addition to himself, operating full time, Roy Dickson, Roy Holm and Don Glass. In the 1940's things started changing when the United States became involved in WWII and the demand for pilots increased. As the military demand for instructors and other pilots grew, the civilian operators were losing their best pilots.

At the end of WWII, Art incorporated Pacific Northern Airlines in 1945 and eventually merged with Western Airlines in 1967. In 1946 Art brought in the first factory new transport plane, a DC-3 under the colors of PNA.

Art passed away in Bellevue, Washington in 1990.

Jack Waterworth

Steve Mills

Charles Ruttan

Waterworth, Ruttan and Mills

In 1932 Anchorage was making aviation history. Three young men came to Anchorage to establish Alaska's first flying school, Star Air Service. STEVE MILLS, JACK WATERWORTH and CHARLEY RUTTAN were the adventuresome three. Two of the trio brought up a new "Fleet" biplane trainer lashed to the deck of the Alaska Steamer *Yukon*. At Seward's airport they assembled the plane and readied it for flight. They set up their flying school at Merrill Field and soon had many students, with Mills and Waterworth alternating as instructors. In addition to operating the flight school, the three pilots few courtesy flights and stunt exhibitions. Waterworth was an excellent acrobatic flier and put on many air shows, some very exciting. In 1933 Mary Barrows, wife of PIA Manager Joe Barrows, soloed to become the first woman to learn to fly in Alaska. Her instructor was Steve Mills.

It soon became evident that there was business in the bush, flying miners, trappers, mail and freight. Star Air Service started expanding and adding airplanes and routes. The name changed to Alaska Star Airways, and investors were attracted to the operation. McGee merged with Star and so on until it evolved into Alaska Airlines, which operates today.

CHARLEY RUTTAN and EVELYN MEYER were married in 1935. Evelyn was the daughter of the Pioneer John Meyer family who owned the North Pole Bakery. She and Charley moved to Victoria, British Columbia in 1941 so Charley could join the Canadian Navy in WWII. Charley died in 1994 in Victoria, British Columbia.

Lilly Johansen Waterworth

Pilot instructor STEVE MILLS was born in Dayton, Wyoming in 1896. After WWI he moved to Seattle, Washington where he learned to fly in 1928. He was an instructor at Boeing field prior to his coming to Alaska. In 1936 he flew a charter fishing party to the Russian River in the Star Bellanca for a day's fishing. His passengers were Mr. and Mrs. George Markle, Mr. and Mrs. Lawrence David and Augustus Teik. They took off from Upper Russian Lake on their return trip and crashed into a mountain. All were killed instantly.

JACK WATERWORTH was born in Olewein, Iowa and moved west to Washington after the death of his parents. After three years of studying pharmacology at the University of Washington, he left college to learn how to fly. He trained at Boeing field in Seattle and then left for Anchorage with his two compatriots, Steve Mills and Charley Ruttan.

In 1935 Jack and Lilly Johanson were married in Anchorage. That same year they moved to Seattle where Jack and George Kennedy established a hardware store in 1943 and operated it until 1951. Jack then joined the Boeing Aircraft Company and stayed with them until his death in 1969.

CHAPTER XVI

1933

Anchorage's new mayor was TOM MCCROSKY.

New Councilmen were:

IKE BAYLES
CHRIS ECKMAN
RAY E. MCDONALD

The big news was the price of gold went to thirty-five dollars per ounce, up from twenty dollars sixty-seven cents, and the first air mail service to the States started going from Anchorage to Juneau, and then by boat to Seattle.

The other big news was the 1933 earthquake that shook Anchorage, the most severe ever felt here to date. At 4:30 PM on April 27, 1933 it hit with a roar. Looking west down 4th Avenue from A Street, it looked like swells of the ocean. You could see the water, and then you couldn't. There was not too much damage, just broken windows on some store fronts, lots of goods on the floor in the stores, and pilots reported some fissures opened up on the Susitna flats.

Mayor Tom
McCrosky

The quake ranged for almost two thousand miles and lasted from two to three minutes. It was reported from Seward, Dutch Harbor, McGrath, Healy and all points on the Railroad. The Railroad reported some bridge and culvert damage. After-shocks lasted for a year on an almost daily basis. Students in the old grade school, which had a high ceiling and chain hanging globes, were exited from the classrooms constantly for fear of crashing globes. The teachers finally gave up, and every day, after the first quake of the day, classes were excused and everyone went home. There was no Richter Scale in those days, but the University of Washington seismic lab reported the epicenter to be 100 miles off-shore from Seward.

Anchorage High School graduated sixteen students, seven girls and nine boys: (Peter King not pictured.)

Eileen Bagoy

Marjorie Balhiser

John Borges

Raymer Brown

Harry Bowman

| Catherine Cavanaugh | Roy Holdiman | Roy Kinsell | Harry Mikami | Paul Miller |

| Elsie Peterson | Verna Reed | Doris Reynolds | Vivian Stoddard | Martin Teresin |

An aviator arrived in Anchorage and signed up with McGee Airways and Bowman Airways. He was JAMES M. DODSON, born in Philadelphia, Pennsylvania in 1902. He first came to Alaska in 1927 to commercial fish in Nushagak in Bristol Bay. He returned to Seattle in the same year and learned to fly in the Naval Reserve at Sand Point Naval Air Station and in Pensacola,

James M. Dodson

Florida. After spending a year on active duty on the carriers *Saratoga* and *Lexington*, he came back to Alaska at Ketchikan to fly for Pioneer Airways and then moved on to Anchorage where he flew for McGee Airways and Bowman Airways. In 1935 Dodson and Mildred Cole were married in Seward, and in that same year he moved to Fairbanks and flew for Wien Air Alaska. In 1936 Jim started his own operation under the title of Jim Dodson Air Service, and in 1947 he, with four other outfits, joined together to form Northern Consolidated Airlines.

In 1950 Jim and family moved to Alberta, Canada, in 1955 to Colorado, and in June 1959 moved back to Anchorage permanently. He had been past President of the Anchorage Chapter of the Air Force Association and vice-president of Alaska Aggregate Company. Jim passed away in Anchorage in 1969. He and Mildred had three children, daughter Abigail Smith and sons James, Jr. and Warren.

The year 1933 brought another pilot/mechanic to Anchorage to work for McGee Airways. ARLOE W. KESSINGER was a half brother to Mac McGee and joined his operations until 1937 when McGee merged with

Home at 940 West 11th Avenue

Arloe and Esther Kessinger

Alaska Star Airways. Arloe was born in Medaryville, Indiana in 1911, and after leaving the airline he worked for the Alaska Road Commission and also for McGee in his mining operations. Arloe was a heavy-duty mechanic and worked on diesel engines of any size. He later was employed by the CAA at various remote sites in Alaska, and his last employment was as a mechanic for Airport Machinery Company until he retired.

Arloe and ESTHER ALTON BROWNE were married in Wasilla in 1939. She was born in Remsen, New York in 1918 and came to Alaska with her family in 1928 to settle in Kasilof, where her father had a fox farm. After about a year they moved on to Nenana, where her father worked for the Alaska Railroad as station manager and telegrapher. In 1934 the family moved to Wasilla, where she met Arloe. In 1940 Arloe and Esther moved to Anchorage, and Esther worked for the Bank of Alaska until she retired in 1989.

Herman and Laine Hermann

Arloe and Esther had two daughters. Laine, the eldest, married Herman Hermann, a Wien pilot. They had three daughters all living in Anchorage: Debbie Hermann McGonegal, Teresa Hermann Robbins and Barbara Hermann. Daughter Arla married Jim Butcher, and they had six children. Linda, George, Robert, Charla and James all live in Anchorage. Anita lives in Naknek, and Martha lives in Fort Smith, Arkansas. Arloe died in 1989, Esther died in 1997, and daughter Laine died in 1990.

Jim and Arla Butcher

A high-powered and ambitious young salesman appeared on the Anchorage scene sometime in 1933, making calls on local businessmen. MILTON W. ODOM was born in Sanford, Mississippi in 1908 and attended grade school there. He finished high school in Longview, Washington and attended the University of Oregon and Washington State University, which he left to take a job with Long Bell Lumber Company in the sales department. He later left Long Bell and acquired a position with the McKesson Robbins Drug Company. His territory included not only the Pacific Northwest, but all of Alaska as well.

Milton Odom

He first arrived in Alaska at Juneau in 1933 and made his first appearance in Anchorage that same year. He had a keen sense of marketing and saw great opportunities in Alaska. In 1934 he acquired the local Anchorage firm of Anchorage Fruit and Produce Company and changed the name to Anchorage Cold Storage. Milt still stayed with McKesson for the next four years as his produce company was still struggling and needed his income to survive.

He saw an opportunity in the liquor business in Alaska after prohibition. The local drug stores in Anchorage, Fairbanks, Juneau, and other towns were all good outlets for liquor. He started the Odom Company in Seattle in 1938 and by this time was well on his way to success.

Julie Odom

Milt was an Alaskan entrepreneur in the true sense. His ability as a salesman and businessman put him in the same class as A. E. "Cap" Lathrop. It was not long before he became the franchise holder for Coca-Cola, 7-Up, Dr. Pepper, and Canada Dry. He acquired a working ranch in eastern Oregon to supply his own beef to his outlets in Anchorage and Seattle. He branched out to Arizona where he sold wholesale liquor in Phoenix, Tucson, Flagstaff, and Yuma. He bought Alaska Freight Lines and formed his own transportation company, handling his own freight as well as the public's. The Odom Company and the Anchorage Cold Storage Company were the big names in the liquor, produce and meat business in Alaska.

In 1982 Milt took on Jesse Carr, the powerful leader of the Teamsters local 959 in Anchorage. It was a titanic struggle where some one hundred twenty workers walked off the job in 1981. They established picket lines and made every attempt to destroy Anchorage Cold Storage. Odom, however, refused to knuckle under and continued to operate, defeating the union which finally withdrew in 1986, one year after the death of Jesse Carr. (Article from the *Anchorage Times*.)

Milt married CORRINE "JULIE" JUELSON, who was the chief

Milt Odom with Boys

stewardess for Northwest Airlines and was born in Fertile, Minnesota. She and Milt had four sons: Michael, John, William, and James. Julie was killed in a plane crash of Pacific Northern Airlines in 1960 when she was returning from a visit to Minnesota. In 1965 Milt and Marilyn Atwood were married, and this union produced three sons, Robert, Paul, and Milton III. Milt and Marilyn divorced in later years.

Although Milt spread his wings outside the borders of Alaska, he still maintained Anchorage as his home and was a true Alaskan entrepreneur. He died of a heart attack while vacationing in Hawaii in 1988. Son Milton III died in Seattle, and former spouse Marilyn Atwood Odom died in 1994.

Another well-known Anchorage businessman came on the Anchorage scene in 1933. GEORGE H. VAARA was born in Ada, Minnesota in 1899. His first job in Anchorage was clerking in the Piggly Wiggly store downtown. He soon ventured on his own and opened Vaara Varieties, a notions store. He operated this successfully for several years, and in 1943 he acquired the Pepsi-Cola franchise and built a plant at the corner of 5th Avenue and I Street, which is now occupied by the Catholic Church Library.

George and Mabel Vaara

George was elected Mayor in 1940 when Anchorage started to blossom out economically due to the onset of WWII and the establishment of Fort Richardson. He served on the Anchorage Port Commission, was Chairman of the United Good Neighbors and President of the first Lions Club, and was a member of the School Board and YMCA. In 1958 he sold his interests in Anchorage and moved to Seattle, Washington.

George and Mabel Vaara had two daughters, Betty Louise Vaara Drumheller, who lives in Seattle, and Jean Alys Bailey, who lives in Phoenix, Arizona. Betty Drumheller had four children, all living in Washington. Karen and Susan live in Kent; Ellen lives in Olympia; and Michael lives in Seattle. Jean Alys Bailey had four children. Carol Bailey Strunk lives in Phoenix, Arizona; Mary Ann Bailey Bush lives in Omaha, Nebraska; James lives in Chandler, Arizona; and Nancy

Betty and Kirk Drumheller and John and Jean Bailey

Ann Lange

Norman Lange and Son, John

Bailey Newton lives in Gilbert, Arizona. George Vaara died in Seattle in 1976, and Mabel died in 1994. They are both buried in Evergreen Cemetery in Seattle.

Another victim of the great depression who found his way to Anchorage looking for the opportunity to make a decent living, NORMAN G. LANGE was born in Amherst Township, Eire County, New York in 1907. He made his way to Alaska and landed in Anchorage in 1933 where he found employment working in the Reliance Grocery for Bill Taylor and Ev McPhee. Norman homesteaded just west of Anchorage beyond Merrill Field and subdivided the homestead piece-meal. Whenever he saved a few dollars he would hire a surveyor to survey the lots, and, in 1940 when the military was arriving in Anchorage, he saw the opportunity to sell small lots at ten dollars down and ten dollars per month to people working on the construction of Ft. Richardson and Elmendorf Field.

Lange's First Store

He sold his lots up and down 4th Avenue to local business people and named the streets after them. He named the area Mountain View, and all of his original streets were named after local businessmen.

First Home in Mountain View

Home on Taylor Street

Taylor and McPhee Streets were named after his employers. Meyer was named for John Meyer, who owned the North Pole Bakery; Schodde was named for Fred Schodde who

New Lange Store in Mountain View

owned the Green Front Store at 4th Avenue and C Street; Price was named for Tom Price, the local commissioner; Bragaw was named after Bob Bragaw, who owned a photo shop; Mumford was named for George Mumford of the Bank of Alaska. Erwin is misnamed; it should be "Ervin," after Win Ervin of the First National Bank. Parsons was named after Fred Parsons of the Parsons Hotel; Bliss was named after Harold Bliss, a local contractor and builder; Lane was named for Harry Lane of the Lane Hotel; Peterkin was named after Tom Peterkin of Peterkin Dairy; Klevin was named for Nels Klevin, a local homesteader; Hoyt was named after Harry Hoyt of Hoyts Garage; Thompson was named after J. Thompson, a local attorney; Tarwater was named after J. H. Tarwater, vice-president of the Bank of Alaska. Wells Street was originally named after Cecil Wells of Wells Garage, but was later changed to Bunn. Pope Street was originally named after Henry Pope of Anchorage Sheet Metal Works but was later changed to Klevin. Odermat Street was named after Charley Odermat, a local restauranteur, but was later changed to Flower, after Joe Flower of the Owl Bar. Romig was changed to Peterkin. Thus Mountain View was born.

Norman Lange with His Beard for the Fur Rondy Contest

In 1938 Norman met ANN ROE, and they were married in Anchorage in 1939. Ann was born in Harrison, Idaho in 1909 and came to Anchorage in 1937 to teach elementary school. Together, Norman and Ann worked many long hours and days in developing Mountain View to bring their dream to fruition. They opened a small store and eventually opened a larger store selling artifacts, food and anything that the military families moving into the area would buy. They had a library of over six hundred Alaska books and a museum that sold original paintings by Laurence, Zeigler, Crumrine, Kehoe and Hamill. Ann was the postmistress, and she and Norman still had time to raise two children.

In 1956 Norman and Ann had sold most of their interests in Mountain View and were living in Seattle. Each summer Norman would come up and sell lots in the Soapstone Road area north of Palmer where he had developed another homestead. Yours truly bought five acres from him for six hundred dollars at ten dollars per month at six percent interest.

These were two of the hard working Pioneer-spirited people who really helped develop Anchorage. With little or nothing financially but with determination and guts, they got the job done.

Norman and Ann raised two children. Daughter Ann Lange Gerstenberger lives in Yakima, Washington, and son John lives in Spokane. Ann Gestenberger had four children. Bruce Cullerton lives in Belize, Central America; Maureen Cullerton Andreas lives in Yakima,

Washington; Tony Cullerton lives in Federal Way, Washington; and Kerry Cullerton lives in West Richland, Washington. Norman died in 1992, and Ann died in 1996, both in Seattle. They are buried in Hollywood Cemetery in Seattle, Washington.

Ed Coffey, 1935   Ruth Coffey, 1935

A man of many talents arrived in Anchorage in 1933. EDWARD DAN COFFEY was born in Chelsea, Oklahoma in 1897 in the Indian Territory of

Oklahoma. He served in WWI, and after the war he did not stay long in Oklahoma as he heard much about the Alaska Territory during the depression years. He first came to Juneau via steerage on the *Queen*. He worked various jobs in the A. J. Mine and had a partnership in the electrical business. He owned and operated the Bergman Hotel dining room and contracted road work with the Bureau of Public Roads in Juneau.

Coffey worked the cyanide plant at the Chichagoff Mine, contracted painting at the Kennecott, worked for the Copper River and Western Railway, and dug clams on the beaches of Cordova. In Fairbanks he drove points for the F. E. Company, fished and packed herring in Kodiak, commercial fished for a few years in Bristol Bay, and was the commissary manager for the Alaska

Road Commission in Palmer. He was superintendent of the commissary for the Alaska Rural Rehabilitation Corporation in Palmer, first President of the Palmer Chamber of Commerce and past general treasurer of the Bristol Bay Fishermen's Union. His political career began with serving two terms in the

Ruth Coffey, 1995   Ruth Coffey and Family

Territorial House of Representatives and two terms in the Senate. He spent his first year in Anchorage in 1933, headquartering there during the winter from Bristol Bay.

With all of this going on with this man, he still had time to marry RUTH KELLY. Ruth was born in Chalfont, Bucks County, Pennsylvania in 1912. She graduated from high school in 1929 and from nursing school in Abington, Pennsylvania in 1933.

Her first job was surgical nurse, and she trained at the same time that Dr. Earl Albrecht was in residency at the Abington Hospital. Dr. Albrecht came to Alaska in 1934, and in 1935 he went to Palmer in response to a scarlet fever epidemic. The colonists built a hospital, and nurses were needed, and this is where Ruth came in at Dr. Albrecht's request. Ruth and Ed met in Palmer on a blind date, and they were married in 1936. They then moved to Anchorage permanently and started an insurance business. They were the first agency to have their customers insured by Lloyds of London. Over the years they had two partners in the insurance business, Louis Odsather and Louis Simpson. Their motto was "Coffey insures everything, remember?" The insurance company was renamed later to the Coffey Simpson Insurance Company.

Ed passed away in 1987 and is buried in the Pioneer Tract of Anchorage Memorial Park Cemetery. Ed and Ruth had one son, Dan Coffey, who, with his spouse Pauline, had four sons, Kevin, Shane, Ryan and Edward, who all live in Anchorage. Ruth still lives in Anchorage with her son Dan and family.

———

One of Anchorage's best-known and most popular local pilots, HAKON "CHRIS" CHRISTENSON, better known as the "Flying Dane," was born in Prastbro, Denmark in 1902. He was educated in Denmark and immigrated to the United States sometime between 1910 and 1917. His brother lived in Eagle Grove, Iowa, and Chris joined him there where the two of them opened a garage. In 1917 he learned to fly and barnstormed the midwest as an acrobatic pilot, flying anything that would fly.

He first came to Anchorage in 1933 and then moved on to Fairbanks where he had gotten a flying job with Ed Lerdahl. He flew in and out of mining camps from Fairbanks, and in 1934 he bought a Curtis Robin and set up business and headquarters in Cantwell. He flew freight and passengers in and out of the Valdez Creek and Peters Creek mining areas as well as Anchorage and Fairbanks.

Hakon "Chris" Christenson

In 1935 Chris and LEONA ELLEN "TINY" DARLO were married in Algona, Iowa. Tiny, as she was fondly called, met Chris during his barnstorming days, and after the two were married they returned to Alaska and set up housekeeping in Cantwell in a cabin on the airstrip. Tiny was born in Butler, Missouri in 1902.

Chris Christenson and Plane at Jean Lake

In 1937 Chris bought a Waco A biplane, which replaced his Curtis Robin. He became a familiar figure in Anchorage, spending more time here than in Cantwell. He finally set up an office downtown and started operating as Christenson Air Service. He and Tiny moved permanently into Anchorage and lived at 1007 5th Avenue. In 1939 Chris acquired a Grumman Widgeon and expanded his operations. He hired Eddie Bowman as another pilot and started flying to Seward and Cordova.

Chris had a jovial personality and was full of good humor. His ability as a pilot was unexcelled. To serve his clients in the mining country in the spring of the year when the snow had left Anchorage but the mines still had snow, Chris took off from the mud flats at Bootleggers Cove on skis so he could land in the high mountain levels of the mines. Many times he could be seen taking off from the mud flats and then banking around and washing the mud off his skis as he skimmed up and away. He did the same routine on Lake Spenard. His contemporaries admired his ability as a flier. He was a past master of the short field approach.

Chris had a deep interest in the youth of Anchorage and was a soft touch for any kid who wanted a ride. His interest was getting more young people interested in flying, and he succeeded in many cases. Yours truly had a delightful experience with Chris, and I shall never forget him and the several trips I made with him. One in particular stands out in my mind. In the fall of 1940, I was returning to Anchorage from Flat after working there for the summer. Weather was bad from McGrath to Anchorage, so, rather than stay in McGrath, I caught Pan American's Pilgrim into Fairbanks with the idea to catch Lavery Airways down to Anchorage. Lavery was not flying into Anchorage because of the weather, and I was forced to lay over in Fairbanks. I was checking into the Nordale Hotel when, lo and behold, there was Chris checking out. He said, "What are you doing here?" And I said, "Trying to get home." He said, "I am leaving right now if you want a ride," and I left. It was a ride from Fairbanks to Cantwell, where we stopped for lunch and Tiny checked the weather in Anchorage. The clouds were lifting, and we came into Merrill Field, low and safe. I did not have the money to pay Chris at the time and said I would cash my check the next day and come by. The next day I met him in his office and said, "How much?" He said, "Did you enjoy the trip?" And I said, "Yes." And he said, "You owe me nothing. I am glad you liked it." I flew with Chris several times thereafter, to Seward and to Kenai Lake in his Widgeon and his Waco on floats. He was quite a guy.

Chris flew his Widgeon down to Texas for complete overhaul and on the return trip picked up his good friend WELLS ERVIN in Seattle in April 1956. They stopped over in Yakutat for fuel and were on the next leg of their journey into Cordova when they got caught in a snow squall. In whiteout conditions, Chris crashed just outside of Cordova. He was killed instantly, and Wells later died in the Cordova Hospital.

Wells was a well-known businessman in Anchorage and a member of the Win Ervin family whose history is already written. He was an officer of Alaska Sales and Service, President of Turnagain, Inc., an apartment house complex, co-owner of Reed Store, and co-owner of Kenai Commercial Company and many other businesses. He was civic-minded in his volunteering for public service such as the Chair of the Heart Association, and he served on the Salvation Army Board of Directors. Wells was married to Doris Lawson "Doady" Ervin who survived him, and they had two children, Clayton Ervin and Betty Lou Broderick.

Chris and Tiny had no children. Tiny died in 1965, and they are both buried in Angelus Memorial Park. Thus ended the legend of "The Flying Dane," a great pilot and a great guy.

A man who became a prominent banker and attorney came to Anchorage from Valdez in 1933. WARREN N. CUDDY was born in Abbington, Maryland in 1886. He earned his law degree at the University of Puget Sound in 1911 and was admitted to the Washington Bar in 1912. In 1914 he landed in Valdez, took his first job as a grocery clerk in the small town, and eventually became owner of the Valdez Mercantile Company.

In 1916 a young schoolteacher arrived to take over as principal of the Valdez High School. Her name was LUCY HON, and she was born in Waldron, Arkansas in 1889. She had five years of teaching experience when she arrived in Valdez, a town of five hundred people, eight high school students, a courthouse, a boarding house, and four men for every woman. It was not long before she met Warren Cuddy, and the two were married in Ft. Smith, Arkansas in 1917.

Warren was practicing law and became clerk of the U.S. District Court in Valdez from 1921 to 1928. He later was appointed district attorney for the third division. In 1933 he moved his family to Anchorage where he took over the law practice of J. S. Truitt who was appointed attorney general for the Territory.

During the thirties he became an officer of the Anchorage Light and Power Company and was an officer in various other enterprises. During the late thirties he assumed the presidency of the

Lucy and Warren Cuddy in Their Early Years

Warren and Lucy Cuddy

David Cuddy

Betty and Dan Cuddy

First National Bank of Anchorage; however, he still maintained his law practice.

Lucy took an active interest in the Anchorage community. She served as Chairman of the Girl Scouts from 1935 until 1941. She was a member of the University of Alaska Board of Regents from 1956 to 1962, and in 1956 she was appointed Campaign Chairman of the Greater Anchorage United Fund Drive. The Lucy Cuddy Center at the University of Alaska Anchorage is named in her honor in recognition of her service on the Board of Regents, as well as the of the financial assistance given to the University by Lucy and Warren.

Warren, as an attorney and also president of a local bank, enjoyed the distinction of being both counsel and a representative of anyone who sought his advice on the law and on finances.

The Dan Cuddy Family

When WWII broke out, eldest son Dave was inducted into the Army and was trained with the First Special Service Forces, a commando style outfit consisting of specially trained Canadian and American soldiers. He was a First Lieutenant and in 1943 was killed at Anzio, Italy. Son Dan served in the ETO in the Army Engineers and upon his return practiced law with his father for a short time. After the death of his father he became president of the bank, and Lucy became chairman of the board.

Dan and wife Betty Jane Puckett had six children. David, Betsy Lawer, Gretchen Coady, Jane Klopfer and Laurel Stutzer all live in Anchorage, and Lucy Mahan lives in Homer. Warren Cuddy died in 1951, and Lucy died in 1981. They are both buried in the Masonic Tract of Anchorage Memorial Park Cemetery.

A man honored and respected by all old-time Alaskans as the one man who worked diligently and consistently for the good of Alaska, ANTHONY J. DIMOND was a man of integrity, a gentleman, a competent lawyer and a powerful spokesman for the Territory of Alaska. Tony, as his friends called him, was born in Palatine Bridge, New York in 1881. After a brief career as a teacher, following his attendance at St. Mary's Catholic Institute in Amsterdam, New York, he set out for Alaska in 1904.

He arrived in Valdez in 1904 and followed the gold trails out of Valdez until 1913, when he started his law practice. His public career started the same year when he was appointed U. S. commissioner at Chisana in 1917, and then served as U. S. attorney for the third division in Valdez. His popularity got him elected as Valdez Mayor, and he served two terms, until he was elected to the Territorial Senate in 1923. He was re-elected again in 1925, 1929 and 1931.

During his prospecting years Tony followed many trails in the Territory not yet accurately mapped. As a prospector, amateur explorer and public servant, he had several near fatal accidents, one of which left him a semi-cripple. He accidentally shot himself in the knee, and this left him with a stiff leg.

A. J. Dimond

In 1916 he married DOROTHEA FRANCIS MILLER, who was his most ardent supporter. She was born in Seattle, Washington in 1891. When she was ten years old, she moved with her family to Valdez, where she met Judge Dimond.

His career as delegate to Congress began in 1933, and he was returned for twelve consecutive years by Alaska voters. During his tenure in Washington he gained national prominence in his quest for Alaska statehood and the development of the Territory. He became a familiar figure on the streets of Anchorage in 1932 and '33. Although his permanent residence was not in Anchorage until his retirement from Congress, he was considered a member of the community.

He retired from the political arena, however, not from public service. He was appointed a federal judge. He accomplished his mission of making life better for all Alaskans, and his life is inseparable from the story of the development of Alaska. His work will be a monument to good and will be long remembered by true Alaskans. As a memorial to his career as an Alaskan advocate, Dimond High School and Dimond Boulevard in Anchorage are named in his honor.

Tony and Dorothea had three children. Son John passed away in Juneau, and daughter Ann Reilly died in Anchorage in 1971. Daughter Sister Marie Therese, a Catholic Nun, lives in Washington, D.C. Dorothea died in 1949, and Tony died in 1953. They are buried with their daughter Ann in the Catholic Tract of Anchorage Memorial Park.

In 1933 a fifty-four year Alaskan moved to Anchorage from Kodiak. Captain CHARLES

Henry, Mabel and Son

Paul Swanson

SWANSON was born in Goteborg, Sweden in 1855 and, as a teenager, stowed away on a ship bound for Australia. He managed to get off the ship in San Francisco and settled in Nutchuk on Hinchinbrook Island. He married PAULINE KVASNIKOFF in 1889. She was born in 1871 in Kodiak, and she and Captain Swanson moved about when he was the skipper of various crafts plying the waters of Prince William Sound. They lived in Nutchuk, Valdez, Mineral Creek, Sitka, Kodiak and finally in Anchorage.

Pauline and Charley had ten children. Emanuel was born in 1889 and died in Valdez in 1955; Anne was born in Nutchuk in 1891; Paul R. was born in Nutchuk in 1898 and died in Kodiak in 1956; Zenia Alice was born in Nutchuk in 1900; George was born in Valdez in 1901; Mary was born in Nutchuk in 1903 and died in 1959 in Fairbanks; Adrei was born in Mineral Creek in 1904 and died in 1907; Charles Augustus was born in Mineral Creek in 1912 and died in San Diego in 1970; Walter Bennett was born in Mineral Creek in 1912 and died in Anchorage in 1985; Henry E. was born in Valdez in 1914 and died in Escondido, Califoirnia in 1991.

Walt and Charles Swanson

All of the Swanson brothers were musicians. Henry played the saxophone with the "Serenaders," and Walter played the trumpet and banjo with the same group. Paul became bandmaster in Anchorage and was adept at many instruments. Charley played drums, however was an accomplished painter and concentrated on painting rather than music.

Henry and Gene Smith

Paul worked for Brown and Hawkins in Anchorage in its early years and then worked for Empress Grocery from 1931 to 1939. He moved to Kodiak and worked for the O. Kraft store until 1955 when he passed away. Walter was a lifelong commercial fisherman on Cook Inlet,

The Serenaders

The Serenaders in Casual Attire

headquartered in Anchorage. He was an electrician by trade and worked for the CAA and the FAA as well as for private contractors in Anchorage. Charley was also a commercial fisherman and worked part time for the Empress Grocery. He was an accomplished artist and many of his paintings still hang in homes in Anchorage. Henry graduated from high school in Anchorage, worked for Z. J. Loussac for many years and played with the Serenaders on KFQD and at local dances. In WWII he joined the Navy as a Pharmacist Mate and remained in the service until he retired in 1969.

Very little is known of the rest of the Swanson family, but suffice it to say they left their mark in early Anchorage history. Charles, Sr. is buried in the Pioneer Section of Anchorage Memorial Park.

JOHN H. PALMER was born in Elsworth, Maine, where he grew up and lived prior to coming to Alaska in 1933 with his wife EMILY KLEINER PALMER. She was born in Germany in 1885 and lived in Massachusetts prior to coming to Alaska with her husband. John obtained employment as a conductor with the Alaska Railroad. The marriage of John and Emily produced four children. Son Everett retired to Garden Grove, California after a career as a locomotive engineer with the ARR. The three daughters all live in California.

Emily and John Palmer

Emily and John Palmer

Beverly lives in Antioch; Carol Roberts lives in Merced; and Louise Palmer Nichols lives in Escondido. Emily died in 1968; John died in 1983; son Everett died in 1998. All are presumably buried in Garden Grove, California.

Everett and Louise Palmer

CHAPTER XVII

1934

The new Mayor was OSCAR GILL.

The new Councilmen were:

DENNY HEWITT
CARL MARTIN
M. J. MACDONALD

Anchorage High
School graduated
sixteen seniors,
nine boys and
seven girls: (Mary
Black not pictured.)

Mayor Oscar Gill

Bob Barnett

Bonnie Bell

Virginia Berg

Bill Bittner

Maxine Blunt

Thelma Carlson

Laurence Johanson

Evelyn Landstrom

Asa Martin

Orrin Nichols

Vera Nordby

Leo Saarela

Harry Seller

Jack VanZanten

Ralph Wood

The most exciting event in 1934 was the arrival of Army Air Corps bombers, under Colonel Hap Arnold, that flew into Anchorage for the first time. The second most exciting event was that Nome was decimated by fire. The third most exciting event was the completion of the road from Palmer to Eklutna. The fourth most exciting thing was the discovery that wanted murderer Thomas Johnson, known as "Blueberry Tommy," was arrested in Brooklyn, New York. He was wanted for the murder of "Fiddler John" Holmgren and "Dutch Marie" Schmidt in the Koyokuk in 1912.

Nick Sopoff

A placer miner from Flat brought his family to Anchorage to take up residency in 1934. NICK SOPOFF was born in Vladikvkaz, Russia in 1891 and immigrated to the United States in 1911. He and his partner, Harry Scott, developed mining ventures in the Iditarod and Stuyahok areas as well as in Ft. Yukon. Nick came to Alaska in 1914, arriving in Seward, where he started his overland hike to Flat. It was an ardous trip, taking over seventeen days. He found that staking a claim was almost impossible, as all of the good ground was taken. He worked for wages and did prospecting on the side, and it was not until 1923 that he and his partner were able to develop their own property.

In 1922 Nick married MATILDA PETERSON of Anvik Mission, and they make their home in Flat. Matilda operated a bathhouse and laundry while Nick worked in the placer mines. Nick and his partner sold their mining interests in the Stuyahok to Vance Hitt in 1930 and spent the next four years in Flat prior to moving to Anchorage.

Nick and Matilda had three children, Nina, Anita, and Marian. In 1938 Nick was working for a contractor in Anchorage laying pipe for a new sewer system when he was accidentally killed when a section of pipe fell into the ditch and landed on him. Matilda died in 1973. She and Nick are both buried in Anchorage Memorial Park.

A sportsman who came to Alaska in 1924 and settled in Seward until he moved to Anchorage in 1934, LEONARD HOPKINS was born in San Francisco in 1895. After his discharge from the Army at the end of WWI, he went to Seward. In the same year he arrived, he was elected Department Commander of the American Legion. He further served as the secretary of the Seward Chamber of Commerce. Leonard opened a sporting goods store at 607 West 4th Avenue and displayed record rainbow trout caught in Kenai and Skilak Lakes. He sponsored basketball teams and baseball teams for several years, and his teams were usually winners. Leonard sold out the store in early 1951 and became a sales representative for various sporting goods manufacturers. He was very active in the Boy Scouts and served a term on the Anchorage School Board.

He met Eleanor at the San Marcos bowling alley in Santa Barbara, California and married her in 1962. He had one son, Jack, who lived in California. Leonard died in 1988 in California. He was the last surviving member of the original Isaak Walton League.

A road builder who landed in Seward in 1933, CLAUDE E. ROGERS was born in Jennings, Kansas in 1912. He came to Alaska looking for a new start and hoping to find something other than the "No Help Wanted" signs he found in the states. He moved to Anchorage in 1934 and found work with the Alaska Road Commission. He worked in McKinley Park, Kodiak, and Anchorage in road construction and became road foreman in Kodiak. In 1945 he was promoted to general foreman of construction on the Sterling Highway at Homer.

During the next ten years he was area foreman for Pioneer Construction on the Denali Highway, the McKinley Park road and the Taylor and Richardson Highways. When the BPR took over operations of the Alaska Road Commission, he continued to work for them until 1960 and then moved to the Alaska Highway Department after statehood. Claude retired in 1973 after thirty-eight years of combined federal and state service.

An old-timer who made the rush to the Klondike and remained there for over thirty years, GEORGE LIGHT was born in Plattsburg, New York in 1862. He entered Alaska at St. Michael in 1896 and spent the next thirty years in the Klondike and the Koyukuk region. He owned and operated a trading post at Hughes for many years, and in 1934 he retired in Anchorage. He never left the territory after he first arrived. George died in 1948 and is buried in the Pioneer Tract of Anchorage Memorial Park.

HOWELL and RHEA ROBERTS DEAVER arrived in Anchorage with their two daughters in May 1934. They drove from Colorado to Seattle in a Model A Ford and from Seattle took the Alaska Steamship line to Seward.

Howell had been a hard-rock miner in Colorado until doctors advised him that he had better quit before he developed miners' consumption. The family set out for Alaska, as they knew there was clean air up here. Howell worked odd jobs for the first year until he got on as a carpenter on one of the ARR bridge crews. The family built their own home on the corner of 8th Avenue and M Street and established a showplace garden.

As the town and the military establishment grew and WWII was in the offing, Howell and Rhea opened a tent and awning shop near 5th Avenue and C Street. Howell suddenly died in 1949, and Rhea stayed on in her home, being active in a painting group and the Womans Club. When the quake hit in 1964 she had to abandon her home, and she moved to Seattle.

Howell and Rhea Deaver
with Grandchildren

Deaver Family

Deaver Home After the 1964 Earthquake

Howell and Rhea had two daughters, Barbara and Betty. Betty contracted tuberculosis and passed away in Los Angeles in 1997. Barbara married Vance Halvorson, and they had four children. Eileen, Connie, Kay and Clarke all live in Washington near Seattle. Barbara and Vance were divorced in 1970. She went on to college at Portland State University, received a degree in accounting, and became a CPA.

Rhea passed away in Seattle in 1980 and is buried in Mt. Pleasant Cemetery with her daughter Betty. Barbara lives in Renton, Washington and is retired. Howell is buried in the Masonic Tract of Anchorage Memorial Park Cemetery.

HARRY WILLIAM HOYT came to Alaska in 1907 to join his father, who had come over the Valdez trail in 1904 and opened a roadhouse at Gulkana. His father saw the opportunity of business with the miners and stampeders coming through and felt a good roadhouse would be successful. Harry was born in Rochester, New York in 1897 and was raised in New York until he was ten years old and made the trip to Alaska.

Harry and Norma Hoyt

Harry worked for the Alaska Road Commission from 1917 until 1936. He was master mechanic for the ARC and was stationed at McKinley Park when he met NORMA JORDET. Norma was born on a farm in Steele County, North Dakota. She was working at the McKinley Park Hotel in 1931 on her summer break from teaching second grade in Fairbanks. She and Harry were married in 1934 and moved to Anchorage that same year. They bought out Jack Callan Motors in 1936 and started Hoyt Motor Company. Harry kept his road commission job to keep the cash flow going while they

Hoyt Motors

Norma Hoyt

developed their business. Their venture proved a success, and in 1947 he made history by bringing in a convoy of new cars and trucks over the Alaska Highway. It proved to be a test case in international relations, as Canadian customs held up the cars for two weeks. Harry and Norma ran the Hoyt Motor Company from 1936 until 1962. Harry was elected to the board of the Alaska State Bank in 1959 prior to his retirement.

Norma was a founding member of the Anchorage Museum of History and Art and one of two Alaskan representatives to the National Trust for Historic Preservation. In 1979 she donated her collection of Alaskan books to the City Library, and the Mayor proclaimed that day Norma Hoyt Day. In 1985 the Anchorage School District nominated her for the Governor's Volunteer Award in recognition of her presentations on Alaska history. She was a trustee of the Sheldon Jackson College in Sitka for ten years. In the meanwhile Harry was flying his Cessna 180 around Alaska, which he loved to do, and spending time at his cabin on Big Lake. Harry and Ray Wolfe built the Wolhoy apartments at the corner 9th Avenue and D Street, and Norma and Harry had an apartment there for many years.

Harry Hoyt and Plane

Harold, Jr. and Carol Hoyt, 1988

Harry and Norma had one son, Harold W., who married Carol BeHanna, and they live at Big Lake. Their daughter Lisa Hoyt Battas and son Edward P. live in California. Harry died in the Fairbanks Pioneer Home in 1977, and Norma died in Anchorage in 1989 and is buried in the Pioneer Tract, Anchorage Memorial Park.

Another one of Anchorage's early bush pilots who arrived in 1934 to fly for the Alaska Exploration and Mining Company in Cantwell, Alaska, ROY SHELTON DICKSON was born in Roddy, Texas in 1901 and attended Whitman College in Walla Walla, Washington. There he

Roy Dickson

Ethel with Dorothy and Roy, Jr.

met ETHEL ALICE MEANS, and after graduation they were married and moved to Halfway in eastern Oregon where they started a sheep ranch. Ethel was born in Hamburg, Iowa in 1903, and her college training was as a high school math and science teacher.

In 1928 the couple moved to Portland, Oregon where Roy learned to fly at Tex Rankin's School of Flying. He barnstormed for a few years and then started flying miners and equipment into the Salmon River country of Idaho. He owned a Ryan B-l airplane and flew the canyons and gorges to deliver the goods. This experience resulted in a contact from the Alaska Exploration and Mining Company in Cantwell, Alaska offering him a job. In 1934 he and his mechanic, Sam Bell, boarded the *S.S. Alaska* with the Ryan on the deck load and headed north. They loaded their plane on the ARR and shipped it to Anchorage where they reassembled it on skis. They then flew into Cantwell and started their run from Cantwell into Valdez Creek. By

Roy Dickson and His Waco

Roy Dickson with Roy Holm in Naknek

the time the mine closed down in the fall they had made one hundred seventy-five trips and carried over sixty tons of cargo.

Roy was out of a job, and, while he was staying at the Parsons Hotel in Anchorage,

Mac McGee offered him a job flying a mail run with all flights being on floats and skis. He sold his Ryan to Bowman Airways and started flying for McGee Airways. On his first trip on the mail run he got lost in a snow-storm and was forced down. He walked out for help, got some gas, and was again on his way.

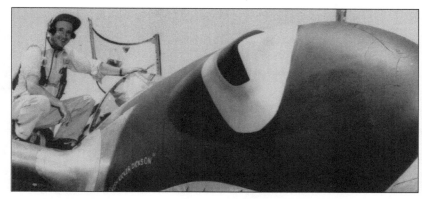

Roy as WWII Lockheed Test Pilot

In 1935 he founded Bering Sea Airways, and Roy was president of the company and chief pilot. Ethel was the bookkeeper and office manager and handled the company business for the investors. Roy was sent out to Seattle to fly back a new Waco five-place plane. In May 1937 Art Woodley made an offer to buy out Bering Sea Air, and Roy went to work for Art. In that same year Roy met Roy Holm, who had come up to deliver the first Taylor Cub to Anchorage. Roy told Woodley about Holm, and Holm was hired immediately. When Dickson went to work for Star, Holm inherited Dickson's favorite Flying W Travel Air 6000.

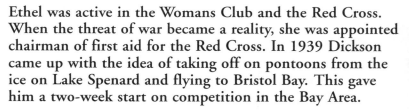

Dorothy Dickson and Husband

Ethel was active in the Womans Club and the Red Cross. When the threat of war became a reality, she was appointed chairman of first aid for the Red Cross. In 1939 Dickson came up with the idea of taking off on pontoons from the ice on Lake Spenard and flying to Bristol Bay. This gave him a two-week start on competition in the Bay Area.

During Rendezvous time there were more bush pilots in Anchorage than at any other time. Accordingly, a meeting was held, and thus was born the Alaska Air Pilots Association with Roy Dickson as president, Bert Ruoff vice-president and Ralph Savory secretary.

Roy Dickson, Jr. and Wife

In 1941 Star sent Roy to New York to fly back a Tri-motor Ford. He stopped in Burbank, California to have it rebuilt, when he was offered a job as test pilot for Lockheed. From 1941 to 1945 he flew and tested a wide variety of planes. After the war, the family moved to Bartlesville, Oklahoma where Roy became a corporate pilot for Phillips Petroleum Company. After thirteen years with Phillips, Roy and his co-pilot were killed in a tragic crash in 1958 when his plane disintegrated at ten thousand feet in severe weather over Mississippi.

Roy and Ethel had two children. Dorothy Jean Dickson McLaren and Roy Shelton, Jr. Dorothy had two children, Scott Alan and Sharon Ann McLaren Brady live in Atlanta, Georgia. Roy also had two children. Roy Shelton III lives in Kansas City, Kansas, and Julia Kay Dickson Skelton lives in Oklahoma City, Oklahoma. Ethel died in 1980 in Bartlesville, Oklahoma.

The year was 1908, and the cry heard in Fairbanks that Christmas week was "gold strike in the Iditarod." On Christmas Day 1908 JOHN BEATON and partner WILLIAM A. DYKEMAN discovered gold in the bottom of a prospect hole on Otter Creek, a tributary of the Iditarod River. It became the largest gold strike in Alaska, rivaled only by the strikes in Nome and Fairbanks.

Beaton Family

John and partner Dykeman purchased a small stern-wheeler named the *K.P.M.* in Holy Cross and put their outfit together to head up the Innoko River. The family states that the name Iditarod means "the river is deep enough." John Beaton supposedly used a rod to measure river depth until he found a spot deep enough to moor the boat for the winter. When he found that spot, he turned to his partner and, in his thick Gaelic brogue, said, "Pull ashore, I dit a rod." And that is the Beaton answer to how Iditarod got its name. Bill Dykeman was the first man officially up the completed and surveyed Iditarod Trail on December 27, 1910.

John Beaton was born at St. Ninian, Inverness County, Nova Scotia in 1875. He was married to Florence MacLennana of Broad Cove, Inverness County, who was born in 1890.

Florence arrived in Iditarod to join John in 1910 when the town was first settled. In 1918 John sent Florence and their two children, six-year-old Loretta and four-year-old Neil, back to Nova Scotia for a visit. He planned to join them in the spring. Florence and the children boarded the *S.S. Princess Sophia* in Skagway for its last trip for the season. On the night of October 23, 1918 the *Sophia* ran aground in Lynn Canal on Vanderbilt Reef. There were three hundred fifty-three people aboard of whom sixty-five were crew members. Many rescue boats circled the *Sophia,* ready to take off the passengers and crew. A storm was in progress and the water was rough, so the decision was made to wait until morning for the rescue. During the night the storm worsened, and in the morning the *Sophia* was gone with all living souls with it. The only survivor was a dog that managed to swim to shore. The bodies of daughter Loretta and mother Florence were reported found. However, after John Beaton arrived in Juneau in December, he found to his dismay that the girl was not his daughter. The children were never found, and John took the body of his wife to Port Hood, Nova Scotia and buried her in the Catholic Cemetery overlooking the Gulf of St. Lawrence.

Ten years later John married
Mary Mae MacDonald Grant, a
widow from Aarisaig,
Antiagonish County, who had a
daughter named Eunice Jean
Grant. John moved his new
family to Iditarod, and Mae
and John had a son together,
Neil Daniel.

Neil Beaton

Penny Beaton

John Beaton was a quiet man
and small of stature but big of
heart. He was instrumental in getting the Matanuska Valley settlers to Alaska and was another investor in the original Alaska Airlines. John suffered great personal tragedy in the loss of
his first family in the Sophia disaster, and it scarred him
for life.

In 1934 Mary Mae persuaded John to move the family to
the bustling city of Anchorage. They built a home on 3rd
Avenue and K Street. John sold his mining holdings,
however continued to prospect with a new partner, A. A.
Shonbeck. Using Anchorage as their headquarters, John
and Art Shonbeck were doing some mining on Gaines
Creek in the Ophir district. In 1945 the truck they were
driving skidded off the bridge on Gaines Creek, and both
were drowned.

Eunice Jean Grant Beaton married Joe Ramstad, and they
had four children: Joel, who died young, Loretta, Phil and
Stuart. Jean and Joe were later divorced. She married
Francis Syzmanski, and they had four children: Collin,
RoseMary, Duncan and Mike.

Ramstad and Syzmanski Families

Son Neil continued in the mining
game in the Gaines Creek area. There
he met widow Penelopie Dorthey
Agnas Marie Bertha Liba MacDonald
and her daughter Judy. Penelopie was
a cook, and she and her partner, Marie
Burso, owned and operated the Ophir
Restaurant and Tavern. Neil and
Penelopie were married, and then had
five children. Lauretta May, John
Andrew, Pencis Rose, Neil Daniel, Jr.,

The Neil Beaton Children

and Timothy Douglas all live in Anchorage. John Beaton, May and adopted daughter Jean are all buried in the Catholic Tract, Anchorage Memorial Park.

The year 1934 was still a depression year in the United States. Young men looking for a future were coming to Alaska and the new frontier. One of many was HAROLD LANGDON SWANK. Harold was born in Ballard, Washington in 1912.

At the age of sixteen he started working in a bakery in Ballard and learned the trade. He spent his younger years employed in the bakery until he met GERTRUDE KRAJEWSKI, a young lady who was also employed in a Seattle bakery. Gertrude was born on a homestead about three miles from Republic, Washington in 1909. Her parents were Polish immigrants, and she was the first American-born child of the family.

Gertrude and Harold began dating in 1931. Harold, in the meanwhile, bought a vegetable stand in Ballard and sold it to a brother who wanted to get into the business. After the sale of his stand, Harold decided Alaska was the place to go, and in 1934 he was all set to go. However, Gertrude was not about to let him go without her, so she also booked passage to Juneau. When they arrived in Juneau they were married in the home of a friend.

Gertrude and Harold Swank

Harold decided to go on to Anchorage where he had heard of a baking job opening, so he proceeded to stow away and was helped along the way by a good Samaritan. Upon arriving in Anchorage he went to work for John Meyer in the North Pole Bakery and remained in his employ until 1944. John Meyer sold the bakery to Nels Stensland in 1944, and in 1946 Harold and Gertrude bought the bakery from Stensland. (See John Meyer history.)

They operated the bakery successfully until 1952. They were doing a wholesale and retail business, selling to the military and to retail stores in town, with lunch sales and show cases in the store front. In 1952 Harold sold the bakery business, converted the front of the building into the Polar Bar, and sold it a year later.

The couple built their permanent home in 1937 at 8th Avenue and E Street, after living in three different places over the years.

Gertrude at First Home

North Pole Bakery

House on 7th Avenue

In 1957 a new bowling alley was being built on Minnesota and Spenard Roads, and Harold leased space to open "Harolds Spare Room Lounge." Harold and Gertrude operated the lounge until 1976 when they decided it was time to retire. Harold died in 1979 in Seattle where he went seeking medical care. Gertrude remained in

Gertrude Swank with Daughter Jeanette, Son-in-Law Ronald Smyth and Child

Daughter Jeanette with Harold

their home in Anchorage until she moved to Edmonds, Washington in 1989 to be with her daughter. Gertrude died in 1993 in Edmonds. Both she and Harold are buried there in Restlawn Cemetery.

The union of Harold and Gertrude produced one daughter. Jeannette Agnes Swank married Ronald Smyth, and they had three children, Harold, Victoria and Eric who all live in the Seattle area.

1934 was still a year in which numbers of young pilots were coming to Anchorage to make history and build an empire. The success story of RAYMOND I. PETERSEN has been told many times. Ray was born in York, Nebraska in 1912 and was raised on a Wyoming ranch prior to moving to Chicago with his family. Ray got a ride with a barnstorming pilot and was hooked on flying. He learned to fly by the time he was twenty years old. He met a pilot

Ray and Toni Petersen   Toni Petersen

Petersen Family

from Alaska who told him of the opportunities of flying in the north. Ray made his way to Seattle and booked steerage on the Alaska Steamship Line. He arrived in Anchorage on April Fools' Day in 1934 and landed his first job with Star Air Service, flying the Lucky Shot Mine route in Hatcher Pass. His next job was in Bethel where he worked for Marsh Airways, and then shortly thereafter he launched his own airline, Ray Petersen Flying Service in 1937.

He flew the bush out of Bethel, carrying fish and fishermen in the season, and miners and gold all over the Kuskokwim and the Yukon River routes. In 1939 after some time of courtship, Ray and ANTOINETTE "TONI" SCHODDE were married. (See Schodde segment.)

The Ray Petersen Flying Service evolved through a series of mergers and acquisitions to the Northern Consolidated Airlines of which Ray became president and CEO. He also became pioneer concessionaire of Katmai National Monument, operating five fishing lodges in what is now Katmai National Park. In 1968 NCA merged with Wien Air Alaska, and Ray retired as president in 1979. In 1982

Flying Out of Anchorage

First Hangar in Anchorage

Ray and his son purchased the Katmai Lodges from the airline. Raymond F. "Sonny" Peterson became owner/president, and Ray became vice-president and treasurer of Katmailand, Inc.

Ray and Toni had four children, Susan, Raymond F., Rose Marie and Charles Edward. Toni passed away in 1980 and is buried in the Pioneer Tract of Anchorage Memorial Park Cemetery. Ray is still going strong with Katmailand at the ripe young age of eighty-nine.

Ray Petersen Fishing in Bristol Bay

Italian immigrant MAURICE MORINO was lured to Nome in 1900, like thousands of other would-be millionaires. In 1916 he gave up on mining, and, hearing of the new railroad being built from Seward to Fairbanks, he headed for McKinley Park where he saw tourist opportunities and built a roadhouse on Riley Creek. McKinley Park was established in 1917, and the Riley Creek roadhouse was in a prime location to serve the AEC crews and forthcoming tourists.

In 1920 Maurice filed on a one hundred sixty acre homestead, and in 1921 he began building a new roadhouse on the bluff overlooking the bridge. The Railroad had built a station house, and then in 1922 the Alaska Road Commission moved in, creating more business for Maurice. He had contracts to feed and house work crews, and his meals were interesting, to say the least. He would buy a case of whatever, as an example, eggs. He would then feed the men eggs morning noon and night until the eggs were gone, and so on and on.

In 1934 Maurice was in ill health, and it was necessary for him to leave for Seattle to seek medical help. His nephew, EUSEBIO JOSEPH MORINO, came to Anchorage in 1934 and went to the Park to relieve his uncle while he was in Seattle. Joe Morino was born in Blairmore, Alberta, Canada in 1914. Joe was just twenty years old when he took over the operation of the roadhouse and post office. In 1936, after Maurice returned, Joe moved down to Anchorage.

Maurice Morino

When he arrived in Anchorage, Joe became the first employee of Milt Odom's Anchorage Cold Storage Company. He worked every branch of the company for forty-seven years. He started the first organized hockey team in Anchorage in 1937 and was the coach and lead player until he was transferred to Kodiak at the outbreak of WWII.

Joe established the Coca Cola plant in Kodiak for the Odom Company to serve the Navy and civilian population. In 1943 he and Alice Willits were married and settled in to raise their family. Two children were born in the years they spent in Kodiak, and finally in 1948 they were moved back to Anchorage. They bought a home at 533 D Street and lived in the "big

Alice and Joe Morino

Morino Family

1937 Aces Hockey Team

city" for eight more years until three more sons were born. They bought land on the old Tudor and Muldoon Roads, seven miles from downtown, and built a large comfortable home for their growing boys.

Joe continued working until 1983. He suffered from asthma for many years and started taking it easy. He was remembered by all sports fans in those days, especially hockey fans, as the father of the Anchorage Aces Hockey Team. He was given the "Gold Pan Award" by the Chamber of Commerce for his contribution to the sport of hockey in Anchorage.

Joe and Alice had nine children, eight boys and one girl: Fred, Tony, Joe, Jr., Bill, Jim, Mike, John, Paul, and Mary. Son John David passed away at the age of thirty-two, and Joe, Sr. died in 1996. Alice still lives in the big house and chases her fifteen grandchildren.

———

The patriarch of the sea-going Anderson family, Captain JACK CONRAD ANDERSON, was born in Bergen, Norway in 1901. He served before the mast when he was nine years old on a voyage to Australia on his father's square rigger. In 1924, after service in the

United States Navy and the Merchant Marine, he came ashore in Seldovia, Alaska. He was known as Captain Jack and soon had a mail and passenger service operating from Cook Inlet points to Kodiak and points on the Aleutian Chain. In 1934 he acquired the mailboat *Princess Pat* and operated up and down Cook Inlet carrying mail and passengers.

His son Jack Anderson, Jr. was introduced to deep water sailing also at the age of nine when he accompanied his father on a trip from Cook Inlet to Dutch Harbor. The younger Jack received his captain's papers when he was fifteen years old and was described by Robert Ripley's *Believe It or Not* as the youngest captain with his own boat in the country. Young Jack was qualified for one thousand tons in any waters.

The Anderson operation was held in abeyance when WWII broke out. Young Jack was in the service in the Aleutians and Jack, Sr. was relaxing in Seattle. After WWII Anderson and Sons Transportation started operations as Cook Inlet Tug and Barge. The Andersons built Anderson Dock, a cargo terminal in Anchorage. When Sealand and Tote began bringing in seven hundred fifty foot container ships, they needed tugboat service.

In 1970 Captain Jack, Sr. retired, sold four of his tugs to the Red Stack Line, and passed the balance of the fleet and equipment on to Captain Jack, Jr. They sold the Anderson Dock and Terminal to North Star Stevedoring and concentrated on the tugboat business.

Helen Hampton Anderson

Jack Anderson, Sr.

Dorothy Anderson

Jack Anderson, Jr. at 18

Lois Anderson

Jack Anderson, Jr., 1989

Captain John C. Anderson

Captain Carl Anderson

Princess Pat

Captain Jack, Jr. and Lois Erickson were married in 1943, and they had three children, one daughter and two sons. The two sons were rapidly indoctrinated into the tugboat business in their youth. The third generation Anderson boys, John C. III and Carl are also licensed tugboat captains.

In October 1964 two tankers collided off the Anchorage Terminal and burst into flames. The Danish *Sirrah* was not bad off, however the *Santa Maria* was in flames seventy feet high and trailing flames in the water. Captain Jack and Lois were in the tug Westwind, which also caught fire. Lois took the controls while Jack put out the fire. They then went to the aid of the *Santa Maria*, which was drifting with the tide. Son, John, was in the *Arctic Wind* and rushed to the assistance of the *Sirrah*, getting some men off the ship. Captain Jack put the *Westwind* alongside the *Santa Maria*, turned the controls over to Lois, and assisted thirty-seven men off the burning tanker. The heat was so intense that that the paint was blistering on the tug. The Carnegie Hero Fund awarded Jack and Lois the Carnegie Silver Medals, and John Anderson III was awarded the Bronze medal.

A third generation Anderson boy, John C. III, operates a tug service in Seward. Third generation Captain Carl "Andy" Anderson operates the tug service in Anchorage.

Helen I. Hampton Anderson passed away in 1950; Captain Jack C. Anderson, Sr. passed away in 1992. Jack C. Anderson, Jr. passed away in 1994; his sister, Dorothy, passed away in 1946. Lois Anderson lives in a retirement home in Seattle, and the daughter of Jack C. and Helen Anderson, Annalee Anderson Hill, lives in Wasilla.

CHAPTER XVIII

1935

OSCAR GILL was serving his third term as Mayor.

The new Councilmen were:

FRANCIS LARUE and EMIL PFEIL.

The big news was that the Palmer Highway was open to the Eklutna River, and an ice dam flooded the Eklutna power house. The Railroad fire department living quarters burned.

Anchorage High School graduated fourteen students, eight girls and six boys:

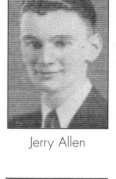

Jerry Allen

Glen Barnett

Esther Browne

Harold Culver

Dorothy Cunningham

Helve Enatti

Frank Kimura

Stanley McCutcheon

Marjie Nelson

Kathleen Schuetz

Hazel Seaburg

Fay Stoddard

Genevieve Strandberg

Max Wells

The big national news was that on August 15, 1935 world travelers Wiley Post and Will Rogers were killed in a plane crash at Point Barrow.

Other big local news was that the first contingent of the Matanuska Valley settlers arrived in Anchorage enroute to their new location in Palmer.

The newcomers were still arriving in 1935, and LEE LAUGHLIN was one of them. He arrived in Anchorage on April 2, 1935. He took a part-time job with the post office department as a temporary clerk and retired in 1970 as assistant postmaster. He was born in Yamhill, Oregon in 1905, and when he arrived in Anchorage he homesteaded on Fire Lake with his brother, Ken Laughlin. He was known as "Mr. Post Office" or "Cigar," a name that evolved from the cigar that seemed a part of him. Lee died in 1987.

Peggy and Ben Peterson

Another of the 1935 arrivals, OLIVER "BEN" PETERSON first landed in Haines in 1932 aboard the *S.S. Admiral Rogers*. He worked at odd jobs in Haines for almost two years and then moved on to Juneau where he worked for a contracting firm constructing a dock at Gustavus. Then he moved back to Juneau and got a job working on the construction of the Juneau-Douglas bridge across the channel. He moved to Anchorage in 1935 to join the Alaska Road Commission in the construction of the Knik River Bridge.

Ben was born in Drummond, Bayfield County, Wisconsin in 1905. In 1936 he and LEONA MARY "PEGGY" GEHLEN were married in Palmer, Alaska. Peggy was born in Glencoe, Minnestoa in 1903 and was raised there. She left Minnesota to go to Alaska in search of employment and met Ben in Haines. Peggy worked as a waitress in the original Hewitts Lunch Counter and was also employed by Nellie Brown in the old Nellie's Diner. She and Ben lived in McKinley Park and Palmer during his years with the ARC, and in 1940 they moved permanently to Anchorage.

The union of Ben and Peggy produced one daughter, Helen Marie. She and spouse Jerry Burkes had two daughters. Teresa Dawn Burkes Atkinson lives in Ashburn, Virginia. Christin Marie Burkes Sweet lives in

Jerry and Helen Burkes

First Home in Anchorage

Anchorage. Peggy died in 1973, and Ben died in 1979. They are buried in Angelus Memorial Park in Anchorage.

A young man of seventeen arrived in Alaska with his parents in 1918. GEORGE ARCHIE LINGO was born in Anaconda, Montana in 1901. His parents brought him to Alaska in 1918, first settling in Ketchikan and then moving on to Latouche, Cordova, Kennecott, Chickaloon, Fairbanks and finally Anchorage. His parents operated roadhouses in these localities. In 1927 George graduated from the University of Alaska with a degree in mining engineering. He moved to Anchorage in 1935 as manager of the land office, a job he held until 1952. Following his resignation from that post he spent his time developing the Forest Park Golf and Country Club and opened it in 1951. He served on the Board of Regents for the University of Alaska in Fairbanks for a term and served in the 1933-35 Territorial legislature.

He married JOAN TROY, the daughter of former Governor Troy of Alaska. Joan was born in Port Angeles, Washington in 1901. She moved to Skagway with her parents when she was six months old and then returned to Washington where she continued her schooling. In 1912 her father purchased the *Daily Alaska Empire* newspaper in Juneau, and she finished high school there. She worked as a newspaper reporter on her father's paper in Juneau. When she and George were married and moved to Anchorage, she was the original agent for Northwest Airlines when they started operations into Anchorage.

She worked with her husband in developing the Country Club in Anchorage. They retired to California in 1960, and, after George passed on in 1976, Joan moved back to Anchorage to be with her daughter in 1990. She passed away in 1993 in Anchorage.

She and George had one daughter, Joan Lingo Moore, who lives in Anchorage. Joan had two sons, John and Michael Farleigh, who both live in Anchorage.

ROBERT B. ATWOOD died on January 10, 1997. Rather than relate his life story, I will take excerpts from the "Voice of the Times" obituary of January 11, 1997, as it says it all.

Dorothy and George Lingo

Joan Moore and Spouse

Atwood Family

Headline: "Alaska Loses a Visionary."

From the first day he arrived in Anchorage on June 15, 1935, Bob Atwood was a community leader. It was because he was the new editor in town and barely 28 years old, he was eager to make a little newspaper get bigger. People looked to him to see what this new owner of the newspaper could do. They soon found out, as he became active in every aspect of community and business life. He proved himself by hard work and by bringing to Anchorage the professional skills he developed at his first newspaper jobs in Massachusetts and Illinois.

He was born in Chicago, Illinois in 1907 and was raised in the suburbs of Chicago. He was supposed to become a lawyer like his father or a geography professor like his uncle. After graduating from high school in Winnetka, Illinois, he went east to Massachusetts to study journalism at Clark University. In 1930 he moved back to Illinois and worked as a reporter for the State Journal in Springfield.

There he met a young social worker from Alaska, MAUDE EVANGELINE RASMUSON, who was born in Sitka. Evangeline had recently graduated from the University of Chicago with a master's in social work. In 1932, she and Bob married and went to Worcester where the two of them worked on his old newspaper, the Worcester Telegram.

In 1935, Evangeline's father, Edward A. Rasmuson, who was now President of the Bank of Alaska, advised them that the local Anchorage Times newspaper was available. They accepted the offer and that began the saga of Bob Atwood.

Much of what exists in Anchorage today was shaped by Bob Atwood. Clearly Alaska achieved statehood through the efforts of Atwood. There were many people involved in this, however his newspaper was at the forefront of the battle. He was Chairman of the Alaska Statehood committee and was the champion of the cause.

Of his many credits that exist today due to his editorialism, we can say that without his efforts the International Airport would not have become a reality, nor would the Port of Anchorage. He helped found the Alaska Methodist University, which is now Alaska Pacific University. His relationship with the military in Anchorage was one of good will and support of his newspaper. He was a driving force behind the development of Alyeska Ski Resort and a supporter of the Matanuska Colony development, which coincided with his arrival in Anchorage in 1935.

Bob Atwood will be long remembered as will his wife Evangeline. She was a compiler of Alaska history and had written many books, among them, *Who's Who in Alaska Politics* and *They Shall Be Remembered*. She was named Historian of the Year by the Cook Inlet Historical Society in 1975. She was a past President of the Anchorage Womans Club, the Alaska Federation of Womens Clubs, and the Alaska Statehood Association. She had organized the Anchorage League of Women Voters and also became a member of the board of the Territorial Board of Public Welfare.

Robert B. Atwood

Evangeline Atwood

Evangeline was born in Sitka in 1906 and died in Anchorage in 1987. She and Bob had two daughters, Marilyn and Elaine. Daughter Marilyn had three sons with Milton Odom, and daughter Elaine never married. Marilyn passed away in 1994.

The year l935 brings to an end the Legends and Legacies chronology. If at some future date some ambitious historian wants to continue this history, he has the names of most of the grandchildren to start with. If no one ever does, at least we have saved this amount of true Pioneer history. I sign this off with "A Tribute to the Pioneers" by Anthony J. Dimond.

A Pioneer — is one who goes ahead, who marches in front
Into the wilderness of land or sea—of thought or
Action—and explores and clears the land, makes the
Roads, builds the bridges, so that others may safely follow.

Not for the Pioneers are the easy ways or the soft
Things in life, not for him the paved road or the
Lighted path. His body and mind must be hardened and
Inured to something sterner and more rigorous. He must
Always face the unknown. He is ever between the main
Body of civilized society and the enemy.

The Pioneer has performed his function, done his duty,
And been successful—if he has made the road safe for
Those who will come after him.

And if he dies in the service—is not his death a
Fulfillment of his life? What failure is there in that?
If he desired to live safely, acquire wealth, and knew
Only the soft and tender things of life, he would not
Have been a Pioneer.

Anthony J. Dimond — 1923

INDEX *

* *Only Alaskan geographic names, businesses and primary family members names are included. "Alaska Railroad" has not been indexed as references to it appear on nearly every page. In the publishing process a few page references may have moved to the previous or following page.*